STUDIES IN PHILOLOGY

Texts and Studies, 1971-1972

GENERAL EDITOR

Dennis G. Donovan

SPENSER ALLUSIONS

In the Sixteenth
and
Seventeenth Centuries

COMPILED BY

Ray Heffner
Dorothy E. Mason
Frederick M. Padelford

EDITED BY

William Wells

The University of North Carolina Press
Chapel Hill

PREFACE

Forty years ago Ray Heffner proposed the publication of a Spenser allusion book, with a first volume to be devoted to allusions of the sixteenth and seventeenth centuries. In 1931 the Spenser Group of the Modern Language Association undertook its preparation through an editorial committee of three, Hardin Craig, A. C. Judson, and Mr. Heffner. As chairman, Mr. Heffner assumed the responsibility of formulating editorial policy and directing the compilation. A good beginning had been assured by books already in print: Frederic Ives Carpenter's *Reference Guide to Edmund Spenser,* and collections of allusions, to Shakespeare by John Munro, to Chaucer by Caroline F. E. Spurgeon, and to Jonson by J. F. Bradley and J. Q. Adams.

The project was very substantially advanced in 1935 when Miss Dorothy Mason, assisted by a grant from the American Council of Learned Societies, undertook a systematic search for Spenser allusions hitherto uncollected, particularly those before the eighteenth century. Her success is clearly reflected in the pages of this compilation. Subsequently, while working on the *Variorum Spenser* in England, she was able to check many of the items submitted by interested scholars.

In 1940, when illness interrupted Mr. Heffner's editorship, Frederick Morgan Padelford of the University of Washington undertook the task. Mr. Padelford, whose interest in Spenserian influence had already expressed itself in his continuing study of Spenser's reputation, made a detailed review of that influence to serve as an introduction to the text of the allusions. To the sizable number already collected he added many which he had noted in his own wide reading. Because the proposed introduction followed a chronological scheme, Mr. Padelford planned an alphabetical arrangement for the allusions themselves. Following Mr. Padelford's death I accepted the invitation offered by Hardin Craig for the allusion book committee to assume the editorship.

The question " What is an allusion? " is deceptive, and the rigorous application of whatever definition one may elaborate is likely to be unsatisfactory at one time or another to everyone, including the elaborator himself. Yet the naming of sufficient, if not necessary, conditions for inclusion in the collection can be useful to editor and user alike.

In the first volume of *Shakespeare & Jonson: Their Reputations in the Seventeenth Century* (1945), Gerald Eades Bentley proposes objective tests to answer the question:

> On the one hand, an acceptable allusion must mention the name of Jonson or Shakespeare or the name of one of their compositions or characters, or it must contain at least one line from their works. About 98 per cent of the 3,269 Shakespeare and Jonson allusions which I have accepted and classified conform to these requirements. In the other 2 per cent, exceptions have been allowed because external evidence makes clear that one of the dramatists or his work is referred to, even though no names are mentioned. . . .
>
> On the other hand, certain types of passages which specifically mention the playwrights have been systematically excluded. Title pages of men's own works, Stationers' Register entries of those works, publishers' advertisements, and sale catalogues have all been eliminated. (Pp. 10-1)

Application of objective tests usually is preferable to the passing of subjective editorial judgment. Certainly Mr. Bentley's preparation for his statistical comparison of Shakespeare and of Jonson allusions, the heart of his study, demanded tests as nearly objective and as precisely defined as possible. Yet the editor of a collection of allusions may respect his own judgment that some parallels are too close to be mechanically excluded. Indeed if he rejects all quotations failing to meet the requirements of his definition, he very probably will reject what many readers with good judgment would consider to be intentional variations upon the original or half-remembered quotations. He may not hope that strict definition will necessarily reveal the author's intent in a passage under review as containing an allusion, but he is obliged to be alert to evidence of intent, or lack of it— evidence which cannot be supported by the sufficient conditions he has set. Of the 1200 entries in this collection, several dozen, somewhat more than the 2 per cent Mr. Bentley allows himself, do not meet the tests requiring the naming of Spenser or of one of his compositions or characters or the quotation of at least one line from his works. Excluded are citations of title pages and entries in the Stationers' Register, and references to Spenser as government official and landowner. Passages included relate to Spenser the writer and his literary works.

As the present chronological arrangement suggests, there has been an attempt to indicate the earliest known appearance of each allusion. Regularly, passages from a manuscript appear under the year of composition and from a book, under the year of publication. Departures from this practice are noted in specific editorial notes. The general procedure has been to furnish a secondary reference to a modern edition, to indicate the specific passage by Spenser wherever borrowing or imitation is recognized, and to provide necessary explanatory notes. Normalizing of quotations has been held to a minimum: original spelling and punctuation have been retained and only manifest errors, such as inversion of letters, have been corrected. *W, w,* and *s* have replaced *UU, uu,* and *ſ*; common forms of abbreviations, such as those of Latin *-que,* have been normalized. In the transcription of passages, set mainly in italics, as for example those from prefaces, italic and roman type have been interchanged.

Initials in parentheses belong to the contributor of the allusion. If two sets of initials appear together, the second contributor has provided a significant supplement. An uninitialled allusion is to be credited to the contributor whose initials next appear. There may be errors in acknowledgment, since very few original notes by occasional contributors were among the papers I have examined.

The generous assistance of many interested persons accounts in large measure for the value this collection may have. Material support has come from a number of sources. Early in the undertaking, microfilm and secretarial help was provided through a grant by the Carnegie Foundation, administered by the Graduate School of the University of North Carolina. A leave of absence from the University and a grant-in-aid by the Trustees of Amherst College facilitated study at the Folger Shakespeare Library in 1952. The Duke-University of North Carolina Cooperative Program in the Humanities authorized a grant for preparing the index. I owe special thanks to Mrs. Ray Heffner for making available her husband's papers relating to the project, and to Mrs. F. M. Padelford, who lent copies of the introduction and text as prepared by Mr. Padelford shortly before his death. Miss Dorothy Mason graciously provided her very extensive file of allusions. The patient wisdom of Miss Georgia Faison, for many years Head Reference Librarian of the University of North Carolina at Chapel Hill, characterizes the benefits I have enjoyed from association with staff members of the several libraries where I have worked. For assistance of many kinds I am indebted to Mrs. William M. (Shirley Graves) Cochrane, Warren Austin, Richmond P. Bond, Leicester Bradner, Hardin Craig, Giles E. Dawson, Dennis Donovan, D. D. Griffith, William Haller, C. Hugh Holman, Alexander C. Judson, James G. McManaway, Dougald MacMillan, Charles G. Osgood, D. D. Pierson, Harry K. Russell, E. A. Strathmann, Thomas B. Stroup, Kester Svendsen, and Louis B. Wright. I am especially grateful to my colleague, Ernest W. Talbert, Editor of *Studies in Philology,* for his sustaining encouragement and to Matthew Hodgson, Director of the University Press, for timely helpfulness.

W. W.

The University of North Carolina

CONTRIBUTORS

Dorothy F. Atkinson (Evans)	(DFA)
Warren B. Austin	(WBA)
Phyllis Bartlett	(PB)
Josephine Waters Bennett	(JWB)
Richard Boys	(RB)
J. Franklin Bradley	(JFB)
Leicester Bradner	(LB)
Douglas Bush	(DB)
Lily B. Campbell	(LBC)
Frederic Ives Carpenter	(FIC)
Arthur William Craver	(AWC)
Charles Crawford	(CC)
Giles E. Dawson	(GED)
Austin C. Dobbins	(ACD)
Mark Eccles	(ME)
G. Blakemore Evans	(GBE)
Edwin Greenlaw	(EG)
Frederick Hard	(FH)
Ray Heffner	(RH)
Brice Harris	(BH)
Virgil B. Heltzel	(VBH)
Hoyt H. Hudson	(HH)
Francis R. Johnson	(FRJ)
Alexander C. Judson	(ACJ)
Rudolf Kirk	(RK)
Paul Kocher	(PK)
Emil Koeppel	(EK)
Kathrine Koller	(KK)
Abram Barnett Langdale	(ABK)
Thorleif Larson	(TL)
Lucy Lawrence	(LL)
John B. Leishman	(JBL)
John Leon Lievsay	(JLL)

Dorothy E. Mason   (DEM)
James G. McManaway   (JGM)
C. Bowie Millican   (CBM)
John Robert Moore   (JRM)
John Munro   (JM)
Frederick M. Padelford   (FMP)
Frank A. Patterson   (FAP)
Richard H. Perkinson   (RHP)
Hyder E. Rollins   (HER)
Helen E. Sandison   (HES)
Georg Schoeneich   (GS)
George F. Sensabaugh   (GFS)
William E. Simeone   (WES)
G. Gregory Smith   (GGS)
Caroline F. E. Spurgeon   (CFES)
Harold Stein   (HS)
James W. Stevenson   (JWS)
George Winchester Stone   (GWS)
Ernest A. Strathmann   (EAS)
Kathleen Tillotson   (KT)
Ruth Wallerstein   (RW)
William Wells   (WW)
George W. Whiting   (GWW)
Franklin B. Williams, Jr.   (FBW)
Elkin C. Wilson   (ECW)
Frances Yates   (FY)

ABBREVIATIONS

Am.	*Amoretti*
As.	*Astrophel*
Bel.	*Visions of Bellay*
Col.	*Colin Clouts Come Home Againe*
Comp.	*Complaints*
Daph.	*Daphnaida*
Epith.	*Epithalamion*
F. Q.	*Faerie Queene*
Gn.	*Virgils Gnat*
H. L.	*Hymne in Honour of Love*
H. B.	*Hymne in Honour of Beautie*
H. H. L.	*Hymne of Heavenly Love*
H. H. B.	*Hymne of Heavenly Beautie*
M. H. T.	*Mother Hubberds Tale*
Mui.	*Muipotmos*
Pet.	*Visions of Petrarch*
Proth.	*Prothalamion*
R. R.	*Ruines of Rome*
R. T.	*Ruines of Time*
S. C. Jan.	*Shepheardes Calender, January*
S. C. Feb.	*Shepheardes Calender, February*, etc.
T. M.	*Teares of the Muses*
Van.	*Visions of the Worlds Vanitie*

Atkinson: Dorothy F. Atkinson, *Edmund Spenser A Bibliographical Supplement*, Johns Hopkins Press, 1937.

Bentley: Gerald Eades Bentley, *Shakespeare and Jonson*, Univ. Chicago Press, 1945.

Bradley: Jesse Franklin Bradley and Joseph Quincy Adams, *The Jonson Allusion-Book*, Yale Univ. Press, 1922.

Chalmers: Alexander Chalmers, *The Works of the English Poets from Chaucer to Cowper*, 21 vols., 1810.

Koeppel: Emil Koeppel, *Ben Jonson's Wirkung auf zeitgenössissche Dramatiker und andere Studien zur inneren Geschichte des englischen Dramas, Anglistische Forschungen*, vol. 20, Heidelburg, 1906.

Lee: Sidney Lee, *Elizabethan Sonnets*, Westminster, 1904.

Munro: John Munro, *The Shakspere Allusion-Book*, 1909; *Notes and Queries*, 10 (July-Dec., 1904). 121.

Nichols: John Nichols, *The Progresses and Public Processions of Queen Elizabeth*, 1823.
Saintsbury: George Saintsbury, *Minor Poets of the Caroline Period*, Oxford: vol. 1, 1905; vol. 2, 1906; vol. 3, 1921.
Smith: G. Gregory Smith, *Elizabethan Critical Essays*, Oxford, 1904.
Spingarn: J. E. Spingarn, *Critical Essays of the Seventeenth Century*, Oxford, 1908.
Spurgeon: Caroline F. E. Spurgeon, *Five Hundred Years of Chaucer Criticism and Allusion*, Chaucer Soc. Pub., 1914; also Cambridge Univ. Press, 1925.
STC: A. W. Pollard and G. R. Redgrave, *Short-Title Catalogue of Books Printed in England . . . 1475-1640*, 1926 [also 1946];
————: Donald Wing, *Short-Title Catalogue of Books Printed in England . . . 1641-1700*, Columbia Univ. Press: vol. 1, 1945; vol. 2, 1948; vol. 3, 1951.

NOTE

Unless otherwise noted, all allusions that are referred to in Carpenter are credited to (FIC); and allusions that are recorded in Bradley, Munro, and Spurgeon, are credited respectively to (JFB), (JM), and CFES). It should be remembered, however, that many of the allusions assigned to Munro had appeared in earlier collections of Shakespeare allusions, and that J. Q. Adams was joint author with Mr. Bradley of *The Jonson Allusion-Book*.

If the place of publication of a book is unnamed, *London* is to be understood.

Part I: 1580-1625

SPENSER ALLUSIONS

1580-5.   Abraham Fraunce. *The Sheapheardes Logike: conteyning the præcepts of that art put downe by Ramus; examples fet owt of the Sheapheards Kalender,* in B. M. MS Add. 34,361, fols. 3-28.

[Quotations from *S. C.* are numerous. Under 1588 below, note extract from Fraunce's prefatory comment in *The Lawiers Logike* and the list of quotations from *S. C.* in that work.] (FIC)

1580?-1600? Gabriel Harvey. *Marginalia.*
[Ed. G. C. Moore Smith, Stratford Upon Avon, 1913, quoted below.]

To 1542 ed. of Quintilian's *Institutes,* p. 122:
   Tria viudissima Britannorum ingenia, Chaucerus, Morus, Juellus: Quibus addo tres florentissimas indoles, Heiuodum, Sidneium, Spencerum.

To 1572 ed. of Twine's translation of Dionysius Periegetes, *The Surueye of the World,* p. 161:
   M. Digges hath the whole Aquarius of Palingenius bie hart: & takes mutch delight to repeate it often.
   M. Spencer conceiues the like pleasure in the fourth day of the first Weeke of Bartas. Which he esteemes as the proper profession of *Urania.*

Ibid., p. 162:
   Sæpè miratus sum, Chaucerum, et Lidgatum tantos fuisse in diebus illis astronomos. Hodiernos poetas tam esse ignaros astronomiae: praeter Buclæum, Astrophilum, Blagravum: alios perpaucos, Uraniæ filios.
   Pudet ipsum Spenserum, etsi Sphæræ, astrolabique non planè ignarum; suæ in astronomicis Canonibus, tabulis, instrumentisque imperitiæ.

To Gascoigne's *Certaine notes of Instruction,* p. 168:
   ye difference of ye last verse from ye rest in euerie Stanza, a grace in ye Faerie Queen.

Ibid., pp. 168-9:
   The reason of manie a good uerse, marred in Sir Philip Sidney, M. Spenser, M. Fraunce, & in a manner all our excellentest poets: in such words, as heāuen, euil, diuĕl, & ye like; made dyssyllables, contrarie to their natural pronunciation.
[Commenting on Gascoigne's observation that Chaucer's lines are not of the same number of syllables, but that the longest verse to the ear will correspond with that which has fewer syllables:]

3

So M. Spenser, & Sir Philip, for yᵉ most part.
Our poems only Rymes, and not Verses.
Aschami querela. Et mea post illum Reformatio; post me,

Sidneius, Spenserus, Francius.
. . . Monasyllables ar good to make upp a hobling and hudling verse.
Sir Philip Sidney, & M. Spenser of mie opinion.

Ibid., pp. 169-70:
Spenser hath reuiued, vncouth, whilom, of yore, for thy.
[On forms allowed by poetical license such as " *Ydone, adowne, orecome, tane, power for powre, heauen for heavn, thewes for good qualities* ":]
All theise in Spenser, & manie like: but with discretion: & tolerably, thowgh sumtime not greatly commendably.

To *The Traveiler of Ierome Turler*, 1575, p. 173:
Ex dono Edmundi Spenserij, Episcopi Roffensis Secretarij. 1578.

Notes following Speght's 1598 ed. of Chaucer, p. 231:
Not manie Chawcers, or Lidgates, Gowers, or Occleues, Surries, or Heywoods, in those dayes: & how few Aschams, or Phaers, Sidneys, or Spensers, Warners or Daniels, Siluesters, or Chapmans, in this pregnant age.

Ibid., p. 232:
And now translated Petrarch, Ariosto, Tasso, & Bartas himself deserue curious comparison with Chaucer, Lidgate, & owre best Inglish, aunctient & moderne. Amongst which, the Countesse of Pembrokes Arcadia, & the Faerie Queene are now freshest in request: & Astrophil, & Amyntas ar none of the idlest pastimes of sum fine humanists.

Ibid., p. 233:
[Dyer's] Amaryllis, & Sir Walter Raleighs Cynthia, how fine & sweet inuentions? Excellent matter of emulation for Spencer, Constable, France, Watson, Daniel, Warner, Chapman, Siluester, Shakespeare, & the rest of owr florishing metricians. (FIC)

About 1581.　*Pedantius. Comoedia, Olim Cantabrig. Acta in Coll. Trin.,* 1631.

[STC 19524. Ed. G. C. Moore Smith, Bang's *Materialen*, Louvain. 1905. Moore Smith, p. xlv, thinks that Leonidas, referred to as the pupil of Pedantius (Gabriel Harvey) represents Spenser.] (FIC)

About 1581.　Sir Philip Sidney. *The Defence of Poesie . . . Printed for William Ponsonby,* 1595.

[STC 22535. Ed. Albert S. Cook, Boston, 1890; rptd Fascimile Text Soc., 1928. Cf. also *An apologie for Poetrie . . . Printed for Henry Olney,* 1595 (STC 22534). Ed. J. Churton Collins, Oxford, 1907.]

Sig H 3ᵛ (Cook, p. 47); cf. *An Apologie*, sig. I 4ᵛ (Collins, p. 51):
I account the Mirrour of Magistrates, meetly furnished of bewtiful partes. And in the Earle of *Surries Lirickes*, manie thinges tasting of a Noble

birth, and worthie of a Noble minde. The Sheepheards Kallender, hath much *Poetrie* in his Egloges, indeed woorthie the reading, if I be not deceiued. That same framing of his style to an olde rusticke language, I dare not allow: since neither *Theocritus* in Greeke, *Virgil* in Latine, nor *Sanazara* in Italian, did affect it. Besides these, I doo not remember to haue seene but fewe (to speake boldly) printed, that haue poeticall sin-newes in them. (FIC)

1582.   Thomas Blenerhasset. *A Reuelation Of the True Minerua.*

[STC 3132. Ed. Josephine Waters Bennett, Scholars Facsimiles and Rpts, 1941.]

Sig. C 4:

> Take Lute in hand, tune to the waters fall.

[Cf. S. C. *Apr.* 36]

Sig. D:

> And I before I hence depart, will frame
> A comely Coronet of goodly greene,
>   which shall right well become a maiden Queene.

[Cf. S. C. *Apr.* 56-63]

[In three stanzas praising the Queen (sig. C 4 - C 4ᵛ) Blenerhasset adopts the verse form of Colin's eulogy in *Apr.* and several of his rimes; cf. Bennett, pp. x-xi.] (JLL, JWB)

1582.   William Vallans. Verses in B. M. MS Harleian 367.

Fol. 129:

The Laboringe man whose paynfull lyms / dothe till the fertile grounde,
To recompence his taken toyle / small profyte dothe redounde.
The sheapeheard feedes his grazynge flocke / wᵗʰ great excedynge care
Yet scarce a Lam & seldome that / falls out vnto his share.
And what falls out for hym (good man) / that wrytes this paynfull
  booke   [5]
Nay gaynfull for the comon wealthe / and suche as theron looke.
But only for to beate the bushe / whylst others catche the burde
To cracke the shell yet vnto vs / the carnell to affoorde.
To treade, and smoothe, the crooked pathe / and make a redye waye
ffor suche as do or after shall / lkye argument assaye   [10]
What payns to seek olde wrytten bookes / what charge to buye the most
What care to kepe old monuments / that els had bene but lost.
But last of all what recompence / remaynes for this and more
But only wᵗʰ his handy worke / for to mayntayn his stoore
Lament, Lament, good aged man / Augustus he is gone   [15]
Maecoenas dead and layd in grave / and patrons there be none.
Thy age at last requyreth east / thy studye quyet rest,
Vnles the gayns wold quyte the payns / to leave I hold it best
Let Caesar wryte his dreadfull warrs / let noble men alone
To tell there predecessors actes / that now are dead and gone   [20]

Let Cytezyns them selves declare / what dedes there mayors have
 done
What Benefactors they have had / what honor they have wonn
And though yor selfe a Cytezyn / regard there lastyng fame
Yet reason is they should reward / or recompence the same.
[Signed, " q^d Wm Vallans Salter. 1582." Cf. *S.C. Oct.*; especially 17
and 61-2 with ll. 7 and 14-5, above.] (WBA)

1583. Claude Desainliens. *To others that shall happen to write in his
commendacion,* verses prefixed to *Campo di Fior, or else the Flourie Field
of Foure Languages.* [STC 6735.]

Sig. iiij^v:
        Although my Floure be waxt a wethered weede.
[Possible echo of *S. C. June* 109.] (FY, DFA)

1583. Brian Melbancke. *Philotimus. The Ware betwixt Nature and
Fortune.* [STC 17801.]

P. 12 (sig. B ii^v):
 And thou *Melpemmone* the mournefulst Muse of nyne, if I haue euer
daunced to thy doleful tunes . . . then deigne to dropp thy heauenly dew.
[Cf. S. C. Nov. 53.]

P. 213 (sig. Ee ij):
I loued a Lasse (alas why did I so?) which made many a swearing
promise.
[Cf. *S. C. Jan.* 61.] (FMP)

1584. Thomas Lodge. *An Alarum against Vsurers. Containing tryed
experiences against worldly abuses.*
[STC 16653. *Complete Works,* ed. Edmund Gosse, Hunterian Club,
Glasgow, 1883.]

Trvths Complaint ouer England, p. 37 (sig. L; Gosse 1. [4th piece] 85):
        My mournfull Muse *Melpomine* drawe neere.

[Cf. *S. C. Nov.* 53.] (FIC)

1584. George Peele. *The Araygnement of Paris. A Pastorall.*
[STC 19530. *Works,* ed. A. H. Bullen, 1888; Malone Soc. Rpts, 1912.]

Act 3, sc. 1, sig. Cij (Bullen, act 3, sc. 1, l. 34; Malone, ll. 581 ff.):
 Colin thenamored sheepeherd singeth his passion of loue.

Act 3, sc. 2, sig. Ciiij (Bullen, act 3, sc. 1, l. 35; Malone, ll. 601 ff.):
        [Enter] *Hobinol, Digon, Thenot.*
        Hob. Poore *Colin* wofull man, thy life forespoke by loue,
            What vncouth fit, what maladie is this, that thou dost proue.
                (FIC)

About 1585. John Dove. *Poimenologia, que vulgo calendarium pastorum e
versu Anglicano in latium traducta. Huic accessit epicedium sub nomine*

Iakues pastoris, in obitum Algrindi archipoimenos, de quo toties occurit mentio in hoc libro, MS translation of S. C. at Gonville and Caius College.

[*Catalogue of MSS in the Library of Gonville and Caius College,* Cambridge, 1908, 2.627. Dove ascribes the poem to an unknown author: " ut hoc opusculum jam pene deletum et quasi sepultum, de novo vestrae lectioni secundo commendarum."] (FIC)

1586.   William Webbe. *A Discourse of English Poetrie.*
[STC 25172. Rptd Edward Arber, 1871; Smith 1.226-302.]

Sig. Biii (Arber, p. 23; Smith 1. 232):
Wherevnto I doubt not equally to adioyne the authoritye of our late famous English Poet, who wrote the *Sheepheards Calender,* where lamenting the decay of Poetry, at these dayes, saith most sweetly to the same.

> *Then make thee winges of thine aspyring wytt,*
> *And whence thou camest flye back to heauen apace. §c.*

Whose fine poeticall witt, and most equisite learning, as he shewed abundantly in that peece of worke, in my iudgment inferiour to the workes neither of *Theocritus* in Greeke, nor *Virgill* in Latine, whom hee narrowly immitateth: so I nothing doubt, but if his other workes were common abroade, which are as I thinke in ye close custodie of certaine his freends, we should haue of our own Poets, whom wee might matche in all aspects with the best.   And among all other his workes whatsoeuer, I would wysh to haue the sight of hys *English Poet,* which his freend *E. K.* did once promise to publishe, which whether he performed or not, I knowe not, if he did, my happe hath not beene so good as yet to see it. (FIC)

Sig. C iiiᵛ (Arber, p. 33; Smith, 1. 242):
Next hym I thynke I may place master *George Gaskoyne,* as painefull a Souldier in the affayres of hys Prince and Country, as he was a wytty Poet in his wryting: whose commendations, because I found in one of better iudgment then my selfe, I wyl sette downe hys wordes and suppresse myne owne, of hym thus wryteth *E. K.* vppon the ninth *Æglogue* of the new Poet.

[Quotes from Gloss to S. C. *Nov.*: " Master George Gaskoyne . . . appeare in him abundantly."] (DEM)

Sigs. Ciiiiᵛ-D (Arber, pp. 35-6; Smith 1. 245-6):
This place haue I purposely reserued for one, who if not only, yet in my iudgement principally deserueth the tytle of the rightest English Poet, that euer I read: that is, the Author of the Sheepeheardes Kalender, intituled to the woorthy Gentleman Master *Phillip Sydney:* whether it was Master *Sp.* or what rare Scholler in Pembroke Hall soeuer, because himself and his freendes, for what respect I knowe not, would not reueale it, I force not greatly to sette downe: sorry I am that I can not find none other with whom I might couple him in this *Catalogue,* in his rare gyft of Poetry: although one there is, though nowe long since,

seriously occupied in grauer studies, (Master *Gabriell Haruey*) yet, as he was once his most special freende and fellow Poet, so because he hath taken such paynes, not onely in his Latin Poetry (for which he enioyed great commendations of the best both in iudgment and dignity in thys Realme) but also to reforme our English verse, and to beautify the same with braue deuises, of which I think the cheefe lye hidde in hatefull obscurity: therefore wyll I aduenture to sette them together, as two of the rarest witts, and learnedest masters of Poetrie in England. Whose worthy and notable skyl in this faculty, I would wysh if their high dignities and serious businesses would permit, they would styll graunt to bee a furtheraunce to that reformed kinde of Poetry, which Master *Haruey* did once beginne to ratify. . . .

As for the other Gentleman, if it would please him or hys freendes to let those excellent *Poemes*, whereof I know he hath plenty, come abroad, as his Dreames, his Legends, his Court of *Cupid*, his English Poet with other: he should not onely stay the rude pens of my selfe and others, but also satisfye the thirsty desires of many which desire nothing more, then to see more of hys rare inuentions. (FIC)

[On sig. D^v (Arber, p. 37; Smith 1. 247) in censure of "the rabble of ryming Ballet makers, and compylers of senselesse sonnets," Webbe quotes the Epistle accompanying S. C.: "I scorne and spue out the rakehelly rout of our ragged Rymers. . . . *Os rabidum fera corda domans* &c."] (WW)

Sigs. Eiiii-F (Arber, pp. 52-5; Smith, 1. 263-5):
But nowe yet at ye last hath England hatched vppe one Poet of this sorte, in my conscience comparable with the best in any respect: euen Master *Sp*: Author of the *Sheepeheardes Calender*, whose trauell in that peece of English Poetrie, I thinke verely is so commendable, as none of equall iudgment can yeelde him lesse prayse for his excellent skyll, and skylfull excellency shewed foorth in the same, then they would to eyther *Theocritus* or *Virgill*, whō in my opinion, if the coursenes of our speeche (I meane the course of custome which he woulde not infringe) had beene no more let vnto him, then theyr pure natiue tongues were vnto them, he would haue (if it might be) surpassed them. What one thing is there in them so worthy admiration, whereunto we may not adioyne some thing of his, of equal desert? Take *Virgil* and make some little comparison betweene them, and iudge as ye shall see cause.

Virgill hath a gallant report of *Augustus* couertly comprysed in the first *Æglogue*: the like is in him, of her Maiestie, vnder the name of *Eliza*. *Virgill* maketh a braue coloured complaint of vnstedfast freendshyppe in the person of *Corydon*: the lyke is him in his 5. *Æglogue*. Agayne behold the pretty Pastorall contentions of *Virgill* in the third *Æglogue*: of him in ye eight *Eglogue*. Finally, either in comparison with them, or respect of hys owne great learning, he may well were the Garlande, and steppe before ye best of all English Poets that I haue seene or hearde: for I thinke no lesse deserueth (thus sayth *E, K* in hys commendations) hys wittinesse in deuising, his pithinesse in vttering, his complaintes of loue so louely, his discourses of pleasure so pleasantly, his Pastrall rudenes, his Morrall wysenesse, his due obseruing of *decorum* euery where, in personages, in season, in matter, in speeche, and generally in all seemely simplicity, of handling hys matter and framing hys wordes. The occasion of his worke is a warning to other young men, who being intangled in loue and youthful vanities, may learne to looke to themselues in time, and to auoyde inconueniences which may breede if they be not in time preuented. Many good Morrall lessons are therein contained, as the reuerence which young men owe to the aged in the second *Eglogue*: the caueate or warning to beware a subtill professor of freendshippe in the fift *Eglogue*: the commendation of good Pastors, and shame and disprayse of idle & ambitious Goteheardes in the seauenth, the loose and retchlesse lyuing of Popish Prelates in the ninth. The learned and sweet complaynt of the contempt of learning vnder the name of Poetry in the tenth. There is also much matter vttered somewhat couertly, especially yᵉ abuses of some whom he would not be too playne withall: in which, though it be not apparent to euery one, what hys speciall meaning was, yet so skilfully is it handled, as any man may take much delight at hys learned conueyance, and picke out much good sence in the most obscurest of it. Hys notable prayse deserued in euery parcell of that worke, because I cannot expresse as I woulde and as it should: I wyll cease to speake any more of, the rather because I neuer hearde as yet any that hath reade it, which hath not with much admiration commended it. Only one thing therin haue I hearde some curious heades call in question: *viz*: the motion of some vnsauery loue, such as in the sixt *Eglogue* he seemeth to deale withall, (which say they) is skant allowable to English eares, and might well haue beene left for the Italian defenders of loathsome beastlines, of whom perhappes he learned it: to thys obiection I haue often aunswered and (I thinke truely) that theyr nyce opinion ouershooteth the Poets meaning, who though hee in that as in other thinges, immitateth the auncient Poets, yet doth not meane, no more did they before hym, any disordered loue, or the filthy lust of the deuillish *Pederastice* takē in the worse sence, but rather to shewe howe the dissolute life of young men intangled in loue of women, doo neglect the freendshyp and league with their olde freendes and familiers. Why (say they) yet he shold gyue no occasion of suspition, nor offer to the viewe of Christians, any token of such filthinesse, howe good soeuer hys meaning were: wherevnto I oppose the simple conceyte they haue of matters which concerne learning or wytt, wylling them to gyue Poets leaue to vse theyr vayne as they see good: it is their foolysh construction, not hys wryting that is blameable. We must prescrybe to no wryters, (much lesse to Poets) in what sorte they should vtter theyr conceyts.

[On sigs. Fiii-Fiiiiᵛ (Arber, pp. 59-61, 65; Smith 1. 270-2, 276) " the different sortes of verses " are illustrated from *S. C.*: *Jan.* 1-2, *Feb.* 1-2, *Mar.* 1-6, *Apr.* 37-45, *Aug.* 53-6 and 151-7, *Nov.* 53-62. On sigs Iii-Iiiii (Arber, pp. 81-4; Smith 1. 286-90) appears Colin's praise of Eliza (*Apr.* 37-152) turned into English " *Saphick* verse."] (FIC)

1587. Angell Daye. *Daphnis and Chloe . . . The Shepheards Holidaie.*
[STC 6400. Ed. Joseph Jacobs, 1890]

Pp. 36-7 (Jacobs quoted):
> Ye deintie tuned fowles whose notes do decke the spring
> > Confesse in hearing of her soundes, your sweets small
> > > pleasure bring
> Ye christall sacred springs, ye vales and mountaines hie,
> > Whose pleasant walkes her passage decks, and spreading
> > > fauours die
> Agree with me in this, my sweete (surpassing far)
> > Excels the sweetnes of you all, and doth your pleasure bar.

[Cf. *S. C. Apr.* 37-153. The full title of STC 6400 is *Daphnis and Chloe
interlaced with the praises of a most peerlesse Princesse, wonderful in
Maiestie, and rare in perfection, celebrated within the same Pastorall, and
therefore termed by the name of The Shepheards Holidaie.*] (DEM)

1587? George Whetstone. *Sir Phillip Sidney, his honorable life, his
valiant death, and true vertues.*
[STC 25349. Rptd Alexander Boswell, *Frondes Caducae*, Auchinleck
Press, 1816.]

Sig. B 2ᵛ (Boswell, sig. B 2):

The last shep-pards calendars the reputed worke of S. Phil. Sydney a work of deepe learning, iudgment & witte disguised in Shep. Rules	What else he [Sidney] wrote, his will was to suppresse, But yet the darke, a *Dyamond* cannot drowne: What be his workes, the finest wittes doe gesse, The Shepheards notes, that haue so sweete a sounde. With Laurel bowghes, his healme, long since haue Cround, And not alone, in *Poesie* he did passe: But eu'ry way, a learned Knight he was. (FIC)

1588. Abraham Fraunce. *The Arcadian Rhetorike: Or The Præcepts of
Rhetorike made plaine by examples, Greeke, Latin, English, French,
Spanish.*
[STC 11338. Ed. Ethel Seaton, Luttrell Soc. Rpts 9, 1950.]

[On sig. C 4 (Seaton, pp. 32-3) quotes the 21-line *Iambicum Trimetrum*
of the Spenser-Harvey correspondence, beginning " Vnhappie verse the
witnes of my vnhappie state "]

Sig. D 7ᵛ (Seaton, p. 53):
> Spenser taketh the words one after an other.

[Quotes *S. C. Aug.* 151-62]

Sig. E 3 (Seaton, p. 60):
> Spencer in his Fairie Queene. 2. booke. cant. 4.

[Quotes stanza 35 entire] (GGS, FIC)

1588. Abraham Fraunce. *The Lawiers Logike, exemplifying the præcepts of Logike by the practise of the Common Lawe.* [STC 11343]

To The Learned Lawyers of England, especially the Gentlemen of Grays Inne, sig. ¶ᵛ:

Yet, because many loue Logike, that neuer learne Lawe, I haue reteyned those ould examples of the new Shepheards Kalender, which I first gathered, and therevnto added thease also out of our Law bookes, which I lately collected. (FIC)

Sig. Ii-iij - Ii.iijᵛ:

For our Kalender, although shepheardes bee not woont to binde themselues to any ouerstrict methode in speaking, yet that song of *Colyn Clowt* rehearsed by *Hobbynoll* in May, may make us beleeuve, that euen shepheardes, by the light of nature, did, asmuch as in them lay, expresse this methode in their speeches. For there he, after a poetical inuocation, and generall proposition of that which he hath in hand, I meane the prayses of *Elysa*, commeth nearer yᵉ matter, and first putteth downe the causes, then adi[u]nctes, and other arguments, incident to *Elysa*.

[Fraunce draws illustrations constantly from S. C.: Cijᵛ-Ciij quotes *July* 145-8; Dij, *June* 115-6 and *Sept.* 106-7; Diijᵛ- Diiij, *June* 1-8, *Jan.* 49-54, *Apr.* 91-2, *July* 18-24 and *May* 117-9; Eiijᵛ - Eiiij, *Aug.* 26-7, *Dec.* 67-70 and 77-80; Giij - Giijᵛ, *Aug.* 26-36, *Feb.* 65-6, 71-6, 143-6 and *May* 71-2; I - Iijᵛ, *Feb.* 169-86, *May* 9-14, 39-44, *July* 53-6, *Oct.* 91-6, *Dec.* 19-36 and *Mar.* 61-101; Lij - Lijᵛ, *Feb.* 41-4, *Apr.* 37-45 and 55-63; Mᵛ- Mij, *Jan.* 7-9 (again, 7-8), *Feb.* 17-8, *Mar.* 10-1, *July* 113-6, 129-32, 169-77, *Aug.* 61-72, *Nov.* 115-6 and 128; Niij, *Apr.* 136-44; Niiij - Niiijᵛ, *May* 164-7, 168, 227-8, *Dec.* 53-4 and *Aug.* 5-6; Qij, *Sept.* 150-3; Qiij, *Apr.* 64-72 and *Sept.* 80-5; Qiiij - Qiiijᵛ, *May* 43-4 and 45-50; Riij - Riijᵛ, *Feb.* 102-14, *May* 182-8 and 235-48; S - Sij, *May* 268-9, *July* 9-2, 57-60, 97-100, *Aug.* 25-42 and *Sept.* 90-3; Tiiij - Tiiijᵛ, *Sept.* 44-6, 58-61, 120-1, *May* 95-100, 205-6, *Feb.* 3-6, 87-90 and *Jan.* 31-6; Uijᵛ - Uiij, *July* 145-8 and *June* 9-16; Uiijᵛ - Uiiij, *July* 101-4 and *Aug.* 137-8; Xᵛ, *Sept.* 128-9 and 134-5; Xiiij, *Aug.* 69-72 and *Nov.* 93-4; Aaiijᵛ, *Jan.* 54, *Nov.* 58 and 169; Bbiij, *July* 173 and *Nov.* 169; Bbiijᵛ, *May* 121; Ccij, *July* 153-6 and *Jan.* 41-2; Cciij - Cciijᵛ, *June* 17-8, *May* 195-7 and *Dec.* 19-20; Cciiijᵛ, *Sept.* 1-2; Ddᵛ, *Dec.* 91-4; Ffiiij - Ffiiijᵛ, *Nov.* 183-92, *Sept.* 236-41 and *Jan.* 17-8; Gg - Ggᵛ, *Jan.* 67-72, *July* 53-6 and *Apr.* 55; Ggij - Ggijᵛ, *May* 215-26 and *Mar.* 115-7; Ggiijᵛ - Ggiiij, *June* 93-112; Hh, *Sept.* 2. Sig. Kiij alludes to, but does not quote *July* 39-52; Likewise Nij refers to *Jan.* 55-60, and Ffij - Ffiij, to *May* 39-54 and *July* passim.] (DEM)

1588. Henry Lyte. *The Light of Britayne. A Recorde of the honorable Originall & Antiquitie of Britaine.*
[Rptd at the Press of Richard and Arthur Taylor, 1814.]

To the . . . *Princesse Elizabeth,* sig. A 4 (Taylor quoted):

Most dread soueraigne Ladie Elizabeth, by the grace of God: The

Phænix of the worlde: The Angell of Englande: The bright Britona of Britayne: euen Britomartis President of Britaine.
[Similar references to Elizabeth as " Britomartis the president of Britayne " to be found on sigs. A 6, A 7ᵛ, A 8ᵛ, B 2.] (FIC)

1589.   William Byrd. *Songs of sundrie natures.*
[STC 4256. Rptd A. H. Bullen, *Some Shorter Elizabethan Poems*, Westminister, 1903.]

No. 23 (Bullen, p. 38):
> Philon the shepherd late forgot,
> siting besides a Christall fountaine,
> In shadow of a greene Oke tree,
> vppon his pipe this song plaid hee.

[In the Spenserian manner. Cf. *S. C. Dec.* 1-2, *Gn.* 237-8; *Col.* 56-60.] (DEM)

1589.   Robert Greene. *Menaphon.*
[STC 12272. *Menaphon By Robert Greene and A Margarite of America by Thomas Lodge*, ed. G. B. Harrison, Oxford, 1927.]

Sig. Hᵛ (Harrison, p. 79):
Our *Arcadian* Nimphs are faire & beautifull, though not begotten of the Suns bright rayes.
[Cf. *F. Q.* 3.6.6.] (JGM)

1589.   Thomas Lodge. *Scillas Metamorphosis: Enterlaced with the vnfortunate loue of Glaucus.*
[STC 16674. *Complete Works*, ed. Edmund Gosse, Hunterian Club, Glasgow, 1883]
Sig. A 3ᵛ (Gosse 1. [5th piece] 10):
> Nimphes, flie these Groues late blasted with my plainings,
> For cruell *Silla* nill regard my truth:
>> And leaue us two consorted in our gronings,
>> To register with teares our bitter monings.
> The flouds doo faile their course to see our crosse,
> The fields forsake their greene to heare our griefe,
> The rockes will weepe whole springs to mark our losse,
> The hills relent to store our scant reliefe,
>> The sire repines, the penciue birds are heauie,
>> The trees to see vs paind no more are leauie.
> Ay me, the Shepheards let their flockes want feeding,
> And flockes to see their palie face are sorie,
> The Nimphes to spie the flockes and shepheards needing
> Prepare their teares to heare our tragicke storie.

[Cf. *S. C. Jan.*]

Sig. C 4 (*ibid.*, p. 27):
Furie and *Rage*, *Wan-hope*, *Dispaire*, and *Woe*

From *Ditis* den by *Ate* sent, drawe nie:
Furie was red, with rage his eyes did gloe,
Whole flakes of fire from foorth his mouth did flie,
   His hands and armes ibath'd in blood of those
   Whom fortune, sinne, or fate made Countries foes.
Rage, wan and pale upon a Tiger sat,
Knawing upon the bones of mangled men;
Naught can he view, but he repinde thereat:
His lockes were Snakes bred foorth in Stigian den,
   Next whom, *Dispaire* that deepe disdained elf
   Delightlesse liude, still stabbing of her self.

[Cf. *F. Q.* 1.4.33-5, 1.9.35 ff.] (DEM)

In praise of the countrey life, sig. D 4ᵛ (*ibid.,* p. 36):
   The Nimphes amidst the vales and groues to take delight,
   To dance, to leap, to skip, with sweet and pleasant grace.

[Cf. *S. C. Apr.* 115 ff., *June* 28-34]

In commendation of a solitary life, sig. E (*ibid.,* p. 37):
   What fruites of former labours doo I finde?
   My studious pen dooth traffique for a scorne:
   My due deserts are but repaid with winde;
   And what I earne, is nought but bitter mourne. . . .
   Euen such as earst the shepheard in the shade
   Beheld, when he a Poet once was made.

[Cf. *S. C. Oct.* The " shepheard in the shade " might be Spenser.] (FIC)

Sundrie sweet Sonnets, 6, sig. F (*ibid.,* p. 45)
      My faintfull flocke dooth languish and lament
      To see their master mourning his mischance
         this iolly season.
      My bag pip's broke, my roundelaies are blent.

[The entire poem should be compared with *S. C. Jan.,* in particular with lines 43-8.] (DEM)

1589.   Thomas Nashe. *To the Gentlemen Students of both Universities,* prefixed to Robert Greene's *Menaphon.*
[STC 12272. *Works of Thomas Nashe,* ed. R. B. McKerrow, 1910]

Sig. A 2 - A 2ᵛ (McKerrow 3.323):
As for pastorall Poëmes, I will not make the comparison [with the works of foreign, particularly Italian, writers], least our countrimens credit should be discountenanst by the contention, who although they cannot fare, with such inferior facilitie, yet I knowe would carrie the bucklers full easilie, from all forreine brauers, if their *subiectum circa quod,* should sauor of anything haughtie: and should the challenge of deepe conceit, be intruded by any forreiner, to bring our english wits, to the tutcsthone of Arte, I would preferre, diuine Master *Spencer,* the miracle of wit to bandie line for line for my life, in the honor of *England,* gainst

Spaine, France, Italie, and all the worlde. Neither is he, the only swallow of our summer.
[Nashe goes on to name, " as for example, *Mathew Roydon, Thomas Atchelow and George Peele.*"] (FIC)

1589.   George Peele. *A Farewell. Entituled to . . . Sir Iohn Norris & Syr Frauncis Drake . . . Whereunto is annexed: A tale of Troy.*
[STC 19537. *Works,* ed. A. H. Bullen, 1888; David H. Horne, *The Life and Minor Works of George Peele,* Yale Univ. Press, 1952]

Sig. B (Bullen 2.244; Horne, p. 186):
> So couth he [Paris] sing his layes among them all
> And tune his pype vnto the waters fall.
[Cf. *S. C. Apr.* 33-6.] (DEM)

1589.   George Peele. *An Eglogue. Gratvlatorie Entituled: To . . . Robert Earle of Essex.* [STC 19534]

[Use of characters *Piers* and *Palinode*; employment of rustic dialect clearly reminiscent of *S. C.* Bullen 2.269-77; cf. Horne, p. 164, 224-30. Thorlief Larson, " The Early Years of George Peele, Dramatist, 1558-1588," *Trans. Royal Soc. Canada,* 22 (1928), sec. 2, lists a number of archaisms in *A Tale of Troy* from *S. C.*] (TL, DEM)

1589.   George Puttenham. *The Arte of English Poesie.*
[STC 20519. Ed. Gladys Doidge Willcock and Alice Walker, Cambridge Univ. Press, 1936.]

P. 51 (sig. I; Smith 2.65; Willcock and Walker, pp. 62-3):
That for Tragedie, the Lord of Buckhurst & Maister *Edward Ferrys* . . . do deserue the hyest price. . . . For Eglogue and pastorall Poesie, Sir *Philip Sydney* and Maister *Challenner,* and that other Gentleman who wrate the late shepheardes Callender. (FIC)

1590-94.   *John of Bordeaux or The Second Part of Friar Bacon,* Alnwick Castle MS.
[Ed. W. L. Renwick, Malone Soc. Rpts, 1936.]

Renwick, pp. 43-4, ll. 1060-88:
> Enter ij sheapherd Correbus and Damon
> tell me Corebus tell me Ientell swayne
> what hath befallne vnto thy flockes of latte
> >y dropest thow thus or wher for art thow s<
> where ar thy meri song*es* thy rundelayes
> which on thy pipe thow wonted wert to playe
> I fer I fear some fayre fast geerle hath cought
> they tender hart and the regardeth nought
> Damod beleve me but thow gessest all a wry
> no love hath w[o]rought in me this hevines
> and to resoulve the lend thy listening eare

I will vnfould to the my cas of care
as lat vnto the Cittie I did go
to buy such nedfull thing*es* as I did wante
        >d vp and doune the toune
th<t> Rossalin a chast and vertious Dame
wif to Ser Iohn of Burdiox that brav knight
som say for treson is condemd to die
and with her Inglish Bacon worthi man of arte
vnles with in one munth the Chance to fynd
a champian forth that will defend the case
that wo is me for that good ladies sacke
to thincke her vertious case thers non doth vndertake
Damō peace peace Correbus hould and say no more
        tis wisdom still to kep a hatch befor the dore
        let those thinges rest and let ous tend or shepe
        him counpt I wise that well his tung can kepe
Corebus that wate I well and ther with all I know
        that good men offten greve at good mens woe Exent
[General influence of *S. C.*] (JGM)

1590. Thomas Lodge. *Rosalynde. Euphues golden legacie.*
[STC 16664. *Complete Workes,* ed. Edmund Gosse, Hunterian Club,
Glasgow, 1883.]

P. 66 (sig. S 2; Gosse 1. [6th piece] 66):
If you gather any frutes by this Lagacie, speake well of *Euphues* for
writing it, and me for fetching it. If you grace me with that fauour, you
encorage me to be more forward: and assoone as I haue ouerlookt my
labours, expect the *Sailers Kalender.*
                                    T. Lodge.
[The projected *Sailers Kalender* may have been inspired by Spenser's
S. C.] (DEM)

1590. Christopher Marlowe. *Tamburlaine the Greate . . . Deuided into
two Tragicall Discourses.*
[STC 17425. *Works,* ed. C. F. Tucker Brooke, Oxford, 1910, quoted
below; *Tamburlaine the Great,* ed. U. M. Ellis-Fermor, 1930 (in *Works
and Life,* R. H. Case, gen. ed.); cf. Charles Crawford, *N & Q,* 9th S.,
7.61-3, 101-3, 142-4, 203-5, 261-3, 324-5, 384-6; Georg Schoeneich,
Der Litterarische Einfluss Spensers auf Marlowe, Diss. Halle-Wittenburg,
Halle a. S., 1907. The following quotations are illustrative: in addition
to these, Schoeneich notes a number of others.]

Pt. 1, 1.2.393 (Schoeneich, p. 18; Brooke, p. 19; Ellis-Fermor, p. 87):
        Ioue sometime masked in a Shepheards weed.
[Cf. *F. Q.* 1. proem 1. 1-2.]

Ibid., 2.3.617-9 (Schoeneich, pp. 18-9; Brooke, p. 25; Ellis-Fermor,
p. 100):

And bullets like *Ioues* dreadfull Thunderbolts,
Enrolde in flames and fiery smoldering mistes,
Shall threat the Gods more than Cyclopian warres.

[Cf. *F. Q.* 1.8.9.1-4.]

Ibid., 3.3.1215-21 (Schoeneich, pp. 24-5; Brooke, p. 41; Ellis-Fermor, p. 130):

Tam. Zenocrate, the loueliest Maide aliue,
Fairer than rockes of pearle and pretious stone,
The onely Paragon of *Tamburlaine*,
Whose eies are brighter than the Lamps of heauen,
And speech more pleasant than sweet harmony:
That with thy lookes canst cleare the darkened Sky:
And calme the rage of thundring *Iupiter*.

[Cf. *F. Q.* 1.3.4.6-8, 1.proem 4.3-4, 1.4.8.5-9, 1.10.55.4-5.]

Ibid., 5.2.1902-4 (Schoeneich, p. 17; Brooke, p. 59; Ellis-Fermor, p. 160):

I will not spare these proud Egyptians,
Nor change my Martiall obseruations,
For all the wealth of Gehons golden waues.

[Cf. *F. Q.* 1.7.43.9.]

Ibid., 1916-35 (Schoeneich, pp. 33-6; Brooke, p. 60; Ellis-Fermor, pp. 161-2):

Ah faire *Zenocrate*, diuine *Zenocrate*,
Faire is too foule an Epithite for thee,
That in thy passion for thy countries loue,
And feare to see thy kingly Fathers harme,
With haire discheweld wip'st thy watery cheeks: 1920
And like to *Flora* in her mornings pride,
Shaking her siluer treshes in the aire,
Rain'st on the earth resolued pearle in showers,
And sprinklest Saphyrs on thy shining face,
Wher Beauty, mother to the Muses sits,   1925
And comments vollumes with her Yuory pen:
Taking instructions from the flowing eies,
Eies when that *Ebena* steps to heauen,
In silence of thy solemn Euenings walk,
Making the mantle of the richest night,   1930
The Moone, the Planets, and the Meteors light.
There Angels in their christal armours fight
A doubtfull battell with my tempted thoughtes,
For Egypts freedom and the Souldans life:
His life that so consumes *Zenocrate*.   1935

[Cf. 1916-7 with *F. Q.* 2.2.22.1-3; 1920 with 2.1.13.6-9; 1921 with 2.12.50.5, 9; 1925-7 with 2.3.25.1-3; 1928-35 with 2.5.33.3 and 2.3.23.1-4.]

Ibid., 1941-54 (Schoeneich, pp. 34-6; Brooke, pp. 60-1; Ellis-Fermor, pp. 162-3):

> What is beauty saith my sufferings then?
> If all the pens that euer poets held,
> Had fed the feeling of their maisters thoughts,
> And euery sweetnes that inspir'd their harts,
> Their minds, and muses on admyred theames: 1945
> If all the heauenly Quintessence they still
> From their immortall flowers of Poesy,
> Wherein as in a myrrour we perceiue
> The highest reaches of a humaine wit.
> If these had made one Poems period   1950
> And all combin'd in Beauties worthinesse,
> Yet should ther houer in their restlesse heads
> One thought, one grace, one woonder at the least,
> Which into words no vertue can digest.

[Cf. *F.Q.* 2.3.25.8-9 and 3.proem 2.6-9.]

Ibid., 2036-44 (Schoeneich, pp. 38-9; Brooke, p. 63; Ellis-Fermor, pp. 167-8):

> *Bai.* O life more loathsome to my vexed thoughts,
> Than noisome parbreak of the Stygian Snakes,
> Which fils the nookes of Hell with standing aire,
> Infecting all the Ghosts with curelesse griefs:
> O dreary Engines of my loathed sight,   2040
> That sees my crowne, my honor and my name,
> Thrust vnder yoke and thraldom of a thiefe.
> Why feed ye still on daies accursed beams,
> And sink not quite into my tortur'd soule?

[Note use of *parbreak* in 2037 and *F. Q.* 1.1.20.9; cf. 2040-1 with *F. Q.* 1.7.22.1-2.]

Ibid., 2071-9 (Schoeneich, pp. 39-40; Brooke, p. 64; Ellis-Fermor, p. 169):

> O highest Lamp of euerliuing *Ioue*,
> Accursed day infected with my griefs,
> Hide now thy stained face in endles night,
> And shut the windowes of the lightsome heauens.
> Let vgly darknesse with her rusty coach   2075
> Engyrt with tempests wrapt in pitchy clouds,
> Smother the earth with neuer fading mistes:
> And let her horses from their nostrels breathe
> Rebellious winds and dreadfull thunderclaps.

[Cf. *F. Q.* 1.7.23.1-5.]

Ibid., 2083-5 (Schoeneich, p. 40; Brooke, p. 64; Ellis-Fermor, p. 169):

> Then let the stony dart of sencelesse colde,
> Pierce through the center of my withered heart,
> And make a passage for my loathed life.

[Cf. *F. Q.* 1.7.22.7-9] (CC, GS)

Pt. 2, 3.5.3650-1 (Brooke, p. 111; Ellis-Fermor, p. 240):

> How now ye pety kings, loe, here are Bugges
> Wil make the haire stand vpright on your heads.

[Cf. *F. Q.* (1590 text) 2.3.20.5.] (JGM)

Ibid., 4.1.3860-71 (Schoeneich, pp. 53-4; Brooke, p. 117; Ellis- Fermor, p. 249):

> Ile make ye roare, that earth may eccho foorth
> The far resounding torments ye sustaine,
> As when an heard of lusty Cymbrian Buls,
> Run mourning round about the Femals misse,
> And stung with furie of their following
> Fill all the aire with troublous bellowing: 3865
> I will with Engines, neuer exercisde,
> Conquer, sacke, and vtterly consume
> Your cities and your golden pallaces,
> And with the flames that beat against the clowdes
> Incense the heauens, and make the starres to melt,
> As if they were the teares of *Mahomet*.

[See *F. Q.* 1.8.11.2-8; also cf. 3864-9 with *F. Q.* 1.8.9.5-8 and 1.6.6.4-5.]

Ibid., 4.3.4090-111 (Schoeneich, pp. 57-9; Brooke, p. 123; Ellis-Fermor, pp. 258-9):

> For there my Pallace royal shal be plac'd:
> Whose shyning Turrets shal dismay the heauens,
> And cast the fame of *Ilions* Tower to hell.
> Thorow the streets with troops of conquered kings,
> Ile ride in golden armour like the Sun,
> And in my helme a triple plume shal spring   4095
> Spangled with Diamonds dancing in the aire,
> To note me Emperour of the three fold world,
> Like to an almond tree ymounted high,
> Vpon the lofty and celestiall mount,
> Of euer greene *Selinus* queintly dect   4100
> With bloomes more white than *Hericinas* browes,
> Whose tender blossoms tremble euery one,
> At euery little breath that thorow heauen is blowen:
> Then in my coach like *Saturnes* royal son,
> Mounted his shining chariot, gilt with fire   4105
> And drawen with princely Eagles through the path,
> Pau'd with bright Christall, and enchac'd with starres,
> When all the Gods stand gazing at his pomp.
> So will I ride through *Samarcanda* streets,
> Vntil my soule disseuered from this flesh,   4110
> Shall mount the milk-white way and meet him there.

[Cf. 4090-1 with *F. Q.* 1.4.4.1-6; 4092 with 1.10.58.9; 4094-103 with 1.7.32.1-9; 4104-9 with 1.4.17.1-9; 4110-1 with 1.2.19.7-9.] (CC, GS)

[Mainly on the basis of an examination of classical sources available to Marlowe and a reconstruction of his use of them, Professor T. W. Baldwin (" Spenser's Borrowings from Marlowe," *ELH*, 9 (1942). 157-87) rejects the generally accepted view that Marlowe used *F. Q.* as a subsidiary source for *Tamburlaine*, and strongly maintains Spenser's indebtedness. Professor Watkins (" The Plagiarist: Spenser or Marlowe? " *ELH*, 11 (1944). 249-65) notes a fact which by itself challenges Professor Baldwin's conclusion: the presence of the alexandrine with the terminal c-rime of the Spenserian stanza in the first and most elaborately discussed of Professor Baldwin's seven instances of connection between *Tamburlaine* and *F. Q.* (Part 2, 4.3.4094-103 and 1.7.32.1-9).]

1590. Sir Walter Raleigh. Verses appended to *The Faerie Queene.*
    [STC 23080-1ª]

A Vision vpon this conceipt of the Faery Queene p. 596:

> Me thought I saw the graue, where *Laura* lay,
> Within that Temple, where the vestall flame
> Was wont to burne, and passing by that way,
> To see the buried dust of liuing fame,
> Whose tombe faire loue, and fairer vertue kept,
> All suddeinly I saw the Faery Queene:
> At whose approch the soule of *Petrarke* wept,
> And from thenceforth those graces were not seene.
> For they this Queene attended, in whose steed
> Obliuion laid him downe on *Lauras* herse:
> Hereat the hardest stones were seene to bleed,
> And grones of buried ghostes the heuens did perse.
> > Where *Homers* spright did tremble all for griefe,
> > And curst th'accesse of that celestiall theife.

Another of the same, p. 596:

> The prayse of meaner wits this worke like profit brings,
> As doth the Cuckoes song delight when *Philumena* sings.
> If thou hast formed right true vertues face herein:
> Vertue her selfe can best discerne, to whom they writen bin.
> If thou hast beauty praysd, let her sole lookes diuine
> Iudge if ought therein be amis, and mend it by her eine.
> If Chastitie want ought, or Temperaunce her dew,
> Behold her Princely mind aright, and write thy Queene anew.
> Meane while she shall perceiue, how far her vertues sore
> Aboue the reach of all that liue, or such as wrote of yore:
> And thereby will excuse and fauour thy good will:
> Whose vertue can not be exprest, but by an Angels quill.
> > Of me no lines are lou'd, nor letters are of price,
> > Of all which speak our English tongue, but these of thy deuice.

(FIC)

1590. William Vallans. *A Tale of Two Swannes. Wherein is compre-*
hended the original and increase of the riuer Lee commonly called Ware-
riuer: together, with the antiquitie of sundrie places and townes seated
vpon the same. [STC 24590]

Sig. A 2:
Yet hereby I would animate, or encourage those worthy Poets, who haue
writtē *Epithalamion Thamesis,* to publish the same: I haue seen it in
Latine verse (in my iudgment) wel done, but the Author I know not
for what reason doth suppresse it: That which is written in English,
though long since it was promised, yet is it not perfourmed: so as it
seemeth, some vnhappy Star enuieth yᵉ sight of so good a work: which
once set abroad, such trifles as these would vanish, and be ouershadowed,
much like the Moon and other starres, which after the appearing of the
Sunne are not to be seene at all. (FIC)
[Are " those worthy Poets " Camden and Spenser?]

Sig. A 3 - A 3ᵛ:
      To *Ware* he comes, and to the Launde he flies,
    Where *Venus,* like the Goddesse of great Loue,
    Sate louely by the running riuer side,
    Tuning her Lute vnto the waters fall.

[Cf. *S. C. Apr.* 36; *F. Q.* 6.10.7.9.]

Sig. B 2ᵛ:
    A Swane of *Thames* inuites the King and Queene
    Vpon a day prefixt, to see and celebrate
    The marriage of two Riuers of great name.

[Cf. marriage of Medway and Thames, *F. Q.* 4.11.] (DEM)

1590. Thomas Watson. *Melibœus Thomæ Watsoni, siuè Ecloga in*
Obitum F. Walsinghami.
[STC 25120. *Poems,* ed. Edward Arber, 1870.]

Sig. D (Arber, p. 172):
    Sed quìd eam refero, quæ nostro carmine maior,
    Est cantanda tuo, dulcis Spencere cothurno,
    Cuius inest numeris Hiblæi copia mellis.
    Tu quoque nobiscum (quoniàm tu noster Apollo)
    Lugentem solare Deam, quotiès Melibœi
    Tristia lacrymulis preciosis funera deflet.
    Dic illi (tu namquè potes fœlice camæna)
    Arcadas innumeros, quanquam Melibœus obiuit,
    Praestantes superesse viros, similes Melibœi.
    Damœtam memora, quo non præclarior alter,
    Non quisquam ingenio melior, non promptior ore,
    Non grauior vultu, nec arma paratior extat:
    Ille est *Damætas,* qui iuris corrigit iram,
    Quem vocat Hattonum Triuiæ venerabile Numen.

1590.   Thomas Watson. *An Eglogue Vpon the death of the Right Honorable Sir Francis Walsingham.* [STC 25121]

Sigs. C 3ᵛ - C 4 (Arber, p. 173):

> Yet lest my homespun verse obscure hir worth,
>   sweet *Spencer* let me leaue this taske to thee,
> Whose neuerstooping quill can best set forth
>   such things of state, as passe my Muse, and me.
> Thou *Spencer* art the alderliefest swaine,
>   or haply if that word be all to base,
> Thou art *Apollo* whose sweet hunnie vaine
>   amongst the Muses hath a chiefest place.
> Therefore in fulnes of thy duties loue,
>   calme thou the tempest of *Dianaes* brest,
> Whilst shee for *Meliboeus* late remoue
>   afflicts hir mind with ouerlong vnrest.
> Tell hir forthwith (for well shee likes thy vaine)
>   that though great *Meliboeus* be awaie:
> Yet like to him there manie still remaine,
>   which will vphold hir countrie from decaie.

[Watson's English version of preceding entry.] (FIC)

1591.   Thomas Bradshaw. *The Shepherds Starre.* [STC 3508]
[A Theocritean contention between Corydon and Tityrus, somewhat in the style of *S. C.*, perhaps influenced by it. Amaryllis, a witness to the contention, answers it, but not in the role of judge.] (DEM)

Sig. E 2ᵛ:
It is not of the necessitie . . . of your Arte to discerne more than you see apparent in the face. And that you describe out of your shepherdes Calender: Whereby you can tell, if you see a cloud, that it is a signe of a showre, and many starres bring a frost: and the euening red, a faire morning: and the morning gray, a faire euening.
[From the context, reference to *S. C.* appears unlikely.] (WW)

1591.   John Florio. *Florios Second Frutes.* [STC 11097]
The Epistle Dedicatorie, sig. A 3 - A 3ᵛ:
   The maiden-head of my industrie I yeelded to a noble Mecenas (renoumed Lecester) the honour of Englād, whom thogh like Hector euery miscreāt Mirmidō dare strik being dead, yet sing *Homer* or *Virgil,* write frend or foe, of *Troy,* or *Troyes* issue, that *Hector* must have his desert, the General of his Prince, the Paragon of his Peeres, the watchman of our peace,

> *Non so se miglior Duce o Caualliero.*

as *Petrarke* hath in his triumph of fame; and to conclude, the supporter of his friends, the terror of his foes, the *Britton* Patron of the Muses.

> *Dardanias light, and Troyans faithfulst hope.*

But nor I, nor this place may halfe suffice for his praise, which the

sweetest singer of all our westerne shepheards hath so exquisitely de-
painted, that as Achilles by Alexander was counted happy for hauing
such a rare emblazoner of his magnanimitie, as the Meonian Poete; so
I account him thrice-fortunate in hauing such a herauld of his vertues as
Spenser; Curteous Lord, Curteous Spenser, I knowe not which hath
perchast more fame, either he in deseruing so well of so famous a scholler,
or so famous a scholler in being so thankfull without hope of requitall to
so famous a Lord. (FIC)

1591.　Grant of Spenser's Pension, Feb. 25. *Patent Roll,* 33 *Eliz.* Pt. 3,
no. 1364.
[Transcript by H. R. Plomer in Carpenter, p. 70.]

1591.　Sir John Harington. *Orlando Furioso in English Heroical Verse.*
[STC 746]

P. 373 (sig. Ii iiij):
　The hosts tale in the xxvviij book of this worke, is a bad one: M.
Spencers tale of the squire of Dames, in his excellent Poem of the Faery
Queene, in the end of vij. Canto of the third booke, is to the like effect,
sharpe and well cōceyted; In substance thus, that his Squire of dames
could in three yeares trauell, find but three women that denyed his lewd
desire: of which three, one was a courtesan, that reiected him bcause he
wanted coyne for her: the second a Nun, who refused him because he
would not sweare secreacie; the third a plain countrie Gentlewoman,
that of good honest simplicitie denyed him. (HER)

1591.　Thomas Nashe. Preface to Sidney's *Astrophel and Stella.*
[STC 22536. *Works,* ed. R. B. McKerrow, 1910.]

McKerrow 3.329 quoted:
The chiefe Actor here is *Melpomene,* whose dusky robes, dipt in the ynke
of teares, as yet seeme to drop when I view them neere.
[Reference to *Comp.,* just published; and to *T. M.* in particular? " It
is hardly extravagant in this context for Nashe to have conceived of
Melpomene's robes as the sheets or pages of a printed book, since the
whole figure he has been developing involves the metaphorical comparison of the book of *Astrophel and Stella* with the representation of a
tragedy presided over by Melpomene."] (WBA)

About 1592.　Sir Walter Raleigh. *The 11th: and last booke of the Ocean
to Scinthia,* Hatfield MS, Cecil Papers, 144.
[*The Poems of Sir Walter Raleigh,* ed. Agnes M. C. Latham, 1951.]

Latham, pp. 34-5:
　　　Thos streames seeme standinge puddells which, before,
　　　Wee saw our bewties in, so weare the cleere.
　　　Bellphebes course is now obserude no more,
　　　That faire resemblance weareth out of date.

Latham, p. 37:
> a Queen shee was to mee, no more Belphebe. (RH)

1592. Nicholas Breton. *The Pilgrimage to Paradise, ioyned with the Countesse of Penbrookes loue.* Oxford.

[STC 3683. Ed. A. B. Grosart, Chertsey Worthies' Library, 1879] Sig. F 3 (Grosart 1.16a):

> I founde that cost was often kindely taken,
> And costly kindnes was a common thing,
> I found the needy friend was soon forsaken,
> And he that had the crownes was halfe a king:
> I founde that flattry was a fine conceite,
> And gold was seru'd, where better gifts did waite.
>
> I found faire beauty like a blasing starre,
> But oftentimes, the Moone was in a mist,
> And many a one, was with his wits at warre,
> while reason reade the rules of had I wiste:
> I found sweet Musicke sounde in many a place,
> while empty purses were weeping case. . . .

[Cf. *Col.*]

Sig. G^v (Grosart 1.17a):

> Where, walking on, they met on their rigt hande,
> A worlde of people, making pitteous mone . . .
>
> The Courtier, hee, complainde, of loues disgrace,
> The souldier, he cried out, of lacke of paie. . . .

[Cf. *Col.*] (DEM)

1592. Samuel Daniel. *Delia. Contayning certayne Sonnets: with the complaint of Rosamond.*
[STC 6253. *Complete Works*, ed. A. B. Grosart, 1885.]

Sonnet II, sig. B^v (Grosart 1.38):

> Goe wailing verse, the infants of my loue,
> Minerua-like, brought foorth without a Mother:
> Present the image of the cares I proue,
> Witnes your Fathers griefe exceeds all other.

[Cf. Spenser's verses *To his Booke* at the beginning of S. C.]

[*Sonnet XXX*, sig. G 3^v (Grosart 1.60, no. 35) employs the Spenserian sonnet rime scheme.] (DEM)

Sonnet XLVI, sig. G 3^v (Grosart 1.73, no. 55):

> Let others sing of Knights and Palladines,
> In aged accents, and vntimely words:
> Paint shadowes in imaginary lines,
> Which well the reach of their high wits records. (FIC)

1592. *A Declaration of the True Causes of the Great Troubles, Presupposed to be intended against the realme of England.* Cologne? [STC 10005]

P. 68:

Prosopopoia or Mother Hubberds tale

And because no man dare frame an endytement against him [Burghley], I will heere omit many other articles of highe treasõ, but yf any will vndertake to iustifie his actions in his course of gouernment, let him know, that there is sufficiēt matter of reply reserued for him, which is not extracted out of *Mother Hubberds* tale, of the false fox and his crooked cubbes, but is to be vttred in plaine prose, and shal lay open to the world, his birth, his lyf, and perhaps his death, seing his detestable actions are such, as do aske vengeance of heauen and earth. (HS)

1592. Abraham Fraunce. *The Third Part of the Countesse of Pembrokes Iuychurch: Entituled Amintas Dale.* [STC 11341]

Sig. Nᵛ (leaf 47ᵛ) [Illustrating the fable of Achilles' heel and the love of Polyxena—a story explained in the gloss of *S. C. Mar.*]:
In imitation whereof, the good *Thomalin* in the new Shepheards Kalender, singeth thus of the winged boy.
[Quotes *S. C. Mar.* 94-102.] (DB)

1592. Gabriel Harvey. *Foure Letters and Certaine Sonnets.* [STC 12900. *Complete Works*, ed. A. B. Grosart, 1884-5; ed. G. B. Harrison, 1922.]

The second Letter, p. 7 (sig. B; Grosart 1.164; Harrison, pp. 15-6):
I must needs say, Mother-Hubbard in heat of choller, forgetting the pure sanguine of her sweete Faery Queene, wilfully ouer-shott her malcontented selfe: as elsewhere I haue specified at larg, with the good leaue of vnspotted friendshipp. Examples in some ages doe exceedingmuch hurt. *Salust,* and *Clodius* learned of *Tully,* to frame artificial Declamations, & patheticall Inuectiues against *Tully* himselfe, and other worthy members of that most-florishing State: if mother Hubbard in the vaine of *Chawcer,* happen to tel one Canicular Tale; father *Elderton,* and his sonne *Greene,* in the vaine of *Skelton,* or *Scoggin,* will counterfeit an hundred dogged Fables, Libles, Calumnies, Slaunders, Lies for the whetstone, what not & most currishly snarle, & bite where they should most-kindly fawne, and licke. Euery priuate excesse is daungerous: but such publike enormities, incredibly pernitious, and insupportable: and who can tell, what huge outrages might amount of such quarrellous, and tumultous causes?

The third Letter, p. 18 (sig. C 2ᵛ; Grosart 1.180; Harrison, pp. 30-1):
Signor Immerito (for that name will be remembred) was then, and is still my affectionate friend, one that could very wel abide Gascoignes Steele glasse, and that stoode equallie indifferent to either part of the state Demostratuie: many communications, and writings may secretlie

passe betweene such, euen for an exercise of speech, and stile that are not otherwise conuenient to be disclosed: it was the sinister hap of those infortunate Letters, to fall into the left handes of malicious enemies, or vndiscreete friends: who aduentured to imprint in earnest, that was scribled in iest, (for the moody fit was soone ouer:) and requited their priuate pleasure with my publike displeasure: oh my inestimable, and infinite displeasure. (FIC, DEM)

Ibid., p. 29 [for 26] (sig. D. 2; Grosart 1.191; Harrison, p. 41):
Euen *Gwicciardines* siluer History, and *Ariostos* golden Cantoes, grow out of request: and the Countesse of Pembrookes Arcadia is not grene inough for queasy stomacks, but they must haue *Greenes* Arcadia: and I beleue, most eagerly longed for *Greenes* Faery Queene.

Ibid., p. 36 (sig. E 3ᵛ; Grosart 1.205; Harrison, pp. 54-5):
. . . they can lash poore slaues, and spurgall Asses mightily: they can tell parlous Tales of Beares, and Foxes, as shrewdlye as mother Hubbard, for her life.

Ibid., p. 44 (sig. F 2ᵛ; Grosart 1.212; Harrison, pp. 61-2):
. . . the verse is not unknowen: & runneth in one of those vnsatyricall Satyres, which M. *Spencer* long since embraced with an ouerloouing Sonnet: A token of his Affection, not a Testimony of hys Iudgement.

Ibid., pp. 48-9 (sigs. F 4ᵛ - G; Grosart 1.217-8; Harrison, pp. 67-8):
Good sweete Oratour, be a deuine Poet indeede: and vse heauenly Eloquence indeede: and employ thy golden talent with amounting vsance indeede: and with heroicall Cantoes honour right Vertue, & braue valour indeede: as noble Sir Philip Sidney and gentle Maister Spencer haue done, with immortall Fame. . . . Such liuely springes of streaming Eloquence: & such right-Olympicall hilles of amountinge witte: I cordially recommend to the deere Louers of the Muses: and namely to the professed Sonnes of the-same; *Edmond Spencer, Richard Stanihurst, Abraham France, Thomas Watson, Samuell Daniell, Thomas Nash,* and the rest.

The Fourth Letter, p. 59 (sig. H 2; Grosart 1.234; Harrison, p. 82):
[Many contemporary writers] are fine men, & haue many sweete phrases: it is my simplicity, that I am so slenderly acquainted with that dainty stile: the only new fashion of current Eloquēce in Esse: far surpassing the stale vein of *Demosthenes,* or *Tully: Iewel,* or *Harding: Whitgift,* or *Cartwright: Sidney,* or *Spencer.*

Sonnet X, p. 66 (sig. Iᵛ; Grosart 1.244; Harrison, p. 92):
A more particular Declaration of his Intention.
    Yet let Affection interpret selfe:
    Arcadia braue, and dowty *Faery Queene*
    Cannot be stain'd by *Gibelin,* or *Guelph,*
    Or goodliest Legend, that Witts eye hath seene.
    The dainty Hand of exquisitest Art,
    And nimble Head of pregnantest receit,

Neuer more finely plaid their curious part,
Then in those liuely Christals of conceit.

Sonnet XXII, p. 73 (sig. K; Grosart 1.252; Harrison, p. 100):

L'*Enuoy; or an Answere to the Gentleman that drunke to Chaucer* . . .
Some Tales to tell, would I a Chaucer were:
Yet would I not euen-now an Homer be:
Though Spencer me hath often Homer term'd. (FIC, FMP)

1592.   Thomas Nashe. *Pierce Penilesse His Svpplication to the Diuell.*
[STC 18371-3. *Works*, ed. R. B. McKerrow, 1910.]

Pp. 39-40 (sig. L 4 - L 4ᵛ; McKerrow 1.243-4; STC 18371 quoted):

And here (heauenlie *Spencer*) I am most highly to accuse thee of
forgetfulnes, that in that honourable Catalogue of our English *Heroes*,
which insueth the conclusion of thy famous Fairie Queene, thou wouldest
let so speciall a piller of Nobilitie [the Earl of Derby?] passe vnsaluted.
The verie thought of his farre deriued discent, and extraordinarie parts
wherewith hee asto[ni]eth the world, and drawes all harts to his loue,
would haue inspired thy forewearied *Muse* with new furie to proceede
to the next triumphs of thy statelie Goddesse, but as I in fauor of so
rare a Scholer, suppose with this counsaile, he refraind his mention in
this first part, that he might with full saile proceede to his due commendations in the second. Of this occasion long since I happened to
frame a Sonnet, which being wholy intended to the reuerence of this
renoumed Lord, (to whom I owe all the vtmost powers of my loue and
duetie) I meante heere for variety of stile to insert [.]

Perusing yesternight with idle eyes,
    The Fairy Singers stately tuned verse:
And viewing after Chap-mans wonted guise,
    What strange contents the title did rehearse.
I streight leapt ouer to the latter end,
    Where like the queint Comædians of our time,
That when their Play is doone do fall to ryme,
    I found short lines, to sundry Nobles pend.
Whom he as speciall Mirrours singled fourth,
    To be the Patrons of his Poetry;
I read them all, and reuerenc't their worth,
    Yet wondred he left out thy memory.
But therefore gest I he supprest thy name,
Because few words might not cōprise thy fame.

Beare with mee gentle Poet, though I conceiue not aright of thy
purpose, or be too inquisitiue into the intent of thy obliuion: for how
euer my coniecture may misse the cushion, yet shall my speech sauour
of friendship, though it be not allied to Iudgement. (FIC)

1592.   Thomas Nashe. *Strange Newes, Of the intercepting certaine Letters, and a Conuoy of Verses, as they were going Priuilie to victuall the
Low Countries.*

[STC 18377-7ᵃ. *Works*, ed. R. B. McKerrow, 1910.]

Sig. E - Eᵛ (McKerrow 1.281-2):

As touching the libertie of Orators and Poets, I will conferre with thee somewhat grauely, although thou beest a goose-cappe and hast no iudgement.

A libertie they haue, thou sayst, *but no liberty without bounds, no license without limitation.* . . .

That libertie, Poets of late in their inuectiues haue exceeded: they haue borne their sword vp where it is not lawfull for a poynado that is but the page of prowesse to intermeddle.

Thou bringst in *Mother Hubbard* for an instance. Go no further, but here confesse thy selfe a flat nodgscome before all this congregation; for thou hast dealt by thy friend as homely as thou didst by thy father.

Who publikely accusde or of late brought *Mother Hubbard* into question, that thou shouldst by rehearsall rekindle against him the sparkes of displeasure that were quenched?

Forgot hee the *pure sanguine of his Fairy Queene*, sayst thou?

A *pure sanguine* sot art thou, that in vaine-glory to haue *Spencer* known for thy friend, and that thou hast some interest in him, censerest him worse than his deadliest enemie would do.

If any man were vndeseruedly toucht in it, thou hast reuiued his disgrace that so toucht in it, by renaming it, when it was worn out of al mens mouths and minds.

Besides, whereas before I thought it a made matter of some malicious moralizers against him, and no substance of slaunder in thruth, now, when thou (that proclaimest thy selfe the only familiar of his bosome, and therefore shouldst know his secretes) giues it out in print that he ouershotte himselfe therein; it cannot chuse but be suspected to be so indeed.

Immortal *Spencer,* no frailtie hath thy fame, but the imputation of this Idiots friendship: vpon an vnspotted *Pegasus* should thy gorgeous attired *Fayrie Queene* ride triumphant through all reports dominions, but that this mud-born bubble, this bile on the browe of the Vniuersitie, this bladder of pride newe blowne, challengeth some interest in her prosperitie.

Sig. E 2ᵛ (McKerrow 1.283):

Did not you in the fortie one Page line 2. of your Epistles to *Collin Clout* vse this speech?

Sig. F 4 (McKerrow 1.294):

Not the least, but the greatest Schollers in the WORLD haue not only but exceedingly fedde him fate in his humor of *Braggadochio Glorioso.*

> *Yea* Spencer *him hath often* Homer *tearmd,*
> *And Mounsier* Bodkin *vowd as much as he;*
> *Yet cares not* Nashe *for him a halfepeny.*

Sig. G (McKerrow 1.295-6):

Signior Immerito (so called because *he was and is his friend* vndeseruedly) was counterfeitly brought in to play a part in that his Enterlude of Epistles that was hist at, thinking his very name (as the name of *Ned Allen* on the common stage) was able to make an ill matter good.

I durst on my credit vndertake, *Spencer* was no way priuie to the committing of them to the print.

Sig. G^v (McKerrow 1.296):

I will not lye or backbite thee as thou hast done mee, but are not these thy wordes *to the curteous Buyer*.

Shew mee or Immerito *two English letters in print, in all pointes equall to these*.

Sig. G 3 (McKerrow 1.299):

Homer, and Virgil, two valorous Authors, yet were they neuer knighted, they wrote in Hexameter verses: *Ergo*, *Chaucer*, and *Spencer* the *Homer* and *Virgil* of England, were farre ouerseene that they wrote not all their Poems in Hexamiter verses also.

Sig. K 3^v (McKerrow 1.321):

If this (which is nothing else but to swim with the streame) be to tell tales as shrewdly as mother *Hubbard*, it should seeme mother *Hubbard* is not great shrewe, however thou, treading on her heeles so oft, she may bee tempted beyonde her ten commandements.

Sig. L (McKerrow 1.323):

Thy Hexameter verses, or thy hue and crie after *a person as cleare as Christall*, I do not so deeply commend, for al *Maister* Spencer *long since imbrast it with an ouer-louing sonnet*.

Why should friends dissemble one with another, they are very vgly and artlesse. You will neuer leaue your olde trickes of drawing M. *Spencer* into euerie pybald thing you do. If euer he praisd thee, it was because he had pickt a fine vaine foole out of thee, and he would keep thee still a foole by flattring thee, til such time as he had brought thee into that extreame loue with thy selfe, that thou shouldst run mad with the conceit, and so be scorned of all men.

Sig. L 2 (McKerrow 1.325):

Then thou goest about to bribe mee to giue ouer this quarrell, and saist, if I will holde my peace, thou wilt bestowe more complements of rare amplifications vpon mee, than euer thou bestowdst on Sir *Philip Sidney*, and gentle Maister *Spencer*.

Thou flatterst mee, and praisest mee.

To make mee a small seeming amendes for the iniuries thou hast done mee, thou reckonest mee up *amongst the deare loueres and professed sonnes of the Muses, Edmund Spencer, Abraham France, Thomas Watson, Samuell Daniell*.

Sig L 2^v (McKerrow 1.326-7):

Onely I will looke vpon the last Sonnet of M. *Spencers* to the right worshipfull Maister *G. H.*, Doctour of the lawes: or it may so fall out that I will not looke vpon it too, because (*Gabriell*) though I vehemently suspect it to bee of thy owne doing, it is popt foorth vnder M. *Spencers* name, and his name is able to sanctifie any thing though falsely ascribed to it. (FIC)

1593.   Barnabe Barnes. *Parthenophil and Parthenope*. [STC 1469]

[Sonnet 23 (Lee 1.182) follows Spenser's sonnet scheme.]

Sonnet 60 (Lee 1.205 quoted):

> Some, valiant Roman wars 'bove stars do mount,
> With all their warlike leaders, men of might:
> Whilst some, of British *Arthur's* valour sing.

[Reference to the Arthur of *F. Q.*?] (DEM)

Canzon 2, st. 8.6-7 (Lee 1.275 quoted):

> Here *Colin* sits, beneath that oaken tree!
> *Eliza* singing in his lays! (FIC)

Ode 7, st. 2.1-2 (Lee 1.282 quoted):

> *Eliza's* praises were too high!
> Divinest Wits have done their best! (DEM)

1593.   Thomas Churchyard. *Churchyards Challenge*.
[STC 5220. Rptd S. Egerton Brydges, *Censura Literaria*, 1805-9; comment by Thomas Corser, *Collectanea Anglo-Poetica*, Manchester, 1869, 4.379.]

Sig. **$_{**}$**^{v} (Brydges 2.308-9):

> *A newe Kinde of a Sonnet.*
> In writing long, and reading works of warre,
> That *Homer* wrote and *Vergils* verse did show:
> My muse me led in ouerweening farre,
> When to their Stiles my pen presumde to goe.
> *Ouid* himselfe durst not haue vaunted so,
> Nor *Petrarke* graue with *Homer* would compare:
> *Dawnt* durst not think his sence so hye did flow,
> As *Virgils* works that yet much honord are.
> Thus each man saw his iudgement hye or low,
> And would not striue or seeke to make a iarre:
> Or wrastle where they haue an ouerthrow.
> So that I finde the weakenes of my bow,
> Will shoot no shaft beyond my length I troe:
> For reason learnes and wisdome makes me know.
> Whose strength is best and who doth make or marre:
> A little Lamp may not compare with Starre.
> A feeble head where no great gifts doo grow:
> Yeelds vnto skill, whose knowledge makes smal shew.
> Then gentle world I sweetly thee beseech:
> Call *Spenser* now the spirit of learned speech. (FIC)

1593.   Michael Drayton. *Idea. The Shepheards Garland, Fashioned in nine Eglogs*. [STC 7202. *Works*, ed. J. W. Hebel, Oxford, 1931-41.]

The Second Eglog, p. 8 (Hebel 1.52):

> Now am I like the knurrie-bulked Oke,
> Whome wasting eld hath made a toombe of dust,
> Whose wind-fallen branches feld by tempest stroke,
> His barcke consumes with canker-wormed rust.
>
> And though thou seemst like to the bragging bryer,
> As gay as is the mornings Marygolde,
> Yet shortly shall thy sap be dried and seere,
> Thy gaudy Blossomes blemished with colde.

[Cf. *S. C. Feb.*] (DEM)

Ibid., p. 9 (Hebel 1.52):

> O diuine love, which so aloft canst raise,
> And lift the minde out of this earthly mire.

[Cf. the entire song in the *Eglog* with *S. C. Oct.* 79-96.] (FMP)

Ibid., p. 10 (Hebel 1.53):

> Now hath this yonker torne his tressed lockes,
> And broke his pipe which sounded erst so sweet.

[Cf. *S. C. Apr.* 12, 14-5.]

The Third Eglog, p. 13 (Hebel 1.55):

> In thy sweete song so blessed may'st thou bee,
> For learned *Collin* laies his pipes to gage,
> And is to fayrie gone a Pilgrimage:
> the more our mone. (FIC)

Ibid., p. 15 (Hebel 1.56):

> O thou fayre silver Thames: ô cleerest chrystall flood.

[With the song beginning thus, cf. Colin's Laye of fayre Eliza, *S. C. Apr.* 38-154.] (DEM)

The Fourth Eglog, p. 24 (Hebel 1.63):

> *Melpomine* put on thy mourning Gaberdine.

[With the song beginning thus, cf. Colin's lament for Dido, *S. C. Nov.* 53 ff.] (FMP)

The Fifth Eglog, p. 29 (Hebel 1.66):

> I may not sing of such as fall, nor clyme,
> Nor chaunt of armes, nor of heroique deedes,
> It fitteth not poore shepheards rurall rime,
> Nor is agreeing with my oaten reedes,
> Nor from my quill, grosse flatterie proceedes.

[Cf. *S. C.* June 65-80; Oct. 85-6, 115-8.]

The Sixt Eglog, p. 44 (Hebel 1.76):

> Long may *Pandora* weare the Lawrell crowne,
> The ancient glory of her noble Peers,
> And as the Egle: Lord renew her yeeres,

Long to vpholde the proppe of our renowne,
   long may she be as she hath euer been,
   the lowly handmaide of the Fayrie Queene.
[Cf. *Am.* 80.]

The Eighth Eglog, p. 61 (Hebel 1.88):
Her feature all as fresh aboue,
   As is the grasse that growes by Doue,
   as lyth as lasse of Kent.
[Cf. *S. C. Feb.* 74.]

Ibid., p. 63 (Hebel 1.90):
Thy sheepe quoth she cannot be leane,
That haue a a iolly shepheards swayne,
   the which can pipe so well.
Yea but (sayth he) their shepheard may,
If pyping thus he pine away,
   in loue of *Dowsabell.*
Of loue fond boy take thou no keepe,
Quoth she, looke well vnto thy sheepe,
   lest they should hap to stray.
[Cf. *S. C. Jan.*]

Ibid., p. 64 (Hebel 1.90):
   And I to thee will be as kinde,
   As *Colin* was to *Rosalinde.* (DEM)

[These quotations illustrate rather than define Drayton's use of *S. C.* in
the composition of *The Shepheards Garland.* The *First* and *Ninth*
Eglogs (pp. 1-4, 66-70; Hebel 1.47-9, 92-4) follow *Jan.* and *Dec.* so
closely in verse form, tone, subject, and turns of speech that Drayton
would seem to be inviting the reader's comparison of the love-stricken
shepherds Rowland and Colin. A number of parallels between Drayton's
eclogues and *S. C.* not given above are noted in Hebel 5.7-12.] (WW)

1593.   Gabriel Harvey. *A New Letter of Notable Contents.*
[STC 12902. *Complete Works,* ed. A. B. Grosart, 1884-5]

Sig. 4 4ᵛ (Grosart 1.226):
Is not the Prose of *Sir Philip Sidney* in his sweet Arcadia, the embrodery
of finest *Art* and daintiest *Witt*? Or is not the Verse of M. *Spencer* in
his braue Faery Queene, the Virginall of the diuinest Muses, and the
gentlest Graces? Both delicate Writers: alwaies gallant, often braue, continually delectable, somtimes admirable. What sweeter tast of Suada,
than the Prose of the One: or what pleasanter relish of the Muses, then
the Verse of the Other? (FIC)

1593.   Gabriel Harvey. *Pierces Supererogation or A New Prayse of The*
Old Asse.
[STC 12903. *Complete Works,* ed. A. B. Grosart, 1884-5]

To my Very Gentle, and Liberall frendes, M. Barnabe Barnes . . . , sig.
**** 3ᵛ (Grosart 2. 15):
Be thou Barnabe, the gallant Poet, like Spencer, or the valiant souldier,
like Baskerville. (DEM)

*To the Right Worshipfull, his especiall deare frend, M. Gabriell Harvey,
Doctour of Lawe, sig.* ***** 3ᵛ (Grosart 2.24):

Sonet.
Harvey, or the sweet Doctour.
Hetcher, with silence whom I may not misse:
Nor *Lewen,* Rhetoriques richest noblesse:
Nor *Wilson,* whose discretion did redresse
    Our English Barbarisme: adioyne to this
Diuinest morall *Spencer:* let these speake
    By their sweet Letters, which do best unfould
Harveys deserued praise: since my Muse weake
    Cannot relate somuch as hath bene tould
By these *Fornam'd.*

[signed: Parthenope.]

P. 15 (sig. C; Grosart 2.50):
But euen since that flourishing transplantation of the daintiest, and
sweetest lerning, that humanitie ever tasted; Arte did but springe in such,
as Sir Iohn Cheeke, and M. Ascham: & witt budd in such, as Sir Phillip
Sidney, & M. Spencer; which were but the violetes of March, or the
Primeroses of May. (FIC)

P. 18 (sig. C 2ᵛ; Grosart 2.54):
Though I be not greatly employed, yet my leisure will scarsely serve to
moralize Fables of Beares, Apes, and Foxes: (for some men can give a
shrewd gesse at a courtly allegory:) but where Lordes in expresse tearmes
are magnifically contemned, Doctours in the same stile may be courage-
ously confuted. (DEM)

P. 39 (sig. F; Grosart 2.83):
I speake not onely to M. Bird, M. Spencer, or Monsieur Bodin whom
he nothinge regardeth: (yet I would his owne learning, or iudgmente
were anye way matchable with the worst of the three). (FIC)

P. 46 (sig. E 4ᵛ; Grosart 2.193):
Petrarck was a delicate man, and with an elegant iudgement gratiously
confined Loue within the limits of Honour, Witt within the boundes of
Discretion; Eloquence within the termes of Ciuility: as not many yeares
sithence an Inglishe Petrarck did, a singular Gentleman, and a sweete
Poet, whose verse singeth, as valour might speake, and whose ditty is an
Image of the Sun voutsafing to represent his glorious face in a clowde.
(DEM)

P. 136 (sig. Sᵛ; Grosart 2.216):
Where the Veine of Braggadocio is famous, the arterie of Pappadocio
cannot be obscure.

P. 140 (sig. S 3ᵛ; Grosart 2.223):

So then of Pappadocio: whom neuerthelesse I esteeme a hundred times learneder, and a thousand times honester, then this other Braggadocio. [First cited by Jakob Schömbs, *Ariosts Orlando Furioso in der englischen Litteratur des Zeitalters der Elisabeth,* Soden, 1898, p. 59.] (JGM)

P. 173 (sig. Y 4; Grosart 2.266):
Come diuine Poets, and sweet Oratours, the siluer streaming fountaines or flowingest witt, and shiningest Art: come Chawcer, and Spencer; More, and Cheeke; Ascham, and Astely; Sidney, and Dier. (FIC)

P. 199 (sig. Cc; Grosart 2.301-2):
For his smug, and Canonicall countenance, certainly he mought have bene S. Boniface himselfe: for his fayre, and formall speach, S. Benedict, or S. Eulaly: . . . for his pastoral devotion, a Shepheardes Calender: for his Fame, an Almanache of Saincts. (DEM)

1593. Thomas Lodge. *Phillis: Honoured with Pastorall Sonnets, Elegies, and amorous delights.*
[STC 16662. *Complete Works,* ed. Edmund Gosse, Hunterian Club, Glasgow, 1883.]

The Induction, sig A 4ᵛ (Gosse 2 [5th piece] 6):

As moderne Poets shall admire the same,
I meane not you (you neuer matched men)
Who brought the Chaos of our tongue in frame,
Through these Herculean labours of your pen:
   I meane the meane, I meane no men diuine,
   But such whose fathers are but waxt like mine.

Goe weeping Truce-men in your sighing weedes,
Vnder a great *Mecænas* I haue past you:
If so you come where learned *Colin* feedes
His louely flocke, packe thence and quickly haste you;
   You are but mistes before so bright a sunne,
   Who hath the Palme for deepe inuention wunne. (FIC)

[For examples of Lodge's employment of Spenserian pastoral diction, see the first and last stanzas of *Egloga Prima,* sigs. D 4, E 2ᵛ (Gosse 2. [fifth piece] 27, 32):

Demades. Now scourge of winters wracke is welnie spent,
And sunne ginnes looke more longer on our clime,
And earth no more to sorrow doth consent
Why beene thy lookes forlorne that view the prime?
   Vnneth thy flockes may feed to see thee faint,
   Thou lost, they leane, and both with woe attaint.
Damon . . . Come you my carefull flocke fore goe your maister,
Ile fold you vp and after fall a sighing,
Wordes haue no worth my secret woundes to plaister,
Nought may refresh my ioyes but *Phillis* nighing.

Farewell old *Demades, DE. Damon* farewell.
How gainst aduise doth headlong youth rebell.] (WW)

1593.   Thomas Nashe. *Christs Teares Over Ierusalem.*
[STC 18366. *Works,* ed. R. B. McKerrow, 1910]

Dedication to *The Most Honored, and Vertuous Beautified Ladie,
The Ladie Elizabeth Carey,* sig ⁎ 2ᵛ (McKerrow 2.10):
Fames eldest fauorite, Maister *Spencer,* in all his writings hie prizeth
you. (FIC)

To the Reader, sig. 2⁎ᵛ (McKerrow 2.181):
Indeede I haue heard there are mad men whipt in Bedlam, and lazie
vagabonds in Bridewell; wherfore me seemeth there should be no more
difference betwixt the displing of this vaine *Braggadochio* [Gabriel Har-
vey], then the whipping of a mad man or a vagabond. (FMP)

Ibid., sig. 2⁎ 3 (McKerrow 2.185):
    Madde heads ouer a dish of stewd prunes are terrible mockers: ô but
the other pint of wine cuts the throat of *Spencer* and euerie body. (FIC)

1593.   Henry Peacham (fl. 1577). *The Garden of Eloquence Conteining
The Most Excellent Ornaments, Exornations, Lightes, flowers, and formes
of speech.* [STC 19498.]

Onomatopeia, p. 15 (sig. D 4):
    . . . Touching this part I will refer the Reader to *Chaucer* & *Gower,*
and to the new Shepherds calender, a most singular imitation of ancient
speech. (FIC)

1593.   George Peele. *The Honour of the Garter.*
[STC 19539. *Works,* ed. A. H. Bullen, 1888; David H. Horne, *The
Life and Minor Works of George Peele,* Yale Univ. Press, 1952]

Ad Mæcenatum Prologus, sig. A 4 - A 4ᵛ (Bullen 2.318; Horne, p. 246):
        Augustus long agoe hath left the world:
        And liberall Sidney, famous for the love
        He bare to learning and to Chiualrie;
        And vertuous *Walsingham* are fled to heauen.
        Why thether speede not *Hobbin* and his phieres?
        Great Hobbinall on whom our shepheards gaze. (FIC)
[Like Bullen, Horne, p. 279, identifies *Hobbin* with Spenser.]

1594.   R. B. *Greenes Funeralls. By RB. Gent.*
[STC 1487. Ed. R. B. McKerrow, 1911.]

Sig. A 4 (McKerrow, p. 71):
    For iudgement *Ioue,* for Learning deepe, he still *Apollo* seemde:
    For floent Tongue, for eloquence, men *Mercury* him deemde.
    For curtesie suppose him *Guy,* or *Guyons* somewhat lesse:
    His life and manners though I would, I cannot halfe expresse.

Sig. B 2 (McKerrow, p. 75):

> Come from the Muses well *Minerua*
> Come and bring a Coronet:
> To crowne his head, that doth deserue,
> A greater gift than *Colinet.*

[R. B. may be Richard Barnfield, though the objections against attributing this work to Barnfield are strong; cf. McKerrow, pp. viii-x] (FIC)

1594. Richard Barnfield. *The Affectionate Shepheard.*
[STC 1480. A. H. Bullen, *Some Longer Elizabethan Poems,* Westminster, 1903.]

The Shepheards Content, sigs. E^v - Eij (Bullen, p. 171):

> Of all the kindes of common Countrey life,
> Me thinkes a shepheards life is most Content;
> His State is quiet Peace, deuoyd of strife;
> His thoughts are pure from all impure intent,
> His Pleasures rate sit at an easie rent:
>   He beares no mallice in his harmles hart,
>   Malicious meaning hath in him no part.
>
> He is not troubled with th'afflicted minde,
> His cares are onely ouer silly sheepe;
> He is not vnto Iealozie inclinde,
> (Thrice happie Man) he knowes not how to weepe.

[Cf. *F. Q.* 6.9.19 ff.]

Sig. Eiij (Bullen, p. 177):

> By thee great *Collin* lost his libertie,
> By thee sweet *Astrophel* forwent his ioy.

[Cupid is addressed.] (DEM)

1594. George Chapman. *The Shadow of Night: Containing Two Poeticall Hymnes.*
[STC 4990. *Poems,* ed. Phillis B. Bartlett, New York & London, 1941.]

Sig. B^v (Bartlett, p. 23):

> The golden chaine of Homers high deuice
> Ambition is, or cursed auarice.

[Cf. *F. Q.* 2.7.46. In all probability Chapman's immediate source is neither Homer nor *F. Q.* but the " De Iunone " of Natalis Comes' *Mythologiae*; note Bartlett, p. 425.] (DEM)

1594. Samuel Daniel. *Delia and Rosamond augmented. Cleopatra.*
[STC 6254. *Complete Works,* ed. A. B. Grosart, 1885.]

To the Right Honourable, The Lady Marie, Countesse of Pembrooke, prefixed to *The Tragedie of Cleopatra,* sig. H 7 (Grosart 3.26-7):

> Whereby great SYDNEY & our SPENCER might,
> With those Po-singers beeing equalled,

Enchaunt the world with such a sweet delight,
That theyr eternall songs (for euer read,)
May shew what great ELIZAS raigne hath bred.
What musique in the kingdome of her peace,
Hath now beene made to her, and by her might,
Whereby her glorious fame shall neuer cease. (FIC)

1594. Hadrian Dorrell. *To the gentle & courteous Reader,* prefixed to *Willobie his Auisa.* [STC 25755. Ed. G. B. Harrison, 1926.]

Sig. A 2ᵛ (Harrison, pp. 14-5):
For the composition and order of the verse: Although hee [Henry Willobie] flye not alofte with the winges of *Astrophell,* nor dare to compare with the Arcadian shepheard, or any way match with the dainetie Fayry Queene; yet shall you find his wordes and phrases, neither Tryuiall nor absurd. (FIC)

1594. Michael Drayton. *Matilda. The faire and chaste Daughter of the Lord Robert Fitzwater.*
[STC 7205. *Works,* ed. J. W. Hebel, Oxford, 1931-41.]

Sig. B 2ᵛ (Hebel 1.215):
And thou ô *Beta,* Soveraigne of his thought,
Englands *Diana,* let him thinke on thee,
By thy perfections let his Muse be taught,
And in his breast so deepe imprinted be,
That he may write of sacred Chastitie:
  Though not like *Collin* in thy *Britomart,*
  Yet loues asmuch, although he wants his arte. (DEM)

1594. Lewis Lewkenor. *The Resolued Gentleman,* translated from the French of Oliver de La Marche. [STC 15139.]

P. 45 (sig. N 3):
[Queen Elizabeth's] rareness being such, that she shall with the highnesse of her vertue, drawe vp (as the heate of the Sunne doth vapours from the earth) the excellent wittes of her time to so high a pitch, that the following ages among millions of other noble workes penned in her praise, shall as much admire the writer, but farre more the subiect of the fairie Queene, as euer former ages did *Homer* and his *Achilles,* or *Virgill* and his *Æneas,* such worthy, rare, and excellent matter, shall her matchelesse and incomparable vertue yeelde them to ennoble their pennes, & immortalize their fames. (FBW)

1594. *The Masque of Proteus,* in Harleian MS 541.
[Rptd *Gesta Grayorum,* ed. W. W. Greg, Malone Soc. Rpts, 1915.]

Fol. 145ᵃ (Greg, p. xxi, quoted):
        The song at yᵉ ending
Shadowes before yᵉ shining sunne do vanish

The iron forcing Adamant doth resigne
His vertues where yᵉ Diamond doth shine
Pure holines doth all enchantment banish
　　And cullors of false Principality
　　Do fade in presence of true majesty.
[Cf. *F. Q.* 1: Arthur, as Holiness, with his diamond shield.
Greg reprints the first extant (1688) ed. of *Gesta Grayorum* (STC
C444) containing a printed version of the masque; for the song, cf.
p. 65 (sig. Kᵛ; Nichols 3.318).] (DEM)

1594. Thomas Nashe. *The Vnfortunate Traueller. Or The life of Iacke
Wilton.*
[STC 18380. *Works*, ed. R. B. McKerrow, 1910.]

Sig. C (McKerrow 2.226):
So it was, that the most of these aboue-named goose-quill Braggadoches
were mere cowards and crauens. (JGM)

1594. I. O. *The Lamentation of Troy, for the death of Hector. Wherevnto is annexed an Olde womans Tale in hir solitarie Cell.*
[STC 18755. S. Egerton Brydges, *Censura Literaria*, 1850-9.]
The Prologue, sig. A 3ᵛ (Brydges 2.349) [Troy's ghost seeks a poet to
recount the events of her misfortune]:

Yet had she rather Spencer would haue told them,
For him she calde that he would helpe t'vnfold them.
But when she saw he came not at hir call
She kept hir first man that doth shew them all.

Sig. B 2 (Brydges 2.349):

O then good *Spencer* the only *Homer* liuing,
Deign for to write with thy fame-quickeninge quill:
And though poore *Troy* due thanks can not be giuing,
The Gods are iust and they that giue them will.
　　Write then O *Spencer* in thy Muse so trim,
　　That he in thee and thou maiest liue in him.

Although thou liuest in thy *Belphaebe* faire,
And in thy *Cynthia* likely art to shine,
So long as *Cynthia* shineth in the ayre:
Yet liue and shine in this same Sunne of mine.
　　O liue in him that whilom was my Sun,
　　But now his light and so my life is done. (FIC)

1594. *The First part of the Tragicall raigne of Selimus.*
[STC 12310ᵃ. Ed. W. Bang, Malone Soc. Rpts, 1908.]
[Charles Crawford, *N & Q*, ser. 9, 7(1901).142-4, 202-5, 261-3, notes
many verbal parallels between *Selimus* and *F. Q.* Noted below, each of
the references, with line numbers of Bang's text, is followed by the
citation, in parentheses, of its parallel passage in *F. Q.*: 17-9 (1.1.5.5-6),

37-8 (2.9.7.5-6), 154 (2.7.37.2), 214-5 (1.8.44.8), 249 (1.9.36.9), 319-21 (1.5.48.1-4), 441-7 (1.5.18.1-6), 540 (1.8.17.8-9), 667 (2.8.28.5), 740 (2.10.24.7), 1277 (2.1.36.3), 1293-4 (2.1.40.1, 9), 1317-8 (1.5.22.5), 1483-4 (1.8.10.8-9), 1489-91 (2.5.8.6-7), 1764-83 (3.4.8-10), 1807 (1.5.22.2), 1810-1 (1.7.23.4-5), 1910-5 3.11.1.1-8), 2218-21 (1.9.22.6-7), 2414-6 (1.6.35.5-6), 2468 (1.1.23.1-5). As illustrative, lines 1754-83, adapted from Britomart's address to the raging sea of love, read as follows:

> *Baia[zet]*. . . .
> You swelling seas of neuer ceasing care,
> Whose waues my weather-beaten ship do tosse,
> Your boystrous Billowes too vnruly are
> And threaten still my ruine and my losse:
> Like hugie mountaines do your waters reare,
> Their loftie toppes, and my weake vessell crosse.
> Alas at length allaie your stormie strife,
> And cruell wrath within me rages rife.
> Or else my feeble barke cannot endure,
> Your flashing buffets and outragious blowes,
> But while thy foamie floud doth it immure,
> Shall soone be wrackt vpon the sandie shallowes.
> Griefe my leaud boat-swaine stirreth nothing sure,
> But without stars gainst tide and wind he rowes,
> And cares not though vpon some rock we split,
> A restlesse pilot for the charge vnfit.
> But out alasse, the god that vales the sea,
> And can alone this raging tempest stent,
> Will neuer blow a gentle gale of ease,
> But suffer my poore vessell to be rent.] (FIC)

1594. *Zepheria.*
[STC 26124. Rptd Lee 2.153-78.]

[Sonnet-sequence, which employs a number of characteristically Spenserian words: well-thewed (Canzon 1.2), emprized (Canzon 2.5), pursuivants (Canzon 3.2), jouissance (Canzon 4.1), souvenance (Canzon 14.6), chevisance (Canzon 19.14) and others.] (DEM)

About 1595. Richard Carew. *The Excellencie of the English tongue by R. C. of Anthony Esquire to W. C.,* in Camden's *Remains, concerning Britaine,* 1614. [STC 4522.]

P. 44 (Munro 1.27):
    Will you reade Virgill? take the Earle of Surrey, *Catullus?* Shakespheare and Barlowes fragment, Ouid? Daniell, Lucan? Spencer, Martial? Sir Iohn Dauies and others: will you haue all in all for Prose and verse? take the miracle of our age Sir Philip Sidney. [For the passage as it appears in B. M. MS Cotton F. xi. (beginning fol. 265), see Smith 2.293.] (JM)

1595. Francis Bacon. " The Speeches drawn up by Mr. Francis Bacon for the Earl of Essex in a device exhibited by his Lordship before Queen Elizabeth, on the anniversary of her accession to the throne, November 17, 1595," in *Letters, Speeches, Charges, Advices, &c of Francis Bacon . . . Now first published by Thomas Birch,* 1763.

P. 14 (Nichols 3.378):
And as for you, untrue Politique, but truest bondman to *Philautia,* you, that presume to bind occasion, and to overwork fortune, I would ask you but one question. (DEM)

1595. Richard Barnfield. *Cynthia. With Certaine Sonnets, and the Legend of Cassandra.*
[STC 1483. Rptd A. H. Bullen, *Some Longer Elizabethan Poems,* Westminster, 1903.]

To the curteous Gentlemen Readers, sig. A 4ᵛ (Bullen, p. 190):
   Thus, hoping you will beare with my rude cōceit of *Cynthia,* (if for no other cause, yet, for that it is the first imitation of the verse of that excellent Poet, Maister *Spencer,* in his *Fayrie Queene*) I will leaue you to the reading of that, which I so much desire may breede your Delight. (FIC)

[The language of *Cynthia* is Spenserian as well as the stanza; e. g. sig. B 2ᵛ (st. 7.9 and 8.4; Bullen, p. 195): " Thus was his Blisse to Bale, his Hony turn'd to gall " and " As one that inly joy'd, so was she glad." On sig. B 4ᵛ (st. 2.9; Bullen, p. 197) Elizabeth is described as " of Beauty fairest Fayrie Queene."] (FMP)

Sig. Bᵛ (st. 3.1; Bullen, p. 194):
   Downe in a Dale, hard by a Forrest side.
[Cf. *F. Q.* 1.1.34.2.] (WW)

Sonnet 20, sig. C 7ᵛ (Bullen, p. 209):
   Ah had great *Colin* chiefe of sheepheards all,
   Or gentle *Rowland,* my professed friend,
   Had they thy beautie, or my pennance pend,
   Greater had been thy fame, and lesse my fall. (DEM)

1595. E. C. *Emaricdulfe.*
[STC 4268. Rptd in *A Lamport Garland,* Roxburghe Club, 1881.]
Sonnet 40, sig. C 7ᵛ:
   Some bewties make a god of flatterie,
     And scorne *Eliziums* eternall types,
   Nathes, I abhorre such faithles prophesie,
     Least I be beaten with thy vertues stripes,
   Wilt thou suruiue another world to see?
     Delias sweete Prophet shall the praises singe
   Of bewties worth exemplified in thee,

And thy names honour in his sweete tunes ring:
Thy vertues *Collin* shall immortalize,
Collin chast vertues organ sweetst esteem'd,
When for *Elizas* name he did comprise
Such matter as inuentions wonder seem'd.
Thy vertues hee, thy bewties shall the other,
Christen a new, whiles I sit by and wonder. (FIC)

1595. H. C. *Piers Plainness seauen yeres Prentiship*, Bodleian MS Malone 670.

Sig. C 2ᵛ:

Thrasilio that base Braggadoche. (RH)

1595. I. [or J.] C. *Alcilia. Philoparthens Loving Folly.*
[No STC entry (STC 4275: 1613 ed.). Rptd and ed. Wilhelm Wagner, *Sh. Jb.* 10(1875).150-92; rptd A. B. Grosart, *Occasional Issues*, 1879.]

[Wagner (p. 157; cf. Grosart, p. xxvi) thinks Spenser the model for *Alcilia*, mainly on the ground of archaisms, and " da die Alcilia sich auch in der wahl des Metrums an diesen Dichter anschliesst (man vergleiche Spenser's Astrophel), so darf man wohl Spenser in gewissen Bezeihung als den Lehrmeister unsers Dichters bezeichnen."] (FIC)

1595. Thomas Campion. *Epigrammatum Liber*, in *Poemata.*
[STC 4544. *Works*, ed. Percival Vivian, Oxford, 1909.]

Sig. E 6ᵛ (Vivian, p. 341):

Ad. Ed. Spencerum.
Siue canis siluas Spencere, vel horrida belli
Fulmina, dispereā ni te amē, & intimè ame. (RH)

1595. Thomas Churchyard. *A Musicall Consort of Heauenly harmonie (compounded out of many parts of Musicke) called Churchyards Charitie.*
[STC 5245. Rptd Alexander Boswell, *Frondes Caducae*, Auchinleck Press, 1817; cf. Thomas Corser, *Collectanea Anglo-Poetica*, Manchester, 1869, 4.383-5.]

To the Generall Readers, sig. A 4:

If ought amisse, you finde good Reader heere,
His fault it is, that sings ne sweete nor loud:
When he caught cold, and voice could not be cleere,
Because ech note, is cloked vnder cloud,
He craud no helpe, nor stole from no mans song,
One peece nor part, of musicke any waie.
[Cf. *Col.* 396-9.] (DEM)

A praise of Poetrie, some notes thereof drawen out of the Apologie, the noble minded Knight, Sir Phillip Sidney wrate, G 3ᵛ (p. 42):

In Spenser morall fairie Queene
And Daniels rosie mound
If they be throwly waid and seen
Much matter may be found.

[*A praise of Poetrie* has its own title page, sig. (E 3).] (FIC)

1595. Anthony Copley. *Wits Fittes and Fancies. Fronted and enter-medled with Presidentes of Honour and Wisdome. Also Loues Owle: and idle conceited Dialogue between Loue and an Olde-man.*
[STC 5738. Extracts S. Egerton Brydges, *Censura Literaria*, 1805-9.]

To the Gentlemen Readers, sig. A 3 (Brydges 5.357-8; 1596 ed., STC 5739, quoted):

As for my *Loues Owle*, I am content that *Momus* turn it to a tennis-ball if he can, & bandy it quite away: namelie, I desire M. *Daniel*, M. *Spencer*, & other the Prime Poets of our time, to pardon it with as easie a frowne as they please, for that I giue them to vnderstand, that an Vniversitie Muse neuer pend it, though humbly deuoted thereunto. (RH)

1595. William Covell. *Polimanteia . . . Whereunto is added England to Her Three Daughters, Cambridge, Oxford, Innes of Court, and to all the rest of her Inhabitants.* Cambridge and London.
[STC 5883. Rptd S. Egerton Brydges, *The British Bibliographer*, 1810.]

Sig. Q^v (Brydges 1.281):

a fit taske for the finest Scholler. So onely without compare, eternallie should you [Cambridge] liue; for in your children shall the loue-writing muse of diuine *Sydnay*, and the pure flowing streame of Chrystallin *Spenser* suruiue onely: write then of *Elizas* raigne, a taske onely meete for so rare a pen.

Sig. R 2^v (Brydges 1.284):

M. Alablaster. Spenser and others. . . . let the worlde know . . . that *Italian Ariosto* did but shadowe the meanest part of thy muse, that *Tassos Godfrey* is not worthie to make compare with your truelie eternizing *Elizas* stile: let France-admired *Bellaw*, and courtlike amorous Ro[n]sard confesse that there be of your children, that of these latter times haue farre surpassed them.

Lylia clouded, whose teares are making. Let diuine *Bartasse* eternally praise worthie for his weeks worke, say the best thinges were made first: Let other countries (sweet Cambridge) enuie, (yet admire) my *Virgil*, thy petrarch, diuine *Spenser*.

[The roll-call continues with the names of Daniel, Shakespeare, Chaucer, Lydgate, Lyndsay.] (FIC)

1595. Michael Drayton. *Endimion and Phoebe. Ideas Latmus.*
[STC 7192. *Works*, ed. J. W. Hebel, Oxford 1931-41.]

Hebel 1.155 quoted:

> Deare *Collin*, let my Muse excused be,
> Which rudely thus presumes to sing by thee,
> Although her straines be harsh untun'd & ill,
> Nor can attayne to thy divinest skill. (DEM)

1595.   Thomas Edwards. *Cephalus and Procris. Narcissus.*
[STC 7525. Ed. W. E. Buckley, Roxburghe Club, 1882.]

Sig. A 2ᵛ (Buckley, p. 4):

> The teares of the muses haue bene teared from *Helicon*. (FIC)

Sig. Bᵛ (Buckley, p. 10):

> And now bright *Phebus* mounted, gan display
> His Orient sunne-beames, on the liuely day,
> *Aurora* made vnto the Siluan shore,
> Where Satyres, Goat-heardes, Shepheardes kept of yore,
> A sacred and most hallowed cristall spring.

[Spenserian pastoral diction?] (DEM)

Sig. B 2ᵛ (Buckley, p. 12):

> Heroicke Parramore of Fairie land,
> That stately built, with thy immortall hand,
> A golden, Angellike, and modest Aulter,
> For all to sacrifice on, none to alter.
> Where is that vertuous Muse of thine become?

Sig. D (Buckley, p. 25) [Procris referred to as Amoretta]:

> But note the sequel, and vnciuill Swaine,
> That had bene wandring from the scorched plaines,
> Espi'd this *Amoretta* where she lay.

Sig. D 2 - D 2ᵛ (Buckley, pp. 27-8):

> But what is more in vre, or getteth praise,
> Then sweete Affection tun'd in homely layes?
> Gladly would our *Cephalian* muse haue sung
> All of white loue, enamored with a tounge,
> That still *Styll* musicke sighing teares together,
> Could one conceite haue made beget an other,
> And so haue ransackt this rich age of that,
> The muses wanton fauourites haue got [.]

He mindes | Heauens-gloryfier, with thy holy fire,
in respect of | O thrise immortall quickener of desire,
Poets | That scorn'st this* vast and base prodigious clime,
and their | Smyling at such as beg in ragged rime,
fauourites. | Powre from aboue, or fauour of the prince,
> Distilling wordes to hight the quintessence
> Of fame and honor: such I say doest scorne,
> Because thy stately verse was Lordly borne,
> Through all *Arcadia*, and the *Fayerie* land

He thinkes it And hauing smale true grace in Albion,
the duetie of Thy natiue soyle, as thou of sight deserued'st,
eueryone   Rightly adornes one now, that's richly serued:
that sailes, to O to that quick sprite of thy smooth-cut quill,
strike maine- Without surmise of thinking any ill
top, before   *I offer vp in duetie and in zeale,
that great   This dull conceite of mine, and do appeale,
& mighty poet With reuerence to thy [affection.]
COLLYN.   On will I put that breast-plate and there on,
            Riuet the standard boare in spite of such:
            As thy bright name condigne or would but touch[.]
            Affection is the whole Parenthesis,
            That here I strecke, which from our taske doth misse. (FMP)

Sig. H 3ᵛ (Munro 1.25-6; Buckley, p. 62):

> *Collyn* was a mighty swaine,
> In his power all do flourish,
> We are shepheards but in vaine,
>   There is but one tooke the charge,
> By his toile we do nourish,
>   And by him are inlarg'd.

> He vnlockt *Albions* glorie,
> He twas tolde of *Sidneys* honor,
> Onely he of our stories,
>   Must be sung in greatest pride,
> In an Eglogue he hath wonne her,
>   Fame and honor on his side. (JM)

1595. Thomas Lodge. *A Fig for Momus: Containing Pleasant varietie, including Satyres, Eclogues, and Epistles.*
[STC 16658. *Complete Works,* ed. Edmund Gosse, Hunterian Club, Glasgow, 1883.]

[Eglogue 1, sig. B 4 (Gosse 3. [2nd piece] 15) is addressed *To reuerend Colin.*] (FIC)

1595. W. S. *The Lamentable Tragedie of Locrine, the eldest sonne of King Brutus.*
[STC 21528. Ed. R. B. McKerrow, Malone Soc. Rpts. 1908.]

[L. Tieck and R. Brotanek (*Anglia Beiblatt* 11.202-7) list seventeen passages in *Locrine* borrowed outright from the *Complaints*; for example, with R. R. 25.1-2 compare *Locrine*, Act 3, sc. 2, sig. E 3ᵛ (McKerrow, ll. 989-91):

> O that I had the Thracian *Orpheus* harpe
> For to awake out of the infernall shade
> Those ougly diuels of black *Erebus*.

F. G. Hubbard (*Camb. Hist. Eng. Lit.* 5.96-7 adds another; T. Erbe (*Die Locrinesage*, Halle, 1904, p. 71) notes that in both play (ll. 201-9) and *F. Q.* (2.10.17) Gwendolen is married to Locrine before the coming of Estrid, found elsewhere only in Warner; and Carrie A. Harper (*MLR* 8.369-71) observes that she has been able to find no previous mention of Debon, "the eponymous hero of Devonshire," who figures in both play (ll. 174-5) and poem (2.10.11-2; 3.9.50.4), and further remarks that, as opposed to the chronicles, "Brutus makes division of his kingdom before his death, and makes Locrine the chief ruler," in both *Locrine* (ll. 180-91) and *F. Q.* (2.10.13).] (FIC)

1595. Robert Southwell. *St. Peters Complaint.*
[STC 22956-7. *Poems*, ed. A. B. Grosart, Fuller Worthies Library, 1872.]

The Author to the Reader, sig. A 3ᵛ (Grosart, p. 9; STC 22957 quoted):
> This makes my mourning muse resolue in teares,
> This Theames my heauy penne to plaine in prose,
> *Christes* Thorne is sharpe, no head his Garland weare:
> Still finest wits are stilling *Venus* Rose.
> In Paynim toyes the sweetest vaines are spent:
> To Christian workes, few haue their tallents lent.

[First line suggested by *T. M.*?] (DEM)

1595. Joshua Sylvester. *The Epistle Dedicatorie To . . . M. Anthonie Bacon*, prefacing Sylvester's translation, *The First Day of The Worldes Creation: Or Of the first weeke of that most Christian Poet, W. Salustius, Lord of Bartas.*
[STC 21658. *Complete Works*, ed. A. B. Grosart, Chertsey Worthies' Library, 1880.]

Sig. A 2:
. . . this most Christian Poet, and noble *Frenchman Lord of Bartas*, might haue been naturalized amongst vs, either by a generall act of a Poeticall Parliament: or haue obtained a kingly translator for his weeke (as he did for his Furies:) or rather a diuine *Sidney*, a stately *Spencer*, or a sweet *Daniell* for an interpreter thereof. (VBH)

About 1596. William Lisle. *To the Readers*, prefixed to his translation, *Part of Du Bartas, English and French, and in his Owne Kinde of Verse*, 1625. [STC 21663.]

Sig. ¶¶4 - ¶¶4ᵛ:
I was about to end; but may not forget to let you vnderstand, that this Bartassian verse (not vnlike herein to the Latin Pentameter) hath euer this propertie, to part in the mids betwixt two wordes; so much doe some French prints signifie, with a stroke interposed, as here in the first two pages you may see, for example. The neglect of this hath caused many a braue Stanza in the Faerie Queene to end but harshly, which might haue beene preuented at the first; but now the fault may be sooner found then amended. (FMP)

About 1596. Henry Stanford. Presentation Verses in Cambridge Univ. MS D.d.V.75.

Fol. 16:

> In sign y^t thou art fair & matcheles w^thout peere
> I send this fayrie quene & wishe ye a new happie yeare
> And all suche earthly ioyes as hart can wishe or craue
> and after long expense of yeres a seate in heauen to haue

[This follows a sonnet sent with a French history " To Mrs. Elizabeth Carey," New Year's, 1595. Presumably these verses were by Stanford and record a New Year's gift of 1595/6 or 1596/7. For other presentation verses by Stanford, see 1610, below.] (ME)

1596. Robert Bowes. Letter to William Cecil, Lord Burghley, Edinburgh, Nov. 12, *S. P. Scotland, Eliz.* 59. 66.

[Cf. *Cal. State Papers, Scotland, 1509-1603*, ed. Markham John Thorpe, 1858, 2.723-4; extract of letter transcribed by Henry R. Plomer and quoted by Carpenter, pp. 41-2.]

Carpenter, pp. 41-2, quoted:

The K[ing] hath conceaued great offence against Edward Spencer publishing in prynte in the second book ¹ p[ar]t of the Fairy Queene and ix*th* chapter some dishonorable effects (as the k. demeth thereof) against himself and his mother deceassed. He alledged that this booke was passed with previledge of her mats Commission[er]s for the veiwe and allowance of all wrytinges to be receaued into Printe. But therin I haue (I think) satisfyed him that it is not given out wth such p[ri]viledge: yet he still desyreth that Edward Spencer for his faulte, may be dewly tryed & punished.

1 " Book " deleted in MS. (FIC)

1596. B. M. MS Harleian 6910.

[*A Catalogue of the Harleian Manuscripts, in the British Museum*, 1808, 1812]

Catalogue, 3.447, quoted:

A Quarto, containing the following Poems: neatly written & ruled.
1. Spenser's Prosopopoia: or Mother Hubberds Tale . . . [fol.] 1.
2. The Tears of the Muses . . .   20.b.
3. Virgil's Gnat . . .   30.b.
4. Muiopotmos or the Fate of the Butterfly . . .   41.b.
5. The Ruines of Time . . .   48.b.
6. Ruines of Rome, by Bellay.   59.b.
7. Visions of the Worlds Vanity.   67
8. Visions of Bellay.   69.b.
9. Visions of Petrarch.   73

At the end of this is written " Finis 1596 " which is five years after most of them were printed in 4to. . . .

[These entries are followed by Nos. 10-26, of miscellaneous poems, including *H. H. B.*, No. 15, fols. 127b-130.] (RH)

1596.   Thomas Churchyard. *A pleasant Discourse of Court and Wars . . . Written by Thomas Churchyard, and called his Cherishing.*
[STC 5249. Rptd Alexander Boswell, *Frondes Caducae,* Auchinleck Press, 1816.]
Sig. B:
> The platform where all Poets thriue,
> Saue one whose voice is hoarse they say.

[Cf. *Col.* 396-9.] (DEM)

1596.   Anthony Copley. *A Fig for Fortune.*
[STC 5737. Sp. Soc. Pub., no. 35, 1883.]
Sigs. B 2 - C (pp. 3-9; Sp. Soc., pp. 9-15) [the argument of Despair beginning as follows]:
> Thou therefore that doest seem a dolefull wight,
> View me the president of Cares redresse,
> And if that Fortune be aboue thy might
> Yet death is in thy power and readinesse:
>> Disdaine Misfortune then t'insult vpon thee
>> Seeing that to die is all so faire and easie.

[Cf. *F. Q.* 1.9.38 ff.]

Sig. I 3ᵛ (p. 62; Sp. Soc., p. 68):
> There grew the loftie Cedar, and the Pine,
> The peacefull Oliffe, and the martiall Firre
> The verdant Laurell in her shadie-shine,
> The patient Palme, and penitentiall Mirrhe:
>> The Elme, the Poplar, and the Cipresse tree
>> And all trees els that pleasant are to see.

[Cf. *F. Q.* 1.1.8-9.]

Sigs. K 2ᵛ - K 3ᵛ (pp. 68-70; Sp. Soc., pp. 74-6) [description of Doblessa and her evil deeds]:
> But she, oh she accursed Sorceresse
> Would neuer yet beleeue, nor gree their grace
> But still persisteth in her wretchednesse
> Warfaring with bloody broile this happy place;
>> Yea, had she might according to her malice
>> *Sion* had been a ruine long ere this.

> She was a Witch, and Queen of all the Desart
> From *Babell*-mount vnto the pit of Hell,
> She forc'd nor God, nor any good desart,
> She could doe any thing saue doing well:
>> Her law was Libertie, her lust was Pride
>> And all good awe and order she defi'd . . .

For she could quaintly maske in *Sions* guize
And sucke out venum from the Flower of life,
And so retayle it with her subtilties
For purest honey: Such was her deed of strife;
  Her woluish nature in a lamblie hue
  She could disguize, and seeme of *Sions crue* . . .

She had no Altar, nor no Sacrament
No Ceremonie, nor Oblation,
Her school was Cauill, & truthlesse babblement
Riot her Raigne, her end damnation;
  This was the haggard whoore of *Babylon*
  Whose cup inuenym'd all that drunke thereon. (DEM)

[The poem is an elaborate Roman Catholic adaptation of the machinery of *F. Q.*, Book One, turning the tables upon the Anglican Church. The Elizian = the Red Crosse Knight; Catoes ghost = Despair; Catechrysius = Dame Coelia; the House of Devotion = the House of Holinesse; the Angell = Prince Arthur; Doblessa (the Anglican Church) = Duessa; " Una, Militans " (the one Catholic and Apostolic, on earth) = Una. The praise of Eliza is purely a blind.] (FMP)

1596.   Sir John Davies. *Orchestra or A Poeme of Dauncing.*
[STC 6360. *Poems,* reprod. in facsimile by Clare Howard, Columbia Univ. Press, 1941.]
St. 24.3-4, sig. A 7 (Howard, p. 73):
    Like Loue his Sire, whom Paynters make a Boy,
    Yet is he eldest of the heau'nly powers.
[Cf. *H. L.* 50-6.]

St. 64.1-2, sig. B 5ᵛ (Howard, p. 86):
    Thus when at first Loue had them marshalled
    As earst he did the shapelesse masse of things.
[Cf. *H. L.* 74 ff.]

Sts. 74-5, sig. B 7 - B 7ᵛ (Howard, pp. 89-90):
    For Loue, within his fertile working braine
    Did then conceiue those gracious Virgins three,
    Whose ciuill moderation did maintaine
    All decent order and conueniencie,
    And faire respect, and seemlie modestie:
      And then he thought it fit they should be borne,
      That their sweet presence dauncing might adorne.

    Hence is it that these Graces painted are
    With hand in hand dauncing an endlesse round:
    And with regarding eyes, that still beware
    That there be no disgrace amongst them found;
    With equall foote they beate the flowry ground,
      Laughing, or singing, as their passions will,
      Yet nothing that they doe becomes them ill. (FMP)

[Cf. *F. Q.* 6.10.12, 15, 23-4.]

St. 128, sig. C 8 (Howard, p. 107):

O that I had *Homers* aboundant vaine,
I would heereof another *Ilias* make,
Or els the man of *Mantuas* charmed braine
In whose large throat great *Ioue* the thunder spake.
O that I could old *Gefferies* Muse awake,
   Or borrow *Colins* fayre heroike stile,
   Or smooth my rimes with *Delias* seruants file. (FIC)

1596. Charles Fitzgeffrey. *Sir Francis Drake,* Oxford.
[STC 10943. *Poems,* ed. A. B. Grosart, Occasional Issues, vol. 16, 1881.]

Sig. B 5 - B 5ᵛ (Grosart, pp. 21-2):

Then you, sweete-singing Sirens of these times,
Deere darlings of the *Delian* Deitie,
That with your Angels-soule-inchauntinge rimes
Transport *Pernassus* in *Britainie,*
With learnings garland crowninge Poesie;
   Sdaine not that our harsh plaints should beate your eares:
   Arts want may stop our tongues, but not our teares.

SPENSER, whose hart inharbours *Homers* soule,
If *Samian* Axioms be autenticall:
DANIEL, who well mayst *Maro's* text controule,
With proud *Plus ultra* true note marginall:
And golden-mouthed DRAYTON musicall,
   Into whose soule sweete SIDNEY did infuse
   The essence of his Phœnix-feather'd Muse:

Types of true honour, *Phœbus Tripodes,*
Hell-charminge *Orphêi, Sirens* of the sense,
Wits substance, *Ioues* braine-borne *Pallades,*
Soules *Manna,* heauens *Ambrosian* influence,
True centers of renownes circumference,
   The gracefull *Graces* faire triplicitie,
   Of moderne Poets rarest trinarie.

Imbath your Angel-feathers loftie quill
In fluent amber-dropping *Castalie,*
That liquid gold may from your pen distill,
Encarving characters of memorie,
In brasen-leavd bookes of eternitie:
   Be DRAKES worth royalized by your wits,
   That DRAKES high name may coronize your writs.

Let famous RED CROSSE yeld to famous DRAKE,
And good SIR GVION give to him his launce;
Let all the MORTIMERS surrender make

To one that higher did his fame advance;
Cease LANCASTERS, & YORKES iars to enhaunce;
Sing all, and all to few to sing DRAKES fame;
Your Poems neede no laurell saue his name. (DEM)

1596.   Bartholomew Griffin. *Fidessa, more chaste then kind.*
[STC 12367.]

Sig. E 4 (Lee 2.292):
I tooke her to be beauties Queene alone,
But now I see she is a senseles stone.

[Cf. *Am.* 54. For the name *Fidessa,* cf. *F. Q.* 1.2.26.2 and 1.4.2.1-4.]
(DEM)

1596.   Sir John Harington. *A New Discourse of a Stale Subiect, Called The Metamorphosis of Aiax.*
[STC 12779. Rptd Chiswick Press, 1814.]

An Apologie, sigs. Aa^v - A[a] 2 (Chiswick, p. 3):
They descanted of the new Faerie Queene and the old both, and the greatest fault they coulde finde in it was that the last verse disordered their mouthes, and was lyke a trycke of xvii. in a sinkapace. (FIC)

Ibid., sig. Bb 5^v (Chiswick, p. 30) [Addressing Sir John Spencer, "a good substanciall free-holder in Northamptonshire," brother of Lady Elizabeth Carey]:
You haue a learned Writer of your name, make much of him, for it is not the least honour of your honourable family. (EAS)

1596.   Richard Linche. *Diella, Certaine Sonnets, adioyned to the amorous Poeme of Dom Diego and Gineura. By R. L. Gentleman.* [STC 17091.]

Sonnet 9, sig. B 5 (Lee 2.305):
Oh, were thou not much harder then a flint,
    thou had'st ere this, been melted into loue,
In firmest stone small raine doth make a print,
    but seas of teares cannot thy hardnes moue.
Then wretched I must die before my time,
Blasted & spoiled in my budding prime.

[Cf. *Am.* 18.]

[Sonnet 13, sig. B 7 (Lee 2.307) and sonnet 32, sig. D (Lee 2.317) follow the Spenserian sonnet scheme.]

Sonnet 20, sig. C 3 (Lee 2.311):
The strongest Pyne that Queen *Feronia* hath,
    growing within her woody Emperie,
Is soone throwne downe by *Boreas* windy wrath,
    if one roote only his supporter be,
The tallest Ship that cuts the angry Waue,
    and plowes the Seas of *Saturnes* second sunne;
If but one Anchor for a iourney haue,

when that is lost gainst euery Rocke doth runne;
I am that Pyne (faire loue) that Ship am I,
and thou that Anchor art and roote to me,
If then thou faile, (oh faile not) I must die,
— and pine away in endless miserie:
But words preuaile not, nor can sighes deuise,
To mooue thy hart, if bent to tyrannize.

[Cf. *Am.* 56.] (DEM)

1596.   Thomas Lodge. *A Margarite of America.*
[STC 16660. *Complete Works,* ed. Edmund Gosse, Hunterian Club,
Glasgow, 1883; *Menaphon . . . and A Margarite of America,* ed. G. B.
Harrison, Oxford, 1927.]

Sig. F 4 (Gosse 3. [4th piece] 43; Harrison, p. 163):
                    Domus doloris.
Who seekes the cave where horride care doth dwell,
    That feedes on sighes, and drinkes of bitter teares:
Who seekes in life to find a liuing hell,
    Where he that liues, all liuing ioy forbeares:
Who seeks that griefe, that griefe it selfe scarce knowes it,
    Here let him rest, this caue shall soone disclose it.

[Cf. *F. Q.* 4.5.33 ff.] (DEM)

1596.   Thomas Lodge. *Wits Miserie, and the Worlds Madnesse.*
[STC 16677. *Complete Works,* ed. Edmund Gosse, Hunterian Club,
Glasgow, 1883.]

P. 57 (sig. H ii; Gosse 4. [1st piece] 63):
Diuine wits, for many things as sufficient as all antiquity (I speake it
not on slight surmise, but considerate iudgement) to you belongs the
death that doth nourish this poison: to you the paine, that endure
reproofe. LILLY, the famous for facility in discourse: SPENCER, best
read in ancient Poetry: DANIEL, choice in word, and inuention:
DRAITON, diligent and formall: TH. NASH, true English Aretine. (FIC)

1596.   Thomas Nashe. *Have With You to Saffron-Walden.*
[STC 18369. *Works,* ed. R. B. McKerrow, 1910.]

Sig. F 2 (McKerrow 3.35):
For hauing found by much shipwrackt experience, that no worke of his
[Harvey's] absolute vnder hys owne name, would passe, he vsed heretofore to drawe *Sir Philip Sydney, Master Spencer,* and other men of
highest credit into euerie pild pamphlet he set foorth; and now that he
can no longer march vnder their Ensignes, (from which I haue vtterly
chac'd him in my *Foure Letters intercepted*) he takes a new lesson out
of *Plutarch,* in making benefit of his enemie. (FIC)

Sig. M 4ᵛ (McKerrow 3.80):
The iust manner of his phrase in his Orations and Disputation they

stufft his mouth with, & no Buffianisme throughout his whole bookes, but they bolstered out his part with; as those ragged remnaunts in his four familiar Epistles twixt him and *Senior Immerito, Raptim scripta, Nosti manum & stylum,* with innumerable other of his rabble routs. (DEM)

Sig. Q 2 (McKerrow 3.103):
Hee bids Barnabe of the Barnes, *bee the gallant Poet like* Spencer, *or the valiant Souldier like* Baskeruile.

Sig. Q 4ᵛ (McKerrow 3.107):
Hereby hee thought to connycatch the simple world, and make them beleeue, that these and these great men, euerie way sutable to Syr *Thomas Baskeruile*, Master *Bodley*, Doctor *Androwes*, Doctor *Doue*, *Clarencius* and Master *Spencer*, had seperately contended to outstrip *Pindarus* in his *Olympicis*, and sty aloft to the highest pitch.

Sig. R (McKerrow 3.108):
Doctour *Doue* and Clarencius, I turne loose to bee their owne Arbitratours and Aduocates; the one being eloquent inough to defend himselfe, and the other a Vice roy & next Heyre apparant to the King of Heralds, able to emblazon him in his right colours, if hee finde hee hath sustained any losse by him: as also in like sort Master *Spencer*, whom I do not thrust in the lowest place, because I make the lowest valuation of, but as wee vse to set *Summ' tot'* alway vnderneath or at the bottome, he being the *Sum' tot'* of whatsoeuer can be said of sharpe inuention and schollership.

Sig. S 2 (McKerrow 3.116):
Here is another Sonet of his, which he cals Haruey, *or* The sweete Doctour, *consisting of* Sidney, Bodine, Hatcher, Lewen, Wilson, Spencer; *that all their life time haue done nothing but conspire to lawd and honour Poet* Gabriell.

Sig. T 3ᵛ (McKerrow 3.126):
Hee complaines *I doo not regard* M. Bird, M. Spencer, Monsieur Bodin. (FIC)

Sig. V 2 (McKerrow 3.131):
As also in hys Booke he writ against *Greene* and mee, he raild vppon me vnder the name of *Piers Pennilesse*, and for a bribe that I should not reply on him praisd me, and reckond me (at the latter end) amongst the famous Schollers of our time, as S. *Philip Sidney*, M. *Watson*, M. *Spencer*, M. *Daniell*, whom he hartily *thankt* & promised *to endow with manie complements for so enriching our English Tongue*. (DEM)

1596.   D. Rollinson.   *Silvanus*, Bodleian MS Douce 21808.

[A St. John's College play, acted January 13, 1596. Rollinson is named in the catalogue of the Bodleian as the author; the part of Silvanus was taken by D. Rollinson. One of the songs employs the metre and refrain of the roundelay in *S. C. Aug.* Cf. George B. Campbell and Wolfgang

Keller, " Die lateinischen Universitäts-Dramen Englands in der Zeit der
Königen Elizabeth," *Sh. Jbh.* 34 (1898) 294-7. The first stanza of
Silvanus' song in praise of Diana (Churchill and Keller, p. 295, quoted)
runs as follows:

> Cantemus omnes Cynthiam
>   hei ho Cynthia
> venationis dominam
>   Sic incipit melodia.
> quae habitas in saltibus
>   hei ho [repetat], Delia
> ornata nostris laudibus
>   adsis nobis bellula.] (FIC)

1596. William Smith. *Chloris.*
  [STC 22872. Rptd A. B. Grosart, Occasional Issues, vol. 4 [piece 3],
  1877; ed. Lawrence A. Sasek, *The Poems of William Smith*, Louisiana
  State Univ. Press, 1970.]

To the Most Excellent and learned Shepheard Collin Clout, sig. A 2
(Lee 2.323; Grosart, p. 3; Sasek, p. 35):

> *Collin* my deere and most entire beloued,
> My muse audatious stoupes hir pitch to thee,
> Desiring that thy patience be not moued
> By these rude lines, written heere you see,
> Faine would my muse whom cruell loue hath wronged,
> Shroud hir loue labors vnder thy protection,
> And I my selfe with ardent zeale haue longed,
> That thou mightst knowe to thee my true affection.
> Therefore good *Collin*, graciously accept
> A few sad sonnets, which my muse hath framed,
> Though they but newly from the shell are crept,
> Suffer them not by enuie to be blamed.
>   But vnderneath the shadow of thy wings
>   Giue warmth to these yong-hatched orphan things.
>
> Giue warmth to these yoong-hatched orphan things,
> Which chill with cold to thee for succour creepe,
> They of my studie are the budding springs,
> Longer I cannot them in silence keepe.
> They will be gadding sore against my minde.
> But curteous shepheard, if they run astray
> Conduct them, that they may the path way finde,
> And teach them how, the meane obserue they may.
> Thou shalt them ken by their discording notes,
> Their weedes are plaine, such as poore shepheards weare.
> Vnshapen, torne, and ragged are their cotes,
> Yet foorth they wandring are deuoid of feare.
>   They wich haue tasted of the muses spring,
>   I hope will smile vpon the times they sing.
>   Finis. W. Smith.

Sonnet 20, sig. B 4 (Lee 2.335; Grosart, p. 15; Sasek, p. 57):
Yee wastefull woods beare witnes of my woe,
Wherein my plaints doe oftentimes abound:
Yee carelesse birds my sorrowes well do knoe,
They in your songs were wont to make a sound.
Thou pleasant spring canst record likewise beare
Of my designes and sad disparagment,
When thy transparent billowes mingled weare
With those downfals which from mine eies were sent.
The eccho of my still-lamenting cries,
From hollow vaults in treble voice resoundeth,
And then into the empty aire it flies,
And backe againe from whence it came reboundeth.
That Nimphe vnto my clamors doth replie,
Being likewise scornd in love as well as I.
[Cf. Cuddie's song, *S. C. Aug.* 151 ff.]

Sonnet 50, sig. D 3ᵛ (Lee 2.349; Grosart, p. 30; Sasek, p. 87):
Colin I know that in thy loftie wit
Thou wilt but laugh at these my youthfull lines,
Content I am, they should in silence sit,
Obscurd from light, to sing their sad designes:
But that it pleased thy graue shepherdhood
The Patron of my maiden verse to bee,
When I in doubt of raging Enuie stood,
And now I waigh not who shall *Chloris* see.
For fruit before it comes to full perfection
But blossomes is, as euery man doth know:
So these being bloomes, and vnder thy protection
In time I hope to ripenes more will grow,
And so I leaue thee to thy woorthy muse,
Desiring thee all faults heere to excuse.
[" Echoes of Spenser in other sonnets, e. g. 1, 15, 35 "] (FIC)

1596-1600. I. T. *Grim the Collier of Croyden: or, The Devil and his Dame: with the Devil and Saint Dunston,* first printed in *Gratiae Theatrales, or A Choice Ternary of English Plays,* 1662.
[STC G1580. Rptd J. W. Farmer, Tudor Facsimile Texts, 1912.]

Sig. G 3 (Koeppel, pp. 92-3):
Infernal Ioue, great prince of *Tartary,*
With humble reverence poor *Malbecco* speaks
Still trembling with the fatal memory
Of his so late concluded Tragedy.
[With these lines Malbecco's Ghost introduces a forty-seven line account of the events of the Malbecco-Hellenore episode, *F. Q.* 3.9.10. The plot of the play carries out much the same story.] (FIC)

1597. Francis Beaumont (d. 1598). Letter from Francis Beaumont to

Thomas Speght, prefixed to Speght's edition of *The Workes of* . . . *Geffrey Chavcer,* 1598.
[STC 5077-9.]

Sig. A iii[v] (Spurgeon 1.145-6):
But yet so pure were Chaucers wordes in his owne daies, as *Lidgate* that learned man calleth him *The Loadstarre of the English language;* and so good they are in our daies, as Maister *Spencer,* following the counsaile of *Tullie in de Oratore,* for reuiuing of antient wordes, hath adorned his own stile with that beauty and grauitie, which *Tully* speaks of: and his much frequenting of *Chaucers* antient speeches causeth many to allow farre better of him, then otherwise they would. (FIC)

1597.   Michael Drayton. *Englands Heroicall Epistles.*
[STC 7193. *Works,* ed. J. W. Hebel, Oxford, 1931-41.]

Richard the second to Queene Isabell, 1598 ed., STC 7194, quoted (Hebel 2.196):
> There wanton Sommer lords it all the yeere,
> Frost-starued Winter doth inhabite heere;
> A place wherein Despaire may fitly dwell,
> For sorrow best sutes with a cloudy Cell. (DEM)

1597.   Joseph Hall. *Virgidemiarvm, Sixe Bookes. First three Bookes, Of Tooth-lesse Satyrs.*
[STC 12716. *Complete Poems,* ed. A. B. Grosart, Occasional Issues, vol. 9, 1879.]

His Defiance of Enuy, sig. A 5 (Grosart, p. 7):
> Or scoure the rusted swords of Eluish knights,
> Bathed in Pagan blood: or sheath them new
> In misty morall Types: or tell their fights,
> Who mighty Giants, or who Monsters slew.
>> And by some strange inchanted speare and shield,
>> Vanquisht their foe, and wan the doubtfull field.

> Maybe she might in stately *Stanzaes* frame
> Stories of Ladies, and aduenturous knights:
> To raise her silent and inglorious name,
> Vnto a reach-lesse pitch of Prayses hight. (FIC)

Ibid., sig. A 6 - A 6[v] (Grosart, pp. 9-10):
> Would we but breath within a wax-bound quill,
> *Pans* seuenfold Pipe, some plaintiue Pastorall:
> To teach each hollow groue, and shrubby hill,
> Ech murmuring brooke, each solitary vale
>> To sound our loue, and to our song accord,
>> Wearying Eccho with one changelesse word.

> Or list vs make two striuing shephards sing,
> With costly wagers for the victorie,

Under *Menalcas* iudge whiles one doth bring
A caruen Bole well wrought of Beechen tree:
Praising it by the story, or the frame,
Or want of vse, or skilfull makers name.

Another layeth a well-marked Lambe,
Or spotted Kid.

[Cf. *S. C. Aug.* 25-42.] (DEM)

Ibid., sig. A 7 (Grosart, p. 11):

At *Colins* feet I throw my yeelding reed.
But let the rest win homage by their deed.

Lib. 1, sat. 1, p. 2 (sig. B 2ᵛ; Grosart, p. 18):

Nor need I craue the Muses mid-wifry,
To bring to light so worth-lesse Poetry:
Or if we list, what baser Muse can bide,
To sit and sing by *Grantaes* naked side.
They haunt the tyded *Thames* and salt *Medway*,
Ere since the fame of their late Bridall day.
Nought haue we here but willow-shaded shore,
To tell our *Grant* his banks are left forlore.

[Cf. *F. Q.* 4.11.10 ff.]

Lib. 1, sat. 4, p. 11 (sig. B 7; Grosart, p. 27):

But let no rebell *Satyre* dare traduce
Th' eternall *Legends* of thy *Faery Muse*,
Renowmed *Spencer*: whom no earthly wight
Dares once to emulate, much lesse dares despight.
Salust of *France*, and *Tuscan Ariost*,
Yeeld vp the *Lawrell girlond* ye haue lost:
And let all others willow weare with mee,
Or let their vnd[e]seruing *Temples* bared bee. (FIC)

Lib. 1, sat. 6, p. 14 (sig. B 8ᵛ; Grosart, p. 30):

Fie on the forged mint that did create
New coyne of words neuer articulate.

[This criticism may be compared to the well-known one quoted above from *A Defiance of Enuy*, which plainly refers to *F. Q.* However, it is more probable that Stanyhurst's translation of part of the *Aeneid*, rather than *S. C.*, is the object of Hall's satire here.] (DEM)

Lib. 2, sat. 2, p. 32 (sig. Dᵛ; Grosart, p. 45):

Liue we as we may:
Let swinish *Grill* delight in dunghill clay. (FIC)

[For other quotation from *Virgidemiarum,* see below: 1599. Joseph Hall.]

1597. George Kirbye. *The first set Of English Madrigalls to 4. 5. and 6. voyces.*

[STC 15010. E. H. Fellowes, *English Madrigal Verse*, Oxford, 1920.] [On sig. B ij^v (Fellowes, p. 113) S. C. *Nov.* 53-62 set to music.] (FIC)

1597. J. S. *Certaine Worthye Manuscript Poems of great Antiquitie Reserued long in the Studie of a Northfolke Gentleman. And now first published by J. S.* [STC 21499.]

Verso of title-page (no sig.):

> To the worthiest Poet Maister Ed. Spenser.

[Hunter, *Chorus Vatum* 4.470, conjectures that J. S. is Joshua Sylvester.] (FIC)

1597. John Salusbury. Poems included in Robert Parry's *Sinetes Passions Vppon His Fortunes.*
[STC 19338. *Poems by Sir John Salusbury and Robert Chester,* ed. Carleton Brown, Bryn Mawr Coll. Monographs, 14 (1913), reissued as EETS, 113 (1914).]

Poesie XII. *The authors muse vpon his Conceyte,* sig. E 7 (Brown, p. 59):

> Faire, fairest, faire: if passing faire, be faire,
> Let not your deed's obscure your beauties faire.
> The Queene so faire of Fearies not more fayer,
> Which doth excell with fancies chiefest fayer,
> Fayre to the worldes faire admiring wonder,
> Fayrer than Ioves loue that kills with thunder. (FMP)

[DEM notes that sonnets 4, 6, 7, 8, 10 (sigs. F^v - F 4^v; Brown, pp. 62-5) follow exactly or with slight variations the Spenserian sonnet scheme.]

1598. Richard Barnfield. *Poems: In diuers humors.*
[STC 1488. A. H. Bullen, *Some Longer Elizabethan Poems,* Westminster, 1903.]

Sonnet 1, *To his friend Maister R. L. In praise of Musique and Poetrie,* sig. E 2 (Bullen, p. 264):

> *Dowland* to thee is deare; whose heauenly tuch
> Vpon the Lute, doeth rauish humaine sense:
> *Spenser* to mee; whose deepe Conceit is such,
> As passing all Conceit, needs no defence.

A Remembrance of some English Poets, sig. E 2^v (Bullen, p. 265):

> Liue *Spenser* euer, in thy *Fairy Queene*:
> Whose like (for deepe Conceit) was neuer seene.
> Crownd mayst thou bee, vnto thy more renowne,
> (As King of Poets) with a Lawrell crowne.

[The remaining stanzas praise Daniel, Drayton, and Shakespeare.] (FIC)

An Ode, sig. E 2^v (Bullen, p. 266):

As it fell vpon a Day,
In the merrie Month of May,
Sitting in a pleasant shade,
Which a groue of Mirtles made,
Beastes did leape, and Birds did sing,
Trees did grow, and Plants did spring. . . .

[Cf. *F. Q.* 2.6.24.] (DEM)

1598. Samuel Brandon. *The Tragicomoedi of the vertuous Octauia.*
[STC 3544. Malone Soc. Rpts, 1909.]

Act 2, sc. 1, sigs. C 4ᵛ - C 5 (Malone, ll. 895-910):
Nature it selfe dooth most delight in change,
The heauens, by motion do their musicke make:
Their lights by diuers waies and courses raunge;
And some of them new formes doe alwaies take.
Their working power is neuer alwaies one,
And time it selfe least constant is of all:
This earth we see and all that liues thereon,
Without new change, into destruction fall.
Nay what is more, the life of all these things,
Their essence, and perfection, doth consist
In this same change, which to all creatures brings,
That pleasure, which in life may not be mist.
Sith then all creatures are so highly blest,
To taste the sweet of life in often change:
If we which are the princes of the rest,
Should want the same, me thinks t'were very strange.

[Cf. *F. Q.* 7.7.]

Act 5, sc. 1, sig. E 7ᵛ (Malone, ll. 1960-75):
Iul. . . . By nature we are moou'd, nay forst to loue:
And being forst, can we resist the same?
The powerfull hand of heauen we wretches prooue:
Who strike the stroke, and poore we, beare the blame.

[Indebtedness to Spenser very doubtful.] (FIC)

1598. Charles Butler. *Rhetoricae Libri Duo*, Oxford. [STC 4197.]

Sigs. C 3ᵛ - C 4 (Munro 1.473; Spurgeon 1.162):
Numerus poeticus est rhythmus, aut metrum. RHYTHMVS est numerus poeticus certu syllabarum numerum (nulla habita quantitatis ra-
tione) continens. Tales rhythmi naturales sunt in omni natione atꝙ;
gente: etiam in Graecia ante Homerum, & in Italia ante Andronicum
reperti sunt. Hodie autem plerumque Epistrophen soni coniunctam
habent: ut in illo Homeri nostri poemate. [Quotes *R. T.* 400-6]
& paulo post. [Quotes *R. T.* 428-34]
Varia rhythmorum genera* optimorum poetarum observatio optimè pre-
monstrabit.

* *Quales sunt apud* nos *Homero, Maroni, & Ovidio merito æquiparandi, Edmvndvs Spencer, Samvel Daniel,* & *Michael Drayton*: aliiq; ingenio & arte florentes, (quorum hæc ætas uberrima est) Atque inprimis horum omnium magister, unicum caligantis sui seculi lumen, dominus *Galfridvs Chavcer.* (JM, FIC)

1598.   Richard Carew. *A Herrings Tayle.* [STC 4614.]

Sig. B 4ᵛ:

> But neither can I tell, ne can I stay to tell,
> This pallace architecture, where perfections dwell:
> Who list such know, let him *Muses despencier* reede,
> Or thee, whom *England* sole did since the conquest breed,
> To conquer ignorance, *Sidney* like whom endite,
> Euen *Plato* would, or *Ioue* (they say) like Plato write.

[Authorship conjectural; cf. *CBEL* 1.826.] (FIC)

1598.   George Chapman. *The Blinde Begger of Alexandria.* [STC 4965. Malone Soc. Rpts, 1928; in *Comedies,* ed. T. M. Parrott, 1914.]

Sig. B 3 (Malone, ll. 378-9; Parrott, p. 12):

> *Br.* I am signeor *Braggadino* the Martiall spaniardo the aide of *Ægypt* in her present wars.

[A swashbuckling character.] (JLL)

1598.   Edward Guilpin. *Skialetheia, Or, A shadowe of Truth, in certaine Epigrams and Satyres.* [STC 12504. Ed. A. B. Grosart, Occasional Issues, vol. 6, Manchester, 1878.]

Satyra secunda, sig. C 6 (Grosart, p. 41):

> But now I call to mind,
> These can bewitch, and so haue made thee blind;
> A compound mist of May deaw and Beane flowre,
> Doe these *Acrasias* on thy eye lids powre:
> Thou art enchaunted (*Publius*) and hast neede
> Of *Hercules,* thy reason, to be freede. (JGM)

Satyra sexta, sig. E (Grosart, p. 63):

> Some blame deep *Spencer* for his grandam words,
> Others protest that, in them he records
> His maister-peece of cunning giuing praise,
> And grauity to his profound-prickt layes. (FIC)

Ibid., sig. Eᵛ (Grosart, p. 64):

> Nay, euen wits *Caesar, Sidney,* for whose death
> The Fates themselues lamented *Englands* scath,
> And Muses-wept, till of their teares did spring
> Admiredly a second *Castal* spring,

Is not exempt for prophanation,
But censur'd for affectation.
[General allusion to *T. M.*] (DEM)

1598. Giovanni Paolo Lomazzo. *A Tracte Containing the Artes of curious Paintinge*, Oxford.
[STC 16698.]

P. 51 (sig. Ee ij):
But you shall not expresse [all parts of the body] quite naked, to the ende you may moue the greater desire of seeing that which is* covered.

The rest hid vnderneath, him more desirous made. Faery Queene Cant. 12. li.2.

P. 85 (sig. Gg viᵛ):
I holde it expedient . . . to reade the Poets, who in similitudes and examples touch them generally, as we may finde in *Homer, Virgil, Ovid, Horace, Catullus* & all which the worthy *Ariosto* hath imitated in that his incomparable *Furioso*.

*Our English Painters may reade Sir Ph: Sidney, Spencer, Daniel, &c.

[The marginal notes are by " R[ichard] H[aydocke] student in Physik," the English translator of Lomazzo.] (HH)

1598. John Marston. *The Scourge of Villainy.*
[STC 17485. *Works*, ed. A. H. Bullen, 1887.]
Satire 6, *Hem nosti'n*, sig. E 7 (Bullen 3.341):
　　　Another yet dares tremblingly come out,
　　　But first he must invoke good *Colyn Clout*.

Ibid., sig. E 7ᵛ (Bullen 3.341):
　　　Here's one, to get an vndeseru'd repute
　　　Of deepe deepe learning, all in fustian sute
　　　Of ill-plac'd farre-fetch'd words attiereth
　　　His period, that sence forsweareth.

　　　Another makes old *Homer, Spencer* cite
　　　Like my *Pygmalion*, where, with rare delight
　　　He cryes, *O Ouid*. . . . (FIC)

1598. Francis Meres. *Palladis Tamia. Wits Treasury. Being the Second part of Wits Common wealth.*
[STC 17834. Ed. Don Cameron Allen, Scholars' Facsimiles & Rpts, New York, 1938.]
Fol. 278ᵛ (Munro 1.46-8):
　　And our famous English Poet *Spenser,* who in his *Sheepeheards Calender* lamenting the decay of Poetry at these dayes, saith most sweetly to the same.

　　　*Then make thee wings of thine aspiring wit
　　　And whence thou camest fly backe to heauen apace, &c.*

Fol. 280:

As the Greeke tongue is made famous and eloquent by *Homer, Hesiod, Euripedes, Aeschilus, Sophocles, Pindarus, Phocylides,* and *Aristophanes;* and the Latine tongue by *Virgill, Ouid, Horace, Silius Italicus, Lucanus, Lucretius, Ausonius* and *Claudianus*: so the English tongue is mightily enriched and georgeouslie inuested in rare ornaments and resplendent abiliments by sir *Philip Sidney, Spencer, Daniel, Drayton, Warner, Shakespeare, Marlow* and *Chapman.*

Fol. 280ᵛ:

As Sextus Propertius saide; *Nescio quid magis nascitur Iliade*: so I say of *Spencers Fairy Queene,* I knowe not what more excellent or exquisite Poem may be written.

As *Achilles* had the aduantage of *Hector,* because it was his fortune to be extolled and renowned by the heauenly verse of *Homer*: so *Spensers Elisa* the *Fairy Queen* hath the aduantage of all the Queenes in the worlde, to bee eternized by so diuine a Poet.

As *Theocritus* is famoused for his *Idyllia* in *Greeke,* and *Virgill* for his *Eclogs* in Latine: so *Spencer* their imitatour in his *Shepheardes Calender,* is renowned for the like argument, and honoured for fine Poeticall inuention, and most exquisit wit.

Fol. 282 - 282ᵛ

And as Horace saith of his; *Exegi monumentū ære perennius; Regaliq; situ pyramidū altius: Quod non imber edax; Non Aquilo impotens possit diruere; aut innumerabilis annorum series & fuga temporum;* so say I seuerally of sir *Philip Sidneys' Spencers Daniels, Draytons, Shakespeares,* and *Warners workes;*

> *Non Iouis ira: imbres: Mars: ferrum: flamma, senectus,*
> *Hoc opus vnda: lues: turbo: venena ruent.*
> *Et quanquam ad pulcherrimum hoc opus euertendum tres illi Dij conspirabūt, Cronus, Vulcanus, & pater ipse gentis;*
> *Non tamen annorum series, non flamma, nec ensis,*
> *Æternum potuit hoc abolere Decus.*

Fols. 282ᵛ - 283:

As *Homer* and *Virgil* among the Greeks and Latines are the chiefe Heroick Poets: so *Spencer* and *Warner* be our chiefe heroicall Makers.

As *Pindarus, Anacreon,* and *Callimachus* among the Greekes; and *Horace* and *Catullus* among the Latines are the best Lyrick Poets: so in this faculty the best amōg our Poets are *Spencer* (who excelleth in all kinds) *Daniell, Drayton, Shakespeare, Bretton.*

Fols. 283ᵛ - 284:

As these are famous among the Greeks for Elegie, *Melanthus . . . Pigres Halicarnassus;* and these among the Latines, *Mecænas . . . Clodius Sabinus*: so these are the most passionate among vs to bewaile and bemoane the perplexities of Loue, *Henrie Howard* Earle of Surrey, sir *Thomas Wyat* the elder, sir *Francis Brian,* sir *Philip Sidney,* sir *Walter Rawley,* sir *Edward Dyer, Spencer, Daniel, Drayton, Shakespeare, Whet-*

stone, Gascoyne, *Samuell* Page sometimes fellowe of *Corpus Christi* Colledge in Oxford, *Churchyard, Bretton.*

As *Theocritus* in Greeke, *Virgil* and *Mantuā* in Latine, *Sanazar* in Italian, and the Author of *Amyntæ Gaudia* and *Walsinghams Melibæus* are the best for pastorall: so amongst vs the best in this kind are sir *Philip Sidney,* master *Challener, Spencer, Stephen Gosson, Abraham Fraunce,* and *Barnefield.* (JM, FIC)

1598. George Nicolson. Letter to Sir Robert Cecil, Edinburgh, Feb. 25, S. P. Scotland, *Eliz.* 62. 6.
[Cf. *Cal. State Papers, Scotland, 1509-1603,* ed. Markham John Thorpe, 1858, 2.747; extract of letter transcribed by Henry R. Plomer quoted by Carpenter, p. 42.]

Carpenter, p. 42, quoted:
[Walter] Quyn is also answering Spensers booke whereat the K[ing] was offended.
[See: 1596. Robert Bowes, above.] (FIC)

1598. William Rankins. *Seauen Satyres Applyed to the weeke.*
[STC 20700. Quoted J. P. Collier, *Bibliographical Account,* New York, 1866.]

Induction, sig. A 3ᵛ (Collier 3.279):
> Of Loue, of Courtships and of fancies force
> Some gilded Braggadochio may discourse:
> My shaggy Satyres doe forsake the woods, . . .
> To view the manner of this humane strife.
[Cf. *F. Q.,* 2.3.4 ff.]

(RH, EAS)

1598. Thomas Rogers. *Celestiall Elegies of the Goddesses and the Muses, deploring the death of . . . the Ladie Fraunces Countesse of Hertford.*
[STC 21225. Rptd Charles Edmonds, *A Lamport Garland,* 1881.]

[The goddesses and the muses mourn the death of the lady in a manner reminiscent of *T. M.* The verse form, however, is that of the Shakespearean sonnet, and each of the several laments is called *Quatorzain.*] (DEM)

1598. Francis Rous. *Thule, Or Vertues Historie. To the Honorable and vertuous Mistris Amy Avdeley. By F. R.*
[STC 21348. Rptd Sp. Soc. Pub., no. 23, 1878.]

Book 1, Canto 7, sig. G 2 (Sp. Soc. Pub., p. 510):
> When in th' *Ægæum* of thy wandring dayes,
> Fortune full softly fils thy swelling saile,
> Let no *Circœas* hinder quite thy wayes,
> Nor let her cups against thy heart preuaile,
> Then vertue of thy spotted soule decayes,
> Blinded in worldly pleasures clowdy vaile:

This pleasing draught shall so bewitch thy will,
Well mayst thou see the good, but doe the ill.
[With verse 2 compare *F. Q.* 2.7.14.3; with 5-6, *H.H.B.* 137; with 6,
F. Q. 3.3.19.6; and with 7, *F. Q.* 1.9.15.3.]

Ibid., sig. G 3ᵛ (Sp. Soc. Pub., p. 54):
This pecocke irond thus of euery side,
A coward is vnfit of manly speare.
[Cf. *F. Q.* 2.3.6.4.] (FMP)

Ibid., sig. H (Sp. Soc. Pub., p. 57):
At last he sees the flame whose firy dart
Kindles the sulphure of his fueld hart.

About he runnes and cryes I burne I burne,
And in black famine all his bones doth spend:
At last vnto the riuer he doth turne,
Thinking to giue this flame a watry end.
[Cf. *F. Q.* 2.6.41-5.]

Book 2, Canto 3, sig. M 4ᵛ (Sp. Soc. Pub., p. 96):
A voyce she heard that fits her plotted wile,
And thus it faintly beates the yeelding ayre.
Issuing from pangs of woe and deepe despayre.

[Cf. *F. Q.* 3.11.25.7.] (DEM)
[Thule is a mosaic of characters and episodes adapted from the *F. Q.*
The passages quoted are merely illustrative.] (FIC, FMP)

1598. Thomas Speght. *The Workes of our Antient and Learned English
Poet, Geffrey Chavcer, newly Printed.* [STC 5077-9.]

Sig. Ciii - Ciiiᵛ:
And as for men of later time, not onely that learned gentleman M.
William Thynne, in his Epistle Dedicatorie to the Kings Maiestie, but also
two of the purest and best writers of our daies: the one for Prose,
the other for Verse, M. *Ascham* and M. *Spenser*, haue deliuered most
worthy testimonies of their approouing of him . . .
Master *Spenser* in his first Eglogue of his Shepheardes Kalender, calleth
him *Titirus*, the god of Shepheardes, comparing him to the worthinesse
of the Roman Titirus Virgil. In his Faerie Queene in his discourse of
friendship, as thinking himselfe most worthy to be Chaucers friend, for
his like naturall disposition that Chaucer had, hee sheweth that none that
liued with him, nor none that came after him, durst presume to reuiue
Chaucers lost labours in that vnperfite tale of the Squire, but only himselfe: which he had not done, had he not felt (as he saith) the infusion
of Chaucers owne sweete spirite, suruiuing within him. And a little
before he termeth him, Most renowned and Heroicall Poet: and his
Writings, The workes of heauenly wit: concluding his commendation
in this manner:

Dan Chaucer, Well of English vndefiled,
On Fames eternal beadrole worthy to be filed.
I follow here the footing of thy feet,
That with thy meaning so I may the rather meet.

And once againe I must remember M. *Camdens* authority, who as it were reaching one hand to Maister *Ascham*, and the other to Maister *Spenser*, and so drawing them togither vttereth of him these words. *De Homero nostro Anglico illud verè asseram, quod de Homero eruditus ille Italus dixit*:

> –––––––––*Hic ille est, cuius de gurgite sacro*
> *Combibit arcanos vatum omnis turba furores.* (FIC)

1598. Robert Tofte. *Certain Diuine Poems, written by the foresaid Author R. T. Gentleman.* Appended to *Alba. The Months Minde of a Melancholy Lover.*
[STC 24096. *Alba*, ed. A. B. Grosart, Occasional Issues, vol. 12 (2nd piece), 1880.]

Deo, Optimo, Maximo, sig. H 4 (Grosart, p. 119):
> With Teares in Eyes, with drops of Blood from Hart,
> With skalding sighs from inward grieued Soule,
> A CONVERTITE, from Vaine LOVE now I part,
> Whilst, for my *Sinnes*, fore *Heauen* I do condole.
> I know, and knowledge I haue liued wrong,
> And wilfull sought mine owne Destruction long.

> The *Temple* of my Heauenly GOD I haue,
> For *earthly Goddesse*, stainde blasphemously,
> Selling my selfe to *Satan* for his *Slaue*,
> Whilst I transgrest in vile *Apostasie*.
> Banisht my selfe I haue from *Paradize*,
> Through *thriftles Toyes* of *base-borne Vanities*.

Ibid., sig. H 5 (Grosart, p. 121):
> Ah, be not flattred with this poysenous LOVE,
> But call thy former Wits to thee againe.

Ibid., sig. H 7ᵛ (Grosart, p. 126):
> This *earthly Beautie* doth the *Sence* delight,
> But *Heauenly Beautie* doth the *minde* more please.

[General influence of Spenser's *Hymnes*.] (FMP)

1598. William Vaughan. *Poematum libellus.* [STC 24620.]

Inuitantur candidati Poetę ad triumphales cantus . . . Roberti Comitis Essexij, sig. A 4ᵛ:
> Huc Spencere veni qui venâ præditus altâ
> Virgilij plenâ pragmata voce canis.
> Non lamijs Libitina tuis continget acerba
> In mare dum Thamesis nobilis vnda fluat. (LB)

About 1599.   Hugh Holland. *On Spencer y*e *Poett*, B. M. Add. MS 21433. Fol. 177v:

On Spencer ye Poett.

H H

He was & is, see then where lyes the odds
Once God of Poetts, now Poet of the Gods
And though his lyne of life begone aboute
Ye life yet of his lyne shall neuer out.

[" A variant couplet, without suggestion of authorship, is found in Harl. MS 5353, fol. 2."] (HES)

1599.   John Chamberlain. Letter to Dudley Carleton, Jan. 17, *S. P. Dom., Eliz.* 270. 16.
[*Letters*, ed. Sarah Williams, Camden Soc., 1861; *Letters*, ed. Norman Egbert McClure, Philadelphia, 1939; Cf. *Cal. State Papers Dom. Eliz., 1598-1601*, ed. Mary Anne Everett Green, 1869, p. 152.]

Williams, p. 41; McClure 1.64-5 quoted:
. . . The Lady Cope your cousen and mine old mistress left the world (as I heare) on Tw'elvth Even and Spencer our principall poet comming out of Ireland died at Westminster on Satterday last. (FIC)

1599.   Thomas Cutwode. *Caltha Poetarum: or The Bumble Bee.*
[STC 6151. Rptd Roxburghe Club Publications, 1815.]

Sigs. A 4v - A 5 (Roxburghe, sig. A 4v):
For *Homer*, who imitated none, and *Archilocus*, who is compared with *Homer*, because they only finished their workes in their life. And *Virgil*, the curious Ape of *Homer*. *Ouid* the Amorous, *Martiall* the lycentious, *Horace*, the mixt betwixt modest & *Satirique* vaine. The flower of our age, sweete pleasing *Sidney*. *Tasso* the graue. Pollished *Daniel* the Historick *Spencer* the Truthes Faith. (FIC)

1599.   Samuel Daniel. *The Poeticall Essayes of Sam. Danyel.*
[STC 6261. *Complete Works*, ed. A. B. Grosart, 1885]

The Civill Wars of England, The Fowrth Booke, sts. 5-6, p. 69 (sig. T; Grosart, *The Fift Booke*, 2.175):

Why do you seeke for fained *Palladins*
Out of the smoke of idle vanitie,
That maie giue glorie to the true dissignes
Of *Bourchier, Talbot, Neuile, Willoughby?*
Why should not you striue to fill vp your lines
With wonders of your owne, with veritie?
T'inflame their offspring with the loue of Good
And glorious true examples of their bloud.

O what eternall matter here is found!
Whence new immortal *Iliads* might proceed,
That those whose happie graces do abound

In blessed accents here maie haue to feed
Good thoughts, on no imaginary ground
Of hungrie shadowes which no profit breed:
Whence musicke like, instant delight may grow,
But when men all do know they nothing know.

Mvsophilvs: Containing a generall defence of all learning, sig. C 4ᵛ
(Grosart 1.239):

How many thousands neuer heard the name
Of *Sydney*, or of *Spencer*, or their bookes?
And yet braue fellowes, and presume of fame
And seem to beare downe all the world with lookes:
What then shall they expect of meaner frame,
On whose indeuours few or none scarse looks? (FIC)

Ibid., sig. F 2 (Grosart 1.254):

And do not thou contemne this swelling tide
And streame of words that now doth rise so hie
Aboue the vsuall banks, and spreads so wide
Ouer the borders of antiquitie:
Which I confesse comes euer amplifide
With th'abounding humours that do multiplie.

[Cf. opinion expressed here with that in *Delia*, Sonnet 46; see 1592.
Samuel Daniel.] (DEM)

1599.   Sir John Davies. *Nosce Teipsum.*
[STC 6355. *Poems*, reprod. in facsimile by Clare Howard, Columbia
Univ. Press, 1941.]

To my most gracious dread Soueraigne, sig. A 3 (Howard, p. 111):

To that cleare Maiestie, which in the North,
Doth like another Sunne in glorie rise.

[Cf. *F. Q.* 5.3.19; *S. C. Apr.* 74.]

Ibid., sig. A 3ᵛ (Howard, p. 112):

Faire *Soule*, since to the fairest bodie knit,
You giue such liuely life, such quickning power,
Such sweete celestiall influence to it,
As keepes it still in youths immortall flower.

[Cf. *H. B.* 127-133.]

Sig. C 2ᵛ (Howard, p. 124):

But thou bright morning Starre, thou rising *Sunne*,
Which in these later times hast brought to light
Those mysteries, that since the world begun
Lay hid in darknesse, and in eternall night.

[Cf. *H. L.* 57-60.]

Sig. F 4ᵛ (Howard, p. 152):

Her *quickning power* in euery liuing part,
Doth as a Nurse, or as a Mother serue,
And doth employ her *œconomicke Art,*
And busie care, her houshold to preserue.

Here she *attracts,* and there she doth *retaine,*
There she *decocts,* and doth the food *prepare;*
There she *distributes* it to euery vaine,
There she *expels* what she may fitly spare.

[These stanzas followed by others on the various senses. Cf. *F. Q.* 2.9.27 ff.] (DEM)

Sig. I 3ᵛ (Howard, p. 174):

Againe, if by the bodies prop she stand,
If on the bodies life, her life depend,
As *Meleagers* on the fatall brand,
The bodies good she onely would intend.

We should not fine her halfe so braue and bold,
To leade it to the warres, and to the Seas;
To make it suffer watchings, hunger, cold,
When it might feed with plenty, rest with ease.

[Cf. *F. Q.* 2.11.23.] (KK)

1599. Anthony Gibson. *A Womans Woorth, defended against all the men in the world.* [STC 11831.]

To the Honourable Mistresse Margaret Ratcliffe, fol. A 7 (quoted Douglas Bush, *MLN,* 42 [1927], 314):

Had I a *Spencers* spirit, a *Daniels* powers:
Th' extracted quintessence were only yours. (DB)

1599. Robert Greene (d. 1592). *The Comicall Historie of Alphonsus King of Aragon.*
[STC 12233. Ed. W. W. Greg, Malone Soc. Rpts, Oxford, 1926.]

Act 1, sig. A 3ᵛ (Greg, ll. 38-43):

I which was wont to follow *Cupids* games
Will put in ure *Mineruaes* sacred Art,
And this my hand which vsed for to pen
The praise of loue, and *Cupids* peerles power,
Will now begin to treat of bloudie *Mars,*
Of doughtie deeds and valiant victories.

[Cf. *F. Q.* 1. proem 1. A general relation of the prologue to Spenser's *Complaints* (observed by J. C. Collins, *Plays and Poems of Robert Greene,* Oxford, 1905, 1.70-82) can hardly be more than faintly reminiscent.] (FMP)

1599. Joseph Hall. *Virgidemiarvm The three last Bookes. Of byting Satyres.*

[STC 12719. *Complete Poems*, ed. A. B. Grosart, Occasional Issues, vol. 9, Manchester, 1879.]

Lib. 4, sat. 1, p. 5 (sig. B 3; Grosart, p. 89):
 Gird but the *Cynicks* Helmet on his head,
 Cares he for *Talus* or his flayle of lead?
[Cf. *F. Q.* 5.1.12.] (JM)

1599. *The Historie of the two valiant Knights, Syr Clyomon . . . And Clamydes . . . As it hath bene sundry Times Acted by her Maiesties Players.*
[STC 19538. Tudor Facsimile Texts, John S. Farmer, Amersham, 1913.]
Sig. C 2ᵛ:
    Enter Bryan sance foy.
[This play is attributed to George Peele.] (FIC)

1599. John Hoskins. *Direccōns for Speech and Style*, B. M. MS Harleian 4604.
[Ed. H. H. Hudson, Princeton Univ. Press, 1935; ed. Louise Brown Osborn, *Life, Letters and Writings of John Hoskyns*, chap. 9, Yale Univ. Press, 1937.]

Fol. 6 (Hudson, p. 10; Osborn, p. 124):
 Let Spencer tell yoᵂ such a tale of a *ffaery Queene*, & *Ovid* of Diana & then it is a poets tale.
[From internal evidence the MS is to be dated 1599.] (HH)

1599. George Peele. *The Loue of King David and Fair Bethsabe.*
[STC 19540. *Works*, ed. A. H. Bullen, 1888; Malone Soc. Rpts, 1913.]
Sig. Eᵛ (Bullen 2.42; Malone, ll. 864-710:
  Ioab. Beauteous and bright is he among the Tribes,
  As when the sunne attir'd in glist'ring robe,
  Comes dauncing from his orientall gate,
  And bridegroome-like hurles through the gloomy aire
  His radiant beames, such doth King Dauid shew,
  Crownd with the honour of his enemies towne,
  Shining in riches like the firmament,
  The starrie vault that ouerhangs the earth,
  So looketh Dauid King of Israel.
[Cf. *F. Q.* 1.5.2.] (DEM)

1599. *The First Booke of the Preservation of King Henry vij when he was but Earle of Richmond.*
[STC 13076. Cf. J. P. Collier, *Illustrations of Old English Literature*, 1866, vol. 2, and *Bibliographical Account of Early English Literature*, 1866, 4.99-100 n.]

Sig. A 2ᵛ:
 I confesse and acknowledge that we haue many excellent and singular

good Poets in this our age, as Maister *Spencer*, that was, Maister *Gowld-ing*, Doctor *Phayer*, Maister *Harrington*, *Daniell*, and diuers others whom I reuerence in that kinde of prose-rhythme: wherein *Spencer* (with offence spoken) hath surpassed them all. I would to God they had done so well in trew Hexameters: for they had then beautified our language. (FIC)

1599. Robert Roche. *Evstathia or the Constancie of Svsanna*, Oxford. [STC 21137.]

To the Reader, sig. A 3ᵛ:

> Expect not heere, th'invention, or the vaine,
> Of *Lucrece rape-write*: or the curious scan,
> Of *Phillis* friend; or famous fairy-*Swaine*;
> Or *Delias* prophet, or admired man.
> My chicken faethered winges, no ympes enrich,
> Pens not full fum'd, mount not so high a pitch.

> Let *Colin* reare his flight to admiration
> And traine his louely flocke, his pipe to follow.
> Let *Damons* reach, out-reach all imitation;
> And frame melodious hymnes, to please *Apollo*.
> The swaine that pend this pastorall for *Pan*;
> Thought once to end his worke, ere [he] began. (JLL)

1599. John Weever. *Epigrammes in the oldest cut, and newest fashion.* [STC 25223. Ed. R. B. McKerrow, 1911.]

Lectores, quotquot, quales, quicunq; estis, sigs. A 5ᵛ - A 6 (McKerrow, pp. 10-1, quoted):

> Nor haue I spent in *Troinouant* my dayes,
> Where all good witts (some say) are crown'd with Bayes . . .

> I neuer durst presume take in mine hand
> The nimble-tripping Faëries history,
> I cannot, I protest, yet vnderstand
> The wittie, learned, Satyres mystery;
> I cannot moue the sauage with delight,
> Of what I cannot, Reader then I write.

The first weeke, sig. B 1ᵛ (McKerrow, p. 18, quoted):

> Epig. 3. *In Elizabetham*.
> If that *Elizium* be no fained thing,
> Whereof the Poets wont so much to sing;
> Then are those faire fields in this Faërie land,
> Which faire *Eliza* rules with awfull hand.

The fifth weeke, sig. F (McKerrow, p. 81, quoted):

> Epig. 7. *In Braggadochionem*.
> Did *Braggadochio* meete a man in field?
> Tis true, he did, the way he could not shun:

And did he force great *Brundon* weapons yeeld;
Nay there he lies. To vntrusse when he begun,
He stole his weapons and away did run:
Vaine is thy vaunt, and victorie vniust,
Thou durst not stay till he his points vntrust.

[See *F. Q.* 2.2.29.8-9 for the last two lines.] (FIC)

The sixt weeke, sig. F 8 (McKerrow, p. 95, quoted):

Epig. 9. In tumulum Ferdinand. Darbie.
Rest, in vnrest, teares-spitting forge be burning,
Vntil some write *The Muses nine dayes mourning.*

[Possible allusion to *T. M.*] (DEM)

Ibid., sig. G 3 (McKerrow, p. 101, quoted):

Epig. 23. In obitum Ed. Spencer Poetae prestantiss.
Colin's gone home, the glorie of his clime,
The Muses Mirrour, and the Shepheards Saint;
Spencer is ruin'd, of our latter time
The fairest ruine, Faëries foulest want:
When his *Time ruines* did our ruine show,
Which by his ruine we vntimely know:
Spencer therfore thy *Ruines* were cal'd in,
Too soone to sorrow least we should begin. (FIC)

About 1600. John Chalkhill. *Thealma and Clearchus. A Pastoral History, in smooth and easie Verse. Written long since, By John Chalkhill, Esq; An Acquaintant and Friend or Edmund Spencer,* 1683. [STC C 1794.]

P. 3 (sig. B 2; Saintsbury 2.374):

Close by the River, was a thick-leav'd Grove,
Where Swains of old sang stories of their Love;
But unfrequented now since *Collin* di'd,
Collin that King of Shepherds, and the pride
Of all *Arcadia.*

P. 61 (sig. E 7; Saintsbury 2.398):

. . . the beauteous *Florimel*
. . . whose vertue had no paralel.

[Echoes of Spenser on pp. 48-50, 99, 125 (sigs. E - E 2, H 2, I 6; Saintsbury 2.393, 414, 424-5), and in the diction, *passim.*] (FIC)

About 1600. Ellis Catalogue 204, item 330.

Lines written in a contemporary hand at the foot of p. 600 of volume I of *F. Q.,* 1590:

Heroicke Muse (distyld from Joue above,
Inspiringe Spenser wth. so loftie layes,
To treate of woorthies, and of Ladies loue.)
Voutchsafe me leaue to yelde him endlesse prayes,

Whose vertue fayer deserues immortal light.
Then take these lines as erst was widowes mite. (DEM)

About 1600. R. H. *In obitum doctissimi viri venerabilis Mri Spenseri carmen* ἐπικήδικον, Newberry Library MS Phillips 28939.

Mæsta veternoso torquentur pectora luctu:
   in luctu tanto fundis Apollo melos?
Si tua luctisonis quadrabunt metra querelis,
   conquerere exosæ tela cruenta necis.
Spreta pius noster persensit spicula Spenser,
   Spenser mortis ovans vulnera sæva tulit.
Ejus alexicacus suffulsit pectora Christus,
   Christus mors mortis, dum moriburus erat.
In misera quisquis remanes hac luce superstes,

[10]   te superesse putas et superasse necem?
Cur pulchro elatus turgescit corpore fastus?
   fastu forma necis tela domare nequit.
Nervosisne potens confides viribus o vir?
   Vir vi non fregit vincula mortis adhuc.
Longane funestus promittit tempora nummus?
   nummus, vt eripiat te, nihil ipse valet.
Mollia num malesana titillat corda voluptas?
   nec volupe ad vitam vel studiosa valet.
Insigni antiquæ num clares stemmate stirpis?
   stirpis nobilitas mortis ad arma nihil.

[20]   Cælica multivagam retinere scientia mentem,
   mens vt sit semper carcere clausa, nequit.
Nec divina feram superat sapientia mortem,
   ad mortem potius præparat illa viam.
Seria venturæ sic est meditatio mortis,
   ad mortem Spenser, janua facta tibi.
Tenuia vitalis servat spiracula vitæ.
   non vitæ integritas: ergo quid illa valent?
Dum rata venturæ speculatur gaudia vitæ;

[30]   vitam fastidit mens pia in orbe brevem.
Sic divina tuo sedit veneratio corde,
   corde vt sis, Spenser, promptas vbique mori.
Nos tua lugubri celebremus funera versu;
   vertit enim in nostrum mors caput omne malum.
Clarus in ingenua dum amittitur arte magister,
   spem mage concussam defleat ista domus.
Sed tristis nostrum finito Musa dolorem:
   nec dolet in cœlis, nec crucis ille capax.
Mortua nam licet hoc circundat membra feretrum

[40]   viva anima illius fertur ad astra tamen.
Jure igitur cassum lugemus lumine amicum,
   namque bonis Spenser semper amicus erat.

[This MS is a single folio sheet, the poem appearing in two parallel columns, with the last two lines centered below. The capitals are ornamental and the script is Italian. Carpenter suggests that the verses may be a copy of one of the poems thrown into Spenser's tomb, and that the author may be Richard Harvey. Lines 35-6 would seem to support this last conjecture.] (FIC)

About 1600. Sir John Harington. *The Most Elegant and Wittie Epigrams of Sir Iohn Harrington, Knight, Digested Into Foure Bookes: Three whereof neuer before published*, 1618 [2nd ed.].
[STC 12776. *Letters and Epigrams of Sir John Harington*, ed. N. E. McClure, Univ. Pa. Press, 1930.]

The second Booke, sig. G 8ᵛ (McClure, pp. 224-5):

> 93 *Of Monsters. To my Lady* Rogers.
> Strange-headed Monsters, Painters haue described.
> To which the poets strange parts haue ascribed, . . .
> On what seu-n-headed beast the Strumpet sits,
> That weares the scarfe, sore troubleth many wits,
> Whether seu'n sinnes be meant, or else seu'n hils,
> It is a question fit for higher skils.

[In B. M. Addit. MS 12049, the fourth line reads: "That wears the skarlett, poseth many wits." Cf. *F. Q.* 1.7.16-8.] (RH)

Ibid., sig. H 3 (McClure, p. 229):

> 100 Lesbias *rule of praise.*
> So, *Linus* praises *Churchyard* in his censure,
> Not *Sydney, Daniel, Constable*, nor *Spencer.* (DFA)

[In Folger MS 4455, p. 156, dated June 19, 1605, a version reads as follows:

> So Lynus prayses Churchyard in his censure
> Not Sydney, Daniell, Constable, nor Spensure.] (DEM)

[The epigrams quoted do not appear in the first, 1615, ed. For the date of composition, see McClure, p. 52, n. 2.]

About 1600. *Hymnus pastoralis in laudem serenissimae reginae Elizabethae, ex Anglico sermone in Latinum traductus*, B. M. MS Harleian 532.
[A translation into Latin verse of the song in *S. C. Apr.*; not the same as Dove's or Bathurst's. See Leicester Bradner, "The Latin Translations of Spenser's *Shepheardes Calender*," *MP* 33 (1935-6) 26 n.] (LB)

About 1600. *The Pilgrimage to Parnassus*, Bodleian MS Rawlinson D.398.
[*The Three Parnassus Plays*, ed. J. B. Leishman, 1949.]

Act 1, l. 83 (Leishman, p. 98, quoted):

> Let lazie grill snorte till the midst of the day.

[Cf. *F. Q.* 2.12.87.8.]

Ibid., 145-6 (Leishman, p. 102, quoted):
And when oure ruder pipes are taught to singe
The eccoinge wood with thy praise shall ringe.

[Cf. *Epith.* refrain.]

Act 4, ll. 454-5 (Leishman, p. 119, quoted):
Cropp you the ioyes of youth while that you maye,
Sorrowe and grife will come another daye.

[Cf. *F. Q.* 2.12.75.8.] (JBL)

About 1600.   [The First Part of] *The Returne from Parnassus*, Bodleian
MS Rawlinson D 398.
[*The Three Parnassus Plays*, ed. J. B. Leishman, 1949.]

Act 3, sc. 1, ll. 1024-8 (Munro 1.68: Spurgeon 1.144; Leishman,
p. 185, quoted):
Ingenioso My pen is youre bounden vassall to cõmande, but what vayne
woulde it please you to have them in?
Gullio Not in a vaine veine (prettie yfaith); make mee them in two or
three divers vayns, in Chaucers, Gowers and Spencers and Mr Shak-
speares. (JM)

Act 4, sc. 1, ll. 1180-3 (Spurgeon 1.145; Koeppel, p. 86; Leishman,
p. 192, quoted):
Ingenioso   Then you shall heare Spe[n]cers veyne.
A gentle pen rides prickinge on the plaine,
This paper plaine, to resalute my love.

Ibid., lines 1198-1201 (Spurgeon 1.145; Leishman, p. 192 quoted):
Gullio Noe more, I am one that can iudge accordinge to the proverbe,
bouem ex unguibus. Ey marry, Sr, these [lines from *Venus and Adonis*]
have some life in them: Let this duncified worlde esteeme of Spēcer and
Chaucer, Ile worshippe sweet Mr Shakspeare. (CFES)

Ibid., ll. 1211-4 (Leishman, p. 193, quoted):
Ingenioso Why, who coulde endure this post put into a sattin sute, this
haberdasher of lyes, this Bracchidochio, this Ladye munger, this meere
rapier and dagger, this cringer, this foretopp, but a man that's ordayned
to miserie? (FMP)
[See also: 1606. [The Second Part of] *The Returne from Pernassus*.]

1600.   Robert Allott. *Englands Parnassus: or The choysest Flowers of
our Moderne Poets, with their Poeticall comparisons.*
[STC 378. Ed. Charles Crawford, 1913.]

[" A book of elegant extracts, arranged under topics. Quotations from
Spenser appear on almost every page (over 300 entries in all, mostly
from *F. Q.*, but with a fair number from *F. H., S. C.*, and other minor
poems,—some 15 or 20). Following the alphabetical arrangement of
topics are extracts in general classes grouped as Divisions of the Day,

Poetical Descriptions, Poetical Comparisons (Similes), etc., where Spenser's rich art in handling *materia poetica* in its details may profitably be studied in juxtaposition with that of his most esteemed contemporaries.
" Cf. Charles Crawford, N & Q, ser. 10, 11.4, 123, 204, 283, 383, 443, 502; 12.235.
" Cf. *Shakspere Allusion Book* 2.474-5: corrects some of the attributions."] (FIC)

1600. John Bodenham. *Bel-vedére, or The Garden of the Muses.*
[STC 3189. Sp. Soc. Rpts, 1875.]

To the Reader, sigs. A 3ᵛ - A 6 (Munro 1.72-3; Bradley, pp. 7-8):
   Concerning the nature and qualitie of these excellent flowres, thou seest that they are most learned, graue, and wittie sentences; each line being a seuerall sentence, and none exceeding two lines at the vttermost. All which, being subiected vnder apt and proper heads, as arguments what is then dilated and spoken of: euen so each head hath first his definition in a couplet sentence; then the single and double sentences by variation of letter do follow: and lastly Similies and Examples in the same nature likewise, to conclude euery Head or Argument handled . . . I haue set down both how, whence, and where these flowres had their first springing, till thus they were drawne togither into the *Muses Garden,* that euery ground may challenge his owne, each plant his particular, and no one be iniured in the iustice of his merit . . .
[Bodenham lists his sources: speeches to the Queen and poems to her ladies; sentences from the verse of King James of Scotland; poems by " these right Honourable persons ": Surrey, Winchester, the Countess of Pembroke, Sidney; and by " these noble personages ": Oxford, Derby, Raleigh, Dyer, Greville, and Harington. He continues:]
   From diuers essayes of their Poetrie; some extant among other Honourable personages writings; some from priuate labours and translations.

> Edmund Spencer.
> Henry Constable Esquier.
> Samuel Daniel.

[The other poets named in this list headed by Spenser are Lodge, Watson, Drayton, Davies, (Thomas) Hudson, Locke, Marston, Marlowe, Jonson, Shakespeare, Churchyard, Nash, Kyd, Peele, Greene, Sylvester, Breton, Markham, (Thomas) Storer, (Robert) Wilmot, (Christopher) Middleton, and Barnfield] . . . These being Moderne and extant Poets, that have liu'd togither; from many of their extant workes, and some kept in priuat . . .
[There follows a list of five poets who are deceased: Thomas Norton, George Gascoigne, Francis Kindlemarsh, Thomas Atchlow, George Whetstone.] (JM)

[Charles Crawford ("Belvedere, or The Garden of the Muses," *Englische Studien* 43 (1911). 207) notes that out of a total of 2380 quotations, 215 are from Spenser, as compared with 269 from Drayton, 215 from Daniel, and 214 from Shakespeare.]

1600. Nicholas Breton. *Melancholike humours, in verses of diuerse natures.*
[STC 3666. Ed. G. B. Harrison, 1929.]

An Epitaph vpon Poet Spencer, sigs F 3 - F 4 (Harrison, pp. 44-6):

Movrnfvll Muses, sorrowes minions,
Dwelling in despaires opinions,
Yee that neuer thought inuented,
How a heart may be contented
(But in torments alle distressed,
Hopelesse how to be redressed,
All with howling and with crying,
Liue in a continuall dying)
    Sing a Dirge on *Spencers* death,
    Till your soules be out of breath.

Bidde the Dunces keepe their dennes,
And the Poets breake their pennes:
Bidde the Sheepheards shed their teares,
And the Nymphes go teare their haires:
Bidde the Schollers leaue their reeding,
And prepare their hearts to bleeding:
Bidde the valiant and the wise,
Full of sorrowes fill their eyes;
    All for griefe, that he is gone,
    Who did grace them euery one.

Fairy Queene, shew fairest Queene,
How her faire in thee is seene.
Sheepeheards Calender set downe,
How to figure best a clowne.
As for Mother *Hubberts* tale,
Cracke the nut, and take the shale:
And for other workes of worth,
(All too good to wander forth)
    Grieue that euer you were wrot,
    And your Author be forgot.

Farewell Arte of Poetry,
Scorning idle foolery:
Farewell true conceited reason,
Where was neuer thought of treason:
Farewell iudgement, with inuention,
To describe a hearts intention:
Farewell wit, whose sound and sense
Shewe a Poets excellence:
    Farewell all in one togither,
    And with *Spencers* garland, wither.

And, if any Graces liue,

That will vertue honour giue,
Let them shewe their true affection,
In the depth of griefes perfection,
In describing forth her glory,
When she is most deepely sory;
That they all may wish to heere,
Such a song, and such a quier,
As, with all the woes they haue,
Follow *Spencer* to his graue. (FIC)

1600. William Camden. *Britannia.* [STC 4507]

P. 379 (Spurgeon 1.1630):
Quique minimè tacendus Poëtarum Angloru̅ princeps Galfredus Chaucer; & qui ad illum ingenij fælicitate, & diuite Poëseos vena proximè inter Anglicos poëtas accessit Edm. Spencerus (CFES)

1600. William Camden. *Reges, Reginæ, Nobiles, & Alij in Ecclesia Collegiata B. Petri Westmonasterij Sepulti.* [STC 4518.]

In Australi plaga Ecclesiæ, sigs. I 2ᵛ - I 3:
Edwardus Spencer Londinensis, Anglicorum Poetarum nostri seculi facilè princeps, quod eius poemata fauentibus Musis & victuro genio conscripta comprobant. Obijt immatura morte anno salutis 1598. & prope Galfredum Chaucerum conditur quo fælicissimè poesin Anglicis literis primus illustrauit. In quem haec scripta sunt Epitaphia.

> *Hic prope Chaucerum situs est Spenserius, illi*
> *Proximus ingenio, proximus vt tumulo.*
> *Hic prope Chaucerum Spensere Poeta poetam*
> *Conderis, & versu, quàm tumulo proprior.*
> *Anglica te viuo vixit, plausitque Poesis;*
> *Nunc moritura timet, te moriente, mori.* (FIC)

1600. Thomas Dekker. *The Pleasant Comedy of Old Fortunatus.* [STC 6517. Ed. Hans Scherer, Münchener Beiträge, 21, 1901.]

The Prologue at Court, sig. A 2 (Scherer, p. 53; Koeppel, p. 91):
> O vouchsafe,
> Dread Queene of Fayries, with your gracious eyes,
> T'accept theirs and our humble sacrifice. (EK, FMP)

1600. *Englands Helicon.* [STC 3191. Ed. Hyder E. Rollins, Harvard Univ. Press, 1935.]

[Three selections from Spenser appear in this anthology. S. C. Apr. 37-153, S. C. Aug. 53-124, As. 1-8 as Nos. 6, 11, 27 on sigs. Cᵛ - C 3ᵛ, D 2 - D 3, G - Gᵛ (Rollins 1.16-7, 25-7, 47-8).] (FIC)

Sig. B 2 (Rollins 1.9; No. 2):
> *Theorello. A Sheepheards Edillion.*
> You Shepherds which on hillocks sit,

Like Princes in their throanes;
And guide your flocks, which else would flit
Your flocks of little ones. . . .

[The picture of shepherds sitting on hillocks is a familiar one. However, there is a possible implication in the second quoted line which brings to mind Spenser's description of the prelates who aspire to princely place, neglecting their pastoral duties. Cf. *S. C. May, July, Sept. Theorello* is signed with the initials E. B., probably to indicate Edmund Bolton; cf. Rollins 2.25-6] (DEM)

Sig. D 3ᵛ (Rollins 1.28: No. 13):

To Colin Cloute.

[Presumably addressed to Colin Clout of *S. C.* For summary of arguments supporting the identification of Anthony Munday with Sheepheard Tonie, author of No. 13, cf. Rollins 2.31-3, 91.] (WW)

Sig. Hᵛ (Rollins 1:56: No. 35):

The *vnknowne Sheepheards complaint.*
My Flocks feede not, my Ewes breede not,
My Rammes speede not, all is amisse:
Loue is denying, Faith is defying,
Harts renying, causer of this.
All my merry Iiggs are quite forgot,
All my Ladies loue is lost God wot.
Where her faith was firmely fixt in loue,
There a nay is plac'd without remoue.
One silly crosse, wrought all my losse,
O frowning Fortune, cursed fickle Dame:
For now I see, inconstancie
More in Women then in men remaine. . . .

[Rustic element introduced into pastoral by Spenser. According to Rollins (2.25), ascription of No. 35 to Barnfield is based on insufficient evidence.]

[Sig. H 2 (Rollins 1.57-8: No. 36), *Another of the same Sheepheards,* has the first 26 lines of Richard Barnfield's 56-line *Ode,* together with a new concluding couplet. See entry: 1598. Richard Barnfield.] (DEM)

Sig. X 4 (Rollins 1.165: No. 125):

A *Pastorall Song betweene* Phillis *and* Amarillis
two Nimphes, each aunswering other line for line.
Fie on the sleights that men deuise,
  heigh hoe sillie sleights:
When simple Maydes they would entice,
  Maides are yong mens chiefe delights.
Nay, women they witch with their eyes,
  eyes like beames of burning Sunne:
And men once caught, they soone despise,
  so are Sheepheards oft vndone. . . .

[Clearly an imitation of *S. C. Aug.* 53-124, which is reproduced on sigs. D 2 - D 3 (No. 11). The poem, signed H. C., is probably Henry Chettle's; cf. Rollins 2.133, 165.] (HER)

1600. I. F. Verses prefixed to John Weever's *Faunus and Melliflora.* [STC 25225. Ed. A. Davenport, Univ. Press Liverpool, 1948.]

Sig. A 4 (Davenport, p. 5):

If for to write of Loue, and Loues delights,
Be not fit obiects for the grauer sights,
Then stil admired *Chaucer*, thou maist rue
And write thy aunciect stories all anew:
And that same Fayry Muse may rise againe,
To blot those works that with vs do remaine. (HH)

1600. Edward Fairfax. *Godfrey of Bulloigne, or The Recouerie of Ierusalem. Done into English Heroicall verse*, translation of Tasso's *Gerusalemme liberata.*
[STC 23698. Ed. Henry Morley, 1890.]

[" In style and phrasing this translation was deeply influenced by Spenser, just as Spenser was deeply influenced by its original, Tasso. Cf. Morley's *Introduction* and E. Koeppel, Anglia, 1890, 105 ff."] (FIC)

1600-15. J. M. *The Newe Metamorphosis. Written by J. M. Gent.*, B. M. Add. MSS 14824-6.
[Cf. John H. H. Lyon, *A Study of The Newe Metamorphosis*, Columbia Univ. Press, 1919.]

MS 14824, fol. 8:

His tents were picht neere Isis silver streames
where great Gloriana, wth her radiant beames
makes the trees fruitfull, & the earth increase, ...
but fewe there were that knewe of Love the toile
for Cupid never did Fays harte beguile
nor tread a steppe till now in Faiery lande
here Gloriana did alone command.

Fol. 43:

... this gallant lusty lad
fayre Acherasia did inveighe quite
under a wicked & a faynd pretence.

[Cf. *F. Q.* 2.12.72 ff.]

MS 14825, fol. 91:

and noble *Spencer* nowe of fairest fame
whose glorious workes imortalize his name. (RH)

MS 14826, fol. 129^{v}:

His conquering blade up to the hilte I sent
in Braggadochio, and away he wente
to digge for more gold in the mynes of hell.

[Cf. *F. Q.* 2.3, *et freq.*]
[In the poem appear other characters whose names and qualities are reminiscent of Spenser, an amorous Helinore, MS 14824, fols. 28-9, 43-7ᵛ, a cruel Orgoglio, MS 14825, fols. 93-101, and an alluring and virtuous Amoretta, MS 14826, fols. 21-37ᵛ. The author may be Gervase Markham.] (DEM)

1600.   William Kemp. *Kemps nine daies wonder. Performed in a daunce from London to Norwich.*
[STC 14923. Ed. Alexander Dyce for Camden Soc., 1840; ed. G. B. Harrison, Bodley Head Quartos, 1923.]

Sig. D 4ᵛ (Dyce, p. 22; Harrison, p. 33):
Call vp thy olde Melpomene, whose strauberry quill may write the bloody lines of the blew Lady, and the Prince of the burning crowne: and better subiect I can tell ye: than your Knight of the Red Crosse. (JGM)

1600   John Lane. *Tom Tel-Troths Message, and his Pens Complaint.*
[STC 15190. Ed. F. J. Furnivall, New Shak. Soc. Pub., ser. 6, no. 2, 1876.]

P. 9 (sig. B; Furnivall, p. 112):
      Come, sad *Melpomene,* thou tragicke Muse,
      To beare a part in these our dolefull cries.
[Cf. *S. C. Nov.* 53.]

P. 31 (sig. D 4; Furnivall, p. 125):
      Next followes Wrath, Enuies fierce fellow-mate,
      Attired in roring Lions skin.
[Cf. *F. Q.* 1.4.33.]

P 32 (sig. D 4ᵛ; Furnivall, p. 126):
      Wrath puffes men vp with mindes Thrasonicall,
      And makes them braue it braggadochio-like.
[Cf. *F. Q.* 2.3.]

P. 37 (sig. E 3; Furnivall, p. 129) [describing Avarice]:
      She hath been troubled long with one disease,
      Which some a Dropsie call, or drouth of gaine.
[Cf. *F. Q.* 1.4.23, 29.] (EAS)

1600.   *The Maydes Metamorphosis.*
[STC 17188. Ed. A. H. Bullen, *A Collection of Old English Plays,* vol. 1, 1882.]

[Bullen, p. 99: " The writer was evidently an admirer of Spenser, and has succeeded in reproducing on his Pan-pipe some thin, but not unpleasing, echoes of his master's music." Two notable parallel passages are reproduced below.]
Act 2, Bullen, pp. 120-1, quoted:
      Within this ore-growne Forrest there is found

A duskie Caue, thrust lowe into the ground,
So vgly darke, so dampie and [so] steepe
As, for his life, the sunne durst neuer peepe
Into the entrance; which do so afright
Where fennish fogges and vapours do abound
There *Morpheus* doth dwell within the ground. . . .
          the drowsie God
Drowned in sleepe continually doth nod. . . .
To sleepes black caue I will incontinent
And his darke cabine boldly will I shake
Vntill the lumpish God awake.

[Cf. *F. Q.* 1.1.39-40, 42-3.]

Act 5, Bullen p. 156, quoted:

The warbling Birds doo from their prettie billes
Vnite in concord as the brooke distilles,
Whose gentle murmur with his buzzing noates
Is as a base unto their hollow throates.

[Cf. *F. Q.* 2.12.7. The parallel was first pointed out by J. P. Collier.]
(AHB, FIC)

1600. *New Year's Gift, Addressed to the Queen,* Cotton MS Vespasian
E. 8.
A Ryddle of the Princesse Paragon, Parthe VII. Euterpe, Nichols 3.474
quoted:

    I saw marche in a meadowe greene,
    A fayrer wight then feirye queene. (DEM)

1600. Samuel Nicholson. *Acolastus his After-Witte.*
[STC 18546. Rptd A. B. Grosart, Occasional Issues, 1876.]
Sig. C 4:

A thousand lawes the Lyon can alleadge,
To pray vpon poore Asses at his pleasure:
    Yet pollicie perswades him to forbear them,
    Till far frō home, the Wolfe may boldly teare them.

[Carpenter recognizes slight influences of Spenser throughout, of which
this quotation may be taken as an example.] (FIC)

1600. William Shakespeare. *A Midsommer nights dreame.*
[STC 22302. Cf. J. O. Halliwell-Phillips, *Memoranda on the Mid-
summer Night's Dream,* Brighton, 1879, pp. 6-7.]
Sig. B 3 (2.1.2-5):

    Fa. Ouer hill, ouer dale, thorough bush, thorough brier,
Ouer parke, ouer pale, thorough flood, thorough fire:
I do wander euery where; swifter than the Moons sphere:
And I serue the Fairy Queene.

[Cf. *F. Q.* 6.8.31.1.]

Sig. G 3^v (5.1.50-3):
The thrise three Muses, mourning for the death
Of learning, late deceast, in beggery?
That is some *Satire* keene and criticall,
Not sorting with a nuptiall ceremony.
[From the time of Warburton's 1747 ed. of Shakespeare, this passage
has been mentioned as a reference to *T. M.*] (FIC)

1600.   Francis Thynne. *Emblemes and Epigrames*, Huntington MS Ellesmere 34/B/12.
[Ed. F. J. Furnivall, E. E. T. S., 1876.]
[Embleame 61], fol. 35^v (Furnivall, p. 46):
                                 Benefitts.
The Silver Moone, *Diana* virgine bright
on mortall creatours powres her moystening light.
wherwith she doth adorne the Sable nighte,
whose sleeping mantle dimms the peircinge sight;
which gladsome shine she take abundantlie.
from her beloved spowse, who favourablie
doth spredd his goulden beames most liberallie
on that faire *Phebee* full of curtesie
[Spenserian diction.]

[Epigram 30], fols. 49^v - 50 (Furnivall, p. 66):
                                   Enuye.
Thow monster of mankinde, obscurer of good name,
thow hated childe of pride, and autor of thy shame,
whose heares are stinging snakes, whose face is pale & wann,
with scornfull eyes and browes, disdaining euerie mann,
with canker taynted tethe, and poysoned tongue of spight,
with vile detracting lipps, defaming [euerie] wighte,
with breth of Sulphures smell, fedd with revenges desire,
with brests defyld with gall, and hart of flaminge Ire.
whose nayles are harpies clawes, and bodie leane and spare,
which never smiles beinge still opprest with greife & care,
whose frettinge pynes thy hart, and eates thy flesh awaie,
still feeding on thy self till thow dost cleane decaye
like burning *Aetna* monte which with his stinking fumes
feedes on it self and with his flame it self consumes.
thy force ech sowle doth feele thoughe to thy bitter paine,
except the mann deiect, whome fortune doth disdaine.
[Cf. *F. Q.* 1.4.30-2; 5.12.28 ff.] (DEM)

[Epigram 38], fol. 53^v (Furnivall, p. 71):
                         Spencers fayrie Queene.
Renowmed Spencer, whose heavenlie sprite
ecclipseth the sonne of former poetrie:

in whome the muses harbor with delighte,
gracinge thy verse with Immortalitie,
Crowning thy fayrie Queene with deitie,
the famous *Chaucer* yealds his Lawrell crowne
vnto thy sugred penn for thy renowne.

Noe cankred envie cann thy fame deface,
nor eatinge tyme consume thy sacred vayne,
no carpinge zoilus cann thy verse disgrace,
nor scoffinge Momus taunt the with disdaine.
since thy rare worke eternall praise doth gayne.
then live thou still, for still thy verse shall live,
to vnborne poets, which light and life will give. (FIC)

1600.   Cyril Tourneur. *The Transformed Metamorphosis.*
[STC 24152. *Plays and Poems,* ed. John Churton Collins, 1878.]

Sig. C 4ᵛ (Collins 2.206):

In *Delta* that's enuiron'd with the sea,
    The hills and dales with heards are peopled,
That tend their tender flockes upon the lea,
    And tune sweet laies vnto their pipes of reed,
    Meane while their flockes vpon the hillockes feed;
And sometime nibble on the buskie root,
That did his tender bud but lately shoote.

[In spirit of Spenser's pastorals.]

Sig. C 6 (Collins 2.207):

Thus (pricking on the plaine) at last he ey'd
    The grisly beast as in her den she lay.

[General correspondence between the efforts of Mavortio to destroy the beast Hyenna and those of Calidore to exterminate the Blatant Beast, *F. Q.* 6.] (DEM)

1600.   William Vaughan. *The Golden-groue, moralized in three Bookes.*
[STC 24610.]

Book I, chap. 29, *Of Foole-hardinesse,* sig. G 2:
    Foole-hardinesse is the excesse of fortitude, vsed for the most part of Caualeers and tosse-pots. . . .
    Their properties are rather to flaunt like Peacockes, to play the Braggadochians, and to trust most impudently in the hugenesse of their lims, and in their drunken gates.

Ibid., sig. G 3:

Obiection.

An audacious Braggadochian being knocked runneth away: therefore there is no difference betwixt a foolehardy man and a coward.

Aunswere.

Two things are   1. Madhardinesse or rashnes, which
to be respected   leadeth him into daunger.

in a foolhardy   2. Weaknes of nature not agreable to
Braggadochian.   his mind: & this is the cause,
                             why he trusteth sometimes vnto
                             his heeles, rather thē his hands.
                             (JLL)

1600. Thomas Weelkes. *Madrigals of 6. parts, apt for the Viols and voices.*
[Separate title page for second section of *Madrigals of 5. and 6. parts.*
STC 25206. Ed. E. H. Fellowes, *English Madrigal Verse*, Oxford, 1920.]

Sig. C iij^v (Fellowes, p. 221):
     When *Thoralis* delights to walke,
        The Faires doe attend hir.
     They sweetly sing and sweetly talke,
        And sweetly do command hir,
     The Satires leape, and dance the round,
     And make their conges to the ground,
        And euer more their song it is,
        Long maist thou liue, faire Thoralis!

[Cf. *F. Q.* 1.6.12-3.] (DEM)

1600. John Weever. *Favnvs and Melliflora or, The Original of our English Satyres.*
[STC 25225. Ed. A. Davenport, Univ. Press Liverpool, 1948.]
Sig. F 2^v (Davenport, p. 42):
     By some great power or heauenly influence,
     The Faëries proued full stout hardy knights,
     In iusts, in tilts, in turnaments, and fights,
     As *Spencer* shewes. But *Spencer* now is gone,
     You Faëry Knights, your greatest losse bemone. (EG)

1600.   Edward Wilkinson. *E. W. His Thameseidos. Deuided into three Bookes, òr Cantos:* [STC 25642.]

Lib. 1, sig. A iij^v:
                        . . . where the Moone,
     Oft stayde to looke vpon the Latmian Lowne:
     In which did grow the tough and hardie Ashe,
     The builder Oke; Holme fit for Carters lash,
     Chast louely *Daphne* closed vnder rinde,
     Incestuous Mirh, that weepeth still of kind:
     Then peacefull Oliue, and the holsome Pine;
     The sayling Firre, and eke the drunken Vine.

[Cf. *F. Q.* 1.1.8-9.] (WW)

Ibid., sig. A 4:
     For there were Roses with Virmilion died,
     Coole Dasies, and white Lillies; Summers pride:

The Marigold, that doth affect the Sunne,
Hiding her beautie when his light is gonne:
The Bee alluring Thime, the sweete Costmarie,
Gray Lauender, and strong senting Rosmarie,
And what else might be pleasing to the view,
Within this faire and princely Meddow grew.

[Cf. *Proth.* 19-33, and *Mui.* 187-202.]

Lib. 2, sig. D^v:

On one side, the last man bore name of King,
In *Brutes* long raigning race, who thought to bring
From *Amorick* an Host of valiant men,
To foyle the *Saxons*, that had footing then
In *Brittaine* tane, had not him Visions stayde,
That wild to *Rome* his Iorney should be made.
There was that *Rhodericke*, the great surnamde,
Who for deuiding *Wales*, was highly famde:
And *Howel Dha*, who auncient laws corrected,
And Officers to see right done, elected:
With *Griffeth Conon*, who victorious raigned
Full fiftie yeeres; and when he peace had gayned
Vnto his Countrey, dyed: And *Llewelline*,
The braue last Prince of auncient *Brittish* line;
Whose life by them whom he did trust, betrayde;
Alterd the gouernment which they had swayde
Two thousand and foure hundred yeeres and od.

[Cf. *F. Q.* 3.3.40-1, 45.]

Ibid., sig. D 2^v:

Deepe in the *Ocean*, where yet neuer ground,
By longest fadome line could ere be found:
Vnder a hollow Rocke, ther is a vault,
By often beating of great Billowes wrought:
So that it seeme to be the noble acte,
Of some rare Mason, or skild Architect.

[With this description of the cave of Proteus, cf. that in *F. Q.* 3.8.37.1-7.]

Lib. 3, Sig. E - E^v:

Not halfe so fast distressed *Florimel*
Fled from the sight of that *Hiena* fell,
Which the dispightfull Witch after her sent,
To bring her backe, and her in peeces rent.
Nor halfe so fast from *Phoebus Daphne* fled,
As ISIS now, to saue her maydenhead.

[Cf. *F. Q.* 3.7.26.1-5. These quotations are merely illustrative of Wilkinson's indebtedness to Spenser.] (EAS, FMP)

1601.   Richard Carleton. *Madrigals to Five Voyces.*
[STC 4649. Quoted in E. H. Fellowes, *English Madrigal Verse*, Oxford, 1920.]

[*F. Q.* 6.7.1 (ll. 1-4 only), 5.8.1, 5.8.2, 5.7.1, 6.8.1 are set to music in nos. 8, 9, 10, 14, 15 respectively (sigs. C ij, C ij^v - C iij, C iij^v - C iiij, D ij^v - D iij, D iij^v; Fellowes, pp. 70-1).] (FIC, DEM)

1601. Robert Chester. *Loues Martyr: or, Rosalins Complaint. Allegorically shadowing the truth of Loue, in the constant fate of the Phoenix and Turtle.*
[STC 5119. Ed. A. B. Grosart, New Shak. Soc., ser. 8, no. 2, 1878.]

[Note assembly of gods and appeal of Nature (under name of Rosalin) to Jove.] (EG)

1601. Gerard De Malynes. *Saint George for England, allegorically described.* [STC 17226^a.]

The Epistle Dedicatorie (to the Right Honorable Sir Thomas Egerton, Knight, Lord keeper of the Great Seale of England), sigs. A 2 - A 3:
The inuented historie of S. George (right honorable and my singular good Lord) howsoeuer heretofore abused, may conueniently be applied to these our dayes of her Maiesties most happy gouernement, wherin the beames of the Orientall starre of Gods most holy word appeare vnto vs most splendent and transparent, to the singular comfort of all faithfull. For wheras vnder the person of the noble champion Saint *George* our Sauiour Christ was prefigured, deliuering the Virgin (which did signifie the sinfull soules of Christians) from the dragon or diuels power: So her most excellent Maiesty by aduancing the pure doctrine of *Christ Iesvs* in all truth and sincerity, hath (as an instrument appointed by diuine prouidence) bene vsed to performe the part of a valiant champion, deliuering an infinite nūber out of the diuels power, whereunto they were tied with the forcible chaines of darknesse. (FMP)

Sig. E 2:
She came accompanied with a Lambe representing her innocence (WW)

Sig. E 4 - E 4^v:
And the greater was the exployt of Saint George in deliuering her, who like a valiant champion being arriued into this Iland, and vnderstanding of the danger she was in, came with a Princely resolutiō to deliuer her, mounted on a pyball horse of seuerall colours, armed like a conqueror, to fight the cōbat with the shield of faith, hauing on the breast-plate of righteousnesse, the helmet of saluatiō, his loynes girt about with verity, and being adorned with the liuery of the Crosse, did with the sword of the Spirit destroy this monster. (FMP)

1601. Charles Fitzgeffrey. *Affaniae: sive Epigrammatum Libri tres, Ejusdem Cenotaphia,* Oxford.
[STC 10934. *Poems,* ed. A. B. Grosart, Occasional Issues, vol. 16, 1881.]

Liber 1, sig. D 5 (Grosart, p. xix, Spurgeon 1.167):
AD EDMVNDVM SPENSERVM.
Nostrū *Maronē* EDMONDE *CHAVCERUM* vocas?

Male herclè! si tu quidpiā potes male;
Namq; ille noster *Ennius,* sed tu *Maro* (CFES, FIC)

Ibid., sig. D 5 - D 5ᵛ:

DE EODEM.

Tercentum numeret cùm fertilis *Anglia* Vates,
Spenseros nequeat cur numerare duos?
Sic ego; sic contra vati *Thamisinus Apollo*
  (SPENSERVS tituli iussit honore frui)
Græcia *Mæoniden* tantùm dare dicitur vnum,
Virgiliosq; tulit Roma nec ipse duos. (FIC)

Liber 2, sig. D 6 (Grosart, p. xiv):

AD SAMVELVM DANIELVM.

Spenserum si quis nostrum velit esse *Maronem,*
  Tu DAN'IELE mihi *Naso* Britannus eris.
Sin illum potius *Phæbum* velit esse Britannum
  Tum DANIELE mihi tu *Maro* noster eris.
Nil *Phæbo* vlterius; si quid foret, illud haberet
  Spenserus, Phæbus tu *Daniele* fores.
Quippe loqui *Phæbus* cuperet si more Britanno
  Haud scio quo poterat, ni velit ore tuo. (DEM)

Ibid., sig. E 4ᵛ:

DE BROMO OENOPOLA.

Sic nostrū *Bromus* Oenopola *Drachum*
Miratur, perit, osculatur, ardet,
Vt nil tersius elegantius[n]e,
Nil emunctius aut magis politum
Dejerans, idiomate Anglicano
Post natas ais extitisse Musas
Si tantum excipias duos *Marones*
Spenserum geniumq; *Danielis:*
Tantas promere prome parce laudes,
Nam vulgo vt placeant mej libelli
Non poscunt ederæ tuæ corymbos,
Sed *Bacchi* potiùs tui culullos. (RH)

Cenotaphia, sig. N 2 - N 2ᵛ (Grosart, p. xix):

EDMONDO SPENCERO.

Dum tumet inq; suo nimis *Anglia* vate superbit
  Atq; omnes mundi provocat vna sinus,
Et tu *Tasse* taces nec tu *Bartasse* triumphas
  Vlteriùs, cæpit teq; *Arioste* pudor,
Non tantum invidiam populis movet omnibus audax
  Sed cœlum invasit livor, agitq; Deos:
Spenserumq; tibi Superi rapuere poetam,
  Anglia, cùm vatem non habuere parem,
Quantus erat, pro quo non tantum regna, sed ipsos
  Rivales meruit patria habere Deos?

Ibid., sig. N 2ᵛ (Grosart, p. xx; Spurgeon 1.167):

> In eiusdem Tumulum
> *Chaucere vicinum Westmonast.*
> *Spenserus* cubat hìc, *Chaucero* ætate priori
> Inferior, tumulo proximus, arte prior. (CFES, FIC)

1601. Ben Jonson. *Euery Man in his Humor.*
[STC 14766. *Ben Jonson*, ed. C. H. Herford and Percy Simpson, Oxford, 1925-52.]

Act. 3, sc. 2, sig. G (Herford and Simpson 3.240):
Bob[adill]. . . . I haue been in the Indies (where this herbe [tobacco] growes). . . . 'tis most diuine. Further, take it in the nature, in the true kinde so, it makes an Antidote, that, had you taken the most deadly poysonous simple in all Florence, it should expell it, and clarifie you, with as much ease as I speake. And for your green wound, your *Balsamum* and your – – – – are all meere gulleries and trash to it.
[Cf. *F. Q.* 3.5.32-3.] (DEM)

1601. John Lyly. *Loves Metamorphosis, A Wittie and Courtly Pastorall.*
[STC 17082. *Complete Works*, ed. R. W. Bond, Oxford, 1902.]

Act 1, sc. 2, sig. B 3ᵛ (Bond 3.305):
Diuine *Phoebus,* that pursued *Daphne* till shee was turned to a Bay tree, ceased then to trouble her; I, the gods are pittifull: and *Cineras,* that with furie followed his daughter *Miretia,* till shee was chaunged to a Mirre tree, left then to prosecute her.
[Cf. *F. Q.* 3.7.26.1-4. Bond recognizes the general influence of Spenser's personal and political allegory in *Endimion, Sapho and Phao, Midas* and *Loves Metamorphosis*; in particular note his comments, 1.74 and 2.256.] (FMP)
[See 1603. Richard Niccols, for *Expicedium*, attributed to Lyly by Bond.]

1601. Thomas Morley. *Madrigales The Triumphes of Oriana, to 5. and 6. voices: composed by diuers seuerall aucthors.*
[STC 18130. Rptd A. H. Bullen, *Some Shorter Elizabethan Poems*, Westminster, 1903; E. H. Fellowes, *English Madrigal Verse*, Oxford, 1920.]

[Note similarity of the names *Oriana* and *Gloriana.* Much of the verse in this collection in praise of the Queen is reminiscent of Spenser's eulogies. The words of the song by Daniel Norcome are quoted as illustrative:]

Sig. B, 1 of 5 [altus reading followed] (Bullen, p. 155; Fellowes, p. 143):

> With Angels face and brightnesse,
> and orient hew, faire *Oriana* shining,
> with nimble foote she tripped, o're hils & mountaines,
> at last in dale she rested, hard by *Dianas* fountaines:

this is y^t maiden Queene, of Fayrie land,
with scepter in hir hand,
the Faunes and Satiers dauncing,
did shew their nimble lightnes,
Faire *Nais* and ye Nimphs leaue their bowers,
& brought their baskets ful of hearbs & flowers.
Thē sang the shepherds & Nimphs of *Diana,*
Long liue faire *Oriana.* (DEM)

1601. John Weever. *The Mirror of Martyrs, or The life and death of
. . . Sir Iohn Old-castle knight Lord Cobham.*
[STC 25226. Rptd Roxburgh Club, 1873; see Collier, *Bibliographical
Account of Early English Literature,* 1866.]

Sig. B 5^v (Roxburgh, p. 194; Collier 4.231):
But how he courted, how himselfe hee carri'd,
And how the fauour of this *Nimph* he wonne,
And with what pompe *Thames* was to *Medway* marri'd.
Sweete *Spenser* shewes (O griefe that *Spenser's* gone!)
With whose life heauens a while enricht vs more,
That by his death wee might be euer pore.
[See *F. Q.* 4.11.] (FIC)

1602. William Basse. *Three Pastoral Elegies; of Anander, Anetor, and
Muridella.*
[STC 1556. *Poetical Works,* ed. R. W. Bond, 1893.]

To the Reader, sig. A 3^v (Bond, p. 36):
*A Shepheards youth dwelt on the plaines,
That passt the common sort of Swaines,
By how much had himselfe before
Beene nursed vp in* Colins *lore;
Who, while his flocke, ybent to stray,
Glad of the Sunne-shine of the day,
Wanderd the field, and were abroade dispers'd,
He tooke his Pipe and sate him downe and vers'd.*

Elegie 2, sig. C 4^v (Bond, p. 58):
Yet in thy quarraile, dare I say therefore:
Faire is the Portall, but the house is hate,
Poorest the Almes, though purest is the gate.
[Continues with the description of the body; cf. *F. Q.* 2.9.]

Elegie 3, sig. E 3^v (Bond, pp. 73-4):
Whilome when I was *Collins* loued boy,
(Ah, *Collin,* for thee *Collin,* weep I now,)
For thou art dead, ah, that to me didst ioy,
As *Coridon* did to *Alexis* vow.
But (as I sed,) when I was *Collins* boy,
This deare young boy, and yet of yeares inow,

To leade his willing heard along the plaine,
I on his pipe did learne this singing veine.

And oh, (well mote he now take rest therfore,)
How oft in pray'rs and songs he pray'd and sung,
That I (as had himselfe full long before,)
Mought liue a happy shepheard and a young;
And many vowes, and many wishes more,
When he his Pipe into my bosome flung:
And said, though *Collin* ne're shall be surpast,
Be while thou liu'st, as like him as thou maist.

Much was my deare therefore when *Collin* died,
When we (alacke) were both agreed in griefe:
He for his infant swaine that me affide,
Yet happed not to liue to see my priefe.
And I that to his gouernance had tide
My bounden youth, in loosing such a chiefe:
And how wou'd he haue sung, and with what grace?
Ananders Loue, and *Muridellaes* Face.

He wou'd haue blazed in eternall note. (FIC)

1602. Richard Carew. *The Suruey of Cornwall.* [STC 4615.]

Fol. 57 (sig. Q):

. . . which termes [dialect words of Cornwall and Devon], as they expresse our meaning more directly, so they want but another *Spencer,* to make them passable. (FBW)

1602. Francis Davison. *A Poetical Rapsody Containing Diuerse Sonnets, Odes, Elegies, Madrigalls and other Poesies, both in Rime, and Measured Verse.*
[STC 6373. Ed. H. E. Rollins, Harvard Univ. Press, 1931-2.]

I. *Eglogve,* sig. B 10 (Rollins 1.25):

They hung their heads as they to weep would learn. . . .
His pleasant Pipe was broke, (alas the while)
And former meriment was banisht quite.

[Cf. *S. C. Jan.* 77-8 and 72.]

Ibid., sig. C (Rollins 1.31):

But I, who erst (ah woefull worde to say)

[Cf. *S. C. Nov.* 93. I. *Eglogue* " is a close imitation of Spenser, especially of the Jan. and Nov. eclogues." (Rollins 2.104).] (HER)

III. *Eglogve. Made long since vpon the death of Sir Phillip Sidney,* sig. C 4ᵛ (Rollins 1.38):

Thenot.
Ah! where is *Collin,* and his passing skill?
For him fits our sorrow to fulfill.

Perin.
Tway sore extreames our *Collin* presse so neere,
(Alas that such extreames should presse him so)
The want of wealth, and losse of loue so deere,
Scarse can he breathe from vnder heapes of woe,
He that beares heau'n, beares no such weight I trow.
Thenot.
Hath he such skill in making all aboue,
And hath no skill to get, or Wealth, or Loue?
Perin.
Praise is the greatest prise that Poets gaine,
A simple gaine that feeds them ne're a whit.
The wanton lasse for whom he bare such paine,
Like running water loues to charme and flit.

Ibid., sig. C 5 (Rollins 1.39):
Breake me your Pipes that pleasant sound did yeeld,
Sing now no more the Songs of *Collin Clout.* (FIC)

Ibid., sig. C 6 (Rollins 1.41):
Ah *Collin!* I lament thy case,
For thee remaines no hope of grace.
The best reliefe,
Of Poets griefe,
Is dead and wrapt full colde in filthy clay. (DEM)

Ibid., sig. C 7 - C 7ᵛ (Rollins 1.43-4):
Alacke and welladay may shepheards cry,
Our *Willy* dead, our *Collin,* killd with care:
Who shall not loathe to liue, and long to die? (FIC)
[The poem is signed " A. W." A[nonymous]. W[riter]. is a not unlikely explanation; see Rollins 2.53-7.]
IIII. *Eglogve. Concerning olde Age. The beginning and end of this Eglogue are wanting,* sig. C 11ᵛ (Rollins 1.52):
Seest not how free yond Lambkin skips and plaies;
And wrigs his tayle, and buts with tender head;
All for he feeles the heate of youthly dayes,
Which secret law of kinde hath inly bred?
Thilke Ewe from whom Ioy with youth is fled,
See how it hangs the head, as it would weep,
Whilome it skipt, vneathes now may it creep.
[Cf. *S. C. Feb.* 71-84.]
Ibid., sig. C 12 (Rollins 1.53):
Ah *Thenot,* be not all thy teeth on edge,
To see youngths folke to sport in pastimes gay?
[Cf. *S. C. May* 35-6.] (FIC, FMP)
[The poem is signed " *Anomos* "; see Rollins 2.40-1.]

To Samuel Daniel Prince of English Poets, sig. E 9ᵛ (Rollins 1.96):
      So (Learned *Daniel*) when as thou didst see,
      That *Spenser* erst so far had spred his fame,
      That he was Monark deem'd of Poesie,
      Thou didst (I gesse) eu'n burne with Iealousie,
      Lest Lawrell were not left enough to frame,
      A neast sufficient for thine endlesse Name.
      But as that Pearle of *Greece*, soon after past
      In wondrous conquests his renowned sire,
      And others all, whose names by Fame are plac'te
      In highest seate: So hath thy Muse surpast
      Spenser, and all that doe with hot desire,
      To the Thunder-scorning Lawrell-crown aspire.

[*An Elegie in Trimetre Iambickes*, sig. L 6 (Rollins 1.233), beginning
" Vnhappy Verse! the witnes of my vnhappie state," rptd from the Spen-
ser-Harvey correspondence.] (FIC)
[For other quotations from *A Poetical Rapsodie*, see: 1608. Francis
Davison.]

1602-3.   John Manningham. *Diary*, in B. M. MS Harleian 5353.
[Ed. John Bruce, Camden Soc. Pub., 99, 1868.]

Fol. 2 (Bruce, p. 2, quoted):
                  In Spenserum.
      Famous aliue, and dead, here is the ods,
      Then God of Poets, nowe Poet of the Gods.

Fol. 31ᵛ (Bruce, p. 43, quoted):
      When hir Majestie had giuen order that Spenser should haue a reward
for his poems, but Spenser could haue nothing, he presented hir with
these verses:
            It pleased your Grace vpon a tyme
            To graunt me rason for my ryme,
            But from that tyme vntill this season
            I heard of neither ryme nor reason. (FIC)

1602.   John Marston. *The History of Antonio and Mellida, The first part.*
[STC 17473. Ed. W. W. Greg, Malone Soc. Rpts, 1921.]

Induction, sig. A 4ᵛ (Greg, ll. 98-101):
Alb. O! 'tis natiue to his part. For, acting a moderne *Bragadoch* vnder
the person of *Matzagente*, the Duke of Millaines sonne, it may seeme
to suite with good fashion of coherence. (JLL)

1602-3.   Sir John Roe. *To Sir Nicholas Smith*, appearing as *Satyre VI*
in the 1669 (7th) ed. of John Donne's *Poems*.
[STC D1817. *Poems of John Donne*, ed. H. J. C. Grierson, Oxford,
1912.]

P. 138 (Grierson 1.401):

Here sleeps House by famous Ariosto,
By silver-tongu'd Ovid, and many moe,
Perhaps by golden-mouth'd Spencer too pardie,
(Which builded was some dozen Stories high)
I had repair'd.

[Cf. *F. Q.* 1.1.39 ff., The House of Sleep. The fourth line apparently alludes to the plan of *F. Q.*; the Stephens MS of Donne reads " two dozen stories," referring to the original plan of 24 books. For discussion of Roe's authorship of the satire, see Grierson 2.cxxix-cxxxv.] (FIC)

1602.   Samuel Rowlands. *Greenes Ghost Havnting Coniecatchers.*
[STC 12243. *Complete Works,* ed. Sir Edmund Gosse, with Notes and Glossary by Sidney J. H. Herrtage, Hunterian Club, 1880, vol. 1 (6th piece).]

Sig. E 4 (Gosse-Herrtage 1.39):
In the meane time curteous Citizens, let me exhort you to become good exāples to your family: for as the master is, so commonly is the seruant, as witness the old verses in the Shepperds Calender in September.

        Sike as the Sheppards, sike beene her sheepe.
[Cf. *S. C. Sept.* 141.]

Sigs. E 4ᵛ - F (Gosse-Herrtage 1.40-1):
Those that should be guides haue need to be lead; those that should instruct to sobrietie, are inducers to vanitie, according to those verses in Maie. [Quotes *S. C. May* 139-44.]

    Againe, what conscience they vse in bargaining and selling, witnesse the whole world, according to Diggon in *Septemb.* [Quotes *S. C. Sept.* 36-9, 82-3.]

Sig. F 2 (Gosse-Herrtage 1.43):
For these night birdes not vnlike the Syrens, the more you frequent them, the more you shall be intangled, according to these verses, Diggon in *Sept.* [Quotes *S. C. Sept.* 130-5.]

    These may be motiues to all to auoide such infectious plague-sores: but how hard it is to get vp a tyred iade when he is downe, especially in the dirt euery man knowes, and men will haue their swinge do all what they can, according to Thenot in *February.* [Quotes *S. C. Feb.* 11-4.]

    But for my part I am resolued and wish all men of like mind sticking my staffe by Peirse in *Maie.* [Quotes *S. C. May* 164-7.] (FIC)

About 1603.   Richard Niccols. *The Beggars Ape,* 1627.
[STC 18516. Ed. Brice Harris, Scholars' Facsimiles and Rpts, New York, 1936.]

Sig. A 2:

        About that Moneth whose name at first begun
        From great AUGUSTUS, that *Romes* Empire wonne:

Whē the fierce *Dog* of Heauen, begun to rise
To baite the *Lyon* in th'*Olympian* skies.
Whose hot fire-breathing influence did cracke
With too much heate our aged Grandames backe,
Lapping vp Riuers with his blaring tongue
T'allay the thirst which his proud stomacke stung.

[With these opening lines, cf. *M. H. T.* 1-8.]

Sig. A 3:

  Some told of battailes and of bloody fights,
  And some of Ladies and of loues delights
  And some of dire euents and Tragicall
  And some of Iests and loues sports Comicall:
  But 'mongst the rout one well I wot there was
  That all the rest in fluent speech did passe
  Who with good vtterance that became him well
  A pretty story of an *Ape* did tell.
  All which for that it seemeth vnto mee
  Worthy their view whose thoughts delighted bee
  In morrall discipline I will vnfold it
  And in those tearmes in which the Begger told it.

[Cf. *M. H. T.* 28-42.]

Sig. C:

  Let boasting *Bragadochioes* of our time
  And golden-handed Churles, that seeke to clime
  To places of such high credit, inly burne
  And with the vaine Sir *Asse*, the Begger spurne. (JLL)

[*The Beggers Ape* " imitates *M. H. T.*, introducing the ape and the fox."—FIC. The emphasis upon court satire in this as in *M. H. T.* is noteworthy. For a concise account see Brice Harris' comments appended to the reprint of 1936.]

1603. Henry Chettle. *Englandes Mourning Garment: Worne here by plaine Shepheardes; in memorie of their sacred Mistresse, Elizabeth.*
[STC 5121. Ed. C. M. Ingleby, New Shak. Soc. Pub., ser. 4, no. 1, 1874.]

[The names of the shepherds participating in this dialogue are *Thenot* and *Collin*; cf. sig. A 3]
Sig. B 2 (Ingleby, p. 85):
[Rulers] ought, if they be true Pastors, to folow the great *Pan* the Father of al good shepheards Christ, who teacheth euery of his Swaines to tell his brother priuately of his fault.
[Cf. *S. C. May* 54 and Gloss.]

Sig. D 2 (Ingleby, p. 97):
I cannot forget the excellent and cunning *Collin* indeed; (for alas, I confess my selfe too too rude,) complaining that a liberal *Mecænas* long

since dying, was immediately forgotten, euen by those that liuing most
laboured to aduance his fame; and these I thinke close part of his songs:

> Being dead no Poet seekes him to reuiue,
> Though many Poets flattred him aliue.

Somewhat like him, or at least to that purpose, of a person more
excellent, though in ruder verse, I speake.
[The lines from Spenser a misquotation from *R. T.* 222-4.] (DEM)

1603. Michael Drayton. *The Barrons Wars in the raigne of Edward the
second.*
[STC 7189. *Works*, ed. J. W. Hebel, Oxford, 1931-41.]
To the Reader, sig. A 3ᵛ (Hebel 2.5):

The Italians vse Cantos, & so our first late great Reformer Ma.
Spenser, that I assume another name for the sections in this volum
cannot be disgratious, nor vnauowable. (FIC)

The First Booke, st. 1, p. 1 (Hebel 2.9):

> The bloody factions, and rebellious pride
> Of a strong nation . . .
> Me from soft layes, and tender loues doth bring,
> Of dreadful fights, and horred warres to sing.

[Cf. 1619 ed., p. 1: "Of a farre worse, then Ciuill Warre to sing."]
The Sixth Booke, st. 46, p. 137:

> A deepe blacke Caue low in the earth is found,
> Whose duskie entrance like pale Morpheus Cell,
> With strange Meanders windeth vnder ground,
> Where sooty darkness euer-more doth dwell.

[Cf. 1619 ed., st. 47, p. 87 (Hebel 2.115):

> Without the Castle, in the Earth, is found
> A Caue, resembling sleepie MORPHEVS Cell,
> In strange *Meanders* wynding vnder Ground,
> Where Darkenesse seekes continually to dwell,
> Which with such Feare and Horror doth abound,
> As though it were an entrance into Hell.]

Ibid., st. 50, p. 139:

> With torches now attempting the sad Caue,
> which at their entrance seemeth in a fright
> At the reflection that the brightnes gaue,
> As till that time it neuer saw the light,
> where light and darknes, with the power they haue,
> Strongly for the preheminence do fight,
> > And each confounding other, both appeare
> > As to their owne selues they contrary were.

[Cf. 1619 ed., st. 51, p. 88 (Hebel 2.116):

> What time, by Torch-light, they attempt the Caue,
> Which at their entrance seemed in a fright,

With the reflection that their Armour gaue,
As it till then had ne'r seene any Light;
Which, striuing there pre-eminence to haue,
Darknesse therewith so daringly doth fight,
That each confounding other, both appeare,
As Darknesse Light, and Light but Darknesse were.]

[Cf. *F. Q.* 1.1.39 ff.] (DEM)

1603. I. G. *Threno-threambeuticon Academiae Cantabrigiensis ob damnum lucrosum, & infoelicitatem foelicissimam, luctuosus triumphus,* Cambridge. [STC 4493.]

P. 55:

Augustum grandisq; Maro, Nasoq; disertus:
Illam [i. e. Elizabeth] Spencerus, Philisidesq; canunt.

[Signed *I. G. T. C. Cant.*] (LB)

1603. I. Iones. *An Epitaph vpon the Death of . . . Elizabeth, Queene of England,* in *Sorrowes Ioye. or, A Lamentation for our late deceased Soueraigne Elizabeth, with a triumph for the prosperous succession of our gratious King, Iames, &c.* [STC 7598.]

P. 33 (sig. E; Nichols 3.651-2):

Not that wise king of peace K. Dauids sonne
In whome great grace and wisdome great did wonne
Had greater grace, ne more did vnderstond
Then did Eliza Queene of Fayry lond. (RH)

1603. John Lane. *An Elegie vpon the death of the high and renowned Princesse, our late Soueraigne Elizabeth, by I. L.* [STC 15189. Rptd Huth's *Fugitive Tracts,* 1875.]

Huth, 2d ser., no. 2, 2d and 3rd [unnumbered] pages, quoted:

Lament the Lady of the *Faiery*-land . . .
Then sing her Requiem in some dolefull Verse
Or do the songs of *Colin Clout* rehearse. (FIC)

1603. William Leighton. *Vertve Triumphant, Or A Lively Description Of The Fovre Vertves Cardinall.* [STC 15435.]

Sig. A 2, st. 2:

Our earth esteem'd halfe dead through Winters spight,
Grones vnderneath the burden of her spring.

[Cf. *S. C. Jan.* 2.]

Sig. E, st. 123:

Sith golden meane doth temperance out measure,
Happy the man that can the same attaine;
Neither to melt in th' hot desire of pleasure;
Nor frie in heart-breake, griefe, and hardest paine.

The greatest enemie that she doth finde,
Is stubburne perturbation of the minde.
[Cf. *F. Q.* 2.1.58.] (FMP)

1603. Richard Niccols. *Expicedium. A Fvneral Oration, vpon the death of the late deceased Princesse* . . . *Elizabeth,* . . . *Writen: by Infelice Academico Ignoto.*
[STC 18519-20. J. P. Collier, *Bibliographical and Critical Account,* New York, 1866.]

Sig. B 3 (Collier 3.42):
>   Wher's Collin Clout, or Rowland now become,
>   That wont to leade our Shepeards in a ring?
>   (Ah me) the first, pale death hath strooken dombe,
>   The latter, none incourageth to sing.

[Attributed to John Lyly in *Complete Works,* ed. R. W. Bond, Oxford, 1902, 1.388.] (FIC)

1603. Henry Petowe. *Englands Caesar. His Maiesties Most Royall Coronation.*
[STC 19806. Nichols, *Progresses of* . . . *James,* 1828.]

Sigs. C 2ᵛ - C 3 (Nichols 1.241):
>   Then should *Belphœbe* know her subiects loue. . . .

>   Usher his way, my Muse say that he comes,
>   At whose vprise *Phœbus* doeth stand at gaze,
>   Thinking the Heauens had ordeyn'd two Sunnes;
>   One for the earth, which made Heauens Sunne amaze.
>   (DEM)

1603. T. W. *The Lamentation of Melpomene, for the death of Belphæbe our Late Queene. With a Ioy to England for our blessed King.* [STC 24918.]

Sig. A iii - A iii ᵛ:
>   For loe; the Lampe that whilome burnt so cleare,
>   Is quite extinct, and darknesse doth appeare.
>   A glorious Lampe; a goodly Light it was,
>   Which whil'st it burnt, all other did surpasse.
>   No place so farre remote but day, and night
>   It was illuminated with this Light.
>   Whilome it was the chiefest light alone
>   Of England, Fraunce, Ireland, and Calydone.
>   Few Lampes like this (yea few) or none at all
>   Are worthy of the like memoriall.
>   The chast *Belphæbe* is of life depriu'de,
>   Merrour of Chastetie, when she suruide.

[Cf. *F. Q.* 1. proem 4.]

Sig. B^v:

> With thee did die the worldes felicitie:
> With thee decay'd all antique dignitie.

[Cf. *Bel.* 10.5-8.]

Sig. B ii^v:

> Eearthes soueraigne Queene is dead.
> Dead sure she is, imbalm'd, and wrapt in Lead.

[Cf. *S. C. June* 89, *Nov.* 58-9.] (FMP)

Sig. B iii:

> Mount winged Fame, and furrow through the aire
> Make Heauen resound with echoes of dispaire:
> Proclayme sadde tydinges of this lucklesse chaunce,
> And with thy Trumpe awake dull ignoraunce.
> Sound loude, for he is deafe, and nothing knowes,
> He never greeves nor pines at anyes woes,
> He sets, and neither stirres, nor speakes whole dayes.
> He answeres none, nor mindes what any sayes.
> Not farre from *Lethe* this aged Sire doth dwell,
> This *Lethe* a spacious River is in Hell,
> Whose nature is to dull the Memorie
> Of those that drinke thereof; or dwelleth bie.
> Fame spread thy winges in Heauen, in Earth, in Hell,
> To every mister wite, her downefall tell.

[Cf. *F. Q.* 1.8.30-4.] (FH)

Sig. B iiii - B iiii^v:

> The Fates (quoth they) in priuate so decreed,
> That she for whom thou weep'st, by death should bleed,
> And they which by deaths cruell hand are slaine,
> Nor sig[h]es, nor singulfes can reduce againe.

[Cf. *F. Q.* 5.6.13.9. Diction throughout poem is reminiscent of Spenser.] (FMP)

1604.   Robert Dallington. *The View of France.* [STC 6202.]

Sig. C (1605 ed., *A Method of Trauell. Shewed by Taking the view of France. As it stoode in the yeare* . . . 1598, STC 6203, quoted):

Spencer.   I would our Poet, that made a marriage betweene the *Medun* and *Thames* at *Rochester,* had the handling of this matter; for it becomes a Poeme better than a Relation.

[" This matter " is the meeting at Lyons of the masculine *Rhosne* river and the feminine *Soane.*] (FIC, FH)

1604.   Michael Drayton. *The Owle.*
[STC 7211. *Works,* ed. J. W. Hebel, 1931-41.]

Sig. C 3 (Hebel 2.488):

> Few words maie serue a mischiefe to vnfolde,

For in short speech long sorrow may be tolde.
But for my freedome that I vs'd of late,
To lanch th'infection of a poysoned state. . . .
[In B. M. copy of STC 7211, press mark C.39.c.9, these lines are scored, with a note in a seventeenth century hand added: " Exilij Spen: cf "; see Hebel 5.178/1; also 5.177/1.] (KT)

1604. William Harbert. *A Prophesie of Cadwallader last King of the Britaines.* [STC 12752. Ed. A. B. Grosart, *Miscellanies*, Fuller Worthies' Library, 1871.]

To The Maiestie of King Iames, Monarch of all Britayne, sig. H 2ᵛ:
> Albions Mœonian, Homer, natures pride,
> *Spenser* the Muses sonne and sole delight:
> If thou couldst through *Dianas* kingdome glide,
> Passing the Pallace of infernall night,
> (The Sentinels that keepes thee from the light)
> Yet couldst thou not his retchlesse worth comprise,
> Whose minde containes a thousand purities. (FIC)

1604. Gervase Markham. *Marie Magdalens Lamentations.*
[STC 17569. Ed. A. B. Grosart, *Miscellanies*, Fuller Worthies' Library, 1871.]

Sig. Bᵛ (Grosart 2.85):
> If you will deigne with fauour to peruse
> Marie's memoriall of her sad lament
> Exciting Collin in his grauer Muse,
> To tell the manner of her heart's repent:
> My gaine is great, my guerdon granted is
> Let Marie's plaints plead pardon for amisse. (FIC)

1604. Thomas Middleton. *The Ant and the Nightingale: or Father Hubburds Tales.*
[STC 17881. *Works*, ed. A. H. Bullen, 1885-6.]

To the Reader, sig. A 4 - A 4ᵛ (Bullen 8.54):
Why I call these *Father Hubburds Tales;* is not to haue them cald in againe, as the Tale of *Mother Hubburd,* the worlde would shewe litle iudgement in that yfaith, and I should say thē *plena stultorum Omnia;* for I entreat here neither of Rugged Beares, or Apes; no, nor the lamentable downefal of the old wiues Platters, I deale with no such Mettal.

1604. Thomas Middleton. *The Blacke Booke.*
[STC 17875. *Works*, ed. A. H. Bullen, 1885-6.]

Sig. D 4ᵛ (Bullen 8.31):
Each slipt downe his Stockin, baring his right Knee, and so began to drinke a Health, halfe as deepe as Mother *Hubburds* Celler: she that was calde in for selling her working Bottle Ale to Booke-binders, and spurting Froth vpon Courtiers Noses. (FIC)

About 1605. William Bedell. *A Protestant Memorial, or The Shepherd's Tale of the Pouder-Plott. A Poem in Spenser's Style,* 1713. [Ed. from Bodleian MS Rawlinson poet. 154, pp. 11-26, by Karl Reuning, *Beiträge zur Erforschung der Sprache und Kultur Englands und Nordamerikas,* Breslau, 4 (1928), 2.113-54; quoted Spurgeon 4, App. A, 56.] [Alexander Clogie, in his *Speculum Episcoporum,* attributed this poem to Bishop Bedell, and says that it is "conceived in the old dialect of Tusser and Chaucer." Reuning not only questions Bedell's authorship but is inclined to regard the poem as a late seventeenth (or early eighteenth) century imitation of Spenser.] (DEM)

About 1605. Joseph Hall. Prefatory poem to William Bedell's *A Protestant Memorial, or, the Shepherd's Tale of the Pouder-Plott. A Poem in Spenser's Style,* 1713.
[Ed. Karl Reuning, *Beiträge zur Erforschung der Sprache und Kultur und Nordamerikas,* Breslau, 4 (1928). 2.113-54.]
Reuning, p. 123:

Ad Authorem
Willy, thy rhythmes so sweetly runn & rise,
And answer rightly to thy tunefull reed,
That (so mought both our fleecy cares succeed)
I ween (nor is it any vaine device)
   That Collin dying his immortal muse
   Into thy learned breast did late infuse.

Thine be his verse, not his reward be thine,
Ah me! that after unbeseeming care,
And secret want, wch bred his last misfare,
His relicks deare obscurely tombed lien
   Under unwriten stones, that who goes by
   Cannot once read, Lo Here doth Collin ly.

Not all the shepheards of his Calendar
(Yet learned shepheards all, & seen in song)
Theire deepest layes & dittyes deep among,
More lofty song did ever make or leare
   Then this of thine. Sing on; thy task shall be
   To follow him, while others follow thee.

[See note to immediately preceding entry.] (DEM, FMP)

About 1605. *In Calvum Poetam,* a poem in Bodleian MS Add. B97.
Fol. 17:
Well didst yᵘ prayse the noble high conceit
Of yᵗ Arcadian knight and Collin swayne . . . (WBA)

About 1605. Robert Tofte. Verses in Bodleian MS Rawlinson D679.
Preliminary leaf:
This had a Task bin for [Sidney] the Muses Heire . . .

Mr. Spenser.   Or for that Author, of the FAIRIE QVEENE
Whose like, before or since, was neuer seene. (FBW)

1605. William Camden. *Certaine Poemes,* . . . *and Epitaphs of the
English Nation in former Times,* appended to *Remaines concerning
Britaine.* [STC 4521.]

P. 8 (paged separately: Sig. a 4ᵛ; Munro 1.127; Bradley, p. 33):
These may suffice for some Poeticall descriptions of our auncient Poets,
if I would come to our time, what a world could I present to you out of
Sir *Philipp Sidney,* Ed. *Spencer, Samuel Daniel, Hugh Holland, Ben:
Iohnson, Th. Campion, Mich. Drayton, George Chapman, Iohn Marston,
William Shakespeare,* & other most pregnant witts of these our times,
whom succeeding ages may iustly admire. (JM)

1605. I. G. *An Apologie for Women Kinde.* [STC 11497.]

Sigs. A 4ᵛ - B:
Full well I wot, this subject was more fitte
For peerlesse *Homers* or for *Virgils* witte.
The *Florence-Petrarkes, Tassoes,* or *Ronsardes,*
Sidneys or *Spencers;* vnto whome, rewardes,
Garlands of Bayes by Poets graunted are. (JLL)

1605. Joseph Hall. *Mvndus Alter et Idem, sive Terra Australis ante
hac semper incognita,* Frankfort [and London?], 1605. [STC 12685.]

Lib. 1, cap. 6, p. 30:
Spenser.   . . . neque *Verolamium* nostri vatis iustius incuset hominum
Ruin. Temp. temporũque iniuriam, dum hæc noua nomen sibi cum honore
         usurpans, utroque exinde duplicato, *Artocreopolis* nun-
         cupatur. (RK)

1605. R. R. *In Commendation of this worthie Worke,* prefixed to *Bartas.
His Deuine Weekes & Workes Translated . . . by Iosuah Sylvester.* [STC
21649.]

Sig. A 6ᵛ:
Foole that I was; I thought in younger times,
That all the *Muses* had their graces sowne
In *Chaucers, Spensers,* and sweet *Daniels* Rimes;
(So, good seemes best, where better is vnknowne)
while thus I dream't my busie phantasie,
Bod me awake, open mine eyes, and see

How SALUST's English *Sun* (*our* SYLVESTER)
Makes *Moone* and *Starres* to vaile: and how the *Sheaves*
Of all his *Brethren,* bowing, doo *preferre*
His *Fruites* before their Winter-shaken *Leaues:*
So much (for *Matter,* and for *Manner* too)
Hath He out-gon those that the rest out-goe:

Let Gryll be Gryll: let Enuie's vip'rous seed
Gnaw-forth the brest which bred and fed the same.
[Cf. *F. Q.* 2.12.87.8.] (DEM)

1605 (?). John Ross. *Parerga*, Folger MS 800.1 (formerly Phillips MS 9628).

P. 49:

In Edw: Spenseram poetā modernū, Epitaph: 1599
Tu multos, te nemo canit (Spensere) sed est hoc,
Non quia nemo velit, sed quia nemo potest.

[*Parerga* as prepared for the press includes a dedication to King James, dated 1605.] (GED)

1605. Joshua Sylvester. *Bartas. His Deuine Weekes & Workes Translated.*
[STC 21649. *Complete Works*, ed. A. B. Grosart, Chertsey Worthies' Library, 1880.]

Eden, pp. 272-3 (sigs. T 4^v - T 5; Grosart 1.97) [lines added by Sylvester]:

Let This [work] prouoke our modern wits to sacre
Their wondrous gifts to honour thee their Maker:
That our mysterious ELFINE oracle,
Deepe, Morall, graue, inuentions miracle:
My deere sweet Daniel, sharpe-conceipted, briefe,
Ciuill, sententious, for pure accents chiefe:
And our new *Naso*, that so passionates
Th'heroicke sighes of loue-sick Potentates:
May change their subiect, and aduance their wings
Vp to these higher and more holy things.

[For a 17th century confirmation that " our . . . Oracle " is an allusion to Spenser, cf. Kathrine Koller, " Identifications in *Colin Clout's Come Home Againe." MLN* 50 (1935). 155-7.] (KK)

1605-18. Joshua Sylvester. *A Maske Sonnet to Queen Anne, in Du Bartas . . . with A Compleate Collectiō of all the most delight-full Workes . . . by . . . Joshuah Sylvester*, 1633.
[STC 21654. *Complete Works*, ed. A. B. Grosart, Chertsey Worthies' Library, 1880.]

P. 630 (Grosart 2.324):

Hye wee,
Hye wee, Sisters, Fairies
Dead our comfort, deep our Care-is
      While wee misse our Mistresse grace:
      In the mirrour of whose Face,
Majestie and mildnesse meet
Stately shining, smiling sweet;
      In whose bosome

Aye repose-em
All the Honours of Diana;
Say, who saw our Glorie-Anna? (DEM)

About 1606.   John Fletcher. *The Woman's Prize: Or, The Tamer Tamed,*
in *Comedies and Tragedies Written by Francis Beaumont and Iohn
Fletcher Gentlemen,* 1647.
[STC B1581. *Beaumont and Fletcher,* ed. A. Glover and A. R. Waller,
Cambridge, 1905-12.]

Act 1, sc. 3, sig. Nnnnn 2ᵛ (Glover and Waller 8.13; Koeppel, p. 88):
Soph. Fly, fly, quoth then the fearfull dwarfe;
Here is no place for living man.
[Cf. *F. Q.* 1.1.13.8-9.] (EK)

About 1606.   *Threnos,* in Cambridge Univ. MS D.d.V. 77, no 7.

A funerall song or Elegie of yᵉ *right honnorable Ladie* yᵉ *Ladie* ISABEL
late Countess Dowager of RUTLAND [d. Jan. 14, 1605/6], p. 2:

	O! that I could as I would æternize her,
	It rather fitts yᵉ Faery Queenes deuiser,
	Or him who made his Delia of such fame
Josuah	Or English Bartas Siluester by name
Siluester:	Or: haut fitz: Gefferie worthy Drakes Learnd Honʳ

Or if Mellifluous Drayton would bemone her:
Your Siluer Penns can best depaint her honer
Yee Phenix feathered Muses of our Time
Eternise her: with your eternall Rime;
O! shame o! griefe vertue' in obliuiō lyes:
Els had Eliza' had her due Eligies
True Elegies wᶜh: shd: yᵉ skies haue Peirst
Had DANIEL, Drayton, Siluester them verst
Or els Fitz: Gefferie whose muse coelestiall
Would penetrate Heauen, Hell, Sea, Earth, and all.

Ibid., p. 12:

	At Length to Mitigate yᵉ mothers Cross,
	her Noble Daughter': yong beautious Baroness Ross:
	Is mou'd to Marrie whom shee held full deere,
	A Gallant squire Nephew of a mightie Peere
Ed. Spencer.	" And on whose mightie shoulders most did rest,

" the burthen of this Kingdomes gouerment
" As yᵉ wide compass of yᵉ firmament,
" On Atlas mightie shoulders is vpstaid:
Englands wise Nestor, Lord high Tresurer,
                                   late
by's eldest sonn: (now) Earle of Excester.

[For quotation see *F. Q.,* ded. sonnet, *To . . . Lo. Burleigh,* ll. 3-6.]
(ME)

1606. Nathaniel Baxter. *Sir Philip Sydneys Ouránia, That is, Endimions Song and Tragedie, Containing all Philosophie. Written by N. B.* [STC 1598.]

To My Ever-Honored Lady and Mistris Arcadian Cynthia, Maria Pembrokiana, sig. A 2:

>   Worlds wonder, learned, mightie *Cinthia*,
>   Artes Darling, & Times Babe, subiect of fame,
>   Wits obiect, *Arcadian* Pastorella.

Sig. B 2ᵛ

>   I well did view the Coronet she ware,
>   With Diamonds and Saphyres orient,
>   A Carkenet most pretious and rare,
>   Fretized with Carbuncles which *Hebæ* sent,
>   (The same which *Pyrocles* did first inuent)
>   Did circle twise, her sacred necke, & brest,
>   In which the Muses, and the Graces, rest.

[For Pyrocles, cf. *F. Q.* 2.4-6.] (FMP)

Ibid.:

>   Betweene her paps a lustrous Diamond;
>   Link'd to her Carkenet by curious Arte,
>   (Of yore found out by skilfull *Belysond*,
>   Andgiuen by the mightie *Britomarte*)
>   So placed was, that light it might imparte,
>   To all inferiour Orbs in darkest night,
>   When *Phœbus* had with-draw'n his glorious light.

Sigs. B 2ᵛ - B 3:

>   A surcote all of purple silke she wore,
>   Diapred with *Flora's* curious skill,
>   Butned with orientall Pearles before,
>   With golden loops to fasten at her will,
>   Fram'd for her bodie by great *Astrophill.*
>   Such as *Bellona* vsed heretofore,
>   In chasing of the feirce *Adonian Bore.*
>
>   Wauing and wide tuck't vp vnto her knee,
>   Adorned with a frindge of purest gould,
>   Whence parcell of the Lawne I chanc'd to see,
>   That whiter then it selfe, her skinne doth fould; . . .
>
>   Part of her legges gaue lusture to my viewe,
>   As Iuorie pillars bearing vp the frame; . . .
>
>   Her Iuorie legs and feet the buskins hide,
>   Of curious stuffe with gold imbellished, . . .
>
>   And in her hand she bare a dreadefull bowe,
>   To kill the game, if any sould appeere,
>   Or any deadly foe approach too neere.

[This description of Cynthia draws generously upon Spenser's description of Belphoebe, *F. Q.* 2.3.28 ff., and of Radigund, 5.5.2-3.] (FMP)

Sig. C 1:

> And sang the Song of vniuersall *Pan*,
> High Soueraigne God, and Prince of Happines:
> When, where, and how, great *Ioue* this Globe began,
> To shew hs euerlasting Mightines.
> How euerie Orbe his center doth possesse,
> And all things else as now they framed beene,
> In blessed order, comelie to be seene.

[Cf. *S. C. May* 54 and E. K.'s gloss. Baxter further identifies *Pan* with *Christ* in passages following this.] (DEM)

Ibid.:

> I heard him sing a Laye of mickle worth,
> Which I by partes will orderly relate,
> Helpe me great *Cynthia* to set it foorth,
> Being choice Melodie and intricate,
> Prized by Poets at the highest rate,
> A Subject fit for *Sydneys* eloquence,
> High *Chaucers* vaine, and *Spencers* influence. (FIC)

Sig. F 3ᵛ:

> Now hath Queen *Tellus* put her Mantle on,
> *Flora* tryumphing in her Paragon.
> She deckes her Queene with Roses white and red,
> Muske and sweet Roses in *Damasco* bred.
> Fragrant Gilliflowers and Carnation,
> Enamiled with pure Vermilion,
> The purple Violet, and Columbine,
> The silu'red flower of sweet Eglantine,
> The Daisie, Cow-cup, sweet smelling-Wallflower,
> The Flower de Luce: the Raine-bowes Paramour,
> The whitest Lillie, and the Daffadill,
> The Paggle, and the blessed Pimpernill:
> The Marygolde, and partie coloured Pinke:
> The Paunsey, and the Hearts-ease, as Shepheards think.

[Cf. *F. Q.; S. C. Apr.* 36-44.] (FMP)

Sig. F 4-F 4ᵛ:

> The loftie Caedar, and Sable Cypresse,
> Threatening the welkin, with his mounting Tresse
> Sweet smelling Firre, and Saxifrace . . .
> The builders Oake, and Plough-mens Ashen tree:
> Princes, and Souldiers, regard in their Degree.
> The weeping Elme, the Beech, the Byrch, the Playne,
> Haue vertues rare, and were not made in vaine.

[Cf. *F. Q.* 1.1.8-9.] (WW)

Sig. H 4:

For *Hercules* must needs be this mans father,
When he might iustly challenge *Iris* rather.
A fustie golden Braggadochio,
A Lumbardarie scauld Borachio.

[Cf. *F. Q.* 2.3., *et freq.*] (DEM)

Sig. K:

Archbishops, Bishops, Deanes, Prebendaries,
Parsons, Vicars, Curates, Commissaries,
Common-set-prayer, and Citations,
Suspensions, and Excommunications:
Lord Bishops, Barons of Parliament,
Made Iustices of ciuill gouernment.
These are not of Christs institution,
But by corrupt times Reuolution.
Infecting the Church by Popes intrusion,
Poysoning her with wofull confusion.
He saith vnpreaching Ministers been dumbe dogs,
Fitter for plough and seruing of hogs,
Then to taken Christs blessed lore in hand,
Reading the things they doe not vnderstand.
If this be true thou pecuniarie Asse,
Art not thou come to a wofull passe?
That into Christs Church hast thrust thy selfe,
To coffer up this yellow worldly pelfe?

[Cf. *M. H. T.* 419 ff.]

Sig. M 2 - M 2ᵛ:

Her skinne was white as was the Iuorie,
Thinne and smooth as the finest Tiffany,
Where through a man might perfectly beholde,
The azured vaynes, her inward parts to folde.
A reddie intermixt vermilion,
Diffused was pleasant to looke vpon.
Her golden hayre dispersed to her thighes,
Close shrowd's, *Lucina's* sacred Misteries.
Her modest eyes like sparkling Diamonds,
Pure and chaste (vnlike to *Rosamonds*,)
Piercing like *Cupids* fixed fierie Darts,
Sterne, fierce, and bloody, Marble-Martiall-hearts,
Loues mountaines, apples of *Hisperida*,
Such were her brests witnesse my *Cinthia*,
From whence by corall conduits flowing are,
Streames of the sweetest cælestiall Nectare,
Her crimson smyling lipps did make a showe,
That mirth and pleasure in her mouth did growe.
Her teeth euen set by natures curious hand,

As rowes of orientall Pearles did stand . . .
Tender her hands, her fingers long and small,
Fit to delight her Lord, and sport withall.
Thus fram'd she was in just proportion,
Which made the world amaz'd to looke vpon.
But for the Ornaments of her princely minde,
For excellency were not farre behinde.

[For many of the details in this description of Eve, cf. *Am.* 15, 77;
Epith. 171 ff.; *F. Q.* 3.9.20, 4.6.20] (FMP)

Sig. M 3ᵛ:

With that, *Endymion* cast his eyes aside,
And saw a gentle Knight come pricking on,
Swift was his pace, and knightlie did he ride.

[Cf. *F. Q.* 1.1.] (DEM)

1606.   Lodowick Bryskett. *A Discovrse of Civill Life: Containing the
Ethike part of Morall Philosophie. Fit for the instructing of a Gentleman
in the course of a vertuous life.* [STC 3958.]

Pp. 5-6:
I had in the spring of the yeare begunne a course to take some physicke
during a few days. Among which, Doctor *Long* Primate of *Ardmagh*,
Sir *Robert Dillon* Knight, M. *Dormer*, the Queenes Sollicitor, Capt.
Christopher Carleil, Capt. *Thomas Norreis*, Capt. *Warham*, Sᵗ *Leger*,
Capt. Nicolas Dawtrey, & M. *Edmond Spenser* late your Lordships Secre-
tary, & *Th. Smith* Apothecary.

Pp. 25-8:
Yet is there a gentleman in this company whom I haue had often a
purpose to intreate, that as his leisure might serue him, he would vouchsafe to spend some time with me to instruct me in some hard points
which I cannot of my selfe vnderstand: knowing him to be not onely
perfect in the Greek tongue, but also very well read in Philosophie, both
morall and naturall. Neuertheles such is my bashfulnes, as I neuer yet
durst open my mouth to disclose this my desire vnto him, though I have
not wanted some hartning thereunto from himselfe. For of loue and
kindnes to me, he encouraged me long sithens to follow the reading of
the Greeke tongue, and offered me his helpe to make me vnderstand it.
But now that so good an opportunitie is offered vnto me, to satisfie in
some sort my desire; I thinke I should commit a great fault, not to my
selfe alone, but to all this company, if I should not enter my request
thus farre, as to moue him to spend this time which we haue now des-
tined to familiar discourse and conuersation, in declaring vnto vs the
great benefites which men obtaine by the knowledge of Morall Philosophie, and in making vs to know what the same is, what be the parts
thereof, whereby vertues are to be distinguished from vices: and finally
that he will be pleased to run ouer in such order as he shall thinke good,
such and so many principles and rules thereof, as shall serue not only

for my better instructiō, but also for the contētment and satisfaction of you al. For I nothing doubt, but that euery one of you will be glad to heare so profitable a discourse, and thinke the time very wel spent, wherein so excellent a knowledge shal be reueald vnto you, from which euery one may be assured to gather some fruit as wel as my selfe. Therefore (said I) turning myselfe to M. *Spenser*, It is you sir, to whom it pertaineth to shew your selfe courteous now vnto vs all, and to make vs all beholding vnto you for the pleasure and profit which we shall gather from your speeches, if you shall vouchsafe to open vnto vs the goodly cabinet, in which this excellent treasure of vertues lieth locked vp from the vulgar sort. And thereof in the behalfe of all, as for my selfe, I do most earnestly intreate you not to say vs nay. Vnto which wordes of mine euery man applauding most with like words of request, and the rest with gesture and countenances expressing as much, M. *Spenser* answered in this maner.

Though it may seeme hard for me to refuse the request made by you all, whom, euery one alone, I should for many respects be willing to gratifie: yet as the case standeth, I doubt not but with the consent of the most part of you, I shall be excused at this time of this taske which would be laid vpon me. For sure I am, that it is not vnknowne vnto you, that I haue already vndertaken a work tending to the same effect, which is in *heroical verse*, vnder the title of a *Faerie Queene*, to represent all the mortal vertues, assigning to euery vertue, a Knight to be the patron and defender of the same, in whose actions and feates of arms and chiualry, the operations of that vertue, whereof he is the protector, are to be expressed, and the vices and unruly appetites that oppose themselues against the same, to be beatē down & ouercome. Which work, as I haue already well entred into, if God shall please to spare me life that I may finish it according to my mind, your wish (M. *Bryskett*) will be in some sort accomplished, though perhaps not so effectually as you could desire. And the same may very well serue for my excuse, if at this time I craue to be forborne in this your request, since any discourse, that I might make thus on the sudden in such a subiect, would be but simple, and little to your satisfactions. For it would require good aduisement and premeditation for any man to vndertake the declaration of these points that you have proposed, containing in effect the Ethicke part of Morall Philosophie. Whereof since I haue taken in hand to discourse at large in my poeme before spoken, I hope the expectation of that work may serue to free me at this time from speaking in that matter, notwithstanding your motion and all your intreaties. But I will tell you, how I thinke by himselfe he may very well excuse my speech, and yet satisfie all you in this matter. I haue seene (as he knoweth) a translation made by himselfe out of the Italian tongue, of a dialogue comprehending all the Ethicke part of Moral Philosophy, written by one of those three he formerly mentioned, and that is by *Giraldi* vnder the title of a dialogue of ciuil life. If it please him to bring vs forth that translation to be here read among vs, or otherwise to deliuer to vs, as his memory may serue him, the contents of the same; he shal (I warrant you) satisfie you all at the ful, and him-selfe wil haue no cause but to thinke the time well spent in reuiewing his labors, especially in the company of so many his friends, who may thereby reape much profit, and the translation happily fare the better by some mending it may receiue in the perusing, as all writings else may do by the oftē examinatiō of the same. Neither let it trouble him, that I so turne ouer to him againe the taske he wold haue put me to: for it falleth out fit for him to verifie the principall part of all this Apologie, euen now made for himselfe; because thereby it will appeare that he hath not withdrawne himself from seruice of the State, to liue idle or wholly priuate to himselfe, but hath spent some time in doing that which may greatly benefit others, and hath serued not a little to the bettering of his owne mind, and increasing of his knowledge, though he for modesty pretend much ignorance, and pleade want in wealth, much like some rich beggars, who either of custom, or for couetousnes, go to begge of others those things whereof they haue no want at home.

With this answer of M. *Spensers*, it seemed that all the company were wel satisfied: for after some few speeches, whereby they had shewed an extreme longing after his worke of the *Faerie Queene*, whereof some par-cels had bin by some of them seene, they all began to presse me to produce my translation mentioned by M. *Spenser*, that it might be per-used among them; or else that I should (as neare as I could) deliuer vnto them the contents of the same, supposing that my memory would not much faile me in a thing so studied, and aduisedly set downe in writing, as a translation must be.

[Spenser is represented as taking part in the discussion on pages 163, 271-5.] (FIC)

1606. George Chapman. *Monsieur D'Olive.*
[STC 4983. *Comedies*, ed. T. M. Parrot, 1914.]

Sig. G (Koeppel, Act 4, sc. 1, p. 87; Parrott, Act 4, sc. 2, p. 348):
    Pac. Dido is dead, and wrapt in lead.
    Di. O heauy herse!
    Pac. Your Lordships honor must waite vpon her.
    Dig. O scuruy verse! Your Lordship's welcome home: pray
        let's walke your horse my Lord.
[Cf. *S. C. Nov.* 58-62.] (FIC)

1606. Michael Drayton. *Poems Lyrick and pastorall. Odes, Eglogs, The man in the Moone.*
[STC 7217. *Works*, ed. J. W. Hebel, Oxford, 1931-41]

To the Reader, sig. A 4ᵛ (Hebel 2.346):
    And would at this time also gladly let thee vnderstand, what I thinke aboue the rest of the last Ode of the twelue, or if thou wilt Ballad in my Book; for both the great master of Italian rymes *Petrarch*, & our *Chawcer* & other of the vper house of the muses, haue thought their Canzons honoured in the title of a Ballade, which, for that I labour to meet

truely therein with the ould English garb, I hope as able to iustifie as the learned *Colin Clout* his Roundelaye. (DEM)

1606. *The Plough-mans Tale.* [STC 20035.]

P. 4 (Quoted Douglas Bush, *MLN* 42 [1927].314):

2. *They haue the corne,* of such shepheards speakes maister *Spencer* in his Kalender.

[Marginal note to line in text.] (DB)

1606. [The Second Part of] *The Returne from Pernassus: or The Scourge of Simony.*

[STC 19309-10. Rptd *The Three Parnassus Plays,* ed. J. B. Leishman, 1949.]

[On sig. A 3ᵛ (Leishman, p. 217) *Signor Immerito* is named as one of the actors.]

Act. 1, sc. 2, sig. Bᵛ (Leishman, pp. 236-8):

> *Ing.* [Reads the names of the most famous poets, beginning with *Edmund Spencer*] Good men and true, stand togither: heare your censure, what's thy iudgement of *Spencer?*
> *Iud.* A sweeter swan then euer song in Poe,
> A shriller Nightingale then euer blest
> The prouder groues of selfe admiring Rome.
> Blith was each vally, and each sheapeard proud,
> While he did chaunt his rural minstralsye.
> Attentiue was full many a dainty eare.
> Nay hearers hong vpon his melting tong,
> While sweetly of his Faiery Queene he song.
> While to the waters fall he tun'd [her] fame,
> And in each barke engrau'd Elizaes name.
> And yet for all this, vnregarding soile
> Vnlac't the line of his desired life,
> Denying mayntenance for his deare releife.
> Carelesse [ere] to preuent his exequy,
> Scarce deigning to shut vp his dying eye.

> *Ing.* Pity it is that gentler witts should breed,
> Where thickskin chuffes laugh at a schollers need.
> But softly may our [Homer's] ashes rest,
> That lie by mery *Chaucers* noble chest.

[Textual emendations indicated by square brackets are Leishman's, based upon his collation of the 1608 ed. with Folger MS 448.12.]

Act 3, sc. 5, sig. F (Leishman, p. 308):

Stud[*ioso*]. Oh no the sentinell his watch must keepe,
　　　　Vntill his Lord do lycence him to sleepe.

[Cf. *F. Q.* 1.9.41.] (JBL)

Ibid. (Leishman, p. 309):

Phil[*omusus*]. . . . .

Then why should hope our [rent] state abide?
Nay let vs run vnto the [balefull] caue,
Pight in the hollow ribbs of craggy cliffe,
Where dreary owles do shrike the liue-long night,
Chasing away the byrdes of chearefull light:
Where yawning Ghosts do howle in gastly wise,
Where that dull hollow ey'd that staring, syre,
Yclept *Dispaire* hath his sad mansion,
Him let vs finde, and by counsell we,
Will end our too much yrked misery.

[Cf. *F. Q.* 1.9.33.] (FIC)

Act 4, sc. 2, sig. G 2 (Leishman, p. 332):

See how the sprites do houer ore thy head,
As thick as gnattes in summer euening tide.

[Cf. *F. Q.* 1.1.23.1-2; 2.9.16.1-2.]

Act 4, sc. 4, sig. G 4ᵛ (Leishman, pp. 347-8):

But this it is that do[t]h my soule torment,
To thinke so many actiue able wits,
That might contend with proudest birds of *Po*,
Sits now immur'd within their priuate cells.

[Cf. *T. M.* 217 ff.] (JBL)

Act 5, sc. 4, sigs. H 3ᵛ - H 4 (Leishman, p. 360):

Stud[ioso]. Weel teach each tree euen of the hardest kind,
To keepe our woefull name within their rinde:
Weel watch our flock, and yet weele sleepe withall,
Weele tune our sorrowes to the waters fall,
The woods and rockes with our shrill songs weele blesse,
Let them proue kind since men proue pittilesse. . . .

Ing[enioso]. Faith we are fully bent to be Lords of misrule in the worlds
wide [hall]; our voyage is to the Ile of Dogges, there where the blattant
beast doth rule and raigne Renting the credit of whom it please.
[Cf. *Bel.* 10.4; *Pet.* 4.5-8.] (FIC)

1606. Joshua Sylvester. *I Postumous Bartas. The Third Day of His
Second Weeke.*
[STC 21664. *Complete Works*, ed. A. B. Grosart, Chertsey Worthies'
Library, 1880.]

The Vocation, p. 19 (sig. Nn* 2 - Nn* 2ᵛ; Grosart 1.169):

In *Groon-land* fields is found a dungeon
A thousand-fold more dark than *Accheron*,
It hath no dore, least as it turnes about
On rustie hooks, it creake too lowdly out;
But *Silence* serues for Port and Porter there. . . .
In midst of all this Cave so darke and deepe,
On a still-rocking Couch lyes bleare-eyde Sleepe. . . .

Confusedly about the silent Bed
Fantasticke swarmes of Dreames there hovered. . . .
  Silence dislodg'd at the first word he spake,
But deafe dead *Sleepe* could not so soone awake,
Hee's call'd a hundred times, and tugg'd, and touz'd,
And by the Angel often rubb'd and rouz'd:
At length he stirres, and stretching lazily
His legges and armes, and opening halfe an eye,
Foure or five times he yawnes.

[Cf. *F. Q.* 1.1.39-44. An allusion is unlikely, though Sylvester's memory
of *Morpheus* in *F. Q.* possibly is revealed in his choice of words.] (FIC)

1606. *A Pleasant Comedie, called Wily Beguilde.*
[STC 25818. Ed. W. W. Greg, Malone Soc. Rpts, 1912; cf. Koeppel,
p. 89 n.]

Sig. B 3ᵛ (Greg, ll. 254-7):
  Or as the poore distressed Mariner,
  Long tost by shipwracke on the foming waues,
  At length beholds the long wisht hauen,
  Although from farre, his heart doth dance for ioy.

[Cf. *F. Q.* 1.3.31.] (FIC)

Sig. B 3ᵛ (Greg, ll. 263-5):
  But *Lelia* scorn's proud *Mammon's* golden mines,
  And better likes of learnings sacred lore,
  Then of fond Fortunes glistering mockeries.

[Cf. *F. Q.* 2.7.]

Sig. D 3 (Greg, ll. 817-28):
  Lelia. What sorrow seiseth on my heauy heart?
  Consuming care possesseth euerie part:
  Heart-sad *Erinnis* keeps his mansion Here,
  Within the Closure of my wofull breast;
  And black despaire with Iron Scepter stands,
  And guides my thoughts, down to his hatefull Cell.
  The wanton windes with whistling murmure beare
  My pearcing plaints along the desert plaines,
  And woodes and groues do eccho forth my woes,
  The earth below relents in Crystall teares,
  When heauens aboue by some malignant course
  Of fatall starres are authors of my griefe.

[Spenserian diction throughout.] (DEM)

1606. William Warner. *A Continuance of Albions England: By the first
Author. W. W.* [STC 25085.]

To the Reader, sig. A 2 (Spurgeon 1.178):
  The *Musists*, though themselues they please,
  Their *Dotage* els finds Meede nor Ease:

Vouch't *Spencer* in that Ranke preferd,
Per Accidens, only interr'd
Nigh Venerable *Chaucer*, lost,
Had not kinde *Brigham* reard him Cost,
Found next the doore Church-outed neere,
And yet a Knight, Arch-*Lauriat* Heere. (FIC)

1607.   Barnabe Barnes. *The Divils Charter.*
[STC 1466. Ed. R. B. McKerrow, Bangs Materialien, 6, 1904; rptd
Tudor Facsimile Texts, 1913.]

Act 1, sc. 4, sig. B 3ᵛ (McKerrow, p. 14):
If any Cedar, in your forrest spread,
And ouer-peere your branches with his top,
Prouide an axe to cut him at the roote,
Suborne informers or by snares intrap
That King of Flies within the Spiders Webbe;
Or els insnare him in the Lions toyles.

[Cf. *F. Q.* 1.1.8.6, as well as the last stanzas of *Mui.*]

Act 3, sc. 5, sig. F 2ᵛ (McKerrow, p. 44):
. . . by night keepes watch-full centinell
To guaze the pleasures of faire *Claribell.*

[Cf. *F. Q.* 2.4.19-20, 26.]

Act 4, sc. 1, sig. F 4ᵛ (McKerrow, p. 48):
[The "magicall glasse" which Alexander beholds may have been inspired by Merlin's magic mirror. Cf. *F. Q.* 3.2.]

Ibid., sig. Gᵛ (McKerrow, p. 50):
What would great *Alexander* haue with vs
That from our fiery region millions of leagues,
Beneath the sulphurous bottome of *Abisse,*
Where *Mammon* tells his euer tryed gould,
Thou call'st me.

[Cf. *F. Q.* 2.7.] (DEM)

1607.   *The Tragedie of Caesar and Pompey. Or Caesars Reuenge.*
(STC 4339-40. Malone Soc. Rpts. 1911.]

Sig. Fᵛ (Malone, ll. 1451-4):
Ant. The restlesse mind that harbors sorrowing thoughts,
And is with child of noble enterprise,
Doth neuer cease from honors toilesome taske,
Till it bringes forth Eternall gloryes broode.

[Cf. *F. Q.* 1.5.1.1-4.] (FIC)

Sig. G 2ᵛ (Malone, ll. 1820-1):
Cice. And lawrell garlands for to crowne his fame,
The Princely weede [*sic*] of mighty conquerors.

[Cf. *F. Q.* 1.1.9.1.] (WW)

Sig. H 4ᵛ (Malone, ll. 2247-9):
Cassi. The wrathfull steedes do check their iron bits,
And with a well grac'd terror strike the ground,
And keeping times in warres sad harmony.
[Cf. *F. Q.* 1.5.20.] (FIC)

1607. Thomas Dekker. *A Knights Coniuring: Done in Earnest: Discovered in Iest.*
[STC 6508. Ed. F. Rimbault, Percy Society, 1842.]

Sig. K 4ᵛ (Rimbault, p. 75):
Graue Spencer was no sooner entred into this *Chappell of Apollo*, but these elder *Fathers of the diuine Furie*, gaue him a *Lawrer* & sung his *Welcome*: *Chaucer* call'de him his *Sonne*, and plac'de him at his right hand. All of them (at a signe giuen by the whole *Quire* of the *Muses* that brought him thither,) closing vp their lippes in silence, and tuning all their eares for attention, to heare him sing out the rest of his *Fayrie Queenes* praises.
[This appears in the chapter which was added when *Newes from Hell* came out under the new title, *A Knights Coniuring.*] (FIC)

1607. Thomas Dekker. *Whore of Babylon.*
[STC 6532. *Dramatic Works*, ed. R. H. Shepherd, 1873.]

Sig. Aᵛ (Shepherd 2.187; Koeppel, p. 91):
Drammatis *personae.*
Titania the Fairie Queene: vnder whom is figured our late Queene *Elizabeth* . . .
Florimell . . .
Paridel . . .
Sig. E 4 (Shepherd 2.229; Koeppel, p. 92):
Is not the good and politique Satyrane. (EK)

1607. Matthew Gwynne. *Vertvmnus sive Annus Recurrens Oxonii XXIX Augusti, Anno. 1605. Coram Iacobo Rege, Henrico Principe Proceribus.*
[STC 12555.]

Epistola Dedicatoria, sig. A 4:
Quin vt *Plutarchus* ex *Homero* arcana philosophiæ effodiant, ex *Ennio Virgilius* gemmas, e *Virgilio Scaliger* naturam alteram: vt plurimi ex *Ariosto*, *Tassio*, *Spensero*, et ethicas, et physicas allegorias: sic hinc fortassis non obscurè, non modò quæ *Hippocratem* Aphorismorum tota sectione tertiâ, et alibi, sed alios sapiant, et medicorum alia: in quibus *Melancthon* velit. (ECW)

1607. Gervase Markham. *The English Arcadia.*
[STC 17351. See *Directions for Speech and Style* by John Hoskins, ed. H. H. Hudson, Princeton Univ. Press, 1935.]

To the Reader, sig. A 2 - A 2ᵛ (Hudson, p. 95):
Next for mine allusion and imitation, which beareth a colour of much
greater vain-glorie: mine excuse must onely bee the worthinesse of former
presidents, as *Virgill* from *Homer*, *Ariosto* from *Baiardo*, famous *Spencer*
from renowned *Chaucer*, and *I* with as good priuiledge, from the onely
to be admired Sir *Philip Sydney*, . . . who were our age but blest with
his liuing breath, he would himselfe confesse the honie hee drew both
from *Heliodorus*, and *Diana*. (HH)

1607.   Richard Niccols. *The Cuckow*. [STC 18517.]
   P. 2 (sig. A 3ᵛ):
         [Flora.] When mild Zephirus did gently blow
         Delightfull odors round about did throw;
         While ioyous birds beneath the leauie shade,
         With pleasant singing sweet respondence made
         vnto the murmuring streames, that seem'd to play
         With siluer shels, that in their bosom lay.
   [Cf. *F. Q.* 2.127.1.] (WW)

   P. 5 (sig. B):
         [Casta] Was well contented that it should be so
         And with *Dan* Cuckow for this cause did go,
         Vnto the bower of blisse, for so it hight,
         Where then those Nymphes to be did most delight. . . .
         It seated is farre in a pleasant wood,
         Where many a loftie Iouiall tree hath stood,
         Not much vnlike, that wood by thornie groue
         Full of the tree erected vnto *Ioue*,
         Which seated is vpon the Northern Strand,
         Where *Saxon Segberts* sacred tower doth stand.
   [Cf. *F. Q.* 2.5.31.1-5.]

   P. 6 (sig. Bᵛ):
         There many blisseful bowers they did behold;
         Whose dwellers neither vext with heate nor cold
         Did there enioy all things, that might delight
         The curious eie of any liuing wight:
         For plentie there to lauish in her gift
         Furnisht each place in scorne of niggard thrift.
   [Cf. *F. Q.* 2.12.51-2.]

   P. 9 (sig. B 3):
         Where, while they staid, with great delight they spent
         The time in viewing this faire continent,
         This bower of blisse, this paradise of pleasure,
         Where lauish plentie did exceed all measure;
         The inner portch seem'd entrance to intice,
         It fashion'd was with such quaint rare deuice,

The top with cannopie of greene was spred
Thicken'd with leaues of th'Iuies wanton hed,
About the which the *Eglentine* did twine
His prickling armes the branches to combine,
Bearing sweete flowers of more then fragrant odour,
Which stellified the roof with painted colour;
On either side the vine did broad dilate
His swollen veines with wreathings intricate,
Whose bunches to the ground did seeme t'incline,
As freely offring of their luscious wine.

[Cf. *F. Q.* 2.5.29; 2.12.54; *Am.* 76.3.]

Pp. 9-10 (sig. B 3 - B 3ᵛ):

From this same portch, a walke directly lay,
Which to the bower it selfe did leade the way
With fruit-trees thicke beset on either side,
Whose goodly fruit themselues did seeme to hide
Beneath the leaues, as lurking from the eies
Of strangers greedie view, fearing surprise,
Whose arched bowes and leauie twigs together
With true loue knots intangled each in other,

P. 10 (sig. B 3ᵛ):

Passing forth, one loe there they did behold
High lifted vp with loftie roofe of gold
The bower of blisse, in which there did abide
The Ladies selfe, that should their cause decide,
On which the heauens still in a stedfast state
Look't alway blithe, diuerting froward fate,
Not suffering ycie frost, or scorching sunne
To vex th'inhabitants, that there did wonne:
For there eternall spring doth euer dwell.

[Cf. *F. Q.* 2.12.51; 3.6.42.]

P. 11 (sig. B 4):

Vnto this bower *Dan* Cuckow and his mate
Approaching nigh, loe standing at the gate,
Which framed was of purest Iuorie
All painted ore with many a historie,
So sweetly wrought, that arte in them did seeme
To mocke at nature as of no esteeme
Eftsoones they heard a pleasing harmonie
Of musickes most melodious minstralsie,
Where sweet voic'd birds, soft winds and waters fall,
With voice and Violl made agreement all,
The birds vnto the voice did sweetly sing,
The voice did speake vnto the Viols string,
That to the wind did sound now high now low,

The wind to waters fall did gently blow;
Thus birds, voice, Violl, winds and waters all
Did sing, did speake, did sound, did blow, did fall.

[Cf. F. Q. 2.12.43-4, 70-1.]

Pp. 12-3 (sigs. B 4ᵛ - B 5):

The time came on, and th'Opall coloured morne,
Bright-cheekt *Aurora* leauing all forlorne
Old *Tython* in his bed, did vp arise
Opening the gates of the orientall skies,
Through which the daies bright king came dauncing out
With glorious golden lockes bespread about
His shoulders broad; from whence such luster came,
That all the world did seeme a golden flame.

[Cf. F. Q. 1.5.2.3-4.]

Pp. 46-7 (sigs. Gᵛ - G 2):

I only here intend to make report
Of that same counted cuckow sport,
Which by our dames is deem'd a lawfull game,
Though impudence it selfe blush at the same,
(I meane of th' old *Malbeccoes* of our age)
Who iustly beare *Cornuted Vulcans* badge.
In *Troynobant* as to and fro I flie
It hath been oftentimes my chaunce t'espie
An old cold *Ianuarie* iet before
A fresh young *May*, a spreetly *Helinore,*
Vnequall both in yeares and in affection,
And also far vnlike in their condition;
Yet to the blind-ey'd world it did appeare,
That *May* did loue her *Ianuarie* deare;
Which I scarse trusting with a curious eie
Haue closely trackt their steps the truth to trie:
And loe, while he hath set his thoughts vpon
His horded heapes, his *May* being left alone,
He being close at his accounts aboue,
While she beneath sits longing after loue,
In steps me *March* clad like a lustie Knight,
Or pleasant *Aprill* full of sweet delight,
Who in loues wanton art, not wanting skill
Hath slights enow t'assault fresh *May* at will;
But what needs long assault where none doth shield;
For gentle heart she is as prone to yeeld,
As he t'assault, which well this younker knowes,
Though seeming strange a while with her he glose,
For by her touching, stroking, gentle pressing,
Her rubbing, wringing, wrestling, wanton thrusting,
Coy looking, culling and kind intertaine

He finds enough and knowes her meaning plaine:
For gentle *May* no proffer'd time will lose,
When as from home old *Ianuarie* goes,
And then the vnchaste kisses common flies,
Which *Hymens* strongest nuptiall bands vnties,
Then beautie sets the eies of lust on fire,
And fancie breakes forth into strong desire,
And lastly lust doth in a moment space
Make *Ianuaries* browes bud forth apace,
Which neither he, nor any else do see,
Though it be commonly well knowne to me:
For these be obiects common to my sight,
As in my bowers I sit, both day and night.

[Cf. *F. Q.* 3.9-10.]

P. 49 (sig. G 3):

For loe, that Squier, that liues in deepe despaire
Of gaining grace of *Columbel* the faire,
Vnto an endlesse taske by her being ti'd
To wander each where, through the world so wide,
To proue how many damsels he could find,
That chastely did retaine a constant mind,
Did of three hundred dames find but this one,
That vnto loues delight would not be wonne:
Then (gentle *Philomel*) lay by thy griefe,
And of this dame let vs go seeke reliefe.

[Cf. *F. Q.* 3.7.51-61. These passages are illustrative; throughout the
poem, phrasing and episodes are reminiscent of Spenser.] (RH, FMP)

1607. John Stradling. *Ioannis Stradlingi Epigrammatum Libri Quatuor.*
[STC 23354.]

Lib. 1, p. 21 (sig. B 4; Chalmers 3.13):

Ad Edm. Spencer *Homerum*
Britannicum.
Si nos Troiani, noua nobis Troia sit: Ipse
(Vt Græcis suus est) noster Homerus eris. (FIC)

Lib. 3, p. 100 (sig. G 3ᵛ):

Ad Edm. Spencer, *eximium poëtam, de exemplaribus suis quibusdam
manuscriptis, ad Hibernicis exlegibus igne crematis, in Hibernica de-
fectione.*

Ingenij tantum noram tibi flumen, vt ipsum
Absumi flammis non potuisse putem.
Flumen at ingenij partìm tibi sorbuit ignis:
Qualis, qui flumen deuoret, ignis erat?
Syluestris populus syluestres inijcit ignes:
Talibus obsistunt flumina nulla pyris. (FIC, DEM)

Lib. 4, p. 165 (sig. L 4; Chalmers 3.13):

Ad Spencer & Daniel, celeberrimos Poetas.
Diuiditis primas inter vos, atque secundas:
Tertius a vobis quisquis erit, sat habet. (FIC)

1607. Thomas Tomkis. *Lingua: Or The Combat of the Tongue, And the fiue Senses for Superiority. A pleasant Comoedie.*
[STC 24104. Rptd Facsimile Texts, 1913. Cf. M. P. Tilley, " *Lingua* and the *Faerie Queene*," MLN, 42 (1927). 150-7.]

Sig. A 2, *Drammatis Personae* [lists, among others:]
          Phantastes . . .
          Anamnestes, Memorie his Page . . .
                    Psence
Personae quarum mentio tantum fit {Arcasia [sic]
                                      {Veritas
                                       Oblivio

[For Phantastes and Anamnestes, cf. *F. Q.* 2.9.52, 58; for Acrasia, 2 *freq.*] (WW)

Act 1, sc. 1, sig. A 3 (Koeppel, p. 88):
Ling. ' Tis plaine indeed, for Truth no descant needs,
Vna's her name, she cannot be diuided.
[Cf. *F. Q.* 1.]

Act 2, sc. 1, sig. C 3ᵛ [*for* C 2ᵛ] (Koeppel, p. 88):
Mend. I long to see those hot-spur senses at it, they say they haue gallant preparations, and not vnlikely, for most of the soldiers are ready in Armes since the last feild fought against their yearely enemy *Meleager,* & his wife *Acrasia*; that Conquest hath so flesht them that no peace can hold them. But had not *Meleager* been sicke, and *Acrasia* drunke, the senses might haue whistled for the victory. [For Meleager, cf. *F. Q.* 2.11. Other references to Acrasia in *Lingua* appear in Act 5: sc. 1, sig. K; sc. 3, sig. K 2ᵛ; sc. 18, sig. M 3ᵛ; sc. 19, sig. M 4.] (FMP)

1608. Henoch Clapham. *A Pastoral Epilogue, betweene Hobbinoll, and Collin Clout,* appended to *Errour on the Left Hand.* [STC 5342.]
Pp. 102-3:
   Collin.   Good *Hobbinoll,* why hangs thou so thy head;
               hast lost some sheep, or be some lambkin dead?
               Thou Whilome sung vnto thy oten pipe,
                 as Fary-queen could not but loue and like.
[Discussion of existent church evils, etc.] (EG)

1608. Francis Davison. *A Poetical Rapsodie* [2nd ed.].
[STC 6374. Ed. H. E. Rollins, Harvard Univ. Press, 1931-2.]
A Complaint Of which all the staues end with the words of the first, like a Sestine, sig. C 4 (Rollins 1.259):
      Ye ghastly groues, that heare my wofull cries

Whose shady leaues do shake to heare my paine
Thou siluer streame that dost with teares lament
The cruell chance that doth my greefe increase:
Ye chirping birds whose cheereles notes declare
That ye bewaile the woes *I* feele in minde,
Beare witnesse how with care *I* do consume,
And heare the cause why thus I pine away.

[The similarity of this stanza to the initial stanza of Spenser's sestina in the Aug. eclogue leaves no room for doubt that Spenser's verse prompted this experiment.] (FMP)

I. Eglogue intituled Cuddy, sig. D 10ᵛ (Rollins 1.287):

And for they had so long beene pent with paine,
At sight of Sun they seem'd to liue againe.

[Cf. *S. C.* Jan. 4.]

Ibid., sig. D 11 (Rollins 1.288):

The ioyfull Sunne, whom clowdy Winters spight,
Had shut from vs in watry fishes haske.

[Cf. *S. C. Nov.* 14-6, and gloss.]

Ibid., sig. D 11ᵛ (Rollins 1.289):

(Thy knees so weake, thy fleece so rough and rent)

[Cf. *S. C.* Jan. 43-4.]

Ibid., sig. D 12 (Rollins 1.290):

Where been the dapper Ditties that I dight.
And Roundlaies, and Virelayes so soot?
Whilome with Collins selfe compare I might
For other Swaine, to striue was little boote,
    Such skill *I* had in making all aboue
    But all to little skill to conquer Loue.

[Cf. *S. C. Oct.* 13-4, and gloss; *Nov.* 20-1, and gloss.] (FIC, HER)

1608.   John Day. *Humour Out of Breath.*
[STC 6411. *Works,* coll. A. H. Bullen, 1881.]

Act 1. sc. 1, sig. A 4:

*Enter Octauio Duke of Venice . . . Florimell his
daughter.* (RH)

1608-44.   Lord Edward Herbert of Cherbury. Poems: See 1665.

1609.   George Chapman. *Euthymiæ Raptus; or The Teares of Peace.*
[STC 4976. *Poems,* ed. Phillis B. Bartlett, New York & London, 1941.]

Sig. C 2 (Bartlett, p. 183):

Your Intellectiue men, they study hard
Not to get knowledge, but for meere rewarde.
And therefore that true knowledge that should be

Their studies end, and is in Nature free,
Will not be made their Broker; hauing powre
(With her sole selfe) to bring both Bride, and dowre.
They haue some shadowes of her (as of me,
Adulterate outward Peace) but neuer see
Her true, and heauenly face. Yet those shades serue
(Like errant Knights, that by enchantments swerue,
From their true Ladyes being; and embrace
An ougly Witch, with her phantastique face)
To make them thinke, *Truths* substance in their arms:
Which that they haue not, but her shadowes charmes.

[Cf. the Red Cross Knight's desertion of Una for Duessa.] (EG)

1609. Samuel Rowlands. *The Famous Historie of Guy Earle of War-
wick.*
[STC 21378. *Complete Works,* ed. Sir. Edmund Gosse, with Notes and
Glossary by Sidney J. H. Herrtage, Hunterian Club, 1880.]

[This narrative poem may owe something to F. Q.; it is written in six-line
stanzas (ababcc) arranged in twelve cantos, each of which is headed
by a four-line argument similar to those in F. Q.] (FIC)

1609. Joseph Wybarne. *The New Age of Old Names.* [STC 26055.]

To the Reader, sig. A 4 - A 4ᵛ
I suppose, that the bramble of controuersie hath been a meanes to choake
most of our sciences, which stand more on explication of experience,
then in winding and windy arguments, if I haue omitted something in
a matter so variable, remember that I talke of *Errors Denne,* celebrated
by the penne of our second *Chaucer.*
[Cf. *F. Q.* 1.1.13.] (FIC)

Pp. 23-4 (sig. D4 - D4ᵛ):
If you binde a fallacie with the chaines of a distinction, you shall cause
her to appeare in her owne likenesse, like *Duessa* disroab'd by Prince
Arthur.
[Cf. *F. Q.* 1.8.46-50; 2.1.22.]

P. 25 (sig. E):
Hence we conclude that fallacies are *vbiquitaries,* and busie as newes-
mongers, and that as each part of the body hath some disease sent from
the Witch *Acrasia,* which is intemperance: so there is no part or func-
tion of mans life, which may not bee ouergrowen by the brambles of
some fallacie.
[Cf. *F. Q.* 2.1.51-5, *et freq.*] (DEM)

Pp. 66-7 (sigs. Kᵛ - K 2):
Shee [poetry] is now become *Trulla,* I had almost said the Trull of
lewde loues, fancies and passions: redeeme her from this shame, if any
sinew of *Spencer* be left in you, and let it be a capitall fault *in Virginis
choro,* I meane *Pallas, Veneris torum vel nominasse.* (FIC)

Pp. 68-9 (sigs. K 2ᵛ - K 3):

. . . These seeming societies, or rather conspiracies, vsing order in disorder, I meane in the feastes of *Bona Dea,* that is of good fellowship, haue made a Monopoly of all neighbourhood, as if the better sort did liue like *Apri singulares & Solivagi,* solitary wandring Boares, whereas these good Wolues pray together, though it may be, they neuer praied but in a storm, in which if *Bias* had beene with them, hee would haue desired their silence, lest that God hearing their praiers, so contrary to their deedes,

See the Legend should as contrary to their wils drowne them in the seas,
of Phaedria in as they with their wils had drowned themselues in the
the 2. booke of dead sea of pleasure. But here is the error, they cannot
the Fayerie be merry except they laugh a Sardonian laughter, *qui plus*
Queene. *Alloes quam Mellis habet,* which turneth at last to wormwood, or rather to the worme that neuer dyes, and the burning wood, whose consumption shall neuer receiue consummation. . . .

P. 72 (sig. K 4ᵛ):

Vertue according to the Stoickes, was diuided into *Cathecon* and *Catorthoma,* that is, into Vertue meane and possible, or Vertue transcendent and heroycall, such as the
See Spencer, Scripture ascribe to *Sampson,* the Poets their Apes to
lib. 6. *Hercules,* and our writers to Prince *Arthur.* This vertue hath beene three wayes assaulted, First, by calumniation, for actions done by diuine instinct, haue euer found some *Zoylus, Momus, Mastix,* or tongue of blattant beast, so called of βλαπτω, to hurt. (FMP)

P. 113 (sig. Q):

This Antichrist is most poetically figured also by the famous heire Apparant to *Homer* and *Virgil,* in his *Faiery Queene* vnder the names of *Archimagus, Duessa, Argoglio* the Soldane and others, throughout the first and fift Legends. (FIC)

1610.   Giles Fletcher. *Christs Victorie, and Triumph in Heauen, and Earth, over, and after death,* Cambridge.
[STC 11058. *The Poetical Works of Giles Fletcher and Phineas Fletcher,* ed. F. S. Boas, Cambridge, 1908-9.]

To the Reader, sig. ¶ 4ᵛ (Boas 1.11):
. . . thrice-honour'd *Bartas,* & our (I know no other name more glorious then his own) Mʳ. *Edmund Spencer* (two blessed Soules) not thinking ten years inough, layeing out their whole liues vpon this one studie.
[As Carpenter remarks, there are " echoes of Spenser on almost every page." Only some of the more striking passages are cited.]

Christs Victorie in Heaven, p. 14, sts. 46-7 (Boas 1.29):
And on thine eyelids, waiting thee beside,

Ten thousand Graces sit, and when they mooue
To earth their amourous belgards from aboue,
They flie from heau'n, and on their wings conuey thy loue.

All of discolour'd plumes their wings ar made,
And with so wondrous art the quills ar wrought,
That whensoere they cut the ayrie glade,
The winde into their hollowe pipes is caught.

[Cf. F. Q. 3.9.52 and 2.8.5.] (FIC)

Christs Victorie on Earth, p. 27, st. 4 (Boas 1.41):
Downe fell the Lordly Lions angrie mood,
And he himselfe fell downe, in congies lowe;
Bidding him welcome to his wastfull wood,
Sometime he kist the grasse whear he did goe,
And, as to wash his feete he well did knowe,
    With fauning tongue he lickt away the dust,
    And euery one would neerest to him thrust,
And euery one, with new, forgot his former lust.

[Cf. F. Q. 1.3.5-9.] (DEM)

Ibid., p. 30, st. 15 (Boas 1.43):
At length an aged Syre farre off he sawe
Come slowely footing, euerie step he guest
One of his feete he from the graue did drawe,
Three legges he had, the woodden was the best,
And all the waie he went, he euer blest
    With benedicities, and prayers store,
    But the bad ground was blessed ne'r the more,
And all his head with snowe of Age was waxen hore.

[Compare this and the following stanzas with F. Q. 1.1.29 ff.]

Ibid., p. 32, st. 23 (Boas 1.45):
Ere long they came neere to a balefull bowre,
Much like the mouth of that infernall caue,
That gaping stood all Commers to deuoure,
Darke, dolefull, dreary, like a greedy graue,
That still for carrion carkasses doth craue.
    The ground no hearbs, but venomous did beare,
    Nor ragged trees did leaue, but euery whear
Dead bones, and skulls wear cast, and bodies hanged wear.

[The description of Despair and his abode in this and the following
stanzas leans heavily upon F. Q. 1.9.33 ff.]

Ibid., p. 37, sts. 39-40 (Boas 1.49-50):
All suddenly the hill his snowe deouers,
In liew whereof a goodly garden grew,
As if the snow had melted into flow'rs,
Which their sweet breath in subtill vapours threw,

That all about perfumed spirits flew.
For what so euer might aggrate the sense,
In all the world, or please the appetence,
Heer it was powred out in lauish affluence.

Not louely Ida might with this compare,
Though many streames his banks besiluered,
Though Xanthus with his golden sands he bare,
Nor Hibla, though his thyme depastured,
As fast againe with honie blossomed.
Ne Rhodope, ne Tempes flowrie playne,
Adonis garden was to this but vayne,
Though Plato on his beds a flood of praise did rayne.

[The garden of Vaine-Glorie is reminiscent throughout of Acrasia's gardens and bower, even to the Circean-charmed beasts and the song with which the temptress seeks to lull her visitor into acquiescence. Cf. *F. Q.* 2.5.27 ff., 2.12.50 ff.] (FIC)

Ibid., p. 41, st. 55 (Boas 1.53):
O sacred hunger of the greedie eye,
Whose neede hath end, but no end covetise,
Emptie in fulnes, rich in pouertie,
That hauing all things, nothing can suffice,
How thou befanciest the men most wise?

[Cf. *F. Q.* 1.4.29.1-6.] (FMP)

Christs Triumph after Death, p. 70, st. 12 (Boas 1.78):
So fairest Phosphor the bright Morning starre,
But neewely washt in the greene element.

[Cf. *F. Q.* 2.12.65.1-2.] (FIC)

1610. John Fletcher. *The Faithfull Shepheardesse.*
[STC 11068. *Beaumont and Fletcher*, ed. A. Glover and A. R. Waller, Cambridge, 1905-12.]

[E. Koeppel suggests Fletcher's indebtedness to Spenser's Una and Sir Satyrane for the characters of Clorin and the Satyr, to the False Una and the False Florimell for Amarillis, and to the healing of Serena and Timias for the purification of Alexis and Cloe. In act 5, sc. 1 (ll. 213-6; Glover and Waller 2.443), honor is paid to Spenser under the name of Dorus:
Now rise and go; and as ye pass away
Sing to the God of Sheep, that happy lay,
That honest *Dorus* taught ye, *Dorus*, he
That was the soul and god of melody.] (FIC)

1610. John Guillim. *A Display of Heraldrie.* [STC 12500.]
P. 150 (STC 12501, bearing date 1611, quoted):
Toades and Frogs doe communicate this naturall property,

that when they sit they hold their heads steady and without motion: which stately action, *Spencer* in his *Sheapheards Calender* calleth the *Lording* of *Frogs*.

P. 266 (STC 12501 quoted):

This property is obserued to be naturally in the *Frogge,*
Ed. Spenser. whereof *Spenser* the *Poet* making mention, termeth it the
in his *Lording of Frogs*, because in their sitting they hold their
Eglogues. heads steady; looking directly in a kind of *grauity* and *state,*
without any motion at all.
[Cf. *S. C. Dec.* 70 and gloss.] (DFA)

1610. Richard Niccols. *Englands Eliza: or The Victorious and Triumphant Reigne of . . . Elizabeth, Queene of England, France and Ireland, &c.* [Part V of the *Mirrour for Magistrates*]. [STC 13446. Ed. Joseph Haslewood, 1815.]

The Induction, p. 779 (Haslewood, pp. 823-4):

(O) did that Fairie Queenes sweet singer liue,
That to the dead eternitie could giue,
Or if, that heauen by influence would infuse
His heauenlie spirit on mine earth-borne Muse,
Her name ere this a mirror should haue been
Lim'd out in golden verse to th'eyes of men:
But my sad Muse, though willing; yet too weak
In her rude rymes *Elizaes* worth to speak,
Must yeeld to those, whose Muse can mount on high,
And with braue plumes can clime the loftie skie.

P. 783 (Haslewood, p. 828):

Then men did walke in shades of darkesome night,
Whose feeble sight with errors blacke strooke blind,
Could in no place Times faire *Fidessa* find. (FIC)

P. 796 (Haslewood, p. 845):

Meane time Romes dragon rousde his bloodie crest,
And wau'd his wings, from whence that rabble rout,
That hell-hatch'd brood, who, fed on Errors brest
And suck'd her poysonous dugs, came crawling out
As was their woont, to flie the world about.
[Cf. *F. Q.* 1.1.15.]

P. 797 (Haslewood, p. 845):

Vnkindly Impes, euen from your birth accurst,
Destested stock of vipers bloodie brood,
That sought to satisfie your burning thirst
By drinking vp your dying mothers blood,
Making her death your life, her hurt your good;
Your deeds are sunke to *Plutoes* darksom den,
Shame is your portion mongst the sonnes of men.

P. 806 (Haslewood, p. 857):
> When grizly night her iron carre had driuen
> From her darke mansion house, that hidden lies
> In *Plutoes* kingdome, to the top of heau'n,
> And with black cloake of clouds muffling the skies,
> With sable wings shut vp all wakefull eies,
>   Obscur'd with darknesse grim they both did go,
>   To act this stratagem vpon the foe.

[Cf. *F. Q.* 1.5.28 ff.] (DEM)

1610. Henry Stanford. Presentation verses in Cambridge Univ. MS D.d.V.75.

Fol. 19:
> h. st. to yᵉ lady Hunsdon 1610. faery quene
> Hauing no other gift right noble dame
> to testifie my mynde this booke I send
> the autour when he liu'd did beare your name
> & for to honour ladies this he penned
> here may you reade in sugred verse set out
> the praises of *Belphebe* worthie Quene
> & faery landes adventures all about
> wᵗʰ other exploites worthie to be seene
> here Georges holines may vs direct
> to conquer all the monstrous shapes of sin
> & Guions temperance make vs suspect
> the sugred baites of pleasures wanton ginnes
>   Deign it to reade & reape such fruites it beares
>   I still will wishe you long & happie yeares

[See also Henry Stanford, above, under 1596.] (ME)

1611. William Byrd. *Psalmes, Songs and Sonnets: some solemne, others ioyfull, framed to the life of the Words.*
[STC 4255. Rptd A. H. Bullen, *Some Shorter Elizabethan Poems,* Westminster, 1903.]

No. 22 (Bullen, p. 58):
> Crowned with flowers, I saw faire *Amarillis*,
>   by *Thyrsis* sit, hard by a fount of Christall,
> And with her hand more white than snow or Lillies,
>   On sand shee wrote, my faith shall be immortall,
>   And sodainely a storme of winde and weather,
>   Blew all her faith and sand away together.

[Cf. *Am.* 75.] (DEM)

1612. George Chapman. *An Epicede or Funeral Song.*
[STC 4974. *Poems,* ed. Phillis B. Bartlett, New York & London, 1941.]

Sig. B 4ᵛ (Bartlett, p. 257):

Ambition; goulden Chaine
To true mans freedome; not from heau'n let fal
To draw men vp; But shot from Hell to hale
All men, as bondslaues, to his Turckish den.
[Cf. *F. Q.* 2.7.46; note comment above: 1594. George Chapman.]
(DEM)

1612. Michael Drayton. *Poly-Olbion* [Part 1].
[STC 7226. *Works,* ed. J. W. Hebel, Oxford, 1931-41.]

From the Author of the Illustrations, sig. A 2ᵛ (Hebel 4.ix):
Concerning the Arcadian deduction of our *British* Monarchy . . . no
Relation was extant, which is now left to our vse. How then are they,
which pretend Chronologies of that Age without any Fragment of Authors
before *Gildas?*. . . . For my part, I beleeue much in them as I do the
finding of Hiero's Shipmast in our Mountaines . . . or that *Iulius Caesar*
built *Arthurs Hoffen* in *Stirling* Shirifdome; or, that *Britons* were at the
Rape of *Hesione* with *Hercules,* as our excellent wit *Ioseph* of *Excester*
. . . singeth: which are euen aqually warrantable, as *Ariosto's* Narra-
tions of Persons and Places in his *Rowlands, Spensers* Elfin Story, or
Rablais his strange discoueries. (FIC)

Illustrations, the fourth Song, p. 68 (Hebel 4.85):

Some account him [St. George] an allegory of our Sau-
Faery Q. *lib.*1. iour Christ; and our admired Spencer hath made him an
embleme of Religion.

Ibid., p. 71 (Hebel 4.89):

[Merlin's] buriall (in supposition as vncertaine as his
ᶜ*Orland. Furios.* birth, actions, and all of those too fabulously mixt stories)
canto 3. and his *Lady* of the *Lake* it is by liberty of profession laid
See *Spencers* in *France* by that *Italian*ᶜ *Ariosto*: which perhaps is credi-
Faery Q. *lib.*3. ble as som more of his attributes, seeing no perswading
cant. 3. authority, in any of them, rectifies the vncertainty.

Ibid., the fifth Song, p. 84 (Hebel 4.108):
ᵉ*Spencers* His Mother (a Nun, daughter to *Pubidius* K. of Ma-
Faery Q. *lib.*3. thraual, and cald Matilda, as by ᵉ*Poeticall* authority onely
cant.3. I finde iustifiable.

Ibid., the eight Song, p. 123 (Hebel 4.154):

Vnto this referre that suppos'd prophecie of Merlin:

Doctrinae studium quod nunc viget ad vada Boum

Ante finem secli celebrabitur ad vada Saxi.
ᶠSpens. Faery Which you shall have *Englished* in that solemnized mar-
Q. lib.4. *Cant.* riage of Thames and Medway, by a most admired ᶠMuse
11. *Stanz.*35. of our Nation, thus with advantage: [quotes ll. 1-6.]

Ibid., the tenth Song, p. 165 (Hebel 4.210):
ᵇFaery Q. *lib.* Hence questionles was that Fiction of the Muses best

1. Cant.9.*Stanz.* pupil, the noble *Spenser*,[b] in supposing *Merlin* vsually to
4.   visit his old *Timon*, whose dwelling he places

— — — — — — — — —*low in a valley greene*
[quotes ll. 5-9.]

Ibid., the eleuenth Song, p. 183 (Hebel 4.233):
Weuer . . . hath this attribut, & that of the Sea-gods suite to him, and
kind entertainment for his skil in physique, & prophecie; iustifiable in
generall, as wel as to make *Tryphon* the Surgeon which our excellent
Spenser hath done.

Ibid., the sixteenth Song, pp. 253-4 (Hebel 4.323-4):

[c]In his Ruines   Personating the *Genius* of *Verlam*, that euer famous
of Time.   [c]*Spenser* sung

I was that Citie. . . . [quotes ll. 36-42]

As vnder the *Romans*, so in the *Saxon* times afterward
it endured a second Ruine: and, out of its corruption,
after the Abbey erected by K. *Offa*, was generated that of
Saint *Albons*; whither, in later times most of the stone-
workes and whatsoeuer fit for building was by the Abbots
translated. So that

[b]*Spens. vbi supra.*   [b]*Now remaines no Memorie* . . . [quotes ll. 4-7.]
. . . *Gildas*, speaking of S. *Albons* martyrdom and his
miraculous passing through the Riuer at *Verlamcestre*,
calls it *inter ignotum trans Thamesis fluvii alueum:* so by
collection they guest that *Thames* had then his full course
this way, being thereto further mou'd by Anchors and such
like here digd vp. This coniecture hath been followed by
[c]*Spenser.*   that [c]Noble Muse thus in the person of *Verlam*;

[Quotes R. T. 134-40, 148-54.] (FIC)

The Sixteenth Song, p. 245 (Hebel 4.313):
The Argument.
Olde Ver, neere to *Saint Albans*, brings
Watling to talk of auncient things;
What *Verlam* was before she fell,
And many more sad ruines tell. . . .

[" Much of this Song reads like an echo of Spenser's *R. T.* Like that
poem it draws largely on Harrison." Hebel 5.238/2. Harrison's *Description of Britaine* appeared in both the 1577 and 1587 eds. of Holinshed.]
(KT)

Ibid., p. 246 (Hebel 4.314):
Thou saw'st when *Verlam* once her head aloft did beare
(Which in her cinders now lies sadly buried heere)
With Alabaster, Tuch, and Porphery adorn'd,
When(welneare)in her pride great *Troynouant* she scorn'd.

Ibid., p. 252 (Hebel 4.321):

When *Tames* his either Banks, adorn'd with buildings faire,
The City to salute doth bid the Muse prepare.
Whose Turrets, Fanes, and Spyres, when wistly she beholds,
Her wonder at the site, thus strangely she unfolds.

The seuenteenth Song, p. 266 (Hebel 4.339):

Ioues Oke, the warlike Ash, veyn'd Elme, the softer Beech,
Short Hazell, Maple plaine, light Aspe, the bending Wych,
Though Holly, and smooth Birch.

[Cf. *F. Q.* 1.1.8-9.]

The eighteenth Song, p. 285 (Hebel 4.366):

And but that *Medway* then of *Tames* obtain'd such grace,
Except her country Nymphes, that none should be in place,
*In the More Riuers from each part, had instantly been there,
Faiery Then at their Marriage, first, by *Spenser* numbred were. (DEM)
Queene.

1612.   Orlando Gibbons. *The First Set of Madrigals and Mottets of 5. Parts: apt for Viols and Voyces.*

[STC 11826. E. H. Fellowes, *English Madrigal Verse,* Oxford, 1920.]

[No. 10, sig. B 3ᵛ, and no. 11, sig. B 4 (Fellowes, p. 98) quote *F. Q.* 3.1.49, ll. 1-4 and 5-9 respectively.] (FIC)

1612.   Sir Arthur Gorges. *The Olympian Catastrophe,* in Huntington MS Ellesmere 1130.
[Ed. Randall Davies, Cayme Press, Kensington, 1925, with omissions and misreadings.]

Pp. 49-50 (Davies, pp. 58-9):

Hensefoorth (quoth she) lett me no more behold
Pleasure on earth, wch is but false delight . . .

No sleepe (the harbinger of wearye neights)
Shall seaze vpon myne ey-lids any more,
Nor any foode refresh my wasted sprights,
And faylinge powers to former strength restore,
   For I by day will feed on heauy plight,
   And spend wth Philomele the longe-some night.

So will I scorne my selfe whom nature made,
And in her workemanshipp no comfort find:
For tis but fraile, and doth like shadowes faile,
So soone as on it blowes the blastinge wynde
   Of spitefull death, that deemes all dates too longe:
   Yet age to die is right; but youth tis wronge.

Why fell he then amidst his floweringe race,
Whilst yet his bud was greene and fresh his rynde,
Whilst he exceld in euery gifte and grace,

That is admired most in humane kinde
Adorne'd wth wisdom and such pieties,
As made him mynion to the deities?

Wth whom he reste, and wheare I wish to bee:
That I might still enioye his blessed sight.

[Cf. *Daph.* 491-2, 470-6, 393-6, 243, 239-42. The greater part of
" Princess Elizabeth's lament for Prince Henry . . . repeats closely
Alcyon's lament for Daphne; i. e., repeats the words Spenser assigned to
Gorges himself as Alcyon."] (HES)

1612.   Thomas Heywood. *An Apology for Actors.*
[STC 13309. Ed. J. P. Collier, Shak. Soc. Pub., vol. 14, 1841.]

Sig. Gᵛ (Collier, p. 57):
Women likewise that are chaste, are by vs extolled, and encouraged in
their vertues, being instanced by *Diana, Belphebe, Matilda, Lucrece,*
and the Countess of *Salisbury.* (DEM)

1612.   Henry Peacham, *the younger. Minerva Britanna Or A Garden of
Heroical Deuises, furnished & adorned with Emblemes and Impresa's
of sundry natures.* [STC 19511.]

The Author to his Muse, sig. P 4:

Now strike wee Saile, and throw aside our oare,
My wearie Muse, the worst is well nie past:
And take a while, our pleasure on the shore,
Recounting what wee overcame at last.

[Cf. *F. Q.* 1.12.42.] (EAS)

Vlterius durabit, p. 161 (sig. Z 2ᵛ):

The monuments that mightie Monarches reare,
COLOSSO'S statües, and Pyramids high,
In tract of time, doe moulder downe and weare,
Ne leaue they any little memorie,
    The Passengers may warned be to say,
    They had their being here, another day.

But wise wordes taught, in numbers sweete to runne,
Preserued by the liuing Muse for aie,
Shall still abide, when date of these is done,
Nor ever shall by Time be worne away:
    Time, Tyrants, Envie, World assay thy worst,
    Ere *HOMER* die, thou shalt be fired first.

[Cf. *R. T.* 402 ff.] (HES)

Nulli penetrabilis, p. 182 (sig. Cc 1):

A shadie Wood, pourtraicted to the sight,
With vncouth pathes, and hidden waies vnknowne:
Resembling *CHAOS,* or the hideous night,
Or those sad Groues, by banke of *ACHERON*

With banefull *Ewe*, and *Ebon* overgrowne:
Whose thickest boughes, and inmost entries are
Not peirceable, to power of any starre.
[Last lines quotes *F. Q.* 1.1.7.6, substituting *to* for *with*. The second stanza, like the first quoted here, echoes *F. Q.* throughout.] (DFA)

1612. Henry Peacham. *Graphice Or The Most Avncient and Excellent Art of Drawing and Limning.*
STC 19507; also 19508, with the title, *The Gentlemans Exercise. Or An Exquisite practise.*]
P. 27 (sig. E 3):

In his Faery   Feare is described by our excellent *Spencer* to ride in
Queene.   armour, at the clashing whereof he looks deadly pale, as
afeard of himselfe.

P. 114 (sig. Q 2ᵛ):
Dissimulation.
A lady wearing a vizard of two faces, in a long Robe of changeable colour, in her right hand a Magpie, the Poet *Spencer* described her looking through a lattice.

Pp. 134-5 (sigs. S 3ᵛ - S 4) [In describing how the months of the year should be drawn]:
August.
August shall beare the forme of a young man of a fierce and cholericke aspect in a flame colored garment, vpon his head a garland of wheat and Rie, vpon his arme a basket of ripe fruites, as peares, plummes, apples, gooseberries: at his belt (as our *Spencer* describeth him) a sickle, bearing the signe *Virgo*. [Cf. *F. Q.* 7.7.36, description of July.] (FH)

1612. John Taylor. *The Sculler, Rowing from Tiber to Thames.*
[STC 23791. *Works*, rptd from ed. of 1630, Sp. Soc. Pub., 1868-9.]
Epigram 28, sig. E 2 (Sp. Soc. Pub., p. 508):
    Braue *Bragadocio* whome the world would threaten,
    Was lately with a fagot sticke sore beaten:
    Wherefore in kindenes now my Muse must weepe,
    Because his resolution was a sleepe. (FBW)

1613. Francis Beaumont and John Fletcher. *The Knight of the Burning Pestle.* [STC 1674.]
[Carpenter suggests that the play may be in part a satire on the *F. Q.*, with "Dorus" as Spenser; Koeppel (p. 88) that the Squire of Damsels, act 2, sc. 3, line 6, may be reminiscent of the Squire of Dames, *F. Q.* 3.6.51.]

1613. William Browne. *Britannia's Pastorals* [Book 1]
[STC 3914-5. *Poems*, ed. Gordon Goodwin, 1893; also 1894.]
P. 30 (sigs. E 3ᵛ - E 4; Goodwin 1.59-60):

[A tree passage resembling *F. Q.* 1.1.8-9.] (DEM)

P. 50 (sig. H^v; Goodwin 1.88):

> Had *Colin Clout* yet liu'd, (but he is gone)
> The best on earth could tune a louers mone. (FIC)

P. 54 (Sig. H 3^v; Goodwin 1.95):

> Full many a Shepheard with his louely Lasse,
> Sit telling tales vpon the clouer grasse:
> There is the merry Shepheard of the hole;
> *Thenot, Piers, Nilkin, Duddy, Hobbinoll,*
> *Alexis, Siluan, Teddy* of the Glen,
> *Rowly,* and *Perigot* here by the Fen.

[Use of pastoral names made familiar by *S. C.*]

Pp. 82, 89 (sigs. M^v, N; Goodwin l. 132, 142):
[References to *Gerion*; cf. *F. Q.* 5.10.11.] (DEM)

P. 94 (sig. N 3^v; Goodwin 1.150):

> Told how shee knew me well since I had beene,
> As chiefest consort of the *Faiery Queene.* (FIC)

P. 99 (sig. O 2; Goodwin 1.157):

> Where certaine *Death* liu'd, in an Ebon chaire
> The soules blacke homicide meager *Despaire*
> Had his abode: there 'gainst the craggy rockes
> Some dasht their braines out, with relentlesse knockes,
> Others on trees (ô most accursed elues)
> Are fastening knots, so to vndoe themselues.

[Cf. *F. Q.* 1.9.35.] (DEM)

1613. Thomas Dekker. *A Straunge Horse-Race.*
[STC 6528. *Non-Dramatic Works,* ed. A. B. Grosart, 1885.]

Sig. C 4^v (Grosart 3.339-40):
   Then came in two by two, other Troopes, whose onsets, and ouer-
throwes, honours, and disgraces, darings, and dauntings, merit an ample
Chronicle, rather then an *Abstract;* all of which the *Braggadochio-vices*
still got the worst: the *Vertues* departing in Triumph, but not with any
insulting. And thus the glory of the *Race* ended. (PK)

1613. William Drummond. *Teares on the Death of Mœliades,* Edinburgh.
[STC 7257. *Poetical Works,* ed. L. E. Kastner, Edinburgh and London,
1913.]

Sig. A 4 (Kastner 1.79):

> Your greene Lockes, *Forrests,* cut, in weeping *Myrrhes,*
> The deadly *Cypresse,* and Inke-dropping *Firres,*
> Your *Palmes* and *Mirtles* turne; from Shadowes darke
> Wing'd *Syrens* waile, and you sad *Ecchoes* marke
> The lamentable Accents of their *Mone,*

And plaine that braue *Mœliades* is gone.

[For catalogue of trees, cf. *F. Q.* 1.1.8, 9. Kastner (1.215) cites the passage as "redolent of Sidnaean imagery."] (DEM)

1613.   William Gamage. *Linsi-Woolsie. Or, Two Centuries of Epigrammes.* [STC 11544.]

Sig. B 5ᵛ (1621 ed., STC 11545, quoted):
   Epigram 39: *The Shepheards Calenders Arithmeticke.* (HER)

1613.   Edward Heyward. *On him; a Pastorall Ode to his fairest Shepheardesse*, prefixed to William Browne's *Britannia's Pastorals,* Book 1. [STC 3914-5. Rptd *Poems of William Browne,* ed. Gordon Goodwin, 1893; also 1894.]

Sig. A 5 (Goodwin 1.12):
         Him did *Nature* from his birth,
         And the *Muses* single out,
         For a second *Colin Clout.* (FIC)

1613.   Thomas Heywood. *A Marriage Triumphe Solemnized in an Epithalamion, in Memorie of the happie Nuptials between the . . . Count Palatine and . . . the Lady Elizabeth.* [STC 13355. Rptd J. P. Collier, Percy Soc., 1842.]

Sig. C 4ᵛ (Collier, p. 17):
         Behold that Prince, the Empires prime Elector,
         Of the religious Protestants protector, . . .
         The high and mighty *Palsgraue* of the *Rhyne,*
         Duke of *Bauaria,* and *Count Palatyne,*
         With Titles equall, laterally ally'd
         To *Mars* his brood, the Soldiers chiefest pride,
         That from the triple-headed *Gerion* haue
         Kept from a timeless and abortiue graue
         Faire *Belgia,* and her seuenteene daughters, all,
         Doom'd to a sad and mournfull funerall.

[Cf. *F. Q.* 5.10-1.] (DEM)

1613.   S. P. *The Love of Amos and Lavra,* in I. C.'s *Alcilia Philoparthens louing Folly.* [STC 4275.]

Verso of title page, without signature, inserted between sigs. K 3 and K 4:
         The Author to His Booke.
      Go little booke into the largest world,
         And blase the chastnes of thy maiden Muse:
      Regardles of all enuie on thee hurld,
         By the vnkindnes that the readers vse:
      And those that enuie thee by scruples letter,
         Bid them take pen in hand and make a better.

[Cf. *To his Booke,* prelude to S. C.] (RH)

1613. Henry Peacham. *The Period of Mourning. Disposed into sixe Visions.* [STC 19513.]

I. Vision, sig. B^v:

But sodainely the Day was ouercast,
A Tempest hurles the billow to the Skye.

[Cf. *F. Q.* 1.1.6.5-6. The visions are, of course, reminiscent of the visions of Petrarch and Bellay.]

II. Vision, sigs. B^v - B 2:

I saw a Palme, of body tall and striaght,
Vpon whose braunches Crownets did depend. . . .

But at the roote, a fearefull Serpent lay,
(Whose many mischiefes Time forbids me tell,)
That vndermin'd the Body night and day,
That last, it downe with hideous fragor fell,
    To griefe of all; mine eye did neuer see,
    More hopefull Blossomes, or a fairer Tree.

[Cf. *Bel.* 2, 7.]

III. Vision, sigs. B 2 - B 3:

A Wood there was, along the *Stygian* Lake,
Where *Night,* and euerlasting *Horror* dwell,
Herein a Caue, two hollow Rockes did make,
From whence a Brooke as blacke as *Lethe* fell:
    A common roade led thither, with descent
    So steepe, that none return'd that euer went.

It was an vncouth Dungeon, darke and wide,
Where liuing man nere was, or light had shone,
Saue that a little glimmering I espi'de
From rotten stickes, that all about were throwne:
    The Boxe and banefull Eugh-tree grew without,
    All which a stinking ditch did moate about.

Within, there hung vpon the ragged wals
Sculs, shirtes of maiels, whose owners had been slaine
Escotcheons, Epitaphes of Funerals;
In bottles teares of friends, and Louers vaine:
    Spades, Mattockes, models, boltes and barres for strength,
    With bones of Giants of a wondrous length.

Beneath, all formes of Monuments were seene,
Whose superscriptions were through age defac'd,
And owners long agoe consumed cleane
But now as coffers were in order plac'd,
    Wherein inditements lay, charmes, Dead-mens wills
    Popes pardons, pleas, and Pothecaries bills.

In mid'st there sat a meagre wretch alone,
That had in sorrow both his ei'n outwept,

And was with pine become a Sceleton:
I ask'd him why that loathsome Caue he kept,
And what he was: my name (quoth he) is *Death*
Perplexed here, for *Henries* losse of breath. . . .

With that, he bad me to retire in hast,
For neuer any came so neere his dore,
And liu'd: here-with mine eye a side I cast,
Where stood a glue-pot, Canes and quiuers store,
  And on a shelfe, lay many stinking weedes,
  Wherewith, I ghesse, he poison'd arrow heads.

By doubtfull tracks away through Brake and Breere,
I left the Wood, and light at last did view. . . .

[Thoroughly Spenserian and reminiscent of *F. Q.* 1.1, 1.9, and 4.1:
The Wood, Error's den etc.; the cave of Despair; and the cave of Ate,
"hard by the gates of hell." Cf. also 2.11.22, the description of
Maleger.] (FMP)

IIII. Vision, sig. B 34:

          I saw erewhile, conducted forth by *Fame*
*Three of Eng- A carre Triumphall, all of massie Gold,
land and that And *foure fierce Lyons yoaked in the same,
one of Scot-   The which a Virgin, louely to behold,
land   With gentle raine did guide and show the way,
*Vnitie   She *Vna* hight, none else they would obay.

[*V. Vision*, sig. B 4ᵛ, like the other visions, is reminiscent of Spenser's,
but without close verbal parallels.]

Nuptiall Hymnes: In Honour of the Marriage, hymn 4, sig. F 3ᵛ:
A thousand *Amorets* about doe play
(Borne of the Nymphes) these onely wound, they say,
The common people, *Venus* darling hee,
Aimes at the Gods, and awfull Maiestie. (DEM)

1613. John Taylor. *The Eighth Wonder of the World.*
[STC 23750. *Works*, rptd from ed. of 1630, Sp. Soc. Pub., 1868-9.]
Sig. A 3ᵛ (Sp. Soc. Pub., p. 224):
Then as thou lou'st the Fairy Queene thine Aunt,
Daine to vouchsafe this poore and triuiall graunt. (DFA)

1613. George Wither. *Abuses Stript, and Whipt. Or Satirical Essayes
. . . Diuided into two Bookes.*
[STC 25891-4. Rptd *Juvenilia*, Sp. Soc. Pub., 1871.]
Of Despaire (STC 25892-4: *Satyr 11*, sig. H 6; Sp. Soc. Pub. 1.119)
STC 25891: Chap. 14, p. 92 quoted:
No more of feare, for lo his impious bratt,
Looks now to be admitted; this is that

We call *despaire,* with ghastly looks he stands,
And poisons, ropes, or poinyards fills his handes,
Still ready to do hurt; one step no more,
Reaches from hence vnto damnations dore.

[Cf. *F. Q.* 1.9.21 ff. For other quotation from *Abuses Stript, and Whipt*
see below: 1622. George Wither.] (DEM)

1613.   Richard Zouche. *The Dove: or Passages of Cosmography.*
[STC 26130. Rptd Richard Walker, Oxford, 1839.]

To the Reader, sig. E 6ᵛ (Walker, p. 51):
And truely, they who will be pleas'd to credit our owne tongue, and age,
may finde our present, and later Poets, capable of that commendation,
which was giuen the antien[ts] among the Greekes: That if their writings were preserued, no part of Learning should wholy perish. *Spencer,*
hauing as well deliuered Morall, and Heroicall matter for vse and action,
as *Du Bartas* (now ours) Naturall and Diuine, for study and meditation.
(FIC)

1614.   William Browne. *The Shepheards Pipe.*
[STC 3917. *Poems,* ed. Gordon Goodwin, 1893; also 1894.]
[The language of *The Shepheards Pipe* constantly reflects Browne's indebtedness to *S. C.* The verse forms of the first, second, fifth, and sixth
eclogues may be compared with those of *Feb.* (also *May* and *Sept.*),
July (also *Aug.* 53-124), *Mar.,* and *Jan.* (also *Dec.*). Each of the
seven eclogues is prefaced with a verse argument similar to those introducing the cantos of *F. Q.* In the third *Eglogue* the speakers are named
Piers and *Thomalin;* in the fifth, *Willy* (= Browne) and *Cutty;* in the
seventh, *Palinode* and *Hobbinol.*] (FMP, WW)

Sigs. C 6ᵛ - C 7 (Goodwin 2.117-8):
    Well I wot, the man that first
    Sung this Lay, did quench his thirst
    Deeply as did euer one
    In the Muses *Helicon.*
    Many times he hath been seen
    With the Fairies on the Greene,
    And to them his Pipe did sound,
    Whilst they danced in a round. . . .
    Scholler vnto *Tityrus.*
    Tityrus, the brauest Swaine
    Euer liued on the plaine,
    Taught him how to feed his Lambes, . . .
    And with all the skill he had
    Did instruct this willing lad.

[Browne is referring to Occleve as being Chaucer's pupil. For Tityrus
as Chaucer note *S. C. June* 81 and Glosse; for the whole passage cf.
F. Q. 6.10.10-8.] (DEM)

1614. Thomas Campion. *The Description of a Maske: Presented* . . . *At the Mariage of* . . . *the Earle of Somerset: And the right noble the Lady Frances Howard.*
[STC 4539. *Works*, ed. Percival Vivian, Oxford, 1909.]
Sig. A 3 - A 3ᵛ (Vivian, p. 150):
> Great Honors Herrald *Fame* hauing Proclaym'd
> This Nuptiall feast, and with it all enflam'd
> From euery quarter of the earth three Knights
> (In Courtship seene, as well as Martiall fights)
> Assembled in the Continent, and there
> Decreed this night A solemne Seruice here.
> For which, by sixe and sixe embarqu'd they were
> In seuerall Keeles; their Sayles for *Britaine* bent.
> But (they that neuer fauour'd good intent)
> Deformed *Errour* that enchaunting fiend,
> And wing-tongu'd *Rumor* his infernall freind,
> With *Curiositie* and *Credulitie*,
> Both Sorceresses, all in hate agree
> Our purpose to divert.

Sig. A 4 (Vivian, p. 151):
Error [appears] first, in a skin coate scaled like a Serpent, and an antick habit painted with Snakes, a haire of curled Snakes, and a deformed visard.
(Cf. *F. Q.* 1.1.13 ff.] (DEM)

1614. John Davies of Hereford. *An Eclogue between yong Willy the singer of his natiue Pastorals, and old Wernocke his friend,* in William Browne's *The Shepheards Pipe.* [STC 3917.]
Sig. G 3:
> *Wernocke.*
> WILLY, why lig'st thou (man) so wo-be-gon?
> What? been thy rather Lamkins ill-apaid?
> Or, hath some drerie chance thy Pipe misdone?
> Or, hast thou any sheep-cure mis-assaid?
> Or, is some conteck 'twixt thy loue and thee?
> Or, else some loue-warke arsie-varsie tane?
> Or, fates lesse frolick than they wont to be?
> What gars my WILLY that he so doth wane?

[Cf. *S. C Apr.* 1-8.]
Sig. G 4 - G 4ᵛ:
> *Willie.*
> Ah *Wernocke, Wernocke,* so my sp'rits been steept
> In dulnesse, through these duller times missawes
> Of sik-like musicke (riming rudely cleept.)
> That yer I pipe well, must be better cause.
> Ah, who (with lauish draughts of *Aganip*)

Can swill their soule to frolick; so, their Muse,
Whan Courts and Camps, that erst the muse did clip,
Do now forlore her; nay, her most abuse?
Now, with their witlesse, causelesse surquedry
They been transpos'd fro what of yore they were. . . .
For thy tho Songsters are misween'd of all.
Mecœnas woont in blonket liueries
Yclad like chanters; but these miser times
Vncase hem quite. . . .
There nis thilke chiuisance they whilome had
For piping swoote; sith, with an Heydeguies
Pipt by *Tom-Piper*, or a Lorrel-lad,
(So be he clawes hem) they idolatrize.

[Cf. *S. C. Oct.* 55-78; throughout, the poem is reminiscent of the dialogue of Pierce and Cuddie.] (DEM)

1614. Thomas Freeman. *Rubbe, and A great Cast. Epigrams.* [STC
11370.]

[Part 2:] *Runne And a great Cast*, sig. I 3:
Epigram 64.
Of Spencers Faiery Queene.
Virgil from *Homer*, th' *Italian* from him,
Spenser from all, and all of these I weene,
Were borne when *Helicon* was full to th'brim,
Witnes *their* works, witnes our *Faiery Queene*:
That lasting monument of *Spensers* wit,
Was n'er come neare to, much lesse equal'd yet. (JM)

1614. E. Johnson. *Of his Friend Maister William Browne,* prefixed
to Browne's *The Shepheards Pipe.*
[STC 3917. *Poems of William Browne*, ed. Gordon Goodwin, 1893;
also 1894.]

Sig. A 3 (Goodwin 2.81-2):
A Poet's borne, not made: No wonder then
Though *Spencer, Sidney* (miracles of men,
Sole English Makers; whose eu'n names so hie
Expresse by implication Poesy)
Were long vnparaleled: For nature bold
In their creation, spent that precious mould,
That Nobly better earth, that purer spirit
Which Poets as their Birth-rights, claime t'inherite:
And in their great production, Prodigall;
Carelesse of futures well-nye spent her-all. (FIC)

1614. Ben Jonson. *Bartholomew Fayre,* in *The Workes of Benjamin
Jonson,* [1631-] 1640.
[STC 14754. *Ben Jonson,* ed. C. H. Herford and Percy Simpson,
Oxford, 1925-52.]

Act 5, sc. 6, p. 87 (sig. M 4; Herford and Simpson 6.138):
Ius. . . . Now thou *Esquire* of *Dames, Madams,* and twelue-penny *Ladies.*
[Cf. *F. Q.* 3.7.37 ff.] (JGM)

1614. Robert Marston. *Tam Martis quam Artis Nenia; or, The Soldier's Sorrow and Learninge's Losse,* MS, 1614.
[Rptd S. Egerton Brydges, *Restituta,* 1816.]

Brydges 4.345-6 quoted:
> O could his father's genius leaue the graue,
> And reassume the facultys wee haue,
> What surfett of content might hee display
> In viewing him, and in him see dead Gray,
> Long since inter'd, reuiu'd. For Arthur's sonn
> Holds Arthur's spiritt, thou his corps bee donn:
> And what deuinest Spenser erst foretolde,
> Finish'd in him, his eies should cleere beholde.
> Where faire discretion, mixt with dauntless heart,
> Sownds loud his prowess and proclaymes his art.
> Whose infant Muse, succor'd by thy faire wing,
> Had leaue to thriue, and thriuing learn'd to sing
> With voice propheticke in those ruder parts,
> Thyselfe sole patron both of arms and arts.

[Elegy upon the death of Thomas, Lord Grey de Wilton.] (FIC)

1614. Richard Niccols. *The Furies: with Vertues Encomium. or, The Image of Honour. In two Bookes of Epigrammes, Satyricall and Encomiasticke.* [STC 1852.]

Epig. 22, sig. C 2:
> In tunefull accents of a dolefull straine
> Old *Verlams* fall thus *Colin* did complaine:
> *Verlam* I was: what boots it what I was
> Sith now I am but weeds and wastfull grass?
> But liu'd he now to see our townes each day
> Made coats fo[r] sheep: of them he thus might say,
> Townes once we were: what boots it what we were
> Since nothing now but sheepes dung doth appeare?
> Here's neyther greene of wastfull weeds or grasse,
> Our wretched case is worse than *Verlams* was.

[In l. 6, misprint *fot* for *for.* Cf. *R. T.* 41.] (HER)

1614. John Norden. *The Labyrinth Of Mans Life. or Vertues Delight and Enuies opposite.* [STC 18611. Quoted C. L. Powell, *English Domestic Relations, 1487-1653,* Columbia Univ. Press, 1917.]

The Authors farewell to his Booke, sig. A 3ᵛ (Powell, p. 191):
> *Chawcer, Gowre,* the *bishop of dunkell,*
> In ages farre remote were eloquent:

Now *Sidney, Spencer,* others moe excell,
And are in latter times more excellent,
To antique *Lauriats* parallel.

But matters of great admiration
In Moderne *Poesies* are wordes estrang'd
Inuention of hid speculation,
The scope whereof hardly conceiu'd as it is rang'd
But by a *Comentation.*

Who readeth *Chaucer* as a *moderne man,*
Not looking back into the time he wrote,
Will hardly his ambiguous *phrases* scan,
Which in that time were vulgar, well I wote,
Yet we run back where he began.
And all our praised *Poems* art beset,
With *Chaucers* wordes and *Phrases* ancient:
Which these our *moderne ages* quite forget
Yet in their Poems, far more Eloquent,
Not yet from *Gowre* or *Chaucer* fett.

[Does the *Comentation* of the second stanza refer to E. K.'s glosses?]
(FIC)

1614. Thomas Porter. *Thomae Porteri . . . Epigrammata,* MS 436 of the
Earl of Leicester, Holkham Hall, Norfolk.
[Hist. MSS Comm., *Ninth Report*; quoted by Bentley 2.25.]
Report 2.362/1 quoted:
Latin poems dedicated to Sir John Heveningham. On the last page
is written " Per me Thomas Porterum ministrum de 'Hemnall 12 die
Martii' mensis 1614." There are epigrams on (amongst other persons)
Samuel Daniel, Ben Jonson, W. Shakespeare, Edm. Spenser, Sir J.
Harrington, Sir P. Sidney, Sir W. Wade, the Earl of Essex, Sir Hamond
Lestrange, literatissimo Comiti Hen. Howard Com. de Northampton,
Joshua Sylvester, Matthew Burt, Master of Eton School, a most excellent
poet, the Earl of Sussex, Lord Chancellor Egerton, John King, Bishop
of London; King James, Joseph Hall, Sir E. Cooke. (GEB)

1614. Daniel Tuvill. *The Dove and the Serpent In which is conteined
a large description of all such points and principles as tend either to
Conuersation, or Negotiation.*
[STC 24394-4ª.]
Chap. 15, *Of Sentences tending to the beautifying of the Stile,* p. 91
(sig. N 2):
[A sentence] is *Tropicall*: as here;
Now strike your sailes, yee iolly Mariners,   *Spencer, Fa:*
For we be come vnto a quiet rode,   *Qu: lib.* 1.
Where we must land some of our Passengers,   *Cant:* 12.
And light this weary Vessell of her lode.

[Cf. *F. Q.* 1.12.42.] (HH)

1614. Tristram White. *The Martyrdome of Saint George of Cappadocia: Titular Patron of England, and of the most Noble Order of the Garter.* [STC 25409.]

Sig. A 2 - A 2ᵛ:
The Poet in his *Faerie Queene*, playing vpon the Etymologie of this Name, doth also allude to *Tilth*, though after a vaine, but very wittie manner, *thus:

*Lib.1.Cant.   *Thence shee thee brought into this Faerie lond. . . .*
10.Stanz.60.

[Quotes all of st. 66, not 60]
Of S. *Georges* entitulation to the patronage of *England*, that Poet in the person of an holy propheticall Father, instructing the Champion of the crosse, after hee had grauely perswaded to the love of heauenly things, hath these Verses:

*In S. *Georges*
English birth
the Poet fol-
lowes the vul-   *For thou amongst those Saints whom thou dost see,*
gar errour, of   *Shalt be a Saint, and thine *owne Nations friend,*
purpose, to fit   *And* PATRON: *thou S.* George *shalt called be,*
his fabulous   *S.* George *of merry England, the signe of victorie.*
morall argu-
ment the
rather.
[*F. Q.* 1.10.61.6-9.] (FIC)

1614. George Wither. *A Satyre: Dedicated to his most Excellent Maiestie.* [STC 25916. Rptd in *Juvenilia*, Sp. Soc. Pub., 1871.]

Sig. F 2 - F 2ᵛ (Sp. Soc. Pub. 2.445-6):
     For though that many deeme my yeares vnripe,
     Yet I haue learn'd to tune an Oaten pipe,
     Whereon I'le try what musicke I can make me . . .

     There to my fellow Shepheards will I sing,
     Tuning my *Reed*, vnto some dancing *Spring*.
[Cf. *S. C. Apr.* 33; *June* 33 ff.] (DEM)

About 1615. William Camden. *Annales Rerum Anglicarum, et Hibernicarum, Regnante Elizabetha.* 2 tom.: 1615, 1627. [STC 4496.]

Tomus Alter, pp. 171-2:
[Camden will name some noteworthy men who died in the year 1598.]
Nec illi præter Burghleium modo dictum plures quam tres, & ex eruditissimorū quidē numero no minores quam fama feruntur.
     Primus erat Thomas Stapletonus, Sacrae Theologiæ D. . . . Alter, Richardus Cosinus Cantabrigiensis . . . Tertius, Edm. Spenserus, patria Londinensis, Cantabrigiensis etiam Academiæ alumnus, Musis adeo arri-

dentibus natus vt omnes Anglicos superioris æui Poëtas, ne Chaucero quidem conciue excepto, superaret. Sed peculiari Poetis fato semper cum paupertate conflictatus, etsi Grieio Hiberniæ proregi fuerit ab epistolis. Vix enim ibi secessum & scribendi otium nactus, cum à rebellibus è laribus eiectus & bonis spoliatus, in Angliam inops reuersus, statim expirauit, & Westmonasterij prope Chaucerum impensis Comitis Essexiæ inhumatus, Poëtis funus ducentibus, flebilibus carminibus & calamis in tumulum conjectis. (FIC)

[Thomas Browne's English translation of the *Annales* (from 1589) appeared in 1629 (STC 4498); and R. N.'s, of the complete work, in the next year (STC 4500). For Browne's translation of this extract see: 1629. William Camden.]

About 1615.　Joseph Hall. Poem, in Bodleian MS Wood D 32.

Fol. 260, p. 577:

> One fayre Par-royal hath our Iland bred
> Whereof one is aliue and 2 are dead
> Sidney yᵉ Prince of prose & sweet conceit
> Spenser of numbers & Heroick Ryme
> Iniurious Fate did both their liues defeate
> For war & want slew both before their time
> Now tho they dead lodge in a princely roome
> One wants a verse, yᵉ other wants a toome.
>
> Camden thou liuest alone of all yᵉ three
> For Roman stile & Englishe historye
> Englande made them thou makest England knowen
> So well art thou yᵉ prince of all yᵉ payre
> Sithence thou hast an Englande of thine owne
> Less welthy, but a fruitfull and more fayre
> Nor is thine Englande moated wᵗʰ yᵉ maine
> But doth our seas, & firmed lands contain. (HES)

1615.　R. A. *The Valiant Welshman.*
[STC 16. Ed. V. Kreb, *Münchener Beiträge* 23, 1902.]
[The Witch, her son, and the monster created by her to destroy Caradoc at instigation of Gloster (act 3, sc. 4, sigs. E 4 - Fᵛ) presumably suggested by *F. Q.* 3.7.20 ff.] (FIC)

1615.　Richard Brathwaite. *A Strappado for the Diuell.*
[STC 3588. Rptd J. W. Ebsworth, Boston (England), 1878.]
An Epigram called the Courtier, p. 126 (sig. I 7ᵛ):

> The Ornaments which he admires are these,
> To faune, to obserue times, to court, to please . . .
> To dance, to dice, to congie, to salute,
> To stamp, to stalke, to finger well a lute.
> To tremble at a Cannon when it shootes,
> To like, to dislike, and fill his head with doubts.

To be in passion, wind his carelesse armes,
To plie his Mistresse with delightfull charmes.
To be for all, yet ignorant of all,
To be disguisd, and strange fantasticall:
Briefly to be, what all his kind haue beene,
Seeme what they be not, be what least they seeme. . . .
Hauing my complete Courtier thus defin'd,
I haue no more that I can call to minde,
" Saue what is common, and is knowne to all
" *That Courtiers as the tide doe rise and fall.*

[The influence of *M. H. T.* is apparent throughout this epigram-char-acter; the passage above ends with the quotation of Spenser's lines 613-4.] (WW)

An Eglogue betweene Billie and Iockie called the Mushrome, pp. 129-35 (sigs. K - K 4):
[Satire influenced by *M. H. T.*; evidence is not specific.] (FIC)

Vpon a Poets Palfrey, lying in Lauander, for the discharge of his Prouender, p. 158 (sig. L 7ᵛ) [appearing between stanzas referring to Don Quixote's Rozinante and Tamberlaine's pampered Jades]:

> If I had liu'd when that proud fayry Queene,
> Boasted to run with swift wingd *Zephirus,*
> Tripping so nimbly on the leuie greene . . .
>   then my Horse had beene
>   A Horse of price. (DEM)

1615. Thomas Collins. *The Teares of Love: or Cupids Progresse.* [STC 5567.]

P. 47 (sig. G 4):

> *Sidney* and *Spencer,* be you aye renoun'd:
> No time hath pow'r your Pastorals to confound.
> *Drayton,* and all the rest that wrote of yore,
> Adorning time with your delicious store,
> Be euer honor'd, and (till th'end of time)
> On Fames peart tongue be praised for your Rimes.
> You worthy ones, oh, do not you disdaine
> My mournfull Muse, that in this humble vaine
> Dares for to sing, considering these are dayes,
> In which some Criticks will the best dispraise:
> But pardon me, should all be silent; then
> Who should praise Vertue, or check Vice in men? (FIC)

1615. William Drummond. Sonnet prefixed to Patrick Gordon's *His-torye of Penardo and Laissa,* Dort.
[STC 12067. *Poetical Works of William Drummond.* ed. L. E. Kastner, Edinburgh and London, 1913.]

Sig. *8ᵛ (Kastner 2.162):

Thy Syre no Pyick purse is of others witt
Thoise Iewellis be his oune which the adorne
And though thow after greatter ones be borne,
Thow mayst be bold euen midst the first to sitt
For whilst fair Iuliett or the farie quene
Doe liue with theirs thy beautie shall be seene. (DEM)

1615. Patrick Gordon. *The First booke of the famous Historye of Penardo and Laissa other ways callid the warres, of Love and Ambitione,* Dort.
[STC 12067. Discussed by E. A. Strathmann, " A Scotch Spenserian: Patrick Gordon," *Huntington Lib. Quar.* 1.427 ff.]

Chap. 1, sts. 34-7, sig. B 5^v (Strathmann, p. 432):
Her face was lyke the sky bothe cleire and fair
Her cheeks as whyt with vermeil red did show
Lyke roses in a bed of lillies rare
Whill they ambrosiall odours from them throw
Feiding the gaizers sense with double pleasure
Such force his beauties all-celestiall treasure.

In whoes bright eyes two lyuelie lamps did flame
That dairted beam's lyik lightning blasts of thunder
Cupid tho blind still ayming at the same
Thousands of shafts he sende but with great wounder
She breks his wantone dairts with awfull yre
And with dreid maiestie she quensh'd his fyre.

The *Graces* one her ey-lid's seem'd to sitt
Vnder the shadow of her bending browes
Her goldin treases couriouslye was knitt
With *Pelicans* of pearle, and siluer doues
These hair lyke goldin weir one eurye pairt,
Serud as a nett for the beholders hart.

Her yuorie forhead was a table fair
Wheir Loues triumphs were cunninglie ingrapht
All goodnes, honor, dignitie was their
In vertues treasure litle hade she left.
She was the mirrour of celestiall grace
That can not be outrune with tyms swift pace.
[Cf. *F. Q.* 2.3.22-5.]

Chap. 2, sts. 1-2, sig. B (Strathmann, p. 435):
Ther is nothing beneth the sky insearte
More moues my mynd to pitie & compassion
Then for to sie a true and vpright hearte
Wheir faith & trueth has bult hir only statiō
By *Fortuns* snar's and *Enuyes* craftie baits
Dispys'd, disdain'd digrac'd with falce deceats.

And whither it be kyndest pitie loe
Or dutie (which I ow all woman kynd)
I know not, but my hart doeth burst for woe
When harme vnto ther harmeles sexe I find
And my poore eyes Whil as I writting lay
With tears did seeme to washe the lyn's away.

[Cf. *F. Q.* 1.3.1.]

Chap. 10, sts. 1-4, sig. H iiij - H iiij^v (Strathmann, p. 434):

The mightie mynd that harbours hautie deid's
And is conceau'd with, child of glorious gaine
Can rest no wheir but to the birth proceids
Of glorious act's brought furth with endles paine
Such restles thought's *Penardo* did torment
Still longing whil the night were over'spent.

At last *Aurora* shews wheir she was layd
In aiged *Tithons* arm's and vp did spring
Blushing for shame that she so long had stayde
Her goldin loks for haist did lously hing
Her crimsone chariot made no longer stay
From criestal heaun's to chace dark night away.

As *Pilot* one the seas has stay'd his sight
Vpone the fixed *Pole* his course to guyde
Whill foggie smook and tempests cloudie night
The burnisht light of that bright lamp doeth hyde
Then to his compas has recourse, wheirby
He guyds his hollow veshell stedfastly.

[Cf. *F. Q.* 1.5.1; 1.11.51; 2.7.1. The quotations above are illustrative; throughout, the poem draws heavily in phrase and incident from *F. Q.*]
(EAS)

1615-23.   Philip Massinger. *The Copie of a Letter written upon occasion to the Earle of Pembroke Lo: Chamberlaine*, Trinity College, Dublin, MS G. 2.21.
[Transcribed A. H. Cruickshank, *Philip Massinger*, App. 17, Oxford, 1920.]

P. 556 (Cruickshank, p. 210, quoted):

Unimitable Spencer ne're had been
So famous for his matchlesse Fairie Queene
Had he not found a ~~Spencer~~ Sydney to preferr
His plaine way in his Shepheards Calendar.

[In the third line " Spencer " is crossed out.] (JGM)

1615.   Sir Thomas Overbury. *New and Choise Characters, of seuerall Authors: Together with that exquisite and vnmatcht Poem The Wife . . . With many other things added to this sixt Impression.*

[STC 18909. The Overburian Characters, ed. W. J. Paylor, Percy Rpts no. 13, Oxford, 1936.]

Sig. D 3 (Paylor, pp. 18, 145 n.):

A braggadochio Welchman.

Is the Oyster, that the Pearle is in, for a man may be pickt out of him. . . . He . . . courts Ladies with the story of their Chronicle. (JGM)

1615. Henry Peacham. *Prince Henrie revived. or A Poem Vpon the Birth, and in Honor of the Hopefull yong Prince Henrie Frederick, First Sonne and Heire apparant to . . . Frederick Count Palatine . . . And the . . . Princesse Elizabeth.* [STC 19514.]

[" Prefatory verses 'To the same most Excellent Princesse' following a prose dedicatory epistle to Princess Elizabeth. The poem consists of six stanzas, five of which are in the Spenserian stanza. Stanza five is imperfect, consisting of only eight lines. It is possible that an original fifth line has dropped out, but this cannot be proved from the context. The second stanza pays tribute to the late Queen Elizabeth. References to Astrea, 'the righteous Maid,' to the golden age, to Envie 'with canckred tongue,' and certain mannerisms suggest affinity with Spenser."] (FH)

1615. John Stephens. *Essayes and Characters. Ironicall, and Instrvctive. The second impression.* [STC 23250.]

Book 2, Character 14, A *wrangling* Welch Client, p. 351 (sig. Aa 2):

His body is so proportioned to his minde, and his clothes to his body, that you cannot finde a fitter modele of enuy in the most beautifull worke of *Spencer*: For as enuy pines away her carcasse when another thriues, so cannot she be cloathed better then (as a Welch Clyent is) with spoiles of innocence; Frise; or cotton.

[*The Errors of Men*, 1627, STC 10527 and 21502, appears to be another issue, with a new title page, of STC 23250. The allusion quoted above occurs in *The Errors* in exactly the same form on the same page (351).] (EAS)
[The passage quoted does not appear in *A Welch Client* of Stephens' *Satyrical Essayes, Characters and Other*, 1615, STC 23249.]

1615. Robert Tofte. Marginal note in Benedetto Varchi's *The Blazon of Iealousie . . . Translated into English, with special Notes vpon the same, by R. T. Gentleman.* [STC 24593.]

P. 5 (sig. C 3) Note to " Iealousie . . . is no other thing, then . . . *A certaine eager and earnest Desire to enioy the* ⁸*Beauty of one alone, by himselfe onely.*":

⁸Beautie (as a certaine graue and learned Gentleman, our Country-man writeth) is nothing else, but a iust proportion of the parts, with an apt correspondency in clours in these inferiour bodies: of which Subiect, the immortal *Muse*, of our euer memorable SPENSER, singeth thus: [quotes *F. Q.* 5.8.1.] (FIC)

1616. Robert Anton. *The Philosophers Satyrs.*
[STC 686. Extract in E. Egerton Brydges, *British Bibliographer*, 1810-14.]
The Philosophers Sixth Satyr of Mercurie, p. 64 (sig. L 4ᵛ; Brydges
1.532-3n; Bradley, p. 99):

> The *chollericke complexion* hot and drie,
> Writes with a *Seriants* hand most gripingly.
> The *Plegmaticke* in such a *waterie vaine*,
> As if some (*riming-Sculler*) got *his straine.*
> But the sound *melancholicke* mixt of *earth,*
> Plowes with his *wits*, and brings a sollid *birth.* . . .
> Mongst which most massiue *Mettals* I admire
> The most iudicious *Beaumont*, and his *fire*:
> The euer *Colum builder* of his *fame,*
> Sound searching-*Spencer* with his *Faierie-frame*:
> The labor'd *Muse* of *Iohnson.* . . .
> Greeke-thundring *Chapman* . . .
> And Morrall *Daniell* with his pleasing *phrase.* (FIC, JFB)

1616. William Browne. *Britannia's Pastorals. The Seconde Booke.*
[STC 3915. *Poems*, ed. Gordon Goodwin, 1893; also 1894.]
P. 1 (sig. B; Goodwin 1.187):

> The Argument.
> Marina's *freedome now I sing,*
> *And of her new endangering:*
> *Of* Famines *Caue, and then th'abuse*
> *Tow'rds buryed* Colyn *and his* Muse. (DEM)

P. 24 (sig. D 4ᵛ; Goodwin 1.221-2):

> Shew now faire *Muse* what afterward became
> Of great *Achilles Mother*; She whose name
> The *Mermaids* sing, and tell the weeping strand
> A brauer Lady neuer tript on land,
> Except the euer liuing *Fayerie Queene*,
> Whose vertues by her *Swaine* so written beene,
> That time shall call her high enchanced story
> In his rare song, *The Muses chiefest Glory.*

Pp. 26-7 (sigs. Eᵛ - E 2; Goodwin 1.225-6):

> And after reu'rence done, all being set
> Vpon their finny Coursers, round her throne,
> And shee prepar'd to cut the watry Zone
> Ingirting *Albion*; all their pipes were still,
> And *Colin Clout* began to tune his quill,
> With such deepe Art that euery one was giuen
> To thinke *Apollo* (newly slid from heau'n)
> Had tane a humane shape to win his loue,

Or with the *Westerne Swaines* for glory stroue.
He sung th'heroicke Knights of *Faiery* land
In lines so elegant, of such command,
*Orpheus   That had the *Thracian plaid but halfe so well
He had not left *Eurydice* in hell.
But e're he ended his melodious song
An host of *Angels* flew the clouds among,
And rapt this Swan from his attentiue mates,
To make him one of their associates
In heauens faire Quire: where now he sings the praise
Of him that is the *first and last of dayes.*
Diuinest *Spencer* heau'n-bred, happy Muse!
Would any power into my braine infuse
Thy worth, or all that *Poets* had before
I could not praise till thou deseru'st no more.
     A dampe of wonder and amazement strooke
Thetis attendants, many a heauy looke
Follow'd sweet *Spencer*, till the thickning ayre
Sights further passage stop'd. A passionate teare
Fell from each *Nymph*, no Shepheards cheeke was dry,
A doleful *Dirge,* and mournfull *Elegie*
Flew to the shore. When mighty *Nereus* Queene
(In memory of what was heard and seene)
Imploy'd a *Factor,* (fitted well with store
Of richest Iemmes, refined *Indian Ore*)
To raise, in honour of his worthy name
A *Piramis,* whose head (like winged *Fame*)
Should pierce the clouds, yea seeme the stars to kisse,
And *Mausolus* great toombe might shrowd in *his.*
Her will had beene performance, had not *Fate*
(That neuer knew how to commiserate)
Suborn'd curs'd *Auarice* to lye in waite
For that rich prey: (*Gold is a taking baite*)
Who closely lurking like a subtile Snake
Vnder the couert of a thorny brake,
Seiz'd on the *Factor* by faire *Thetis* sent,
And rob'd our *Colin* of his Monument.

P. 86 (sig. M 3ᵛ; (Goodwin 1.313):
     Wherein (as *Mantua* by her *Virgils* birth
     And *Thames* by him that sung her Nuptiall mirth)
     You may be knowne. (FIC)

1616. George Hancocke. *George Hancocke, Somersettensis, to his frende
J. L.,* verses prefixed to John Lane's *Spencers Squiers tale,* Bodleian MS
Douce 170.

Spurgeon 1.190 quoted:
     So ringe the peals of love, truith, iustice out,

as it, into their choire, all heerers chime . . .
as Chaucer, Lidgate, Sidney, Spencer dead,
yett, living*e* swanns, singe out what thow haste sedd? (FIC)

1616. Ben Jonson. *Epicoene, or the silent woman*, in *Workes of Beniamin Jonson*.
[STC 14751. *Ben Jonson*, ed. C. H. Herford and Percy Simpson, Oxford,
1925-52.]

Act 2, sc. 2, p. 541 (sig. Zz; Herford and Simpson 5.182):
Trv: . . . So shee may censure *poets*, and authors, and stiles, and compare 'hem, DANIEL with SPENSER, IONSON with the tother youth, and
so foorth. (FIC)

Act 5, sc. 2, p. 589 (sig. Ddd; Herford and Simpson 5.254):
HAV. . . . you need not feare to communicate any thing with her, for
shee is a FIDELIA.
[Cf. *F. Q.* 1.10.4-20.] (FMP)

1616. Ben Jonson. *The Golden Age Restored*, in *Workes of Beniamin
Jonson*.
[Cf. preceding entry.]

P. 1012 (sig. Qqqq 2ᵛ; Herford and Simpson 7.425; Spurgeon 1.190):
Pal. You farre-fam'd spirits of this happie Ile,
That, for your sacred songs haue gain'd the stile
Of PHOEBVS sons: whose notes they aire aspire
Of th'old *Ægyptian*, or the *Thracian* lyre,
That *Chaucer, Gower, Lidgate, Spencer* hight
Put on your better flames, and larger light,
To waite vpon the age that shall your names new nourish,
Since vertue prest shall grow, and buried arts shall flourish.
(CFES)

1616. John Lane. *Spencers Squiers tale which hath binn loste allmost
three hundred yeers, and sought by manie, is now brought to light by
J. L.*, Bodleian MS Douce 170.
[Ed. F. J. Furnivall, Chaucer Soc. Pub., ser. 2, nos. 23 (1888) and 26
(1890).]

[Lane's continuation of Chaucer's *Squieres Tale*. MS Ashmole 53 contains a revised version which is entitled: *Chaucers Piller beinge his
masterpeece, called the Squiers Tale, which hath binn given [up as] lost,
for all most thease three hundred yeares: but now found out, and brought
to light by Jone Lane*, 1630. In each version the prefatory material contains the entry "The Poet Spencer, concerning this invention of
Chaucers," followed by *F. Q.* 4.2.31-4 and verses 1-4 of stanza 35. Cf.
Furnivall, pp. 8-10.] (FIC, RH)

1616. Thomas Scot. *Philomythie or Philomythologie*. [STC 21869.]

To the Reader, sig. ◖◖ 3 :
> If *Spencer* now were liuing, to report
> His *Mother Hubberts* tale, there would be sport:
> To see him in a blanket tost, and mounted
> Vp to the Starrs, and yet no Starre accounted.
>
> The Ghost of *Virgils* Gnat would now sting so,
> That great Men durst not in the Citie goe
> For feare of petty-Chapmen, with a Seriant,
> And a slie Yeoman, noted in the Margeant. (FIC)

Sig. ◖◖ 6ᵛ:
> Wagers haue been laid
> That let an enemie fart, he would out-run
> An Irishman, for feare 't 'ad been a gun.
> Where learned *Spencer* maketh harnas't *Feare*
> Afraid the clashing of his armes to heare,
> That apprehension he from hence did gaine,
> Our *Monsieur* did, what *Spencer* did but faine. (HER)

1616.   Daniel Tuvill. *Asylum Veneris, or A Sanctuary for Ladies. Iustly Protecting Them, their virtues, and sufficiencies from the foule aspersions and forged imputations of traducing Spirits.* [STC 24393.]

[The dedication, *to . . . the Lady Alice Colville*, sig. A 4, mentions "That seruiceable Loue, wherewith I haue alwaies honoured your noble Familie the Spencers, & their Allies," but without evidence that Tuvill associates the poet with the Spencers.]

[Chap. 2, *Of their Beautie*, p. 16 (sig B 8ᵛ), quotes without reference F. Q. 5.8.1. Chap. 3, *Of their chastitie*, begins (p. 24, sig. C 4ᵛ) by quoting, without reference, F. Q. 3.5.52. *Ibid.*, p. 32 (sig. C 8ᵛ), quotes F. Q. 3.9.2, with "We should not let" for "But neuer let" in the first verse; and marginal note gives reference [*sic*]: "Sp. T Q. Cant. 9."]

Chap. 10, *Of their Courage and Valour*, pp. 136-7 (sigs. I 7ᵛ - I 8): Haue wee not in our owne Confines, that princely *Voadicia*, for in this point I wll not mention any later times, who with her warlike *Amozoneans* maintaind the reputation of her State, and kept it long on foot against the feirce invasion of the *Romanes*? And therefore as our English Poet saith. *Spencer F. Q. lib. 3. Can. 2.* [Quotes st. 1.]

The Epilogue, p. 147 (sig. K 5):
Prohibitions . . . are but prouokings. Besides they are to little purpose. [Quotes F. Q. 3.9.7.4-9.] (GWW)

1617.   *Apollo Christian: or Helicon Reformed.* [STC 708.]

Melos 7, pp. 29-30 (sigs. C 2 - C 2ᵛ):
> Come, let vs sing, that God may haue the glorie,
> Some noble act; and let mine auditorie

Bee of the best: my Lyra now is strung,
And English, which I sing in, is a tongue.
The victory Saint *Michael* did obtaine
Against the Dragon in the open plaine,
And moouing champaine of the triple aër,
As braue a subiect as high heauens are faire . . .
And whither Decasyllabons will you goe?
Great was the combat, great the ouerthrow
Which our Saint *George* did to this Dragon giue,
Whose fame in *Spensers* Red-crosse Knight doth liue:
Thither repair who loue descriptions life,
There hangs the table of the noble strife.
The spirit, and the sense of things our care is.
Wisdome is Queene, who fareth not with Faëries.

Melos 12, p. 35 (sig. C 5):

Greece had her *Sappho,* and her spruce old wagg,
    Anacreon;
Rome her *Catullus,* and the like some bragg,
    Of *Albion.*
And would to God that heerein to seeme lagg,
Were not a cause of absurd shame to many,
Court who court list, bee not wits Ape to any.

Without that noble *Sidney* heere I tax,
    Or *Spensers* pomp:
And gladly granting *Iohnson* nothing lacks
    Of *Phoebus* stamp.
For neuer wits were made of finer wax,
Then *England* hath to vaunt of in these times,
But them I tax whose reason's lost in rimes. (HH, FMP)

1617.   Lady Anne Clifford. *The Diary of Lady Anne Clifford.* [Ed. V. Sackville-West, 1923.]

P. 52:
Jan. 1617. *Rivers* used to read to me in Montaigne's Plays and *Moll Neville* in the Fairy Queen. (RH)

1617.   William Drummond. *Forth Feasting. A Panegyricke To The Kings Most Excellent Majestie,* Edinburgh.
[STC 7252. *Poetical Works,* ed. L. E. Kastner, Edinburgh and London, 1913.]

Sig. A 3 (Kastner 1.143):

And you my Nymphes, rise from your moyst Repaire,
Strow all your Springs and Grotts with Lillies faire:
Some swiftest-footted get her hence and pray
Our Floods and Lakes, come keepe this Holie-day;

What e're beneath *Albanias* Hills doe runne,
Which see the rising or the setting Sunne,
Which drinke sterne *Grampius* Mists, or *Ochells* Snows:
Stone-rowling *Taye, Tine* Tortoyse-like that flows,
The pearlie *Don,* the *Deas,* the fertile *Spay,*
Wild *Neuerne* which doth see our longest Day,
Nesse smoaking-Sulphure, *Leaue* with Mountaines crown'd,
Strange *Loumond* for his floting Isles renown'd:
The irish *Rian,* Ken, the siluer *Aire,*
The snakie *Dun,* the *Ore* with rushie Haire,
The Chrystall-streaming *Nid,* lowd-bellowing *Clyd,*
Tweed which no more our Kingdomes shall deuide:
Rancke-swelling *Annan, Lid* with curled Streames,
The *Eskes,* the *Solway* where they loose their Names,
To eu'rie one proclaime our Ioyes, and Feasts,
Our Triumphes; bid all come, and bee our Guests:
And as they meet in *Neptunes* azure Hall,
Bid Them bid *Sea-Gods* keepe this Festiuall.

[Cf. *F. Q.* 4.11.10 ff.] (FMP)

1617. Henry Fitzgeffery. *Satyres: And Satyricall Epigram's.* [STC 10945.]

Sig. A 7:

> Be there a Citty show: or sight at Court:
> Of Acts Heroicke: or of Princely sport:
> (which right to *write* of, or in Type to tell:
> Might taxe a *Daniels* or a *Spencers* quill.) (FIC)

[This quotation appears in the 1618 and 1620 eds. (STC 7567-8) of *Certain Elegies, done by Svndrie Excellent Wits. With Satyres and Epigrames,* sig. A 7 (p. 25 of the 1620 ed. as reprinted by E. V. Utterson, Beldornie Press, 1843).]

1617. John Lane. Preface to his revision of Lydgate's version of the *History of Guy of Warwick,* B. M. MS Harleian 5243, fol. 4. [Ed. John W. Hales and F. J. Furnivall, *Bishop Percy's Folio Manuscript. Ballads and Romances,* 1868.]

P. 522b, Hales and Furnivall quoted:
In which last, the heroical kind; Homer bestirred him selfe to lead the dawnce. Virgil blasoned the riches of his learninge in the same cloth of arras. the ancient English Poets (meaning allwaies the sownd ones) have delivered them of heroical birthes in this kind; which doe survive of theire deceased parentes glorie, all of them adducinge a complete knight, in the personations of twoe in number; and maie as lawfullie bee instanced in one: and all as well in twoe, as pleaseth the ingenious. For so Mr Edm: Spencer in his allegorical declaratorie, faerely declameth.

P. 524a-b, Hales and Furnivall quoted:

Thus Lidgat faierlie discharginge him selfe, leaveth it apparent, that the meere historien, is of all other infestus! the most malignant toward the Poet historical; whome hee vnderstandeth not: though him the Poet doth, at ann haier, is thearefore the most vnfitt to accuse, or censure the industrious, in the same case, that Prince Hector, and kinge Artur maie also bee doubted of, because they likewise have binn poeticalie historified by poetes prosequutinge ideal veritie, as the historien pretendeth positive truith.
[Apparently Lane has in mind the Letter to Raleigh.] (EAS)

1617. Fynes Moryson. *An Itinerary . . . Containing His Ten Yeeres Travell.* [STC 18205. *Fynes Moryson's Itinerary*, Glasgow, 1907-8.]

II. i. 4 (Glasgow ed. 2.173 quoted) [Land grants in Cork]:

In Cork by patent to Vane Beacher, to Henrie North, to Arthur Rawlins, to Arthur Hick, to Hugh Cuffe, to Sir Thomas Noris, to Warham Sent-leger, to S Thomas Stoyes, to Master Spencer, to Thomas Fleetwood, and Marmaduke Edmunds, and to their heires were granted – – – – – – 88037 Acres with rents five hundred twelve pound seven shillings sixe pence halfe penny sterling. (FIC)
[Moryson's continuation of the *Itinerary*, written 1617-20 (but unpublished until 1903 when it was edited by Charles Hughes under the title, *Shakespeare's Europe*) uses Spenser's *View of Ireland* as a source. Professor Rudolf B. Gottfried ("The Debt of Fynes Moryson to Spenser's *View*," *P. Q.*, 17 (1938). 297-307) has collected convincing evidence to show that Moryson borrowed from the *View* "with careless familiarity."]

About 1618. Edmund Bolton. *Hypercritica; or a Rule of Judgment for writing, or reading our History's,* Oxford, 1722.
[Rptd Joseph Haslewood, *Ancient Critical Essays upon English Poets and Poesy*, 1815.]

P. 235 (Haslewood 2.249; Spingarn 1.109):
In verse there are *Ed. Spencer's* Hymns. I cannot advise the allowance of other his Poems, as for practick *English*, no more than I can do *Jeff. Chaucer, Lydgate, Pierce Ploughman*, or *Laureat Skelton*.
[The *Hypercritica* was first published by Anthony Hall at the end of *Nicolai Triveti Annalium Continuatio*. In a note to *Addresse the Fourth* Haslewood (2.246-7) says: "The following extract from another copy of the work, in a less perfect state, preserved with Rawlinson's MSS Misc. 1, p. 13) is now given as being that portion of the *Hypercritica* which founds its principal claim to insertion in the present collection, and was probably the original outline of Addresse the fourth." To the next paragraph (which is similar to that in Section 1 of *Addresse the Fourth* of the *Hypercritica* as published) is appended a list of writers commended by the author for their English; among them is "Edmund Spencer (the most learned Poet of our Nation,) very litle for the vse of history."] (FIC)

1618. *Certain Elegies, done by Svndrie Excellent Wits.* See: 1617. Henry Fitzgeffrey.

1618. *A maske presented on Candlemas nighte at Coleoverton, by the earle of Essex, the lord Willobie, Sʳ Tho. Beaumont, Sir Walter Devereux, Mr. Christopher Denham, Mʳ Walter T. . . . , Mʳˢ Ann R. . . , Mʳˢ An Burnebye, Mʳˢ Susann Burnebye, Mʳˢ Elizabeth Beaumont, Mʳˢ Katherine Beaumont, Mʳˢ Susann Pilkingetun, to Sʳ William Semer and the ladie Francis Semer,* in South Kensington MS Dyce 28. [Performed Feb. 2, 1618]
[Rptd Rudolf Brotanek, *Die Englischen Maskenspiele,* in *Wiener Beiträge zur Englischen Philologie,* vol. 15, 1902.]

Fol. 7 (Brotanek, p. 333, quoted):

> His name Sʳ Arthur, & in field
> A crowned Lion on his sheild.
> Wisdom and Justice then, wᶜʰ call
> Sʳ Sapient & Artegall
> virtues twines, whose upright hands
> Atlass like uphold all lands,
> Keepe yᵉ world, it does not run
> To the old confusion.
> Next Sʳ Guion doth advance
> The golden Virtue Temperance.
> Last in Ranck, but not the least,
> One that joyned to the rest
> Does relish them and make them right,
> Calidore the curteous Knight.
> Musicke, straine a note devine;
> Appeare, yoᵘ virtues masculine. (FIC)

1619. A. D. B. *The Court of the Most Illvstrious and most Magnificent James, the first, King of Great-Britain, France, and Ireland: &c.* [STC 1022.]

Lines under the title:

> *Principibus placuisse viris, non vltima laus est.*
> To please the Best, best praise I doe it iudge;
> Let Grill be Grill: I passe not Enui's grudge.

[Cf. *F. Q.* 2.12.87.8.] (DEM)

1619. W. B. and E. P. *A Helpe to Discourse.* [STC 1547.]

Pp. 184-5 (1620 ed., STC 1548, quoted):
    Epitaph. 6. In Verolamium, a forgotten Citie, sometimes neare Saint Albons.
[Subject and title possibly suggested by *R. T.*] (FBW)

1619. Edward Coffin. *A Refvtation of M. Ioseph Hall . . . for the Marriage of Ecclesiasticall Persons.* [STC 5475.]

An Advertisement to the Reader, sigs. * 2ᵛ - * 3:
And euen now there is come to my hands a booke written by one
Collins in defence of Doctor *Andrews*. If *Spenser* the Poet were liuing,
he might very well make another *Collins Slowt* vpon his slowterly discourse, so loose & loathsome, as will weary the most patient Reader.
[The " booke written by one Collins " is apparently Samuel Collins'
Increpatio Andreæ Eudæmono-Johannis Jesuitæ, Cambridge, 1612 (STC
5563). In the Folger copy of the *Refutation* the leaves of the *Advertisement*, sigs. * - * 4, are bound with sigs. Aa - Aa 4 at the end of the
volume.] (FBW)

1619.   Michael Drayton. *Poems.*

[STC 7222. *Works*, ed. J. W. Hebel, Oxford, 1931-41.]

*The Legends of Robert Duke of Normandie. Matilda . . . Gaveston . . .
Cromwell*, To The Reader, p. 312 (Hebel 2.382):
    The word LEGEND, so called of the Latine Gerund, *Legendum*, and
signifying, by the Figure *Hexoche*, things specially worthy to be read,
was anciently vsed in an Ecclesiasticall sense, and restrained therein to
things written in Prose, touching the Liues of Saints. Master EDMUND
SPENSER was the very first among vs, who transferred the vse of the
word LEGEND, from Prose to Verse: nor that vnfortunately; the Argument of his Bookes being of a kind of sacred Nature, as comprehending
in them things as well Diuine as Humane. And surely, that excellent
Master, knowing the weight and vse of Words, did completely answer
the *Decorum* of a LEGEND, in the qualitie of his Matter, and meant
to giue it a kind of Consecration in the Title. To particularize the Lawes
of this Poeme, were to teach the making of a Poeme; a Worke for a
Volume, not an Epistle. But the principall is, that being a *Species* of an
Epick or Heroick Poeme, it eminently describeth the act or acts of
some one or other eminent Person; not with too much labour, compasse,
or extension, but roundly rather, and by way of Briefe, or *Compendium.*
(DEM)

Pastorals. Contayning Eglogves, To the Reader of his Pastorals, p. 432
(Hebel 2.518):
    Master EDMVND SPENSER had done enough for the immortalitie of his
Name, had he only giuen vs his *Shepheards Kalender*, a Master-piece
if any. The *Colin Clout* of SKOGGAN, vnder King HENRY the Seuenth, is
prettie: but BARKLEY's *Ship of Fooles* hath twentie wiser in it. SPENSER
is the prime *Pastoralist* of *England*. (FIC)

1619.   William Drummond. *Heads of a Conversation betwixt the Famous
Poet Ben Johnson, and William Drummond of Hawthornden, January,
1619*, in *Works*, 1711.

P. 226 (Munro 1.251):
    The Authors I have seen (saith he [Drummond]) on the subject of Love,
are the Earl of Surrey, Sir Thomas Wyat (whom, because of their

Antiquity, I will not match with our better Times) *Sidney, Daniel, Drayton* and *Spencer*. . . . As to that which *Spencer* calleth his *Amorelli* [*sic*], I am not of their Opinion, who think them his; for they are so childish, that it were not well to give them so honourable a Father. (JM, FIC)

1619.   Alexander Gill. *Logonomia Anglica.* [STC 11873. Rptd Otto L. Jiriczek in *Quellen und Forschungen,* vol. 90, 1903.]

[Gill's treatise is in Latin, but the various figures are illustrated by quotations in English, phonetically spelled, from Spenser. Gill's illustrations are reproduced by Herbert David Rix in his study of *Rhetoric in Spenser's Poetry,* Pennsylvania State College, 1940.] (FIC)

1619.   Ben Jonson. *Conversations with William Drummond of Hawthornden,* from MS of Sir Robert Sibbald, Advocates' Library, Edinburgh. [Ed. G. B. Harrison, Bodley Head Quartos, 1923.]

Fol. 25ᵛ (Harrison, p. 4):
     Spenser's stanzaes pleased him not, nor his matter, the meaning of which Allegorie he had delivered in papers to Sir Walter Raughlie.

Fol. 26ᵛ (Harrison, p. 7):
     He [Jonson] hath be heart some verses of Spensers Calender, about wyne, between Soline & percye.

Fols. 26ᵛ - 27 (Harrison, pp. 8-9):
     That the Irish having robd Spensers goods, and burnt his house and a little child new born, he and his wyfe escaped, and after, he died for lake of bread in King Street, and refused 20 pieces sent to him by my Lord of Essex, and said, He was sorrie he had no time to spend them. That in that paper S. W. Raughly had of the Allegories of his Fayrie Queen, by the Blating Beast the Puritans were understood, by the false Duessa the Q. of Scots. (FIC)

1619.   *Pasquils Palinodia, and His progresse to the Taverne.*
[STC 19454. Rptd J. P. Collier, *Illustrations of Old English Literature,* 1866.

Sig. A 3 (Collier, vol. I, second item):
          Loe! I the man whose Muse whilome did play
          A *horne-pipe* both to country and the citty.
[Parody on the opening lines of *F. Q.*] (FIC)

About 1620.   Thomas Jackson (d. 1640). *Works of Thomas Jackson,* 1673. [STC J90.]
Dominus Veniet. Of Christ's Session at the Right-Hand of God, vol. 3, p. 746 (Spurgeon 3.70):
     As our Posterity in a few years will hardly understand some passages in the *Fairy Queen,* or in *Mother Hubbards* or other Tales in Chaucer, better known at this day to old Courtiers than to young Students. (CFES)

About 1620.   Thomas Robinson. *The Life and Death of Mary Magdalene, Or, Her Life in Sin, and Death to Sin,* B. M. MS Harleian 6211, and Bodleian MS Rawlinson 41.
[Ed. H. O. Sommer, E. E. T. S., E. S. 78, 1899.]

[An allegorical poem imitative of Spenser in form and style. The Palace of Pleasure, folios 57-60, is modeled upon the Palace of Pride, *F. Q.* 1.4; the Bower of Bliss, 2.5.27 ff.; and Castle Joyeous, 3.1.31 ff. The description of the Cave of Melancholy, folios 69-70, echoes that of the Cave of Despair, *F. Q.* 1.9.35 ff. The following passages are illustrative.]

Fol. 60 (Sommer, p. 15):

> So soone this crewe dispers'd: some to their sporte,
> Some in greene arbours spent the *liue longe* day;
> Some staulked round about y⁰ amber court;
> Others to gaminge fell, and such like play, . . .
> And heere and there a drunken louer lay,
> Who, by his giddy, brain-sicke concubine,
> Disgorg'd y⁰ venoum baite of raginge wine.

[Cf. *F. Q.* 3.1.39, 57.]

Fol. 63 (Sommer, p. 21):

> *The* Damaske-roses heere *were brought* a bed,
> Iust opposite y⁰ Lilie of y⁰ Vale:
> The Rose, to see y⁰ Lilie white, wax'd red;
> To see y⁰ rose so red, y⁰ Lilie pale;
> While Zephyre fann'd the[m] with a gentler gale.
>   The woody Primrose and the pretty Paunce,
>   The Pinke, y⁰ Daffodill and Cheuisance,
> All in Perfumed sets, yʳ fragrant heads aduance.

[Cf. *S. C Apr.* 136-44.]

Fols. 69ᵛ - 70 (Sommer, p. 32):

> But loe, within, dull Melancholy sits,
> Proppinge with weary hand his heauy head,
> And lowringe on y⁰ ground in franticke fits,
> With pallid hue hee look'd, as hee were dead,
> Or Death himselfe: for many hee had sped
>   And sent vnto y⁰ graue: rough was his haire,
>   His hollow eyes, Hyæna-like did staire,
> Sparkelinge like fishes scales amid y⁰ cloudy aire.
>
> Long eares, blacke lippes, teeth yeallowe, meagr[e] face,
> Sharpe nose, thin cheekes, chin pendant, vaulted cragge,
> Lean ribbes, bare loynes, lanke belly, snale-like pace,
> Lame feet, dead hands, and all his garments sag[ge:]
> Heere hanges a patch, and ther a tatter'd ragge. (FIC)

About 1620.   Stephen Taylor. *A Whippe for Worldlings Or the Centre of Content,* n. d.

[STC 23818, which misdates the book 1586: Huntington Lib. copy 13657 is dated about 1640; F. B. Williams Jr., *TLS*, Sept. 12, 1935, p. 565, suggests 1620.]

Sig. B:
> If glorie vaine blent not his Reasons eyes.

[Cf. *F. Q.* 1.2.5.7.]

Sig. Bᵛ:
> Heart-burning hate. . . .
> Deceite, whose faire fil'd tongue is ever found
> To his hart discord, sharpe, yet no true sound.

[Cf. *F. Q.* 2.7.22.3 and 2.1.3.6.]

Sig. B 3ᵛ:
> But where vertue cleare
> Or any parts deserving shall appeare,
> Though clad in ragges, & coverd with the scorne
> Of fortunes butterflies, seeming forlorne,
> Them they will honour, and respect much more
> Than thousand Braggadocho's nam'd before.

[Cf. *F. Q.* 2.3. *et freq.*]

Sig. C:
> Yet let not Passions raging tirannie
> Robbe reason of her due regalitie.

[Cf. *F. Q.* 2.1.57.4-5.] (EAS)

1620. *Hæc-Vir: or The Womanish-Man: Being an Answere to a late Booke intituled Hic-Mulier.* [STC 12599.]

Sig. C 4:
We will bee henceforth like well-coupled Doues, full of industry, full of loue, which proceedes from God; whose vnexpressable nature none is able to deliuer in words, since it is like his dwelling, high and beyond reach of humane apprehension; according to the saying of the Poet, in these Verses following:

> Of loues perfection perfectly to speake,
> Or of his nature rightly to define,
> Indeed doth farre surpasse our reasons reach,
> And needs his Priest t'expresse his power diuine,
> For long before the world he was ybore,
> And bred aboue ith hy'st celestiall Spheare,
> For by his power the world was made of yore,
> And all that therein wondrous doth appeare.

[Cf. *Col.* 835-42; note changes in ll. 3 and 6.] (FH)

1620. *Hic Mvlier: or, The Man-Woman; Being a Medicine to cure the Coltish Disease of the Staggers in the Masculine-Femines of our Times.* [STC 13374.]

Sig. C 2 - C 2ᵛ:
 But when they thrust vertue out of doores, and giue a shamelesse
libertie to euery loose passion . . . they care not into what dangers they
plunge either their Fortunes or Reputations . . . according to the saying
of the Poet:

E. S. Such is the cruelty of women-kinde,
   When they haue shaken off the shamefac't band
   Of which wise nature did them strongly binde,
   T'obey the hests of mans well-ruling hand;
   That then all Rule and Reason they withstand
   To purchase a licentious libertie;
   But vertuous women wisely vnderstand,
   That they were borne to milde humilitie,
   Vnlesse the heauens them lift to lawfull soueraintie.

[Cf. *F. Q.* 5.5.25; note change in l. 8 from *base* to *milde.*] (FH)

1620. Henry Peacham. *Thalia's Banqvet: Furnished with an hundred
and odde dishes of newly deuised Epigrammes.* [STC 19515.]

[Epigram 81, sig. C 5, is entitled *Vpon Grantorto.*] (DEM)

1620. Francis Quarles. *A Feast for Wormes.*
[STC 20544. *Works,* ed. A. B. Grosart, 1880.]

Section 7, *Meditatio septima,* sig. G (Grosart 2.18a):
  Charissa hight, (the Almner of the Realme . . .) *Charity
  And gone her water that *Fidessa* made (FIC)   *Faith

1620. Joshua Sylvester (d. 1618). *Epithalamion* [for Martha Nicolson]
appended to *The Wood-mans Bear A Poeme By Io. Syluester.*
[STC 23583. *Complete Works,* ed. A. B. Grosart, Chertsey Worthies'
Library, 1880.]

Sig. C 5 - C 5ᵛ (Grosart 2.314):
  While I in honor of a happy choice,
  To cheerefull Layes tune my lamenting voice;
  Making the mountaines and the vallies ring,
  And all the young-men and the maidens sing,
  *All earthly ioyes, and all heauens blisse betide
  Our ioyfull Bridegroome, and his gentle Bride.*
   Thē, peace cōplaint, & pack thee hence proud sorrow,
  I must goe bid my merry Greeks *good morrow*:
  Good morrow Gallants: thus begins our game:
  What? fast asleep? fie sluggards, fie for shame,
  For shame shake off this humour from your eies.
  You haue ore-slept: 'tis more then time to rise.
   Behold, already in the ruddy East
  Bright *Erycina* with the beaming crest,
  Calles up *Aurora,* and shee rose-like blushing,

Frō aged *Tythons* cold armes, quickly rushing,
Opens the wide gates of the welcome day,
And with a becke summons the Sunne away,
Who quickly mounting on his glistering chaire,
Courseth his nimble Coursers through the aire.

[Cf. *Epith.* and Spenser's characteristic dawn descriptions, e. g., *F. Q.*
1.2.7; 1.4.16; *Gn.* 64-9.] (FIC)

1620.   John Taylor. *Praise of Hemp-seed.*
[STC 23788. *Works*, rptd from ed. of 1630, Sp. Soc. Pub., 1868-9.]
P. 26 (Sp. Soc. Pub., p. 556; Munro 1.278; Spurgeon 1.194; Bradley,
p. 120):

In Paper, many a Poet now suruiues
Or else their lines had perish'd with their liues.
Old *Chaucer, Gower,* and Sir *Thomas More,*
Sir *Philip Sidney* who the Lawrell wore,
Spencer, and *Shakespeare* did in Art excell. (JM)

About 1621.   John Fletcher. *The Wild-Goose Chase,* 1652.
[STC B1616. *Beaumont and Fletcher,* ed. A. Glover and A. R. Waller,
Cambridge, 1905-12.]

Act 4, sc. 3, p. 43 (Glover and Waller 4.371; Koeppel, p. 90):
Ros. . . . Live not 'mongst Men; thou art a Beast, a Monster;
A Blatant Beast.
[Cf. *F. Q.* 5.12.37-43 *et freq.*] (FMP)

1621.   Robert Aylett. *The Song of Songs, Which Was Salomons, Meta-
phrased in English Heroiks by way of Dialogue. With Certayne of the
Brides Ornaments, Viz. Poeticall Essays upon a Diuine Subiect* Books
1-2, By R. A.
[STC 2774. Rptd *Divine, And Moral Speculations in Metrical Numbers
Upon Various Subjects,* by Doctor R. Aylet . . . , 1654 (STC A4284),
quoted below.]

The Song of Songs
[Written in Spenserian stanzas.]
Chap. 7, p. 12, st. 4, l. 9 (sig. B 6ᵛ):
For thee (O my *belov'd*) against our *marriage day.*
[Cf. *Proth.,* l. 17, *et passim.*]

The Brides Ornaments
[Written in Spenserian stanzas.]
The Proeme, p. 15. st. 1 (sig. B 8):
Those sublime Wits that in high Court of Fame
Do seek [t]o rank themselves by Poesie,
Eternizing the glory of their name
By praise of Honour and of Chivalry,
To some great Princes Court their youth applys

Knights honourable actions to behold;
Chaste Ladies loves, and Nobles courtesie.
Of such have *Homer, Virgil, Spencer* told,
And have thereby their names in Fames fair Court enrold.
[Entire poem should be compared with *F. Q.* 1.10.]
Of Humility, p. 37, st. 19, ll. 5-9 (sig. D 3):
      Proud Briar that safe and secure did lie
Under stout *Oaks* most safe protecting arms,
      Supplanted him by treason cunningly,
      Then to Suns heat expos'd and Winters storms,
He's trod down by wild beasts, and eaten up of worms.
[Cf. *S. C. Feb.* 102 ff.]
Of Repentance p. 56, st. 50, ll. 1-2 (sig. E 4ᵛ):
      Ioy after *sorrow*, after labour rest,
And after *shipwrack* the desired Port.
[Cf. *F. Q.* 1.9.40.8.]
Of Hope, p. 78, st. 27, l. 5 (sig. F 7ᵛ):
On left hand stands *Despair* with bloudy knife.
[Cf. *F. Q.* 1.9.29.9.]
Of Truth, p. 103, st. 32 (sig. H 4):
      Divinest *Spencer,* thou didst shadow well
In *Legend* of true *Love* and *Chastity*:
      By *girdle* fair of fairest *Florimell,*
This sacred *Belt* of *Truth* and *Verity,*
      Which none on looser Ladies joints could tie,
Yet their fair Limbs that had liv'd true and chaste,
      It did adorn most rich and gloriously,
      And was most fitting for their slender waste,
But they *Ungirt unblest,* were that had been *unchaste.*
[Cf. *F. Q.* 4.5.6, *et passim.*]
Of Mercy
[With pp. 110-3, sts. 15-26 (sigs. H 7ᵛ - I) cf. *F. Q.* 1.10.34 ff. For
discussion of *The Song of Songs* and *The Brides Ornaments,* see F. M.
Padelford " Robert Aylett," *Hunt. Lib. Bul.* 10 (Oct. 1936). 1-48. Other
quotations from *The Brides Ornaments* appear below: 1625. Robert
Aylett.] (EAS, FMP)

1621. Robert Burton. *The Anatomy of Melancholy,* Oxford.
[STC 4159. Ed. (from text of 6th ed.) Floyd Dell and Paul Jordan-
Smith, New York, 1927.]
Part. 3. Sect. 1. Memb. 3. Sub. 1, pp. 519-20 (Dell and Jordan-Smith,
p. 636):
      Friendship is an holy name, and a sacred communion of

eLucianus   friends. eAs the Sunne is in the Firmament, so is
Toxari. amicitia   friendship in the world, a most diuine and heauenly
vt sol in mundo   band, take this away, and take all pleasure, all ioy,
comfort, happinesse and true content out of the world,
tis the greatest tye, and as the Poet decides [1624 ed.:
as our modern Maro decides it], is much to be pre-
ferred before the rest.

fSpencer Fairy   fHard is the doubt, and difficult to deeme,
Queene lib. 5 [4].   When all three kindes of loue together meet;
cant..9.staffe.1.2.   And doe dispart the heart with power extreme, to wit,
Whether shall waigh the ballance downe, to wit,
The deare affection vnto kindred sweet,
Or raging fire of loue to women kind,
Or zeale of friends combind by vertues meete.
But of them all the band of vertuous minde,
Me thinks the gentle heart should most assured bind.

[This and succeeding stanzas from Spenser are quoted inaccurately from
memory or deliberately altered.]

For naturall affection soone doth cease,
And quenched is with Cupids greater flame,
But faithful friendship doth them both suppresse,
And them with mastering discipline doth tame,
Through thoughts aspiring to eternall fame.
For as the Soule doth rule the earthly masse,
And all the seruice of the body frame
So loue of Soule doth loue of Body passe,
No lesse then perfect gold surmounts the meanest brasse.

Part. 3. Sect. 2. Memb. 2. Subs. 2, p. 555 (Dell and Jordan-Smith,
p. 675):

These other senses, hearing, touching, may much penetrate and affect, but none so much, none so forcible as
Sight. Forma Briseis medijs in armis mouit Achillem,
Achilles was touched in the midst of a battell. Iudith
captiuated that great captaine Holofernes, Dalilah Samp-
nDeleuit omnes   son, Rosamond nHenry the second, Roxalana, Solyman the
ex animo   Magnificent, &c. [1624 ed. adds: A fayre woman ouer-
mulieres.   comes fire and sword.]

oSpencer in   oNought vnder heauen so strongly doth allure,
his Fairie   The sense of man and all his mind possesse,
Queene.   As beauties louliest bait, that doth procure
Great warriers erst their rigor to suppresse,
And mighty hands forget their manlinesse,
Driuen with the power of an heart-burning eye,
And wrapt in flowres of a golden tresse,
That can with melting pleasure mollifie,
Their hardned hearts inur'd to cruelty.

[F. Q. 5.8.1.]

Part. 3. Sect. 2. Memb. 3, p. 621 (Dell and Jordan-Smith, pp. 759-60):
[Love is] the sole subiect almost of all Poetry, all our inuention tends
to it, all our songs, what euer those old *Anacrions, Greeke Epigramma-
tists,* Loue writers, *Anthony Diogenes* the most ancient, whose Epitome
we finde in *Phocins Bibliotheca, Longus Sophista* . . . *Ovid, Catullus,
Tibullus, &c.* Our new *Ariosto's, Boyardes,* autors of *Arcadia, Fairy Q.
&c.* haue written in this kinde, are but as so many Symptomes of Loue.
[For allusions to Spenser added in the 4th ed., see: 1632. Robert
Burton.] (DEM)

1621.   Peter Heylyn. *Microcosmus, or A Little Description of the Great
World.* [STC 13276.]
The Brittish Ilands, p. 250 (sig. Iiv; Spurgeon 1.194):
<table>
<tr><td></td><td>The chiefe in matter of Poesie haue beene 1 Gower. 2</td></tr>
<tr><td>*In the def.*</td><td>Chaucer, of whom Sir P. *Sidney* vsed to say, that hee mar-</td></tr>
<tr><td>*of Poesie.*</td><td>uelled how that man in those mystie times could see so</td></tr>
<tr><td></td><td>cleerely, and how wee in these cleere times go so stumblingly</td></tr>
<tr><td></td><td>after him. 3 Edm. Spencer. 4 Drayton, Daniel, &c. (FIC)</td></tr>
</table>

Egypt, p. 392 (sig. Ccc 4ᵛ):
Here also was the artificiall Towre built by *Ptolomie,* which being by
reason of magicke enchantments impregnable, was by him laid leuell to
the ground with a handfull of beanes; of which thus our Spencer discours-
ing of K. *Rience's* glasse [quotes *F. Q.* 3.2.20.] (JLL)
[For quotations from later editions of the *Microcosmus,* see below under
the dates 1625 and 1652.]

1621.   John Lane. *Tritons Trumphet to the several monethes husbanded
and moralized by John Lane,* B. M. MS Royal 17 B xv.
[Quoted incompletely and inexactly by J. P. Collier, *Works of Edmund
Spenser,* 1862.]

Junes Moral, p. 82:
> From Faerie Lande I come quoth Danus now
> Ha that quoth June mee never chanced to knowe
> Ne could or noold high poet Spencer tell
> (so farr as mote my witt his riddle spell)
> Though none that breatheth livving air doth knowe
> Wheare is that happie land of Faierie
> Wh' I so oft doe vaunt. Yet no wheare showe
> But vouch antiquities which nobodie maie knowe.

[Cf. *F. Q.* 2. proem 1.6-9.] (KK)
P. 102:
> in poet Spencers am[p]le times.

P. 175 (Collier l.cli):
> Whither quoth shee. to England Danus said.
> To England! quoth shee, no: that place me traied,
> so that none theare loves mee. Wᶜʰ I knowe by proof,

how they from my deere *Spencer* stood aloof
When verbale drones of virtuous merit scant,
suffered that gentile poet die of want:
One onlie knowinge generositie,
and findeinge hee woold starre for modestie,
him sent in greatest sicknes, crownes good score,
so *Robert Essex* did (honors decore).
Nathless of pininge griefe, and wantes decaid
hee may thank that stowt Earle, yet thus him said,
the medcine comes too late to the pacient!
he died. and so woold I, if thither went!
Alas! was that his ende, quoth Danus tho,
I pittie him, yet heareof this I kno,
hee ha[th] on him bestowd a funeral,
after the rites of Laureat coronel. . . .
ne had that cost vppon him binn imploid,
but for my lovinge frend Lodowick Lloyd. (FIC, RH)

P. 177:

Don Lidgat! Noble Sidney! Spencer diepe!
By her upcalled arose from deadlie sleepe.
[" The pupils of Cambridge are summoned to do their duty to their visitor
November."]

P. 179:

So forth she made through the satiric route
fr Lidgate Spencer Daniel quite lost out
Through soaringe on that high ideal spirit. (KK)

P. 185:

Spencer because hee had no picture green
Shee bidde goe live in his *Faerie Queene*. (RH)

1621.   William Mason. *A Handfvl of Essaies. Or Imperfect Offers.* [STC
17624.]

Of Envy, sigs. F 4ᵛ - F 5:
   When I behold Enuy (as the Poet describeth her) to haue a pale
face without blood, a leane body without moysture (like one of Pharaohs
leane kine) squint eyes, foule or blacke teeth, a heart ful of gall, a
tongue tipt with poison, neuer laughing but when others weepe; neuer
sleeping because she alwaies thinketh on mischiefe; I then abhorre this
Monster.
[Cf. *F. Q.* 1.4.30-2; 5.12.28-32.] (JLL)

1621.   William Slatyer. *The History of Great Britanie from the first
peopling of this Iland to this present Raigne of . . . K. James.* [STC
22634.]

Lauro, ac Laude Dignis S. P. D., sig. ❡❡ᵛ:

Yet faine I doe admire you, and
Ee'n beg this boone at *Phoebus* hand,
To rest where in th'*Elisian* plaines,
Faire fields, I may heare your sweete straines,
Our *Ennius, Chaucer,* with old *Line,*
Or *Orpheus,* where, *Sidney* deuine
Sits with *Musaeus; Iohnson, Spencer,*
Drayton, Daniel, English Horace, Homer,
Maro, Ouid. (HH)

1621. John Taylor. *Taylor's Motto: Et habeo, Et Careo, Et Curo.*
[STC 23800. *Works,* rptd from ed. of 1630, Sp. Soc. Pub., 1868-9.]
Sig. E 2 (Sp. Soc. Pub., p. 217):
Old *Chaucer, Sidney, Spencer, Daniel, Nash,*
I dipt my finger where they vs'd to wash.
As I haue read these Poets, I haue noted
Much good, which in my memory is quoted. (DEM)

About 1622. William Basse. *On Mr. Wm. Shakespeare. he dyed in Aprill
1616,* in B. M. MS Lansdowne 777.
[*Poetical Works,* ed. R. W. Bond, 1893.]
Fol. 67b (Munro 1.286; Spurgeon 1.196; Bond, p. 115, quoted):
Renowned Spencer lye a thought more nye
To learned Chaucer, and rare Beaumond lye
A little neerer Spenser, to make roome
For Shakespeare in your threefold, fowerfold Tombe. (JM)

1622. Robert Aylett. *Peace with her Foure Garders. Viz. Fiue Morall
Meditations: Concord, Chastitie, Constancie, Courtesie, Grauitie.* [STC
1002. Rptd *Divine, And Moral Speculations . . . By Dr. R. Aylet,* 1654
(STC A4284).]
Of Constancie, p. 31 (sig. C 3; 1654 ed., p. 392, sig. Bb 8v, st. 35):
Paul ready is not onely to be *bound,*
But at *Hierusalem* for *Christ to die,*
He *patient* is in all afflictions found,
Constant in losses, ioy, prosperity:
  Read his imprisonments brave history
  You there shall more diuine *Idea's* find,
  Then *Homer, Virgil, Spencer,* can supply
  Though they in loftiest straines the form have lin'd
Of a most braue, heroick, *constant,* noble mind. (DEM)

Of Courtesie, p. 38 (sig. C 6v; 1654 ed., p. 399, sig. C[c] 4, sts. 18-9):
No flower in Loues fairest garden growes,
That more delights the smell, affects the eye,
But as from roote bright hue and sweetnesse flowes,
So from the heart springs fairest *Courtesie,*

Else as the *Flower* fades, so dyes *Humanity*:
For as a gentle heart it selfe bewrayes,
By doing courteous deeds with free delight,
Eu'n so base dunghill minde it selfe displayes,
In malice, churlishnesse, reuenge and spight.

[Cf. *F. Q.* 6. proem. 4.1-2; 6.7.1.1-4.]

Ibid., p. 42 (sig C 8ᵛ; 1654 ed., p. 403, sig. C[c] 6, st. 64):
No vertue so adornes a valiant man,
Nor vertuous Dame, whom valiant men doe loue,
As courtesie, which best direct them can
To beare themselues in all as doth behoue:
Whether them God hath plast to rule aboue,
Or wait below, it them befits to know
Their Duties, that none iustly may reproue
Their rudenesse, in not giving what they ow:
Who gives each man his due, doth great discretion show.

[Cf. *F. Q.* 1.2.1.] (FMP)

1622.   Robert Aylett. *Susanna: or, The Arraignment of the Vniust Elders.*
[STC 1003. Rptd *Divine, And Moral Speculations . . . By Dr. R. Aylet,*
1654 (STC A4284).]
The first Book, p. 6 (sig. A 6ᵛ; 1654 ed., p. 6, sig. II 5ᵛ):
Yea *Collin Clout* doth breake his Pipe for shame,
To heare the heauenly ditties of his Dame. (RH)

1622.   Robert Aylett. *Thrifts Equipage: viz. Fiue Diuine and Morall Meditations, of 1. Frugalitie. 2. Prouidence. 3. Diligence. 4. Labour and
Care. 5. Death.*
[STC 1004. Rptd *Divine, And Moral Speculations . . . by Dr. R. Aylet,*
1654 (STC A4284).]

[Written in Spenserian stanzas]
Of Death, pp. 57-9 (sigs. D 7 - D 8; 1654 ed., pp. 474-5, sigs. Hhᵛ -
Hh 2):
Oh! there I shall inioy eternall rest,
And happy Peace, which here I craue and misse,
And wander further more and more distrest.
What if some little paine in passage is,
Which makes frail flesh to fear *Deaths* pallid kisse?
That paine's well borne, that endlesse ease doth gaine,
And from Sinnes cruell slavery dismisse.
Sleepe after *Toyle, fair-weather* after *raine,*
Peace after *Warre; ease* is most pleasing after *paine.*

We all are *wanderers* weary of our *way,*
And hasting to the *Graue* our *certaine home*:
This world's the *Flood* which doth our *passage* stay,
ᵃDeath   Tillᵃ *Charons boat* to weft us ouer, come.

Who Life did limit by eternall Doome,
And times for all things hath established,
Appoints each *Centinel* vnto his roome,
And so the termes of Life hath limited,
None may depart, but by their *Captaine* licensed.

Nefarious wretch! who with flagitious hand,
Dares violate the *Temple* God did raise,
A *Mirrour* here of all his Works to stand,
His *wisedome* to commend, and *goodnesse* praise:
　　He that appoints the *great worlds* nights & daies,
From her *Creation* to last *Reuolution,*
Determins all thy *small worlds* workes and wayes,
Who wilfully then hasts his dissolution,
Seekes to gain-say his Makers constant resolution.

The *longer life* I know the *greater sinne;*
The greater *sinne,* the greater *punishment,*
Yet if thou Souldier-like art entred in,
Thou must go on with stoutest hardiment.
　　And not depart without commandement.
Oh lie not downe, and thee to rest betake,
Ensuing ills of *liuing* to preuent,
Though life hath nought that can her loued make,
Yet giues it no iust Cause that thou should'st it forsake:

And yet, O sinfull man! do not desire,
To draw thy dayes forth to the last degree,
Vntill the measure of thy sinfull hire,
Be heaped vp with all impiety,
　　Against the day of Wrath and Ielousie,
Whilst thou this sinfull Body bearst about,
Laden with Sinnes, and foule Iniquity,
Their numbers more and more increase no doubt,
Most happy he whom *Death* the soonest helpeth out.

Despaire not yet, fraile, silly, fleshly wight,
Nor let *Distrust* amate thy manfull heart,
Nor *Satans* malicing dismay thy sprite,
Thous in thy *Sauiours merits* hast a part,
　　Oh why shouldst thou despaire, that certain art
Of Christ thy Sauiour? Lo! in him is *grace,*
From thee for euer to remoue Hels smart.
And that accurst *hand-writing* to deface,
No sinnes can be so great, but *Mercy* may haue place.

How then should any wretched wight be wonne,
To spoil the *Castle* of his *life* and *state?*
Is't not Gods doing whatsoeuer's don
In heau'n and earth? Did he not all create
　　To liue and die by his eternall *Fate?*

Who dares then striue with strong Necessity?
That constant holds the world in changing state,
All ought be willing here to liue or die:
Life, Death, ordained are by heau'nly *Destiny*.

[Cf. *F. Q.* 1.9.40-53, a passage adapted with only slight changes.] (EAS)

1622. William Browne. *To My Honor'd Friend M*ʳ. *Drayton*, prefixed
to *The Second Part* . . . *of Poly-olbion from the Eighteenth Song*.
[STC 7229. Rptd *Poems of William Browne*, ed. Gordon Goodwin,
1893; also 1894; *Works of Michael Drayton*, ed. J. W. Hebel, Oxford,
1931-41.]

Sig. A 3 (Goodwin 2.313; Hebel 4.393):

> *Englands* braue *Genius*, raise thy head; and see,
> We haue a *Muse* in this mortalitie
> Of Vertue yet suruiues; All met not Death,
> When wee intoomb'd our deare *Elizabeth*.
> Immortall *Sydney*, honoured *Colin Clout*,
> Presaging what wee feele, went timely out. (FIC)

1622. Patrick Hannay. *The Nightingale. Sheretine and Mariana. A
Happy Husband. Eligies on the death of Queene Anne. Songs and
Sonnets*.
[STC 12748. Ed. Hunterian Club, 1875.]

Sheretine and Mariana, Canto 2, p. 136 (sig. K 5; Hunterian, pp.
150-1):

> All-woe-begone, He wanders here and there,
> Lookes most for rest when furthest from resort,
> Submits himselfe solely to sad *Despaire*,
> With cheering-comfort He cannot comport:
> At last He came vnto an obscure shade,
> Where mirthlesse *Melancholy* mansion had.
>
> Low on the ground grew Isope, Wormewood, Rew,
> The mourning mounting trees ware Cypresse green,
> Whose twining tops so close together grew,
> They all seem'd as they but one Bow had beene;
> Couering a spacious Tombe where cursed *Care*
> Her selfe had sepulchriz'd with dire *Despaire*.
>
> No wanton Bird there warbled louing layes,
> There was no merry *Merle, Gold-Finch,* or *Thrush*;
> No other hopping Bird in higher sprayes,
> No mourning *Nightingale* in lower bush:
> The carcasse-crauing-*Rauen, Night-Crow, Owle,*
> In this darke groue their hatefull notes did howle.

[Cf. *F. Q.* 1.9.33 ff.] (FIC)

On the Queene, [p. 193] (sig. O 2; Hunterian, p. 207):

The *World's a* Sea *of errors,* all must passe,
Where shelues and sands the purling billow blindes:
Mens bodies are fraile *barks* of brittle *glasse,*
Which still are toss'd with aduerse *tides* & *windes,*
Reason's the *Pylot* that the course directs,
Which makes the vessell (as it's height) hold out,
Passions are partners, a still-iarring rout.
[Cf. *F. Q.* 2.12.]

Songs and Sonnets, song 8, p. 241 (sig. R 2; Hunterian, p. 255):

Next shadie groues where *Delia* hunteth oft,
And light-foot *Fairies* tripping still doe haunt:
There mirthfull *Muses* raise sweet notes aloft,
And wanton birds their chaste loues cheerely chant,
There *Syluian* with his Satyres doth remaine,
There Nymphs doe love and are belou'd againe. (DFA)

1622. Henry Peacham. *The Compleat Gentleman Fashioning him abso-lute in the most necessary & commendable Qualities concerning Minde or Bodie.* [STC 19502.]

Chap. 1. Of Nobilitie in Generall, p. 1 (sig. B 3):
The Lyon we say is King of Beasts, the Eagle chiefe
of Birds; The Whale and Whirle-poole among Fishes, Spenser in his
Jupiters Oake the *Forrests King.* (DEM) Fairy Queene.

Chap. 10. Of Poetrie, pp. 95-6 (sig. O 2 - O 2ᵛ):
In the time of our late Queene *Elizabeth,* which was truly a golden Age (for such a world of refined wits, and excellent spirits it produced, whose like are hardly to be hoped for, in any succeeding Age) aboue others, who honoured Poesie with their pennes and practise (to omit her Maiestie, who had a singular gift herein) were *Edward,* Earle of *Oxford,* the Lord *Buckhurst, Henry* Lord *Paget;* our *Phoenix,* the noble Sir *Philip Sidney,* M. *Edward Dyer,* M. *Edmund Spencer,* M. *Samuel Daniel,* with sundry others; whom (together with those admirable wits, yet liuing, and so well knowne) not out of Enuie, but to auoide tedious-nesse I ouerpasse. Thus much of Poetrie. (FIC)

1622. George Wither. *Abuses Stript, and Whipt: or Satyricall Essayes.* [STC 25898. Rptd *Juvenilia,* Sp. Soc. Pub., 1871.]

To the Reader, sig. B (Sp. Soc. Pub. 1.17; Bradley, p. 127):
Readers; I speake to you that haue vnderstanding; when these first fruits of my infant *Muses* shall come to your iudicious censures; doe not looke for *Spencers* or *Daniels* well-composed numbers; or the deepe conceits of now-flourishing *Iohnson.* (FIC)

1622. George Wither. *Faire-Virtue, The Mistresse of Phil'Arete. Written by Him-selfe.*
[STC 25903. Rptd *Juvenilia,* Sp. Soc. Pub., 1871.]

Sig. F 7ᵛ (Sp. Soc. Pub. 3.796):

> And, because I had no *Muse,*
> Shee her selfe daignd to infuse
> All the skill, by which I clime,
> To these praises in my *Ryme.*
> Which, if she had pleased to add,
> To that Art sweet *Drayton* had,
> Or that happy Swaine that shall
> Sing *Britanias Pastorall;*
> Or to theirs, whose *Verse* set forth
> *Rosalind,* and *Stella's* worth. (FIC)

Sig. M 7ᵛ (Sp. Soc. Pub. 3.892):

> Poore *Collin,* grieues that he was late disdaind.
> And *Cloris* doth for *Willy's* absence pine.
> Sad *Thirsis,* weeps, for his sicke *Phœbe* paind.
> But, all their sorrowes cannot equall mine. (DEM)

1623.   Ben Jonson. Verses prefixed to first folio edition of Shakespeare. [STC 22273.]

Sig. A 6 (Oxford reprod., p. 13; Munro 1.310; Spurgeon 1.198):

> My *Shakespeare,* rise; I will not lodge thee by
>   *Chaucer,* or *Spenser,* or bid *Beaumont* lye
> A little further, to make thee a roome. (JM)

1624.   Edmund Bolton. *Nero Caesar, or Monarchie Depraued.* [Joseph Hunter, *Chorus Vatum,* Harleian MS 24490.]

P. 161 (Hunter, p. 470):

The leuell, or plot of ground vpon which the army of BOADICIA, by the ROMANS forestallment, came to be embatteld, was certainly vpon a *plaine,* of at least *fiue,* or *sixe* miles ouer in breadth, between *two woods*; at either end of the open field one. . . . But whereabout in these parts of BRITAIN, that very place was, vnlesse it were vpon SALIS-BURIE *plaine,* where there is a *black-heath,* and scope enough, is not for mee to imagine. *Edmund Spencer,* who was in his time, the most learned poet of ENGLAND, layes it to haue beene further off; for he names *besides* SEVERN. But without praying in aide of his poems, I seeme to my selfe to haue made it vehementlie probable, that the field was hereabout, by hauing shewed that PAULLINVS was marcht hither-wards. (EAS)

1624.   Robert Burton. *The Anatomy of Melancholy . . . The second Edition.* Oxford. [STC 4160.]

One or two changes introduced by this edition are noted in the extracts from the first; see: 1621. Robert Burton.]

1624.   Thomas Scott. *Robert Earle of Essex His Ghost, Sent from Elizian:*

To the Nobility, Gentry, and Commvnaltie of England. Virtutum Comes
Invidia. Printed in Paradise. [STC 22084.]

P. 13 (sig. B 4) [The ghost of Essex speaks of his own times]:
  Oh the flourishing State of your Faery-Land, in the
dayes of yore, whiles I liued on earth, vnder the Gouernment of that glorious Queene, of eternall memory: The
Christian World did admire her Gouernment, and your
flourishing State; Nay, the very Mahumetane* Monarchs   *Speed, in Hist.
did admire and acknowledge the same.   pag.852.85[3].
[It is uncertain whether the author is identical with the Thomas Scot
who wrote Philomythie or Philomythologie. Cf. D. N. B.] (LBC)

About 1625. William Browne. Original Poems; ed. Sir Egerton Brydges,
   private press of Lee Priory, 1815.
   [Poems, ed. Gordon Goodwin, 1893; also 1894.]

   An Ode, p. 3 (Goodwin 2.213 quoted):
            And if my Muse to Spenser's glory come,
            No King shall own my verses for his tomb. (DEM)

   Caelia, Sonnet 1, p. 35 (Goodwin 2.217 quoted):
            Lo, I the man that whilom lov'd and lost,
            Not dreading loss, do sing again of love.
   [Cf. F. Q. 1 proem 1.1-2.] (FMP)

   Ibid., Sonnet 4, p. 37 (Goodwin 2.219 quoted):
            So sat the Muses on the banke of Thames,
            And pleas'd to sing our heavenly Spenser's wit. (DEM)

   Fido: An Epistle to Fidelia, p. 132 (Goodwin 2.237 quoted):
            I read (as fate had turn'd it to my hand)
            Among the famous lays of fairy land,
            Belphœbe's fond mistrust, whenas she met
            Her gentle squire with lovely Amoret.
   [Cf. F. Q. 4.7.35 ff.] (FIC)

   [Dates of composition of the pieces in Original Poems, most of which
   are printed from B. M. MS Lansdowne 777, range from 1614 to 1637;
   the poems quoted here appear to have been written in the 1620's, though
   the Caelia may be earlier.]

1625. Robert Aylett. The Brides Ornaments, Books 3 and 4.
   [Printed by William Stansby; no STC no.; Book 4 has separate t.-p.
   (sig. D 5). Rptd Divine, And Moral Speculations . . . by Dr. R. Aylet,
   1654 (STC A4284).]
   [Both books are written in Spenserian stanzas.]

   Book 3, Of Temperance, p. 22 (sig. B 5ᵛ; 1654 ed., p. 164, sig. M 2ᵛ,
   sts. 8-9):
            See in her Diet first Sobrietie,

In words and actions true *humiliation,*
Accompany'd with precious *Modesty,*
Last *Continence* from *Lust,* and angry *Passion;*
    The cause of all is *prudent Moderation;*
The aged *Palmer, Spencer, Guyons* trustie guide,
That stands aginst all *stubborne perturbation,*
By whose sage help, secure and safe we slide,
By whirl-pooles and deep gulfes which gape for vs so wide.

For all through this worlds boistrous Sea must passe,
Before we at our quiet Hav'n arriue,
The *Boate* our Body is, as brittle glasse,
Our *Steers-man; Temperance,* it right doth driue,
    Besides the Rocks, that threat this Boat to riue;
Are many *Gulphes* and *Whirl-pooles* of decay
Which wait th'*Affections* and the *Senses* fiue
By force and sweet Allurements to assay,
Some fall by rage and diet, some by lustfull play.

[Cf. *F. Q.* 2.12.1-33.] (DEM)
[With the stanza beginning " It is mans mind that maketh good or ill,"
p. 30 (sig. Cᵛ; 1654 ed. p. 171, sig. M 6, st. 38), cf. *F. Q.* 6.9.30.]
(FMP)

Ibid., Of Bounty, p. 31 (sig. C 2; 1654 ed., p. 173, sig. M 7, sts. 1-3)
beginning:

Now will I raise fair *Alma'*s statly tower
On *Temperance,* her strong and soundest frame;
And goodly deck *Dame Bounty'*s dainty bower,
Whereby all Princes gaine immortall fame.

[Cf. *F. Q.* 2.9.17 ff.] (DEM)

Book 4, Of Wisedom and Prudence, p. 62 (sig. Eᵛ; 1654 ed., p. 202,
sig. O 5ᵛ, st. 30):

Oh sonnes of men that you could but behold!
The wondrous *Beauty* of this heau'nly *Peare;*
But nought on earth her *Beauty* can vnfold
Her Glory in the Heau'ns doth shine most cleare;
    In all Gods workes her splendour doth appeare,
She first from Heau'n vouchsafed to descend
To liue in *Judah,* with her chosen deare:
But now her *Beames* more ample doe extend
To all the Nations of the earth she light doth lend.

[Cf. *H. H. B.* 182 ff.] (FMP)

Vrania, or the Heauenly Muse, p. 112 (sig. H 2ᵛ; 1654 ed., p. 92, sig.
R[r] 7ᵛ):

And as the obiect of our Loue exceeds,
So strikes the *Muse* on high or lower strings;

Who lowly late did maske in Shepheards weeds,
Spencer.   In high Heroiques of *Armes,* and *Honour* sings. (DEM)

1625-35.   William Browne. *Britannia's Pastorals* [Book 3]; ed. T. Crofton
Croker from orig. MS in Salisbury Cathedral, for Percy Soc., 1852.
[*Poems,* ed. Gordon Goodwin, 1893; also 1894.]
P. 26 (Goodwin 2.51):
> Full many a girle,
> Of the sweet faierye ligne, wrought in the loome
> That fitted those rich hangings cladd the roome.
> In them was wrought the love of their great king;
> His triumphs, dances, sports, and revelling:
> And learned *Spenser,* on a little hill,
> Curiously wroughte, laye, as he tun'de his quill. (FIC)

P. 40 (Goodwin 2.66):
> It was a shepheard that was borne by-west,
> And well of *Tityrus* had learnt to sing.

[Use of Spenser's name for Chaucer; *S. C. Feb.* 92, *June* 81-2, *Dec.* 4.]
(DEM)

Ibid. (Goodwin 2.67):
> The little *Cupid* lou'd him for his verse,
> Thoughe lowe and tuned to an oaten reed.

[Cf. *F. Q.* 1. proem 1.4.] (FMP)

1625.   Edward Hall. *An Ode,* inserted in a copy of the 1625 ed. of
William Browne's *Pastorals.*
[Printed in *Poems of William Browne,* ed. Gordon Goodwin, 1893; also
1894.]

Goodwin 2.5-6 quoted:
> What though Roger of the plains,
> Hobinoll and other swains,
> Join'd with Colin of the glen.
> Perigot and other men,
> Warble sweetly, thou when they
> Sung on Pan's last holiday,
> Won'st the chaplet which was made
> Hard by Tavy in a glade. (DEM)

1625.   Samuel Hardinge. *Upon the Occasion of Reading this Complete
Poem,* prefixed to a copy of the 1625 ed. of William Browne's *Pastorals.*
[Printed in *Poems of William Browne,* ed. Gordon Goodwin, 1893; also
1894.]

Goodwin 2.8 quoted:
> Or is your pipe ybroke,
> And 'twill not sound?

Go, go unto the oak
    By yonder mound:
Take Colin's pipe (ther't hangs) in hand. (DEM)

1625.   Peter Heylyn. *Microcosmus.* [STC 13277.]
    The Brittish Ilands, pp. 516-7 (sigs. Ii 5ᵛ - Ii 6):
    These and the othere riuers of principall note, take along with you,
according as I find them registred by that excellent Poet M. *Spencer* in
his *Canto* of the marriage of *Thames* and *Medwaie.* [Quotes *F. Q.* 4.11.
41 and 4.11.44.1-6.] (DEM)

Before 1626.   Edward Alleyn. *A Musical Dialogue.*
[Printed in The Alleyn Papers, ed. J. P. Collier, Shak. Soc. Pub., 1843.]

[The dialogue in thought is reminiscent of *S. C. March* 61 ff., and in
structure of *Aug.* 53 ff. The first of its eleven stanzas is given below from
Collier, p. 29:]
    Man.   It fell upon a sollem hollidaye,
    Boye. Woe me, that the day should be termed holey.
    Man.   When idell wittes had gotten leave to play,
    Boye. Such play ill please the mind that's wean'd from folly. (DEM)

Before 1626.   Sir John Davies. " The Translator to the Reader," before
the translation of Charles Sorel's *The Extravagant Shepherd,* 1654.

Fol. Aᵛ:
    The *Indecorum* of *Homers* gods, the fault in *Virgils* Chronology, *Tasso*
making *Christian* speak like *Heathens,* *Spencers* confusion, and different
choice of names, are things never to be forgiven (HH)

Part II: *1626-1700*

SPENSER ALLUSIONS

1626. Peter Heylyn? *A monethes Iorney into ffrance*, in B. M. MS Sloane 1442.

Fol. 92 (p. 183) [Commenting on one of two women met on a trip from Orleans to Paris]:

As yet I am vncertaine whether the poem of our Arch poet Spencer, intituled the Ruines of Times, was not purposelie intended on her. Sure I am it is very appliable in the title. (RH)

[The MS is dated 1626 in catalogue. Substantially the same passage is found in Peter Heylyn's *A Survey of the Estate of France*, 1656 (STC H1737), p. 160; Heylyn has the same phrasing in his *France Painted to the Life. By a Learned and Impartial Hand*, also 1656 (STC H1710, pp. 308-9, with the omission of the name of the poem, but with space left for it after the word "intituled."] (HH)

1626. Robert Salter. *Wonderfull Prophecies*.
[STC 21630. Cf. C. Bowie Millican, "A Friend of Spenser," *TLS*, Aug. 7, 1937, p. 576.]

Pp. 42-3 [The square brackets in the quotation are Salter's]:

And euen this very *Mysterie* is it, that a right learned and vertuous Gentleman hath so liuely decyphered, in his *Legend* of the *Patron of trew holinesse*, the *Knight of the Red-Crosse;* whereby, and by the rest of those his louely *Raptures*, hee hath iustly purchased the *Lawrel* of *honorable memory*, while the Pilgrimage of those his worthies are to indure.

Hee there hath brought forth our *Noble Saint George;* at the first onely in the state of a *Swayne*, before his *Glorious Queene* cast down on the ground [*Vncouth, vnkest*] *Vnacknowne, vncared off* as a dead trunke, and onely fit for the *fire* (as in our first *Period*).

But when hee had arrayed himselfe in the *Armor* of his Dying Lord, his presence is then become *Gracious*, and his Person promising great things [*as one for sad incounters fit*]. Which hee first *Passiuely* (as in our second *Period*), and after *Actiuely* (as in our third *Period*) doth so victoriously passe through and finish; that at the length (as in our fourth *Period*,) hee is become altogether *Impassible*, whether of *Assalts*

of the fraylety of *Nature* within, or *Affronts* of *Aduersaries* without, as being fully possessed of that Kingdome, against which there is none to stand vp.
[Salter prints this marginal note to the "right learned and vertuous Gentleman" in the first sentence of the quotation:
Mr. Edmund Spencer. The great contentment I sometimes enioyed by his Sweete society, suffereth not this to passe me, without Respectiue mention of so trew a friend.] (CBM)

1626. William Vaughan. *The Golden Fleece Diuided into three Parts.* [STC 24609.]

Pt. 3, chap. 13, p. 93 (sig. Mmm 3):
The next day after this *Sonnet* was sung in the Amphitheater at *Parnassus* by S. *Dauid, Spencer* the *Emperours Atturney* for the *English Poets,* being moued with the vnmannerly and rude interruptions of Scoggin and Skelton, informed against them as Libellers before the *Lady Pallas.* (EG)

1626. Anthony Wotton. *The Art of Logick. Gathered out of Aristotle . . . by Peter Ramus.* [STC 15248.]

[On pp. 48-9 quotes *F. Q.* 4.2.42.1-3; on p. 86, *F. Q.* 6.1.1.1-2; on pp. 106-7, *S. C. Feb.,* 102-14.] (FBW)

1627. William Camden. *Tomus Alter Annalium.* See: 1615. William Camden. *Annales.*

1627. Thomas Dempster (d. 1625). *Historia Ecclesiastica Gentis Scotorum,* Bologna.

Sig. O 2ᵛ:

Bundeuica. 199. . . . Haec Scotorum Regis filia, Britannorum, qui nunc sunt Angli, Regina, multa contra Romanos strenue gessit, Coloniamque deleuit. . . . [lists "works"] . . . Eam extulit eleganti, & suaui versu Edmundus Spenserus Poeta doctissimus in *Ruani temporis.*
[Possibly Dempster was influenced by *R. T.* 106-12 in using this name.] (EAS)

1627. Michael Drayton. *The Battaile of Agincourt . . . The Shepheards Sirena . . . Elegies vpon sundry occasions.* [STC 7190. *Works* ed. J. W. Hebel, Oxford, 1931-41.]

The Shepheards Sirena, p. 146 (Hebel 3.158):
Colin on his *Shalme* so cleare,
Many a high-pitcht Note that had,
And could make the Eechos nere
Shout as they were wexen mad.

Elegies vpon sundry occasions, pp. 205-6 (Hebel 3.228):
To my most dearely-loued friend

HENERY REYNOLDS Esquire, of *Poets and Poesie.*

. . . Graue morrall *Spencer* after these came on
Then whom I am perswaded there was none
Since the blind *Bard* his *Iliads* vp did make,
Fitter a taske like that to vndertake,
To set downe boldly, brauely to inuent,
In all high knowledge, surely excellent. (DEM)

1627. Phineas Fletcher. *The Locusts, or Apollyonists,* Cambridge. [STC 11081. *The Poetical Works of Giles Fletcher and Phineas Fletcher,* ed. F. S. Boas, Cambridge, 1908-9.]

[Phineas Fletcher was so constantly indebted to Spenser that quotation of parallel passages is precluded: we give the tabulation of apparent sources in Spenser noted by Dr. Abram Barnett Langdale in Appendix B of his critical study, *Phineas Fletcher Man of Letters, Science and Divinity,* Columbia Univ. Press, 1937. 1.15 indicates Canto I, stanza 15.]

1.15, p. 36 (Boas 1.132): F. Q. 1.9.21-2; 1.39, p. 44 (Boas 1.139): *Gn.* 344; 2.21-2, p. 52 (Boas 1.145-6): F. Q. 6.12.24; 2.29, p. 54 (Boas 1.148): F. Q. 1.8.47; 2.39, p. 58 (Boas 1.151): F. Q. 2.3.19; 3.9, p. 62 (Boas 1.154): M.H.T. 949 ff.; 3.18-20, p. 65 (Boas 1.157): R. T. 64-77; 3.27, p. 68 (Boas 1.159): F. Q. 1.4.4; 4.11, p. 76 (Boas 1.166): F. Q. 5.10.7-14; 5.14, p. 91 (Boas 1.178-9): F. Q. 4.11.34; 5.32, p. 97 (Boas 1.184): F. Q. 5.10.9. (ABL)

1627. John Speed. *England Wales Scotland and Ireland Described.* [STC 23036.]

The Generall of Great Britaine, chap. 1, sig. A 3ᵛ:
(5) . . . Whatsoever by the goodnesse of God, and industry of man it [Great Britain] is now, yet our English *Poet* hath truely described unto us the first face thereof, thus; [quotes F. Q. 2.10.5.1-4.]
(6) And albeit the Ocean doth at this present thrust it selfe between Dover and *Callis* . . . yet divers have stifly held, that once it was joyned by an arme of land to the Continent of *Gallia.* To which opinion *Spencer* farther alluding, thus closeth his Stanza. [Quotes F. Q. 2.10.5.5-9.] (DEM)

1627. John Stephens. *The Errors of Men.* See: 1615. John Stephens. *Essayes and Characters.*

1628. Phineas Fletcher. *Brittain's Ida. Written by that Renowned Poët, Edmond Spencer.*

[STC 11057. *The Poetical Works of Giles Fletcher and Phineas Fletcher,* ed. F. S. Boas, 1908-9.]

[See headnote to entry 1627. Phineas Fletcher. Apparent sources in Spenser are listed below; 1.1 indicates Canto 1, stanza 1.] 1.1, sig. B

(Boas 2.347): F. Q. 7.6.36; 2.1-6, sigs. B 3 - B 4ᵛ (Boas 2.349-50):
F. Q. 2.12.42; 2.4-5, sig. B 4 (Boas 2.350): F. Q. 2.12.70-1; 3.2, sig.
B 6 (Boas 2.352): F. Q. 2.6.32, 2.12.77; 3.11, sig. B 8 (Boas 2.354):
F. Q. 6.8.43; 3.13, sig. B 8ᵛ (Boas 2.355): 2.12.77; 4.1, sig. C (Boas
2.355): F. Q. 2.12.68. (ABL)

1628.　William Lisle. *To the Worthy Reader*, prefixed to his *Virgil's
Eclogues Translated into English.* [STC 24820.]

Sig. ¶ 5:

. . . onely Master *Spencer* long since translated the Gnat, (a little
fragment of *Virgils* excellence,) giving the world peradventure to conceive, that hee would at one time or other have gone through the rest
of this Poets works: and it is not improbable, that this very cause was
it, that made every man els very nice to meddle with any part of the
Building which hee had begun, for feare to come short with disgrace,
of the pattern which hee had set before them. (FIC)

After 1628.　　Sir Kenelm Digby. *Observations on the 22. Stanza of the
9th Canto of the 2d. Book of Spencers Faery Queene.* See: 1643. Sir
Kenelm Digby, below.

1629.　Samuel Austin. *Austins Vrania, or, the Heavenly Muse.*
[STC 971.]

Austins aduertisement, sig. A 6ᵛ:

. . . and so perchance
They might be drawne from hellish ignorance
Into the glorious light of Grace.

[Cf. *T. M.* 259: "Image of hellish horrour, Ignorance." An allusion
is unlikely.] (FMP)

1629.　William Camden. *Tomus Alter, & Idem: Or the Historie of the Life
and Reigne of that Famous Princesse, Elizabeth.*
[STC 4498, a tr. by Thomas Browne of Book 4 of the *Annales;* cf. 1615.
William Camden.]

Pp. 231-2.
[Browne omits sentence mentioning Burghley.] The first was *Thomas
Stapleton* Doctour of Diuinity. . . . The second was *Richard Cosin* a
Cambridge Man. . . . The Third was *Edmund Spencer,* a Londoner
borne, and a Scholler of *Cambridge,* who was borne to so great a fauour
of the Muses, that he surpassed all our Poets, euen *Chawcer* himselfe
his fellow Citizen. But labouring with the peculiar destiny of Poets,
pouerty; (although hee were Secretary to *Grey* Lord Deputy of *Ireland*)
for there hauing scarse time or leisure to write or pen any thing, he
was cast forth of doores by the Rebels, and robbed of his goods, and
sent ouer very poore into *England,* where presently after hee dyed; and
was buried at *Westminster* neere *Chawcer,* at the charges of the Earle of

Essex, all Poets carrying his body to Church, and casting their dolefull Verses, and Pens too into his graue. [FIC, WW]

1629.   Francis Quarles. *Argalus and Parthenia.*
[STC 20526. *Works*, ed. A. B. Grosart, 1880.]

Book 3, p. 113 (sig. P 4ᵛ; Grosart 3.271):
> The rafters of the holy *Temple* shooke,
> As if accursed *Archimagoes* booke
> (That cursed Legion) had beene newly read.
[Cf. *F. Q.* 1.1.36.]   (FIC)

Before 1630.   John Lane. *Alarvm to Poets*, 1648. [STC L337.]

Sigs. B 2ᵛ - B 3:
> *Averdi*, still as meeke, as calmest day,
> Then soaring for discovery, every way,
> Intended her rath Muses to bestow,
> On some more meet, discreet, and grave below:
> Far kenning from an high point, *Faiery Land,*
> Which sounds encrease, and nourishing, if scan'd,
> Did there reigne her Elixir, which so wrought,
> As that folke, rapt in love, this Dame most sought,
> Whose very light, them strake with admiration,
> To trace her steps from Nation, into Nation,
> And Land, to Land, where so she chose to alight,
> Although it be in *Fairy* Land she pight.

[" Having tried a number of lands which are mentioned by name, and having been frustrated by Delfisa, Averdi seeks England."]

Sig. B 3ᵛ:
> *Delfisaes* Phiol sheds cromatick matters, . . .
> Whereof, blood up to th'orses bridles rose,
> As Poets crying Ruddimane forshewes;
> How first ambitious jealousies did grow,
> 'Bout having, who should more then others know.
[Cf. *F. Q.* 2.3.2.8.]   (EAS)

Sig. B 4:
> Wherefore yee swans of *Thamesis*, what say?
> Which of you hath this anagogick key?
> For Chaucer, Lidgate, Sydney, Spencer, dead,
> Have left this riddle harder to be read.

[" Averdi, sent by Jove to enlighten man, but frustrated in her mission by Delfisa, is asked by the poets to tell them how Delfisa beguiled them. In reply, Averdi throws among them her ' anagogick key,' which is caught by one of the poets. Before throwing the key, Averdi had told the poets that he who could find the way back to her in accents numbered would be her true love. The lines quoted say that, since Chaucer, Lydgate,

Sidney, and Spenser are dead, it is hard to say who has Averdi's key. On the evidence of the prefatory matter in Lane's continuation of the *Squieres Tale* [see: 1616. John Lane, above], I would date the poem before 1630, possibly before 1616. George Hancocke's commendatory poem on Lane's continuation of the *Squires Tale* (ed. Furnivall, p. 8) copies line 3 of the quotation above. Less likely, Lane copies Hancocke."—EAS.] (HH, EAS)

1630. William Camden. *The Historie of the Most Renowned and Victorious Princesse Elizabeth, Late Queen of England.*

[STC 4500, a tr., by R. N., of the *Annales;* in Booke 4, pp. 134-5 (sigs. Rrr 3ᵛ - Rrr 4) appears the tr. of the passage quoted above under: 1615. William Camden. Cf. also: 1629. William Camden.] (FIC, WW)

1630. Michael Drayton. *The Muses Elizium, Lately discouered, by a new way over Parnassus.*

[STC 7210. *Works,* ed. J. W. Hebel, Oxford, 1931-41.]

[The nymph Florimel is mentioned in *the First Nimphall,* p. 9 (Hebel 3.256); in *the Third Nimphall,* p. 21 (Hebel 3.273) she is described as "A Nimph for Beauty of especiall name "; and in *the Seventh Nimphall,* p. 58 (Hebel 3.301) Lelipa addresses her as "The onely Mayden, whom we all admire For Beauty, Wit, and Chastity."] (DEM)

1630. George Hakewill. *An Apologie or Declaration of the Power and Providence of God in the Government of the World.*

[STC 12612, 2nd ed.; quotation does not appear in first, 1627, ed.]

Lib. 3, cap. 8, sect. 3, p. 254 [discussing Virgil's excellence]:
 Yet if I should match him with *Ariosto* or *Torquato Tasso* in *Italian, Bartas* in *French,* or *Spencer* in *English,* I thinke I should not much wrong him. Of the latter of which, our great *Antiquary* in the life of Q. *Elizabeth,* anno 1598, giues this testimonie; *Musis adeo arridentibus natus, vt omnes Anglicos superioris ævi poetas (ne Chaucero quidem conciue excepto) superaret,* hee was borne so farre in favour of the *Muses,* that hee excelled all the *English* Poets of former ages, not excepting *Cha[u]cer* himselfe his fellow citizen. (DEM)

1630. *Pathomachia: or The Battell of Affections. Shadowed by a Faigned Siedge of the Citie Pathopolis. Written some yeeres since, and now first published by a Friend of the deceased Avthor.* [STC 19462. The Epistle Dedicatorie is signed: F. Constable.]

Act 3, sc. 1, p. 23:
 Mal[ice]. We haue found much of that stuffe disperst here, and there in the late conflict betweene the Affections, which Despaire in our hearing did relate: as for other peeces Couetousnesse one of our con-

federates, at my request, stole them out of the common Wardrobe: If these be wanting, I know you could fetch *Proteus, Mestra, Circe,* or *Archimago* the Ieusite, some Taylor from France, or great Brittany to disguise vs in Attire.

Act 4, sc. 2, p. 34:

Iust[*ice*]. . . . Well, disrobe this *Duessa,* locke her vp fast least she breed any new troubles. (JGM)

About 1631. Nicholas Ferrar. *The Story Books of Little Gidding,* B. M. Add. MS 34657.
[Ed. E. Cruwys Sharland, 1899.]

Fols.108v - 109 (Sharland, p. 119):

. . . and now I see ye reason, Why not onely Virgill & Homere, but Ariosto & Spencer & all other bookes of Chevalry, bring in their fayned worthies so defectiue in Patience. Mans witt can well enough, I perceiue, fitt all other weapons of Christian Religion to serue the worlds turnes even against religion; but onely Patience, thats too weighty to bee put on a Counterfeit. Hee must bee a Christian in earnest & not in appearance, that weares this peice of Armour. Which because these famous Deuices want, however compleat in the height of all other vertues they bee made, I cannot allow them to passe for good Examples of vertue amongst Christians.

Fol. 110 v (Sharland, p. 121):

But painted Fire warmes not, howeuer liuely it bee sett forth, nor was euer any man made truely better by meanes of these Deuises.

Who dare truely say that either Temperance, Iustice, Charity or any other Vertue euer tooke rise or heate in his mind or desires from Orlando. Examples or any of ye rest of those Chimaeras? (HH)

1631. Phineas Fletcher. *Sicelides. A Piscatory,* Cambridge.
[STC 11083. *The Poetical Works of Giles Fletcher and Phineas Fletcher,* ed. F. S. Boas, Cambridge, 1908-9.]

[Cf. Act 2, *Chorus,* sigs. D 4v - E (Boas 1.212-3) with *F.Q.* 6.9.19-25; and ll. 19-25 of the *Chorus* with *S. C. Dec.* 83-4. Cf. Act 4, *Chorus,* sigs. I 2v - I 3 (Boas I.246-7) with *Gn.* 433-80.] (ABL)
[The verbal parallels are not close, and the ideas expressed are general.]

1631. Robert Henderson. *The Arraignement of the Whole Creature, At the Barre of Religion, Reason, and Experience.*
[STC 13069.]

P. 186 (sig. Bbv):

Our new *Ariostoes, Boyards,* Authors of *Arcadias* Faery Queene, describe severall beauties, in their *Poems, Love-Stories, Odes, Sonnets, Songs, Fancies, Emblemes, Empressaes, Devises.* (JM)

1631.   Peter Heylyn.   *The Historie of that most Famous Saint and Souldier of Christ Iesus St George of Cappadochia Asserted from the Fictions of the Middle Ages of the Church and opposition of the present.* [STC 13272.]

Syllabus Capitum, pt. 1, chap. 1., sig. B^v [repeated at head of chapter, p. 13 (sig. C 4)]:

   1. Three kindes of Imposture. *2.* The First Author of Scholasticall or fabulous Historie. *3.* The three ages of the Church in these later times. *4. Iacobus de Voragine,* the Author of the *Golden Legend*: his time and qualitie. *5.* His fiction of St. *George's* killing of the Dragon. *6.* The remainder of that legend continues out of *Ovid.* *7.* The fable of St. *George's* Birth in *England.* *8.* Poetically countenanced by *Edm Spencer.* *9.* The legend of the Dragon reiected by the learned Romanists. *10.* Defended by *Geo.* Wicelius. *11.* The Scene thereof removed from *Africke,* into *Asia.*

Pt. 1, chap. 1, pp. 22-3 (sigs. E 4^v - D):

   (8) To this Relation, of his being borne of *English* Parentage, our admir'd *Spencer,* although poëtically, doth seeme to give some countenance: where he brings in his *holy Hermite, heavenly Contemplation,* thus laying to St. *George,* the *Red-crosse Knight,* his Parentage and Country. [Quotes *F. Q.* 1.10.65-6.]

Ibid., chap. 3, p. 42 (sig. E 2^v):

   But now St. *George* must eyther poast away unto the Land of *Faeries;* and there remaine for ever, with other the Chimaeras of an idle head: or which is worse, be layed for all eternitie in the pit of horrour, with *Heretickes* and *Atheists.*

Ibid., Chap. 4, pp. 68-9 (sigs. F 4^v - G):

   Aeneas is not therefore to bee thought a Knight of *Faery Land,* the issue of an idle braine, a fiction or *Non ens;* because the Poëts hath expres'd him, with some additions more than reall. (DEM)

Pt. 2, chap. 1, p. 124 (sig. K 4^v):

   The name of GEORGE, not to proceed in it more Grammatically, is originally Greeke: deriv'd Ἀπὸ τοῦ Γεωργεῖν, which is; To till the Earth, or to play the Ploughman. It signifieth an Husband-man; and therefore Suidas doth expound the name by Γεωπόνος, a Tiller, or Labourer of the Earth. So *Camden,* in his *Remaines, George, gr. Husband-man,* the same with *Agricola*: and thereunto the famous *Spencer* thus alludeth in the wordes before recited; [quotes *F. Q.* 1.10.66.3-6.]   (FRJ)

Ibid., chap. 8, p. 296 (sig. X 2):

From henceforth therefore, we must not looke upon St. GEORGE, as a Saint in generall; but as conceived, (such was the superstition of those times) the speciall Patron of the *English*: of which, the *Pilgrim* in the *Poet,* thus prophecieth unto his *Red-crosse Knight,* as hee there calls him. [Quotes *F. Q.* 1.10.61.]   (DEM)

1631.   Edmund Howes. *Annales, or, A Generall Chronicle of England. Begun by Iohn Stow: Continued And Augmented with matters Forraigne and Domestique; Ancient and Moderne, vnto the end of this present yeere, 1631.* [STC 23340.]

Pp. 811-2 (sig. Yyy 3 - Yyy 3ᵛ; Munro 1.243; Bradley, p. 165):

Our moderne, and present excellent Poets which worthily flourish in their owne workes, and all of them in my owne knowledge liued together in this Queenes raigne, according to their Priorities as neere as I could, I haue orderly set down (viz) *George Gascoigne*, Esquire, *Thomas Churchyard* Esquire, Sir *Edward Dyer* Knight, *Edmond Spencer* Esquire, Sir *Phillip Sidney* Knight.

[Howes continues his list with the names of Harington, Challoner, Bacon, Davie[s], Lily, Chapman, Warner, Shakespeare, Daniel, Drayton, Marlowe, Jonson, Marston, Fraunce, Meres, Sylvester, Dekker, Webster, Heywood, Middleton, and Wither.] (JM)

1631.   Francis Lenton. *Characterismi: Or Lentons Leasures.* [STC 15463. Rptd Leota Snider Willis, *Francis Lenton, Queen's Poet*, Univ. Pa. Diss., 1931.]
[On sigs. Eᵛ - E 3ᵛ the character of *A Bragadotia* is described. Cf. Willis, pp. 76-7.] (FBW)

1631.   John Weever. *Ancient Funerall Monuments, within the Vnited Monarchie of Great Britaine.* [STC 25223.]

A Discourse of Funerall Monuments, chap. 1, p. 3.

Bellay in his ruines of Rome, translated by *Spenser*, makes this demonstration or shew of that citie, to the strange countrey man or traueller:
[Quotes *R. R.* 29-42.]

Ibid., p. 4:

[Of the ruin of ancient buildings] you may reade in learned *Camden*: onely thus much out of famous *Spenser* personating the Genius of Verlame, or Verulam, sometimes a citie neare to S. Albons.
[Quotes *R. T.* 36-42.]

Ibid., p. 5:

But I will conclude this Chapter with these two stanzaes following taken out of *Spensers* poeme aforesaid, speaking of the vanity of such Princes who (*Absolon* like) thinke to gaine a perpetuitie after death, by erecting of pillars, and such like monuments, to keepe their names in remembrance: when as it is onely the Muses works which giue vnto man immortality.
[Quotes *R. T.* 407-13, 400-6, sts. in reverse order.]
[Chap. 8, p. 39, quotes *R. T.* 4-7, with marginal note: *Spns.* Ruines of Time.] (FBW)

Ancient Funerall Monuments within the Diocese of London, p. 491 [on Chaucer]:
    Spenser in his Fairie Queene calleth his writings, The works of heauenly wit. Concluding his commendation in this manner
        Dan Chaucer, Well of English, vndefiled,
        On Fames eternall beadrole worthy to be filed.
[Weever is following Speght. Cf. 1598. Thomas Speght.] (DFA)

About 1632.   Robert Lownes. *A Note-book by Robert Lownes and Francis Clark,* in B. M. Harleian MS 1749.

["In item 5, p. 570, Lownes observes that his 'four chief poets are Chaucer, Spenser, Beaumont, Shakespeare, but he giveth perference to the last.'"] (RW)

1632.   Robert Burton. *The Anatomy of Melancholy . . . The fourth Edition, corrected and augmented by the Author.* Oxford. [STC 4162. Ed. (from text of 6th ed.) Floyd Dell and Paul Jordan-Smith, New York, 1927.]
    Part.3.   Sect.2.   Memb.3.   Subsect.1, p. 508 (Dell and Jordan-Smith, p. 722):
                    As drops from a Still,
        — — —*vt occluso stillat ab igne liquor,*
            doth *Cupids* fire provoke teares from a true Louers eyes,
* Fairy Queene   * *The mighty Mars did oft for Venus shreeke,*
l. 3. cant. 11   *Priuily moistening his horrid cheeke*
                    With womanish teares, . . .
                                        with many
            such like passions.
    [Cf. *F. Q.* 3.11.44.]

    Ibid., p. 525 (Dell and Jordan-Smith, p. 739):
    Diana was not to be compar'd to her [any lover's mistress], nor *Iuno,* nor *Minerua,* nor any Goddesse. *Thetis* feet were as bright as siluer, the ancles of *Hebe* clearer then Cristall, the armes of *Aurora* as ruddy as the Rose, *Iuno's* brests as white as snowe, *Minerua* wise, *Venus* faire; but what of this? Shee is all in all,
†*Angerianus*   — — — — —†*Cælia ridens*
            Est Venus, incedens Iuno, Minerua loquens
†*Fayry Queene Fairest of faire, that fairenesse doth excell.*
cant. 2. lib. 4.
    [Cf. *F. Q.* 4.2.23.4.]

    Ibid., p. 532 (Dell and Jordan-Smith, pp. 746-7):
    Our Knights errant, and the Sr *Lancelots* of these daies, I hope will adventure as much for ladies favours, as the *Squire of Dames, Knight of the Sunne,* Sr *Bevis of Southampton,* or that renowned peire,

ᵏ*Ariost. lib.* ᵏ*Orlando, who long time had loued deare*
1. Cant.1.   *Angelica the fayre, and for her sake*
staff. 5.   *About the world, in nations farre and neare,*
            Did high attempts performe and vndertake,

    he is a very dastard, a Coward, a blocke and a beast, that will
not doe as much, but they will sure, they will; For it is an
ordinary thing for these enamorato's of our times to say and doe
more, . . . to make his corrival doe as much. Tis frequent with
them to challenge them the field for their lady and mistris sake,
to runne a tilt,

†*Fayry Queene* †*That either beares (so furiously they meete)*
cant. 1. lib.4. *The other downe vnder the horses feet.*
& cant.3.
lib.4.

    And then up and to it againe,
   And with their axes both so sorely power,
   That neither plate nor maile sustaind the stour,
   But rivelde wearke like rotten wood a sunder
   And fire did flash like lightning after thunder.
[*F. Q.* 4.1.41.7-8 and 4.3.15.3-8, but quoted inaccurately from memory
or deliberately altered.]

Ibid., p. 537 (Dell and Jordan-Smith, pp. 752-3):
There is no man so pusillanimous, so very dastard, whom loue would
not incense, make of a divine temper, and an heroicall spirit. As hee
said in like case, *Tota ruat cœli moles non terreor, &c.* Nothing can
terrifie, nothing can dismay them, But as Sr. *Blandamor* and *Paridell,*
those two braue Fayrye K[n]ights, fought for the loue of faire *Florimel* in
presence,

   *And drawing both their swords with rage anew,
*Fayrie Qu. *Like two mad Mastiues each on other flew,*
lib.4.Cant.2. *And shields did share, and males did rash, and*
          [*helmes did hew:*
   So furiously each other did assaile,
   As if their soules at once they would haue rent,
   Out of their brests, that streames of blood did rayle
   Adowne, as if their springs of life were spent,
   That all the ground with purple blood was sprent,
   And all their armour stain'd with bloody gore,
   Yet scarcely once to breath would they relent.
   So mortall was their mallice and so sore,
   That both resolued (then yeeld) to dye before.

†[Plato]   . . . . And for that cause †he would haue women follow the
Lib.5. de   Camp, to be spectators and encouragers of noble actions: vpon
legibus.

*Spencers such an occasion; the *Squire of Dames* himselfe, S. *Lancelot,*
Fairie   or Sir *Tristram,* Cæsar, or *Alexander* shall not be more resolute,
Queene   or goe beyond them.
5.book.
cant.8.

[Cf. *F. Q.* 4.2.17-8, but note Burton's alterations. For other allusions to Spenser in the *Anatomy of Melancholy* see: 1621. Robert Burton.] (DEM)

1632. Philip Massinger. *The City Madam, A Comedie,* 1658.
[STC M1046. The Plays of Philip Massinger, ed. W. Gifford, 1813 (1st. ed., 1805); ed. Rudolf Kirk, Princeton Univ. Press, 1934.]

Act 2, sc. 1, p. 29 (Gifford 4.45; Kirk, p. 97):

> Plenty. . . . I have read of a house of pride, and now I
> have found one:
> A whirle winde overturn it.

[Cf. *F. Q.* 1.4.] (EK)

1632. Henry Reynolds. *Mythomystes Wherein a Short Survey Is Taken of The Nature And Value of True Poësy.* [STC 20939.]

P. 8 (Spingarn 1.147):
I must approue the learned *Spencer,* in the rest of his Poëms, no lesse then his *Fairy Queene,* an exact body of the Ethicke doctrine: though some good iudgments haue wisht (and perhaps not without cause) that he had therein beene a little freer of his fiction, and not so close riuetted to his Morall. (FIC)

About 1633. Robert Jegon. *Spencero Posthumo,* verses accompanying Ralph Knevett's *A Supplement to the Faery Queene,* Cambridge Univ. Library MS Ee. 3.53.

[Quoted C. Bowie Millican, " Ralph Knevett, Author of the *Supplement* to Spenser's *Faerie Queene,*" RES 14 (1938), 45.]

Verso of the sixth unnumbered folio:

> Perficere Herculeos pergos (Spencere) labores;
>   Heu finem cæptis invida fata negant,
> At te Pierides prohibent periisse sorores;
>   Vela dabit famæ Posthumus tuæ:
> Et veluti Phariâ Volucris nutritus in orâ,
>   Gaudet axem proprio restituisse rogo:
> Haud aliter nostrum lætantur sæcula Vatem,
>   Spencerum calamo viuificesse suo.
> Dignam te, Musisque refers (rediuiue) poesin,
>   Nec minor est virtus, fama perennis erit.
>   Rob: Iegon
>   Armiger.

[" You strive, O Spencer, to complete Herculean labours; alas, fates hostile to things begun deny the completion, but the Pierian sisters prevent you from perishing; behold, Posthumous will set sail to your fame: and just as the bird nourished on the Pharian shore rejoices to have restored the heavens by his own funeral pile, even so do the ages exult that our poet by his own pen has brought Spencer to life. You are writing poetry, O Renewed One, worthy of yourself and of the Muses: nor is your courage less; your fame will be everlasting." Tr. by Millican, p. 45, n. 2] (CBM)

About 1633. Ralph Knevett. *A Supplement of The Faery Queene in three Bookes. Wherein are allegorically described Affaires both military and ciuill of these times,* Cambridge Univ. Library MS Ee. 3.53.

Fols. vii - ix:

The end of writeing Bookes, should be rather to informe the vnderstanding, then please the fancy: I haue knowne many great witts, as ambitious as Ixion, committ adultery with the clouds, and begett Monsters, either as deformed, as that absurd picture which Horace speaketh of in his Booke de Arte Poet. or like the Thebane Sphinx, vttering vnnecessary ænigmaes. Such volumes, or (like the Ghost of Euridice) vanish as soone as they are view'd, or stand as trophyes, of their Authours vanityes to posterity: But if the sayeing of the Poet stands for an infallible truth:
>Omne tulit punctum, qui miscuit vtile dulci

Then our learned Spencer through whose whole Booke, a Grace seemes to walke arme in arme with a Muse, did merit best an honorarye garlande, from that Tree which Petrarch calleth
>Arbor vittoriosa, triumphale,
>Honor d'Imperadori, e di Poeti.

The worke being such
>Quod nec Cecropia damnent Pandionis arces.

Homer the fountaine of arts, yea from whom graue Philosophy deriues her pedigree, did first deuise that kind of heroicke poesy, which is of force, not onely to temper the affections, but also to rectifye the will, and direct the vnderstanding. Wee reade of Agememnon, that hee beinge ingaged in the Troiane expedition, left a Doricke Musicion to attend vpon his Wife Clytemnestra, who with his graue spondaicke numbers, maintained in her such a coniugall chastity, that Aegisthus the Adulterer, could no way tempt her to lightnes, vntill he had cruelly destroyed this harmonious Guardian of her vertue. Euen so doth diuine Poesye, excite in the ingenious, such an ardent affection of goodnes, and detestation of vice, that precepts taken either from Platos Academye, or Aristotles Lycaeum, produce not the like effects: Therefore did Horace write thus to his friend:

>Troiani belli scriptorem, (Maxime Lolli)
>Dum tu declamas Romæ, Prænesti velegi,
>Qui quid sit pulchrum, quid turpe, quid vtile, quid non,
>Plenius, ac melius Chrysippo, et Crantore dicet.

Homer in his Ilias, hath made Agamemnon . . . the patteren of a wise
Gouernour, and vlysses in his Odysseis . . . the example of a Wise Man.
Virgill after him, in the Person of his Pius Aeneas, described a good
Gouernour, and an honest Man: Ariosto did the like in his Orlando. But
Tasso hath deduced these two regiments of vertues, politicall, and morall,
from two seuerall Persons, makeing Godfredo the fountaine of Politickes,
or those qualityes, which ought to bee inherent in a Gouernour, and
Rinaldo the subiect of Ethickes; vertues pertaineing to a priuate Man.
But our late Spencer building his fabricke vpon the like foundation, hath
contriu'd his worke so symmetrically, that his methode appeareth farre
more exquisite, then theirs, hee haueing designed twelue Bookes, for the
tractation of twelue seuerall vertues: which with their branches, allyes,
and opposites, are so exactly by him handled, in those six Bookes which
he hath written, that I haue seene many treatises fraught with more
sophistry, but few with more sapience.
[Then quotes from the letter to Raleigh. For authorship of *A Supplement,*
see C. Bowie Millican, " Ralph Knevett . . . ," *RES* 14 (1938), 44-
52.] (FIC, CBM)

About 1633. Thomas May. Lines addressed to Sir Kenelm Digby on his
  Observations [on *F. Q.* 2.9.22], in B. M. MS Add. 25303.
  [Cf. Malone MS 16, p. 39, 1633; B. M. Add. MS 21433. Rptd Allan
  Griffith Chester, *Thomas May: Man of Letters,* Thesis, Univ. Penna.,
  1932, p. 52.]

  Fol. 187:
        As wee esteeme the greatest Princes blest
        To haue their worth by ablest Penns exprest
        So may wee thinke best Poets happie then
        When they are read and fam'd by worthy Men.
        Such is thy ffate brave Spencer thou hast found
        A noble knowing Reader that can sound
        Thy misticke depthes, one that can give thy due,
        And make the Age beleive his Censure true:
        A Sydney dy'd to kill thy bleeding hart,
        A Digby lives to fame thy charming Art:
        Braue Sydny's Artes, & Spirrit in him are knowne
        And Hee, no lesse then Sidney is thine owne.
        Such is thy Digby such thy Sidney was
        I could almost beleive Pythagoras. (HES)

1633. Jasper Fisher. *Fvimvs Troes. Aenid. 2. The Trve Troianes.* [STC
  10886.]

  Sig. A 3:
        Braue Souldiers hold the second, clad in steele,
        Whose glittering Armes brighten those gloomy shades,
        In lieu of Starry lights.
  [Cf. *F. Q.* 1.14.4-5.]

Sig. G 3:

But Time may fauour win:
When Hope doth fayle, then Knife or Rope begin.

[Cf. F. Q. 1.9.21 ff.]

Sig. I:

Though I shall passe twelue monsters as the Sunne,
Or twelue Herculean labours on a row:
Yet one kinde looke makes all my iourney sweet,
Thou Fayry-Queene of the Tartarian Court. (DEM)

1633. Phineas Fletcher. *The Purple Island, or The Isle of Man: together with Piscatorie Eclogs and other Poeticall Miscellanies,* Cambridge.

[STC 11082. *The Poetical Works of Giles Fletcher and Phineas Fletcher,* ed. F. S. Boas, Cambridge, 1908-9.]

[See headnote to 1627. Phineas Fletcher. Apparent sources in Spenser are noted immediately below. These lists are followed by quotations of those passages in which direct reference is made to Spenser.]

The Purple Island: 1.2, p. 1 (Boas 2.12): *Col.* 1-9; 1.26-33, pp. 7-9 (Boas 2.17-9): *Gn.* 89-152; 1.44, p. 12 (Boas 2.21-2): *F. Q.* 2.9.22; 2.29, p. 24 (Boas 2.32): *F. Q.* 2.9.28; 2.33, p. 25 (Boas 2.33): *F. Q.* 2.9.31; 2.36-43, pp. 25-7 (Boas 2.33-5): *F. Q.* 2.9.31-2; 3.27, p. 35 (Boas 2.43): *F. Q.* 4.10.37 ff.; 5.2-3, p. 47 (Boas 2.53): *F. Q.* 1.1.1; 5.59, p. 61 (Boas 2.66): *F. Q.* 2.9.26; 5.61-8, pp. 62-3 (Boas 2.66-7): *Gn.* 433-80; 6.2, p. 65 (Boas 2.69): *F.Q.* 6.9.8; 6.5, p. 66 (Boas 2.70): *F. Q.* 4.2.34; 6.13-4, p. 68 (Boas 2.71-2): *F. Q.* 5.9.32, and 5. proem 10-1; 6.18, p. 69 (Boas 2.72-3): *F. Q.* 5.10.1; 6.43, p. 75 (Boas 2.78): *F. Q.* 2.9.48; 6.51, p. 77 (Boas 2.80): *F. Q.* 2.9.18 ff.; 6.52, p. 77 (Boas 2.80): *F. Q.* 2.9.55-8; 6.53, p. 78 (Boas 2.80): *F. Q.* 2.9.52; 6.68-9, pp. 81-2 (Boas 2.84): *S. C. Apr.* 136-44; 7.4-6, pp. 85-6 (Boas 2.87): *R. T.* 64-77; 7.16, p. 88 (Boas 2.89): *F. Q.* 2.12.1; 7.23-6, pp. 90-1 (Boas 2.91-2): *F. Q.* 1.4.24-6; 7.55-7, pp. 98-9 (Boas 2.98): *F. Q.* 1.4.33-5; 7.66-8, p. 101 (Boas 2.100-1): *F. Q.* 1.4.30-2 and 5.12.29-32; 7.80-4, pp. 104-5 (Boas 2.103-4): *F. Q.* 1.4.21-3 and 2.12.86-7; 8.8, p. 108 (Boas 2.106-7): *F. Q.* 6.10.26; 8.10-2, p. 109 (Boas 2.107): *F. Q.* 3.12.12; 8.24-9, pp. 112-4 (Boas 2. 110-1): *F. Q.* 1.4.27-9; 8.27, p. 113 (Boas 2.111): *Col.* 201-9; 8.27-8, p. 113 (Boas 2.111): *F. Q.* 2.7.17; 8.34, p. 115 (Boas 2.112): *F. Q.* 1.4.18; 9.1, p. 122 (Boas 2.119): *F. Q.* 1.5.2; 9.12, p. 124 (Boas 2.121): *F. Q.* 1.10.46-7; 9.19-24, pp. 126-7 (Boas 2.123-4): *F. Q.* 1.10.12-3; 9.30-4, pp. 129-30 (Boas 2.125-6): *F. Q.* 1.10.14; 10.29, p. 142 (Boas 2.136): *F. Q.* 3.2.4; 10.30-8, pp. 142-4 (Boas 2.136-8): *F. Q.* 2.3.22-5; 29; 10.39, p. 144 (Boas 2.138): *F. Q.* 4.6.19-21; 11.48, p. 157 (Boas 2.150): *F. Q.* 2.11.26; 12.1-7, pp. 159-60 (Boas 2.151-2): *F. Q.* 6.9.19-25; 12.20, p. 163 (Boas 2.155): *F. Q.* 4.6.14; 12.24, p. 164 (Boas 2.156): *F. Q.* 1.7.33; 12.26, p. 165 (Boas 2.156-7): *F. Q.* 1.1.22;

12.27-8, p. 165 (Boas 2.157): *F. Q.* 5.11.23-4; 12.38, p. 168 (Boas 2.159): *F. Q.* 2.11.22; 12.44, p. 169 (Boas 2.160-1): *F. Q.* 4.10.45; 12.59, p. 173 (Boas 2.164): *F. Q.* 1.11.8-10,18,54; 12.66, p. 175 (Boas 2.165): *Gn.* 345-52; 12.68-70, pp. 175-6 (Boas 2.166): *F. Q.* 1.12.5-8,22.

Piscatorie Eclogs: 1.7-9, p. 3 (Boas 2.176-7): *S.C. Dec.* 19-50; 1.12, p. 4 (Boas 2.177): *S. C. May* 39-40; 1.13-5, pp. 4-5 (Boas 2.178): *S. C. Apr.* 23-4; 1.18, p. 5 (Boas 2.179): *F. Q.* 6.9.19-25; 2.8, pp. 8-9 (Boas 2.182): *S. C. Apr.* 13-6; 3.1, p. 14 (Boas 2.187): *S. C. July* 81; 3.4, p. 15 (Boas 2.187) *S.C. Jan.* 39-40; 3.20, p. 19 (Boas 2.191): *S. C. Jan.* 72; 4.1, p. 19 (Boas 2.192): *S. C. Aug.* 47-8; 4.14-9, pp. 22-4 (Boas 2.194-5): *S. C. May* 38-54, 121-9; 4.22, p. 24 (Boas 2.196): *S. C. July* 183-203; 5.18, p. 33 (Boas 2.204): *F. Q.* 3.4.43.

Poeticall Miscellanies, An Hymen at the Marriage of most deare cousins Mʳ. W. and M. R.: P. 55 [ll. 13-4] (Boas 2.223): *Epith.* 145-6; pp. 56-7 [ll. 43-9] (Boas 2.224): *Epith.* 185-90.

Ibid., To Mʳ. Jo Tomkins: P. 68 [ll. 28-36] (Boas 2.234): *S. C. Oct.* 116-8.

Elisa or An Elegie Upon The Unripe Decease of Sʳ. Anthonie Irby: 1.7, p. 106 (Boas 2.262): *Daph.* 150-4; 1.16-40, pp. 109-15 (Boas 2.264-9): *Daph.* 262-94; [2.]38-40, p. 127 (Boas 2.280): *R. T.* 50-6. (ABL)

The Purple Island, Canto 1, sts. 19-21, p. 6 (Boas 2.16):

19

*Spencer Witnesse our**Colin;* whom though all the Graces,
  And all the Muses nurst; whose well taught song
  Parnassus self, and *Glorian* embraces,
  And all the learn'd and all the shepherds throng;
   Yet all his hopes were crost, all suits deni'd;
   Discourag'd, scorn'd, his writings vilifi'd:
  Poorly (poore man) he liv'd; poorly (poore man) he di'd.

20

And had not that great *Hart,* (whose honour'd head
  Ah lies full low) piti'd thy wofull plight;
  There hadst thou lien unwept, unburied,
  Unblest, nor grac't with any common rite:
   Yet shalt thou live, when thy great foe shall sink
   Beneath his mountain tombe, whose fame shall stink;
  And time his blacker name shall blurre with blackest ink.

21

O let th'Iambick Muse revenge that wrong,
  Which cannot slumber in thy sheets of lead:
  Let thy abused honour crie as long
  As there be quills to write, or eyes to reade:

On his rank name let thine own votes be turn'd,
Oh may that man that hath the Muses scorn'd,
Alive, nor dead, be ever of a Muse adorn'd!

Ibid., Canto 6, st. 5, p. 66 (Boas 2.70):

5

Two shepherds most I love with just adoring;
That *Mantuan* swain who chang'd his slender reed
To trumpets martiall voice, and warres loud roaring,
From *Corydon* to *Turnus* derring-deed;
 And next our home-bred *Colins* sweetest firing;
 Their steps not following close, but farre admiring:
To lackey one of these is all my prides aspiring.

Ibid., sts. 51-2, p. 77 (Boas 2.80):

51

But let my song passe from these worthy Sages
Unto this Islands highest *Soveraigne,   *Soveraigne,   *The un-
And those hard warres which all the yeare he wages: derstand-
For these three late a gentle sheperd-swain   ing.
 Most sweetly sung, as he before had seen
 In *Alma's* house: his memorie yet green
Lives in his well-tun'd songs, whose leaves immortal been.

52

Nor can I guesse, whether his Muse divine
Or gives to those, or takes from them his grace;
Therefore *Eumnestes* in his lasting shrine
Hath justly him enroll'd in second place:
 Next to our *Mantuan* poet doth he rest;
 There shall our *Colin* live for ever blest,
Spite of those thousand spites, which living him opprest.

Ibid., st. 58, p. 79 (Boas 2.81):

58

Not that great Soveraigne of the *Fayrie* land,
Whom late our *Colin* hath eternized, . . .
Not that great *Glorians* self with this might e're compare.

Piscatorie Eclogs, and Other Poeticall Miscellanies:

To my beloved *Thenot* in answer to his verse, pp. 65-6, sts. 2-3
(Boas 2.231-2):

But if my *Thenot* love my humble vein,
(Too lowly vein) ne're let him *Colin* call me;
He, while he was, was (ah!) the choicest swain,
That ever grac'd a reed: what e're befall me,
Or *Myrtil*, (so'fore *Fusca* fair did thrall me,
Most was I know'n) or now poore *Thirsil* name me,

Thirsil, for so my *Fusca* pleases frame me:
But never mounting *Colin; Colin's* high stile will shame me.

Two shepherds I adore with humble love;
Th'high-towring swain, that by slow *Mincius* waves
His well-grown wings at first did lowly prove,
Where *Corydon's* sick love full sweetly raves;
But after sung bold *Turnus* daring braves:
And next our nearer *Colin's* sweetest strain;
Most, where he most his *Rosalind* doth plain.
Well may I after look, but follow all in vain. (FIC)

1633. Phineas Fletcher. *Sylva Poetica.*
[STC 11084. *The Poetical Works of Giles Fletcher and Phineas Fletcher,*
ed. F. S. Boas, Cambridge, 1908-9.]

[See headnote to 1627. Phineas Fletcher. Apparent sources in Spenser
are noted below.]
Nisa Ecloga: P. 18 (ll. 86-92; Boas 2.304): *S. C. June* 108-12.
Fusca Ecloga: P. 19 (ll. 12-27; Boas 2.305): *S. C. Feb.* 77-83 and
Aug. 16-7; p. 20 (ll. 58-9; Boas 2.306): *S. C. Mar.* 80-2; p. 21 (ll.
84-8; Boas 2.307): *S.C. Mar.* 61-4. (ABL)

1633. Philip Massinger. *The Guardian,* in *Three New Playes,* 1655.
[STC M1050. *The Plays of Philip Massinger,* ed. W. Gifford, 1813
(1st ed., 1805).]

P. 12 (Gifford 4.140-1):
    A Cast of Haggard Falcons, by me man'd,
    Eying the prey at first, appear as if
    They did turn tayl, but with their laboring wings
    Getting above her, with a thought their pinions
    Cleaving the purer Element, make in,
    And by turns bind with her; the frighted Fowl,
    Lying at her defence upon her back,
    With her dreadful Beak, a while defers her death,
    But by degrees forc'd down, we part the fray
    And feast upon her.
[Gifford compares this passage to *F. Q.* 6.7.9.] (JGM)

1633. Francis Quarles. Commendatory Verses appearing in Phineas
Fletcher's *The Purple Island . . . together with Piscatorie Eclogs,* Cambridge.
[STC 11082. *The Poetical Works of Giles Fletcher and Phineas Fletcher,*
ed. F. S. Boas, Cambridge, 1908-9.]

Sig. ¶¶ 2 (Boas 2.8):
    To The Ingenious Composer of This Pastorall,
    The Spencer of this age.
    I vow (Sweet stranger). . . . (EG)

No sig., following p. 130 (Boas 2.284):
> To my deare friend, the Spencer of this age.
> Dear friend,
> No more a Stranger now. . . . (DEM)

About 1635. Philip Papillon. *Euterpe to her dearest Darling W. B.*, inserted in a copy of the 1625 ed. of William Browne's *Pastorals*. [Rptd *Poems of William Browne*, ed. Gordon Goodwin, 1893; also 1894.]

Goodwin 2.3:
> Hearing such madrigals as these
> Astonished is Philisides,
> And vanquished by thy sweeter lays
> Forswears
> Resigns   his pipe; yields thee the bays:
> And Colin Clout his oaten reed,
> Which to us such pleasure breed,
> Resigns to thee; griev'd because his
> Mulla by Tavy vanquish'd is. (DEM)

1635.   William Austin (d. 1634). *Deuotionis Augustinianæ Flamma, or Certaine Deuout, Godly, and Learned Meditations.*

[STC 972. Described in E. A. Strathmann, " William Austin's ' Notes ' on *The Faerie Queene*," *Hunt. Lib. Bul.*, 11 (Apr. 1937). 155 ff.]

In Festo Sancti Michaelis Archangeli: An Essay of Tutelar Angels, p. 249: Wherefore, since *Man* is (here) made a *Spectacle* to *Men and Angels*, fighting against the *World*, the *Flesh*, and the *Devill*, (strong *Enemies*, and *weake warriours*) *therefore hee hath charged these heavenly Soldiers* to ayde us *militant*, against *their*, and our *common-Enemies*: and, to *pitch their Tents round about us; like Fellow-Soldiers*, fighting *one*, and the *same Quarrell.*

[Cf. *F. Q.* 2.8.1-2]

[*Ibid.*, p. 255, quotes *F. Q.* 2.8.1.5-2.9, changing 2.8.1.9 to read " *To guide* us, *where; and keepe* us, *when we goe.*"] (EAS)

1635.   John Gower. *Pyrgomachia, Vel Potius Pygomachia, the Castle Combat.*

[STC 12142.]

[On sig. A 4ᵛ appears a character named Braggadocio.]

A Quære with a Quare concerning Iohn Quis (verses by " Edm. Iohnson "), sig. F 4:
> Thus, by Soule-shifting, *Virgil's* ghost did wend
> To *Spencer's* lodge. Who *Ovid* was before;
> Is *Drayton* since. Thus *Lucan* Fates restore
> In May. Thus *Orpheus* soule doth *Quarl's* attend. (FBW)

1635.   William   Habington.   *Castara.—Carmina   non   prius   Audita,*
Musarum sacerdos Virginibus. The second Edition Corrected and Aug-
mented.

[STC 12584-4ᵃ. Ed. Edward Arber, *English Reprints,* 1870.]

To my most honoured Friend and Kinsman, R. St. *Esquire,* p. 59
(sig. D 6; Arber, p. 50; Spurgeon 1.216):

> Yet doe I not despaire, some one may be
> So seriously devout to Poesie
> As to translate his [Chapman's] reliques, and finde roome
> In the warme Church, to build him up a tombe.
> Since *Spencer* hath a Stone; and *Draytons* browes
> Stand petrefied ith'Wall, with Laurell bowes
> Yet girt about; and nigh wise *Henries* herse,
> Old *Chaucer* got a Marble for his verse (CFES, FMP)

[Not in *Castara. The First Part,* 1634 (STC 12583). For another
reference to Spenser in *Castara,* see: 1640. William Habington.]

1635.   Thomas Heywood. *The Hierarchie of the blessed Angells. Their*
Names, orders and Officers. The fall of Lucifer with his Angells.
[STC 13327.]

Lib. 4, *The Dominations,* pp. 249-50 (sig. X 5 - X 5ᵛ):
    That forrein Authors haue not onely complained of the great scorne
and contempt cast vpon the *Enthusiasmes* and Raptures; as also that no
due respect or honour hath been conferred vpon the Professors thereof;
whosoeuer shall call to minde the all praiseworthy and euer-to-be-
remembred *Spencer,* shall finde that hee much bewailed this inherent and
too common a disease of neglect, which pursueth the Witty, and in-
separably cleaueth to the most Worthy. Witnesse, his *Teares of the*
Muses, his *Collen Clouts, Come home againe,* and diuers other of his
Workes: but more particularly in the tenth Eclogue of his *Shepheards*
Calender, in the moneth entituled October you may reade him thus:
[Quotes ll. 7-18, with marginal note: "*Cuddy* the / Sheepeheard /
speaketh," and 55-78.]

Lib. 7, *The Principats,* pp. 430-1 (sigs. Nn 5ᵛ - Nn 6):

> Imagin him arriv'd vpon the Coast
> Where she whose presence he desired most,
> Waits till the Captaine of the Pyrats can
> Be thither brought; who meagre, pale, and wan,
> Enters, but like the picture of Despaire,

The   His head, browes, cheekes, and chin o'regrowne with haire;
Father   His Cloathes so ragg'd and tatter'd, that alas
appeares   No one could ghesse him for the man he was.
at Court.

[Cf. *F. Q.* 1.9.35 ff.] (DEM)

1635.   Thomas Lloyd. *Invidus in Chauceri interpretem . . . Sermo Britan-nicus in invidum,* prefixed to Sir Francis Kynaston's *Amorum Troili et Creseidae.* [STC 5097.]

Sig. † 4 - † 4ᵛ (Spurgeon 1.214):
        Flamma sic crescat tibi
        Cælestis ignis æmula: auspiciis tuis
        Spencerus olim sentiat sortes pares.
        Extende Linguam patriam. (FIC)

1635.   Philip Massinger. *Sero, sed serio. To the right honourable my most singular good Lord and Patron Philip Earle of Pembrooke and Mont-gomerye, Uppon the . . . death of his Sonne Charles,* B. M. MS Royal 18 A xx, fols. 1-4.
[*The Plays of Philip Massinger,* ed. W. Gifford, 1813 (1st ed., 1805.]

P. 365 [Coxeter's 1761 ed. of Massinger] (Gifford 4.596-7):
        He that would
        Write what he was, to all Posterity, should
        Have ample Credit in himself, to borrow
        Nay make his own the saddest Accents, Sorrow
        Ever expres'd, and a more moving Quill
        Than *Spencer* us'd when he gave *Astrophil*
        A living *Epicedium.* (JGM)

1635.   N. N. *Maria Triumphans.*
[STC 18331. Cf. G. F. Sensabaugh, "A Spenser Allusion," *TLS,* Oct. 29, 1938, p. 694.]

P. 83:
        Spenser . . . the chiefest English poet in this age.
[" The book is a long discussion about Mariolatry, and the author, by quoting from the *F. Q.,* proves to his own satisfaction that, since Spenser is not thought idolatrous in his admiration of Queen Elizabeth, neither should those be thought blasphemous who write deifying the Virgin Mary." Lawrence Anderton may be the author.] (GFS)

1635.   Francis Quarles. *Emblemes.*
[STC 20540. *Works,* ed. A. B. Grosart, 1880.]

Book 5, II, p. 250 (sig. R 3ᵛ; Grosart 2.91):
        Virgins, tuck up your silken laps, and fill ye
        With the faire wealth of *Floras* Magazine;
        The purple Vy'let, and the pale-fac'd Lilly;
        The Pauncy and the Organ Colombine;
        The flowring Thyme, the guilt-boule Daffadilly;
        The lowly Pinck, the lofty Eglentine:
            The blushing Rose, the Queene of flow'rs, and best
            Of *Floras* beauty.
[Cf. *S.C. Apr.* 136-44.] (FIC)

1635. Joseph Rutter. *The Shepheards Holy-Day. A Pastorall Tragi-Comædie.*
[STC 21470. Rptd Dodsley's *Old English Plays,* ed. W. C. Hazlitt, 1875.
" The influence of Spenser may be felt throughout this play. The S. C.
is reflected in various pastoral characters as, for example, the shepherd
complaining of his love. No lines are exactly parallel with Spenser's, but
the general Spenserian spirit is illustrated in the following: "]

Act 2, sc. 1, sig. B 8ᵛ (Dodsley 12.379-80):
        This day the Sunne shot forth his beames as faire
        As ere he did, and through the trembling aire
        Cool *Zephyrus* with gentle murmuring
        Breath'd a new freshnesse on each Tree and Plant.

Ibid., sig. C 3 (Dodsley 12.384):
        Alas, *Mirtillus,* I have broke my Pipe,
        My sighs are all the musicke which I now
        Can make.

[Cf. *S. C. Apr.* 13-6.] (DEM)

1635. George Tooke. *The legend of Brita-mart.*
[STC 24116. Title borrowed from *F. Q.* 3? " Consists of an acute
criticism of the constitution of the English infantry in the form of a
dialogue." *D. N. B.*] (HH)

1635-8. Stephen Taylor. *A Whippe for Worldlings.*
[STC 23818. See pp. 155-6, Stephen Taylor, above. Charles R. Forker,
Library, XXV (1970), 338-44, argues for 1635-8 rather than 1620 as
the date of *A Whippe.*]

Before 1636 (?) E. C. *Vindiciæ, Virgilianæ,* Bodleian MS Ashmole 38.
    Fol. 30, ll. 73-92:
                        Virgil awake . . .
        Spencer a wake thee from thy clayeie bed
        Let tyme throw of deathes dusty coverlid;
        Knocke up thy Tytirus too, that bard of yore
        Who sleeps close by thee, at next marble dore
        Chaucer new scower thy rustye gat, and fyer
        Stricke from his Flinty pate, who first did mare
        The muses garden wᵗʰ his common shere
        And stencht thes flowers, wᵗʰ Nessus poysnous gore,
        That Garden wheare thy choysest flowers grew
        Those flowers from whence thy bees ther honye drew
            Spencer a wake thee see heer's one hos spoyld
        Those Mantuan gemms, and their true Luster soyld
        Those gemms, wher wᵗʰ a round embellisht boon
        Th'embroydred robes of thy blest Fayrie Queen
        Lett hym bee Counted as the mad dog starve
        In thy everlasting sheppardes Calendar,

Spencer a wake the lett this scribler knowe
he doth a scorne to all the muses owe.
Thy tunes heroick for a scourg exchange
And whip from Phoebus hostes this mad doges Mange.
Johnson awake. . . .

[Note at end of poem (fol. 130ᵛ): "Wrighten against John Vicars
the Vsher of the schole of Christs Church-hospitall by E. C."] (PB, RH)

1636.   Edward, Viscount Conway. Viscount Conway and Kiluta to
[George] Gerrard, Aug. 15, 1636.
[Hist. MSS Comm., Fourteenth Report, App., Pt 2. Quoted Marjorie
H. Nicolson, *Conway Letters*, Yale Univ. Press, 1930.]

P. 38 (Nicolson, p. 9):
We tooke a Dutch Captaine prisoner . . . and yet he had a face like
the shield of the Red crosse knight wherein old dints of deepe woundes
did remaine, though he perdy did never fight in field.
[Cf. *F. Q.* 1.1.1.3.] (DFA)

1636.   William Davenant. *The Platonick Lovers. A Tragæcomedy.*
[STC 6305. *Dramatic Works*, ed. James Maidment and W. H. Logan,
Edinburgh and London, 1872-4.]

Sig. B 2ᵛ (Maidment and Logan 2.13):
                    Iust like the parley
    'Twixt Mounsier *Hobbynoll*, and *Collen Clowt.* (FIC)

1636.   Thomas Heywood. *Loves Maistresse: or, The Queens Masque.*
[STC 13352. *The Dramatic Works*, ed. R. H. Shepherd, 1874.]

Act 2, sc. 1, sig. E 2 (Shepherd 5.114; Koeppel, p. 89):
Clowne. But listen to them, and they will fill your heads with a thousand
fooleries; obserue one thing, there's none of you all sooner in love, but
hee is troubled with their itch, for hee will bee in his Amorets, and his
Canzonets, his Pastoralls, and his Madrigalls, to his Phillis, and his
Amorilles.
                    Enter Swaines

1. Swai Where is *Coridon* . . . ?
Clo. I doe not thinke the Clownes will know me when they see mee,
Colin, Dickon, Hobinall, and how is't, how is't? (EK)

1636.   *The King and Queenes Entertainement at Richmond after their
Departure from Oxford.*
[STC 5026. Ed. W. Bang and R. Brotanek, *Materialen*, Louvain, vol.
2, 1903.]

Sig. C 4ᵛ (Bang and Brotanek, p. 24):
Britomart . . . Their Squires, or Dwarfes rather, are some halfe an
houres journey behind, for so it was said of old,

The fearefull Dwarfe did euer lag behind.
[Cf. *F. Q.* 1.1.6.1; quotation is not exact.] (FIC)

1636. William Strode. *The Floating Island: A Tragi-Comedy. Acted before his Majesty at Oxford, Aug. 29, 1636. By the Students of Christ-Church,* 1655.
[STC S5983. *Poetical Works,* ed. B. Dobell, 1907.]

Act 3, sc. 4, sig. D 2 (Dobell, p. 188). Morpheus gives directions to six dreams in a masque, of which the following to Despair is reminiscent of *F. Q.* 1.9.33 ff.]:
> *Despaire* start, stand, and crush thy throat,
> Then stab thy breast and groan death's note.

Act 5, sc. 7, sig. Fᵛ (Dobell, p. 225) [Desperato serves his guests at table]:
> *Am*[*orous*]. What's here? Knives, Bodkins, Daggers?
> *Mal*[*evolo*]. Ropes, silken, hairy, hempen?
> *Tim*[*erous*]. Little papers,
> Of witty, loving, raging, sleeping poysons?

[In answer to his guests' query about the entertainment, Desperato replies in lines reminiscent of Spenser's Despair]:
> Could Art invent, or Wealth procure you better?
> The Greatest, Wisest, Stoutest and the fairest
> Have chose these Gates to relish their last palats:
> Have you not heard of *Mithridates, Cato,*
> Of *Hannibal,* and *Cleopatra?* These?
> These gods on earth have travl'd to their home
> With such provision. Tast. One Tast of these
> Forever frees from Hunger, Thirst, Want, Griefe:
> These are receites for immortality. . . .
> Death to the wretched soul as needful is,
> As sleep unto the weary. Why should men
> Condemnd to misery thus toile to mend
> Their Fates which cannot alter?

Act 5, sc. 7, sig. F 2 (Dobell, pp. 228-9):
> *An Attendant sings in a base.*
> Come heavy souls oppressed with the weight
> Of Crimes, or Pangs, or want of your delight,
>   Come d[r]own in *Lethe's,* sleepy lake
>   Whatever makes you ake.
>   Drink health from poyson'd bowles
> Breathe out your cares together with your souls.
>   Cool Death's a salve
>   Which all may have
> There's no distinction in the grave;
> Lay down your loads before deaths iron dore,
> Sigh, and sigh out, groan once, and groan no more. (DEM)

1637.   William Austin (d. 1634). *Hæc Homo, Wherein the Excellency of the Creation of Woman is described, By way of an Essay.* [STC 974. Described in E. A. Strathmann, "William Austin's 'Notes' on *The Faerie Queene*." *Hunt. Lib. Bul.* 11 (Apr. 1937). 155 ff.]

Cap. 5, pp. 79-80 (sig. E 4 - E 4ᵛ):

(b) Mʳ. Spencer dyed a- bove 30 yeares a- gon.

All which discourse concerning the *severall proportions* of the body, are very elegantly and briefly contracted, by the ᵇ*late dead Spencer,* in his everliving *Fairy Queen;* where, coming to describe the *house of Alma,* (which, indeed, is no *other* but the *body*; the *habitation* of the Soule,) he saith.

[Quotes *F. Q.* 2.9.22.]
[Austin employs other quotations from *F. Q.*: p. 94 (sig. E 11ᵛ), 2.9.32; pp. 96-7 (sigs. E 12ᵛ - F), 2.9.44.8-9 and 2.9.46.1-47.5. P. 97 refers to 2.9.26.] (EAS)

1637.   T. H. *A Curtaine Lecture.* [STC 13312.]

Pp. 20-1 (sigs. B 10ᵛ - B 11) [Comments upon poets who have defended women]:

And of our English, I will only, at this time, memorize two; famous Mʳ. *Edmund Spencer,* magnified in his *Gloriana;* and the most renowned Sʳ. *Philip Sidney,* never to bee forgotten in his *Pamela* and *Philoclea.* [T. H. is identified as Thomas Heywood.] (EG)

1637.   Ralph Knevett. *Funerall Elegies, to the Memory of Lady K. Paston.* [STC 15035. Cf. C. Bowie Millican, "Ralph Knevett, Author of the Supplement to Spenser's Faerie Queene," *RES,* 14 (1938), 44-52.]

[" The third elegy consists of twenty Spenserian stanzas."] (CBM)

1637.   Shackerley Marmion. *A Morall Poem, Intituled the Legend of Cvpid and Psyche.*
[STC 17444-4ᵃ.]

Sigs. D 4ᵛ - E:

> There is a Goddesse flyes through the earths globe
> Girt with a cloud, and in a squalid robe,
> Daughter to *Pluto,* and the silent night,
> Whose direfull presence does the Sun affright.
> Her name is *Ate,* venome is her food,
> The very Furies and *Tartarian* brood
> Doe hate her for uglinesse, she blacks
> Her horrid visage with so many *Snakes:*
> And as her tresses 'bout her necke she hurles,
> The Serpents hisse within their knotty curles.

Sorrow, and shame, death, and a thousand woes,
And discord waites her, wheresoe're she goes.
[Cf. *F. Q.* 4.1.19 ff.] (DEM)

1637.　John Milton. *A Maske Presented At Ludlow Castle, 1634.*
[STC M17937. *Works*, Frank A. Patterson, gen. ed., Columbia Univ.
Press, 1931-40.]

P. 28 (ll. 815-22; *Columbia Milton* 1.115-6):
　　　. . . without his rod revers't,
And backward mutters of dissevering power
Wee cannot free the Ladie that sits here
In stonie fetters fixt, and motionlesse;
Yet stay, be not disturb'd, now I bethinke me,
Some other meanes I have which may be us'd,
Which once of *Melibœus* old I learnt
The soothest shepheard that ere pipe't on plains.

P. 29 (ll. 847-53; *Columbia Milton* 1.116-7):
　　　. . . the shepheards at their festivalls
Carroll her goodnesse lowd in rusticke layes,
And throw sweet garland wreaths into her streame
Of pancies, pinks, and gaudie daffadills.
And, as the old Swaine said, she can unlocke
The clasping charme, and thaw the numming spell,
If she be right invok't in warbled Song.

[Is Meliboeus Spenser? The identification is not improbable, if the free-
ing of the Lady from the charm of Comus by Sabrina reflects the episode
of Amoret's release from the enchantments of Busirane by Britomart.
Cf. especially the first two lines quoted above with *F. Q.* 3.12.36.1-2.

Parallels between *Comus* and Spenser's verse noted in *An Index to
the Columbia Milton*, Frank L. Patterson and French R. Fogle (Columbia
Univ. Press, 1940) 2.1849-50, are listed below. Numbers in parentheses
refer to pages in vol. 1 of the *Columbia Milton*; unless otherwise noted,
F. Q. is the Spenser reference.

Comus 50 (87): 6.10.16.4; 73-4 (87): 2.1.54.1-5; 94 (88):
3.4.51.6-7; 147 (90): 2.12.71.1; 188 (92): 2.1.52.8; 213
(93): H. H. B. 93; 264 ff. (95): 2.3.33; 266 (95): 1.6.16.2-3;
324 (97): 6.1.1.1; 331 (97): 3.1.43.6; 372-3 (99): 1.1.12.9;
412 (100): 3.12.15.1-6; 421 (100): 2.3.29.1-2, st. 31.3-4; 540
(105): 1.1.23.3-4; 693 (111): 5.9.48.1; 744-5 (113): 2.3.39.9;
811 (115): 1.1.47.6; 906 (119): 3.12.31.1; 931 (120):
3.4.18.3-5; 1009 (123): 3.6.48.1-2, st. 49.1, st. 50.]

1637.　James Shirley. *The Lady of Pleasure. A Comedie.*
[STC 22448. *The Dramatic Works and Poems*, ed. Alexander Dyce,
1833.]

Sigs. I 4ᵛ - K (Dyce 4.95):

Lor[d]. . . . The windes shall play soft descant to our feete,
And breathe rich odors to repure the aire,
Greene bowers on every side shall tempt our stay,
And Violets stoope to have us treade upon em.
The red rose shall grow pale, being neere thy cheeke,
And the white blush orecome with such a forehead,
Here laid, and measuring with our selves some banke,
A thousand birds shall from the woods repaire,
And place themselves so cunningly, behinde
The leaves of every tree, that while they pay
A tribute of their songs, thou sha[l]t imagine
The very trees beare musicke, and sweet voyces
Doe grow in every arbour.
[Spenserian imagery.] (FIC)

1638. Henry Adamson. *The Muses Threnodie, or, Mirthfull Mournings, on the death of Master Gall.* King James College, Edinburgh.
[STC 135.]

Sig. C 4ᵛ:

Let Poetaster-parasits, who fain,
And fawn, and crouch, and coutch, and creep for gain. . . .
[Cf. *M. H. T.* 727-8, 905.] (DEM)

1638. Robert Chamberlain. *Nocturnall Lucubrations: or Meditations Divine and Morall. Whereunto are added Epigrams and Epitaphs.*
[STC 4945. Quoted Thomas Corser, *Collectanea Anglo-Poetica,* Chetham Soc., Manchester, 1867.]

On the death of Mr. Charles Fitz-Geffrays, Minister of God's Word, sig. H 6 (Corser, 3.272):

O Thou the saddest of the sisters nine,
Adde to a sea of teares, one teare of thine. (DEM)

1638. Edmund Coleman. Verses prefixed to Robert Farley's *Kalendarium Humanae Vitae. The Kalender of Mans Life.*
[STC 10693.]

Sig. A 3ᵛ:

Th' *Arcadian Shepheards* shall make thee their starre,
And place this next to *Tityrus Calendar.* (FBW)

1638. Dru Cooper. *Vpon Mʳ. James Shirley his Comedy, cal'd The Royall Master,* prefixed to *The Royall Master.*
[STC 22454-4a. Rptd James Shirley, *Dramatic Works,* ed. Alexander Dyce, 1833.]

Sig. A 3ᵛ (Dyce l.lxxxiv):
     When *Spencer* reign'd sole Prince of Poets here,
     As by his Fairy Queene doth well appeare
     There was not one so blind, so bold a Bard,
     So ignorantly proud or foolish-hard
     To encounter his sweete Muse; for *Phoebus* vow'd
     A sharpe revenge on him should be so proud. (FIC)

1638.   William Drummond. *To the Exequies of the Honourable Sʳ Antonye
Alexander Knight. A Pastorall Elegie*, Edinburgh.
[*Poetical Works*, ed. L. E. Kastner, Edinburgh and London, 1913.]

P. 44 (Kastner 2.143, quoted):
     A gentler Shepheard Flocks did never feed
     On *Albions* Hills, nor sung to oaten Reed. (DEM)
[Kastner, 2.141 n., remarks the loss of the unique copy of the elegy,
formerly preserved in the library of the University of Edinburgh.]

1638.   J. Hayward. *To the deceased's vertuous sister the Ladie Margaret
Loder*, in *Obsequies to the memorie of Mr. Edward King, Anno Dom.
1638*.
[STC 14964. Rptd David Masson, *Life of Milton*, 1859-94; and by
Ernest C. Mossner, Facsimile Text Soc., 1939.]

Sig. H 2 (Masson 1.517):
     With joy I recollect and think upon
     Your reverent Church-like devotion;
     Who by your fair example did excite
     Church-men and clerks to do their duty right,
     And by frequenting that most sacred quire,
     Taught many how to heav'n they should aspire.
     For our Cathedralls to a beamlesse eye
     Are quires of angels in epitomie,
     Maugre the blatant beast, who cries them down
     As savouring of superstition.
     [Cf. *F. Q.* 5.12.37 ff., *et freq.*] (RH)

1638.   Franciscus Junius. *The Painting of the Ancients: in three Books.*
[STC 7302.]

Lib. 3, chap. 5, sec. 10, p. 317 (sig. Ss 3):
     Great masters use sometimes to blaze and to pourtray in most excellent
pictures, not onely the dainty lineaments of beauty, but they use also to
shadow round about it rude thickets and craggy rockes, that by the hor-
ridnesse of such parts there might accrue a more excellent grace to the
principall: even as a discord in musicke maketh now and then a comely
concordance: and it falleth out very often, that the most curious spectators finde themselves, I know not how, singularly delighted with such
a disorderly order of a counterfeited rudenesse.
[Cf. E. K.'s epistle to Harvey, prefixed to *S. C.*] (FH)

1638.   John Milton.   *Lycidas*, in *Justa Edovardo King naufrago.* . . .
Obsequies to the memorie of Mr Edward King.
[STC 14964. *Works*, Frank A. Patterson, gen. ed., Columbia Univ.
Press, 1931-40.]

[Parallels between *Lycidas* and Spenser's verse which have been indicated
in *An Index to the Columbia Milton*, Frank L. Patterson and French R.
Fogle (Columbia Univ. Press, 1940) 2.1849-50, are noted below. The
numbers in parentheses refer to pages in vol. 1 of the *Columbia Milton*.
Line 6 (76): *F. Q.* 1.1.53.1; 9 ff. (77): *F. Q.* 3.6.45.6,9; 11 (77):
R. R. 348-9; 15 (77): *T. M.* 53; 55 (78): *F. Q.* 1.9.4.7-8; 65 (79):
S. C. June 67; 103 (80): *F. Q.* 1.3.10.8; 115 (80): *S. C. May* 127;
142 (81): *S. C. Apr.* 62. Also cf. 64 ff. with *S. C. Oct.* 19 ff.]

1638.   Henry Peacham.   *The Truth of our Times: Revealed out of one
Mans Experience, by way of Essay.* [STC 19517.]

Pp. 37-8 (sig. C 7 - C 7ᵛ):
     The famous Spencer did never get any preferment in his life, save
toward his latter end hee became a Clerk of the Councell in *Ireland*;
and dying in *England*, hee dyed but poore. When he lay sick, the Noble,
and patterne of true Honour, *Robert* Earle of *Essex*, sent him twenty
pound, either to relieve or bury him. (FIC)

1638.   Sir John Suckling.   *The Goblins A Comedy*, 1646.
[STC S6129; also published in Suckling's *Fragmenta Avrea*, 1646 (STC
S6126); *Works*, ed. A. H. Thompson, 1910.]

Act 4, p. 45 (sig. C 7; Thompson, p. 198):
               Enter *Poet* and *Theeves.*
     Po. Carer per so lo carer,
     Or he that made the fairie Queene. (MYH)
[*The Goblins* was acted in 1638.]

1638.   Nathaniel Whiting.   *Il Insonio Insonnadado, or a sleeping-waking
Dreame, vindicating the divine breath of Poesie* . . . , annexed to *Le hore
di recreatione: Or the Pleasant Historie Of Albino and Bellama.* [STC
25436-6a; 25436a quoted.]

Sig. H. 3 [for H 5] (Saintsbury 3.544):
     This done, the Pursevant *Apollo* posts
     T'*Elysium*, to call the Poets ghosts
     That payd th'infernall Ferry-man his fee:
     There saw I *Homer* [and other famous poets, from
     Ovid to Boethius].
     Amongst the Modernes came the Fairy Queene,
     Old *Geffrey, Sidney, Drayton, Randolph, Greene,*
     The double *Beaumonde, Drummond, Browne.*
     Each had his chaplet, and his Ivie crowne.

Sig. H 8 (Saintsbury 3.550):
I'rne-sinewed *Talus* with his steely flaile,
Long since ith'right of iustice did prevaile
Vnder the Scepter of the Fairy Queene,
Yet *Spencers* lofty measures makes it greene. (FIC)

1639.   Leonard Lawrence. *A Small Treatise betwixt Arnalte & Lucinda,*
Entituled The Evill-intreated Lover, or The Melancholy Knight. Origi-
nally written in the Greeke Tongue by an unknowne Author. Now
turned into English verse by L. L. [STC 778.]

The Translator tenders his respect to all ingenious Poets, sig. B 2 - B 2ᵛ:

Sweete-ton'd Poesie
Makes men immortall, and doth Deifie
Them by their actions: what was ever writ
By a true Poet, *Fame* eterniz'd it;
Witnesse an *Homer,* or brave *Horace* name,
Propertius, Virgil, or sweete *Ovids* fame:
Or looke but backe to these our Moderne times,
Spencer, though dead, surviveth by his rimes;
Iohnson, and others needlesse to rehearse,
Are eternized by their famous Verse. (HER)

1639.   Sir James Ware. *De Scriptoribus Hiberniae,* Dublin. [STC 25066.]

Lib. 2, Cap. 5. *Scriptores Anglici,* p. 137 (sig. T):
Edmundus Spenserus patriâ Londinensis & academiae Cantabrigiensis
alumnus, Poëtarum Anglorum suæ ætatis princeps, in Hiberniam primùm
venit cum Arthuro *Domino Grey Barone de Wilton,* Hiberniæ Prorege,
cui fuit à Secretis. Obijt Westminasterij an 1599. & ibidem in ecclesiâ
S. Petri, prope Chaucerum sepultus est. Scripsit Anglicè
Poemata varia,
quae excusa in uno volumine extant. Item prosâ, per modum Dialogi, inter
Eudoxum & Irenaeum,
De Statu Hiberniae, Lib. I.
Promisit etiam in eo libro se de antiquitatibus Hiberniae scripturum,
sed an præstiterit nondum reperi, versimile autem est morte præventum
non præstitisse. (FIC)

Before 1640.   William Alabaster. *Epigrammata.* Bodleian MS Rawlinson
D. 293 [also D. 283].

Fol. 19ᵛ (D. 283, fol. 2ᵛ):
In Edouardum Spencerum, Britannicae poesios facile principem
Hoc qui sepulchro conditur siquis fuit
Quaeris uiator, dignus es qui rescias.
SPENCERUS istic conditur, si quis fuit
Rogare pergis, dignus es qui nescias. (FIC)

About 1640. Randle Holme (d. 1699). *The Academy of Armory*, 1688. [STC H2513.]

Pt. I, Book II, p. 205:
Faith is Painted in white Garments in one hand a Cross, and in the other hand a Golden Cup or Chalice, and sometimes a Book.
Hope is a Woman in Blew Garments, with Mantle or Vail red, holding or Supporting a Silver Anchor.
Charity a person in Yellow or Crimson Robes and Vail with a Child in her Arme, and one in her hand by her side; or an enflamed heart in the other hand, with a tyre of Gold and Precious Stones on her head.
[Cf. descriptions of Fidelia, Speranza, and Charissa, *F. Q.* 1.10.4 ff.] (DFA)

1640. Thomas Carew. *Poems.*
[STC 4620. Ed. Rhodes Dunlap, Oxford, 1949.]

A Rapture, p. 83 (sig. G 3; Dunlap, p. 51):
    Then will I visit, with a wandring kisse,
    The vale of Lillies, and the Bower of blisse.
[Cf. *F. Q.* 2.5.27 ff.] (JGM)

[Dunlap, pp. 236-7, is inclined to date the composition of *A Rapture* before 1624.]

1640. William Habington. *Castara . . .The third Edition. Corrected and augmented.*
[STC 12585. Ed. Edward Arber, *English Reprints,* 1870.]

Cogitabo pro peccato meo, p. 222 (sig. L 3ᵛ; Arber, pp. 140-1):
    Growne elder I admired
    Our Poets as from heaven inspired
    What Obeliskes decreed I fit
    For *Spencers* Art, and *Sydnyes* wit?
    But waxing sober soone I found
    Fame but an Idle sound. (FIC)

1640. Ben Jonson (d. 1637). *Ben: Ionson's Execration against Vvlcan with divers Epigrams.*
[STC 14771. *Ben Jonson,* ed. C. H. Herford and Percy Simpson, Oxford, 1925-52.]

To my Detractor, sig. E 3ᵛ (Herford and Simpson 8.408):
    But bark thou on; I pitty thee poor Cur,
    That thou shouldst lose thy noise, thy foame, thy stur,
    To be knowne what thou art, thou blatent beast;
    By writing against me.
[Following Harleian MS 4955, fol. 173b, Herford and Simpson give *bawle* for *bark* in the first line.] (FBW)

1640. Ben Jonson. *Timber; or, Discoveries; Made vpon Men and Matter,* in *The Workes of Benjamin Jonson. The second Volume,* 1640. [STC 14754-4ᵃ. Cf. preceding entry.]

P. 97 (sig. N 3; Herford and Simpson 8.582):
If it were put to the question of the Water-rimers workes, against *Spencers;* I doubt not, but they would find more Suffrages; because the most favour common vices, out of a Prerogative the vulgar have, to lose their judgements; and like that which is naught.

Pp. 116-7 (sigs. P 4ᵛ - Q; Herford and Simpson 8.618):
Spencer, in affecting the Ancients writ no Language: Yet I would have him read for his matter; but as *Virgil* read *Ennius.*

P. 119 (sig. Q 2; Herford and Simpson 8.622):
Words borrow'd of Antiquity, doe lend a kind of Majesty to style, and are not without their delight sometimes. For they have the Authority of yeares, and out of their intermission doe win to themselves a kind of grace-like newnesse. But the eldest of the present, and newnesse of the past Language is the best. For what was the ancient Language, which some men so doate upon, but the ancient Custome? . . . *Virgill* was most loving of Antiquity; yet how rarely doth hee insert *aquai,* and *pictai! Lucretius* is scabrous and rough in these; hee seekes 'hem: As some doe *Chaucerismes* with us, which were better expung'd and banish'd. (DEM)

1640. Ben Jonson. *Underwoods Consisting of Divers Poems,* in *The Workes of Benjamin Jonson. The second Volume,* 1640. [Cf. preceding entry.]

An Epigram To my Muse, the Lady Digby, on her Husband, Sir Kenelme Digby, p. 246 (sig. Kk 3ᵛ; Herford and Simpson 8.263):
 For he doth love my Verses, and will looke
  Upon them, (next to *Spenser's* noble booke,)
 And praise them too. O! what a fame 't will be? (FIC)

1640. Sir John Mennes. *Wits Recreations.* [STC 25870.]
Sig. B 3ᵛ:
        [No.] 17 *On a braggadocio.*
   Don *Lollus* brags, he comes of noble blood,
   Drawn down from *Brutus* line; 'tis very good!
   If this praise-worthy be, each flea may then,
   Boast of his blood more then some gentlemen.
Sig. F:
          [No.] 200 *Phineas Fletcher.*
             5 anagr.
          Hath Spencer life?
          Or Spencer hath life.

That *Spencer* liveth, none can ignorant be,
That reads his worke (*Fletcher*) or knoweth thee.
[See also: 1641. Sir John Mennes.] (FIC)

1640. James Shirley. *St. Patrick for Ireland. The first Part.*
[STC 22455. *The Dramatic Works and Poems,* ed. Alexander Dyce, 1833.]

Sig. A 2ᵛ (Dyce 4.366):
　　　　　The names of the Actors
. . . Archimagus, *The chife Priest, a Magitian.* (FIC)

1640. *The womens sharpe revenge: Or an answer to Sir Seldome Sober.*
[STC 23706.]

Sig. B 11 - B 11ᵛ:
　　A Poet sure hee could not be: for not one of them but with all his
industry strived to celebrate the praises of some Mistris or other: or
for example, Amongst the *Greekes, Aristophanes, Meander,* &c. . . .
Amongst the *Italians, Petrock* his *Laura,* &c. And of our owne Nation,
Learned Master *Spencer* his *Rosalinde,* and *Sam. Daniel* his *Delia,* &c.
(HER)
[This satire on John Taylor names as its author "Mary Tattlewell."]

1641. Thomas Beedome. *Poems, Divine and Humane.*
[STC B1689. *Select Poems Divine and Humane,* ed. Francis Meynell, 1928.]

The Iealous Lover, or, the Constant Maid, sig. C 8 (omitted by Meynell):
　　The hunger-bitten Lyon greedy came,
　　Thinking to seaze her body for a pray,
　　But when he saw her, straight was turned tame,
　　And at her feet for mercy prostrate lay,
　　　　While his dumbe reverence seem'd to tell the Maid,
　　　　He mourn'd to thinke how he made her afraid. (DEM)
[Cf. *F. Q.* 1.3.5 ff.]

Encomium Poetarum ad fratrem Galiel Scot, sig. F 5 (Meynell, p. 19):
　　Nor Spencer to whose verse the world doth owe
　　Millions of thankes can unremembred goe. (DFA)

1641. John Hepwith. *The Calidonian Forest.* [STC H1486.]
[A beast satire on the court of James I, influenced in diction, style and
episode by *M. H. T.* Palace of Politeia is reminiscent of the House of
Temperance, *F. Q.* 2.9.18-60.] (HH)

1641. Sir John Mennes. *Wits Recreations Containing 630. Epigrams.
160: Epitaphs.* [STC M1720.]

Epitaph 141. *On M. Edm. Spencer the famous Poet.*
At Delphos shrine, one did a doubt propound
Which by the Oracle must be released,
Whether of Poets where the best renoun'd
Those that survive, or that that are deceased?
The gods made answer by divine suggestion
While *Spencer* is alive it is no question. (RK)
[See also: 1640. Sir John Mennes.]

1641. John Milton. *Animadversions upon The Remonstrants Defence, Against Smectymnuus.*
[STC M2089. *Works*, Frank A. Patterson, gen. ed., Columbia Univ. Press, 1931-40.]

P. 54 (*Columbia Milton* 3.161-2):
Doe they thinke then that all these meaner and superfluous things come from God, & the divine gift of learning from the den of *Plutus*, or the cave of *Mammon?*

[Cf. *F. Q.* 2.7]

Pp. 58-9 (*Columbia Milton* 3.165-7):
Let the novice learne first to renounce the world, and so give himselfe to God, and not therefore give himselfe to God, that hee may close the better with the World, like that false Shepherd *Palinode* in the eclogue of *May*, under whom the Poet lively personates our Prelates, whose whole life is a recantation of their pastorall vow, and whose profession to forsake the World, as they use the matter, boggs them deeper into the world: those our admired *Spencer* inveighs against, not without some presage of these reforming times.
[Quotes *S. C. May* 103-31.] (FIC)

1641. John Milton. *The Reason of Church-government Urg'd against Prelaty.*
[STC M2175. *Works*, Frank A. Patterson, gen. ed., Columbia Univ. Press, 1931-40.]

P. 63 (*Columbia Milton* 3.275):
Him our old patron St. George by his matchlesse valour slew, as the Prelat of the Garter that reads his Collect can tell. And if our Princes and Knights will imitate the fame of that old champion, as by their order of Knighthood solemnly taken, they vow, farre be it that they should uphold and side with this English Dragon; but rather to doe as indeed their oath binds them, they should make it their Knightly adventure to pursue & vanquish this mighty sailewing'd monster that menaces to swallow up the Land, unlesse her bottomlesse gorge may be satisfi'd with the blood of the Kings daughter the Church. (FIC)
[Cf. *F. Q.* 1.11.]

1641. H. P. *To the Memorie of his friend, Master Thomas Beedome. And upon his Poems,* prefixed to Beedome's *Poems, Divine, and Humane.* [STC B1689.]

Sig. A 7ᵛ:
Then let me weepe a sigh-through-mangled verse,
Steep'd deepe in teares, upon his honour'd hearse,
Tell ye he's gone, whose muses early flight,
Gave hopes to th'world, we nere should see a night
Of Poetry, that th'Widdow of those rare men,
Spencer, and *Drayton,* admir'd *Donne,* great *Ben,*
Should now remarried be. (DEM)

1641. Martin Parker. *The Poet's Blind mans bough, or Have among you my blind Harpers.*
[STC P443. Rptd E. W. Ashbee, *Occasional Facsimile Rpts,* no. 22, 1871; ed. Charles Hindley, *Old Book Collector's Miscellany,* 1873.]

Sig. A 4 (Hindley, vol. 3 [12th piece], p. 4; Spurgeon 1.221; Bradley, p. 273):
All Poets (as adition to their fames)
Have by their Works eternized their names,
As Chaucer, Spencer, and that noble earle,
Of Surrie t[h]ought it the most precious pearle,
That dick'd his honour, to Subscribe to what
His high engenue ever amed at. (CFES)

1642. Sir Francis Kynaston. *Leoline and Sydanis. A Romance of the Amorous Adventures of Princes.* [STC K759.]

St. 1, p. 1 (Saintsbury 2.70):
Fortunes of Kings, enamour'd Princes loves,
Who erst from Royal Ancestors did spring,
Is the high subject that incites and moves
My lowly voice in lofty Notes to sing.
[Cf. *F. Q.* 1. proem 1.] (FIC)

St. 21, p. 6 (Saintsbury 2.73):
But O false world! O wretched state unstable
Of mortal men! O frail condition.
[Cf. *S. C. Nov.* 153-4, *R. T.* 197.] (FMP)

St. 229, p. 59 (Saintsbury 2.110):
Nine times the lusty Prince did come aloft.
[Cf. *F. Q.* 3.10.48.5.] (FIC)

1642. John Milton. *An Apology against a Pamphlet call'd A Modest Confutation of the Animadversions of the Remonstrant against Smectymnuus.*

[STC M2090. *Works*, Frank A. Patterson, gen. ed., Columbia Univ. Press, 1931-40.]

Pp. 16-7 (*Columbia Milton* 3.304):
I betook me among those lofty Fables and Romances, which recount in solemne canto's the deeds of Knighthood founded by our victorious Kings; & from hence had in renowne over all Christendome. There I read it in the oath of every Knight, that he should defend to the expence of his best blood, or of his life, if it so befell him, the honour and chastity of Virgin or Matron. From whence even then I learnt what a noble vertue chastity sure must be, to the defence of which so many worthies by such a deare adventure of themselves had sworne. (FIC)

1642.   Henry More. ψυχωδια *Platonica or a Platonicall song of the Soul.*
[STC M2674. 2nd ed., *Philosophical Poems*, 1647 (STC M2670) quoted. *Philosophical Poems*, ed. G. Bullough, Manchester, 1931.]

Psychozoia, To his dear Father Alexander More, Esquire, sig. A 2ᵛ (Bullough, p. 1):
. . . You deserve the Patronage of better Poems then these, though you may lay a more proper claim to these then any. You having from my childhood tuned mine ears to Spencers rhymes, entertaining us on winter nights, with that incomparable Peice of his, *The Fairy Queen*, a Poem richly fraught within divine Morality as Phansy. (FIC)

Ibid., To The Reader Upon the first Canto of Psychozoia, sig. B 7ᵛ (Bullough, p. 8):
. . . . Why may it not be free for me to break out into an higher strain, and under it to touch upon some points of Christianity; as well as all-approved *Spencer*, sings of Christ under the name of *Pan*? (DEM)
[Cf. *S. C. May* 54, *July* 49.]

Ibid., p. 23 (Bullough, p. 41):
    His name is *Daemon*, . . .
    he's the fount of foul duality.
    That wicked witch *Duessa* is his bride. (FIC)
[Cf. *F. Q.* 1.2, *et freq.*]

Ibid., p. 23 (Bullough, p. 42):
    Duessa first invented magick lore,
    And great skill hath to joyn and disunite.
[Cf. More's note on this passage (pp. 359-60, Bullough, p. 195):
"*Duessa* is the natural life of the body, or the naturall spirit, that, whereby we are lyable to Magick assaults, which are but the sympathies and antipathies of nature, such as are in the spirit of the world."]

Ibid., p. 50 (Bullough, p. 77):
    Then the wise youth, Good Sir, you look too high:
    The wall aloft is rais'd; but that same doore
    Where you must passe in deep descent doth lie:

But he bad follow, he would go before.
Hard by there was a place, all covered o're
With stinging nettles and such weedery,
The pricking thistles the hard'st legs would gore,
Under the wall a straight doore we descry:
The wall hight *Self-conceit*; the doore *Humility*.

[Cf. *F. Q.* 1.10.5-6.]

Ibid., p. 56 (Bullough, p. 85):
On *Ida* hill there stands a Castle strong,
They that it built call it *Pantheothen*.
(Higher resort a rescall rabble throng
Of miscreant wights;)

[Cf. *F. Q.* 1.8.]

Ibid., p. 58 (Bullough p. 88):
Hence you may see, if that you dare to mind,
Upon the side of this accursed hil,
Many a dreadful corse ytost in wind,
Which with hard halter their loathd life did spill.
There lies another which himself did kill
With rusty knife, all roll'd in his own blood,
And ever and anon a dolefull knill
Comes from the fatall Owl, that in sad mood
With drery sound doth pierce through the death-shadowed wood.

[Cf. *F. Q.* 1.9.22-32.]
[The passages quoted above are illustrative; many others are equally
reminiscent of Spenser. See also entry under: 1647. Henry More.]
(FIC, DEM)

Before 1643. Sir Kenelm Digby. *A discourse concerning Edmund
Spencer,* in B. M. MS Harleian 4153, item 1.
   Whosoeuer will deliver a well grounded opinion and censure of any
learned man, must at the least stand vpon the same leuell with him in
matter of iudgement and ability: for otherwise, whiles remaining on
the lower ground he looketh vp at him, he shall haue but a superficiall
view of the most prominent parts, without being able to make any dis-
couery into the large continent that lyeth behind those; wherein vsually
is the richest soyle. This consideration maketh mee very vnwilling to
say anything in this kind of our late admirable poet EDMUND SPENCER
[in red ink], who is seated soe high aboue the wreach of my weake eyes,
as the more I looke to discerne and discry his perfections, the more
faint and dazeled they grow through ye distance and splendour of the
obiect. Yet to comply wth yor [?] desire, I will here briefly deliuer you
(though wth a hoar[s]e voyce and trembling hand) some of those rude
and undigested conceptions that I haue of him; not daring to looke too
farre into that sacrary of the MUSES and of learning, where to handle
anything wth boldness, were impiety. His learned workes confirme me

in the beliefe y^t our NORTHEREN climate may give life to as well
tempered a brain, and as rich a mind as where the sunne shineth fairest.
When I read him methinks our country needth not enuy either GREECE,
ROME or TUSCANY; for if affection deceiue me not very much, their
POETS excell in nothing but he is admirable in the same: and in this
he is the more admirable that what perfections they haue seuerally,
you may find all in him alone; as though nature had striued to shew
in him that when she pleaseth to make a MASTER-PIECE, she can
giue in one subject all those excellencies that to be in height would
seeme to require euery one of them a different temper and complexion.
And if at any time he plucketh a flower out their gardens, he trans-
planteth it soe happily into his owne, that it groweth there fairer and
sweeter then it did where first it sprang vp. his works are such, as
were their true worth knowne aboard, I am perswaded ye best witts and
most learned men of other parts, would study our long neglected language,
to be capable of his rich conceptions and smooth delivery of them. For
certainely, weight of matter was neuer better ioyned wth propriety of
language and wth maiestey and sweetnes of verse, then by him. And
if any should except his reuiuing some obsolete words, and vsing some
ancient formes of speech, in my opinion he blameth that wch deserueth
much prayse; for SPENCER doth not that out of any affection (although
his assiduity in CHAUCER might make his language familier to him)
but only then when they serue to expresse more liuely and more con-
cisely what he would say: and whensoeuer he vseth them, he doth
so polish their natiue rudenes, as retaining the maiesty of antiquity
the[y], want nothing of the elegancy of our freeshest speech. I hope
that what he hath written will be a meanes that the english tongue will
receiue no more alteration and changes, but will remaine & continue
settled in that forme it now hath; for excellent authours doe draw vnto
them the study of posterity, and whosoeuer is delighted wth what he
readeth in an other, feeleth in himselfe a desire to expresse like thinges
in a like manner: and the more resemblance his elocutions haue to his
authours ye neerer he perswadeth himselfe he arriueth to perfection: and
thus, much converstation [*sic*] and study in what he would imitate,
begetteth a habite of doing the like. This is the cause that after the great
lights of learning among the GRÆCIANS their language receiued no
further alterations. and that the LATINE hath euer since remained in
the same state wherevnto it was reduced by CICERO, VIRGILL, and
the other great men of that time; and the TUSCANE toungue is at this
day the same as it was left about 300 yeares agoe by DANTE PETRACHE
and BOCCACE. If it is true that the vicissitudes of things (change being
a necessary and inseperable condicion of all sublimary creatures) and
the mundations of barbarous nations, may overgrow and ouerrune the
vulgar practise of the perfectest languages, as we see of the foremen-
tioned GREEKE and LATINE; yet the vse of those toungues will flourish
among learned men as long as those excellent authours remaine in the
world. Which maketh me confident that noe fate nor length of time

will bury SPENCERS workes and memory, nor indeed alter that language
that out of his schoole we now vse vntill some general innouation
happen that may shake as well the foundations of our nation as of
our speech: from wᶜʰ hard law of stepmother Nature what Empire or
kingdome hath euer yet bin free? And herein SPENCER hath bin
very happy that he hath had one immediately succeeding him of partes
and power to make what he planted, take deepe rootes; and to build vp
that worke whose foundations he soe fairely layd; for it is beyond the
compasse and reach of our short life and narrow power to haue the
same man beginne and perfect any great thing. Noe Empire was euer
settled to long continuance, but in yᵉ first beginnings of it there was
an vninterrupted succession of heroick and braue men to defend and
confirme it. A like necessity is in languages, and in oures we may
promise our selues a long and flourishing age, when diuine SPENCERS
sunne was noe sooner sett, but in JOHNSON a new one rose wᵗʰ as
much glory and brightnes as euer shone withall; who being himself
most excellent and admirable in the iudicious compositions that in
seuerall kinds he hath made, thinketh no man more excellent or more
admirable then this his late praedecessour in the Laurell crowne. To
his wise and knowing iudgement faith may be giuen, whereas my
weake one may be called in quaestion vpon any other occasion then
this, where the conspicuity of truth beareth it out. SPENCER in what
he saith hath a way of expression peculiar to him selfe; he bringeth
downe the highest and deepest misteries that are contained in human
learning, to an easy and gentle forme of deliuery: Wᶜʰ sheweth he is
Master of what he treateth of; he can wield it as he pleaseth: And this
he hath done soe cunningly, that if one heed him not wᵗʰ great attention,
rare and wonderful conceptions will vnperceiued slide by him that
readeth his works, & he will thinke he hath mett wᵗʰ nothing but
familiar and easy discourses but let one dwell a while vpon them and
he shall feele a straunge fulnesse and roundnesse in all he saith. The
most generous wines tickle the palate least; but they are noe sooner in
the stomach but by their warmth and strength there, they discouer
what they are: And those streames yᵗ steale away wᵗʰ least noyse are
vsually deepest, and most dangerous to pass ouer. His knowledge in
profound learning both diuine and humane appeareth to me without con-
troversie the greatest that any POET before him euer had, Excepting
VIRGIL: whom I dare not medle withall, otherwise then (as witty
SCALIGER did) erecting an altar to him; And this his knowledge was
not as many POETS are contented withall; wᶜʰ is but a meere sprinkling
of seuerall superficiall notions to beautify their POEMS wᵗʰ: But he
had a solide and deepe insight in THEOLOGIE, PHILOSOPHY (especially
the PLATONIKE) and the MATHEMATICALL sciences, and in what
others depend of these three, (as indeed all others doe.) He was a
Master in euery one of them: And where he maketh vse of any of them,
it is not by gathering a posie out of others [*sic*] mens workes, but by
spending of his owne stocke. And lastly where he treateth MORALL or

POLITICAL learning, he giueth euidence of himself that he had a most excellently composed head to obserue and gouerne mens actions; & might haue bin eminent in the actiue part that way, if his owne choice or fortune had giuen him employment in the common wealth.

["This MS vol. is made up of Digby Papers and seems to have the original MS of Digby's observations on 22nd stanza. The above is neither dated nor signed and appears to be a copy in the same hand as the others, except MS of observations, which is in an earlier hand." —RH.]

["Digby's copy of Spenser's Works, 1617, with his signature, was advertised in a London book auction sale, April, 1922."—FIC] (FIC, RH)

1643. John Bramhall. *The Serpent-Salve*, Dublin.
[STC B4236. Rptd *Works* (STC B4210), Dublin, 1676; *Works*, ed. A. W. H., Oxford, 1842-5.]

Works, 1676 ed., p. 574, quoted (A. W. H. 3.421-2):
Suppose the people should desire Liberty of Religion for all Sects; should the King grant it, who is constituted by God the Keeper of the two Tables? Suppose they should desire the free exportation of arms, Moneys, Sheep, . . . and that this should be assented to by the Observers advise, would not the present or succeeding ages give him many a black blessing for his labour?
God help the man so wrapt in errours endless train.
[Cf. *F. Q.* 1.1.18.] (DB)

1643. Stephen Bukley. *Tis a plaine Case Gentlemen*, a broadside printed at York, 1643.
   . . . I'le tell you a pretty tale. There grew a tall
A goodly fence of Hawthorn and of Bryer,
That when the Sunne was chollericke and hot
Kept sheepe and yeaning Lambs safe from his rage
Or when the Sky storm'd did his wrath asswage.
This goodly rowe of Bryers still anon,
Would as the Sheep went by, teare from their backs
Rags of their wooly coates, at which the sheepe
(Though by protection of this good old Bryer
They were fed fatt, and therefore were grown proud[)]
Repin'd, and did preferre bills of complaint
Up to the shepheards: The rude hairbrain shepheards
Cryed down with this proud Bryer; the hedging bills
So layd about them down the Bryer did fall,
And what ensued? a tale most tragicall,
Being layd along, they trod on't it in despite,
Put fire unto it, and burnt it in the flame,
The green bows wept, seeing men past ruth or shame

What sorrow next? marry haile, raine, and snow
Beat on the sheepe and Shepherds, cold winds blow
But whers their shelter? gon Then did the heat
So scorch them that they had no liste to eate.
But whers their coole shade now? gon, gon, & then
Others break in and feed, whilest these fed leane.
At last starved wolves and ravenous foxes came,
And eate up all left neither ewe, nor lambe;
The shepherds pin'd to nothing and like men
Made wise by their harmes, wisht th'ole [sic] Bryer agen.
I' have read a Text, preach you upon't 'tis plaine,
They stab themselves, that strike their soveraigne. (HH)
[Cf. *S. C. Feb.*]

1643. Sir Kenelm Digby. *Observations on the 22. Stanza in the 9th Canto of the 2d. Book of Spencers Faery Queene, written by the Request of a Friend.* [STC D1439.]

[Frequently reprinted in eds. of Spenser; e. g., see Todd, 1805 ed., 4.180-9; *Spenser Variorum* 2.472-8. Though not published until 1643, the *Observations* were written, at the request of Sir Edward Stradling, some time after Digby's voyage in the Mediterranean in 1628.] (FIC, RH)

1644. John Milton. *Areopagitica.*
[STC M2092. *Works*, Frank A. Patterson, gen. ed., Columbia Univ. Press, 1931-40.]

Sigs. B 3ᵛ - B 4 (*Columbia Milton* 4.311):
That vertue therefore which is but a youngling in the contemplation of evill, and knows not the utmost that vice promises to her followers, and rejects it, is but a blank vertue, not a pure; her whitenesse is but an excrementall whitenesse; Which was the reason why our sage and serious Poet *Spencer,* whom I dare be known to think a better teacher then *Scotus* or *Aquinas,* describing true temperance under the person of *Guion,* brings him in with his palmer through the cave of Mammon, and the bowr of earthly blisse that he might see and know, and yet abstain. [Cf. *F. Q.* 2.12.42 ff.] (FIC)

1644. *Vindex Anglicus; or, The Perfections of the English Language. Defended, and asserted,* Oxford.
[STC V461. Rptd *Harleian Miscellany,* ed. T. Park, 1808-13.]

Sig. A 3 (Park 2.37-42; Munro 1.494; Bradley, p. 279):
    There is no sort of verse either ancient, or Modern which we ar not able to equall by Imitation, we have our English *Virgil, Ovid, Seneca, Lucan, Iuvenal, Martial,* and *Catullus:* In the *Earle of Surry, Daniell, Johnson, Spencer, Donne, Shakespeare,* and the glory of the rest, *Sandys* and *Sydney.* (JM)

1645.   *The Great Assises Holden in Parnassus by Apollo and his Assessours.*
[STC W3160. Rptd Sp. Soc. Pub., 1885.]

P. 10 (sig. B 4ᵛ; Sp. Soc. Pub., sig. A 2 - A 2ᵛ):
     Then *Edmund Spenser* Clarke of the Assise,
     Read the Edictment loud, which did comprise
     Matters of scandall, and contempt extreme,
     Done 'gainst the Dignitie, and Diademe
     Of great *Apollo.*
[" EDMVND SPENCER, Clerk of the Assises " also appears among the
list of characters, sig. A 2ᵛ. Ink correction on B. M. copy alters date
to 1644. *The Great Assises* is attributed to George Wither.] (JFB, DEM)

1645.   John Milton. *Poems.*
[STC M2160. *Works,* Frank A. Patterson, gen. ed., Columbia Univ.
Press, 1931-40.]

Il Penseroso, ll. 116-21, pp. 41-2 (*Columbia Milton* 1.44):
     And if ought els, great *Bards* beside,
     In sage and solemn tunes have sung,
     Of Turney's and of Trophies hung;
     Of Forests, and inchantments drear,
     Where more is meant than meets the ear.

Mansus, ll. 30-4, pp. 73-4 (*Columbia Milton* 1.288):
     Nos etiam in nostro modulantes flumine cygnos
     Credimus obscuras noctis sensisse per umbras,
     Quà Thamesis latè puris argenteus urnis
     Oceani glaucos perfundit gurgite crines.
[Cf. *Proth.* 11.] (FIC)

[Other significant parallels between verses in 1645 ed. of *Poems* and
Spenser, noted in *An Index to the Columbia Edition,* Frank L. Patterson
and French R. Fogle (Columbia Univ. Press, 1940), are listed below.
The numbers in parentheses refer to pages in vol. 1 of the *Columbia
Milton.*

On the Morning of Christ's Nativity 173 (8) : S. C. *May* glosse, " Great
pan)."
On the death of a Fair Infant 57 (18) : H. H. B. 93.
At a Vacation Exercise 84 (22) : T. M. 301-2
The Passion 4 (23) : F. Q. 3.1.40.1-2.
L'Allegro 1 (34) : T. M. 262.
Il Penseroso 4 (40) : F. Q. 4.7.16.5; 44 (41) : *Epith.* 234.
Arcades 1 ff. (72) : *Epith.* 148 ff.; 13 (72) : F. Q. 5.12.33.4-5;
     16 (72) : F. Q. 5.9.28.6-8.
Elegia secunda 5 (176) : *Proth.* 42-4.
Elegia tertia 47 (182) : *Proth.* 1-4.
Elegia sexta 13 ff. (208) : S. C. *Oct.* 105.
Elegia septima 55 (218) : F. Q. 3.1.43.1-5.

In quintum Novembris 66 ff. (240) : *F. Q.* 1.5.20, 28.
Ad Patrem 105 (276) : *F. Q.* 2.7.25.1-2 and 3.12.25.4; 106 (276) :
F. Q. 5.12.33.4-5.
Epitaphium Damonis 136 (308) : *Col.* 636; 141 (308): *S. C. Dec.*
77.]

1645.   Humphrey Moseley. *The Stationer to the Reader*, prefixed to *Poems of Mr. John Milton.*
[STC M2160. *The Works of John Milton*, Frank A. Patterson, gen. ed.
Columbia Univ. Press, 1931-40.]

Sig. a 4 - a 4ᵛ (Patterson 1.415):
   Let the event guide it self which way it will, I shall deserve of the
age, by bringing into the Light as true a Birth, as the Muses have brought
forth since our famous *Spencer* wrote; whose Poems in these English
ones are as rarely imitated, as sweetly excell'd. (FIC)

1645.   Edmund Waller. *Poems, &c. Written by Mr. Ed. Waller.*
[STC W511. *Poems*, ed. G. Thorn Drury, 1893.]

The Apology of sleep, p. 14 (sig. B 7; Thorn Drury, p. 81):
   I shall no more decline that sacred bower
   Where *Gloriana* their great mistresse lyes.

In Answer to one, &c., p. 18 (sig. Cᵛ; Thorn Drury, p. 25):
   Hast thou not read of fairy *Arthurs* shield,
   Which but disclos'd, amaz'd the weaker eyes
   Of proudest foe, and wone the doubtfull field?
   So shall thy Rebell wit become her prize.
   Should thy Iambecks swell into a book,
   All were confuted with one Radiant look.
[Cf. *F. Q.* 1.7.33-6.]

Of the Misreport of her Being Painted, p. 26 (sig. C 5ᵛ; Thorn Drury,
p. 50):
   So little care of what is done below
   Hath the bright dame whom heaven affecteth so,
   Paints her : 'tis true with the same hand which spreads
   Like glorious colours through the flowry meads.
   When lavish nature with her best attire
   Clothes the gay spring, the season of desire.
[Cf. *Mui.* 163-4.]

Thyrsis. Galatea, p. 50 (sig. Eᵛ; Thorn Drury, p. 41):
   Who with the Royal mixt her Noble blood,
   And in high grace with *Gloriana* stood.
[Said of the Duchess of Hamilton, Lady of the Bedchamber to Henrietta
Maria.] (DEM)

The Battell of the Summer Islands, Canto 3, p. 56 (sig. E 4ᵛ; Thorn
Drury, p. 71):

So with the barbed Javeling stung, he raves,
And scourges with his tayl the suffering waves:
Like fairy *Talas* with his iron flayl,
He threatens ruine with his pondrous tayl.
[*F. Q.* 5, *freq.*] (FIC)

Puerperium, p. 70 (sig. F 3ᵛ; Thorn Drury, p. 82):
Great *Gloriana*: faire *Gloriana*. (DEM)

[On pages 29 and 74 (sigs. C 7, F 5ᵛ; Drury, pp. 83, 58) are poems addressed to " Amoret," according to Thorn Drury the name under which Waller celebrated Lady Anne Cavendish, later Lady Rich.]

1646.   John Cleveland. *The Kings Disguise*. [STC C4678.]

Sig. A 2ᵛ (Saintsbury 3.55):
Scribling Assasinate, thy lines attest
An eare-marke; Cubbe of the Blatant Beast,
Whose breath before 'tis syllabled for worse
Is Blasphemy unfledg'd, a Callow curse. (EG)

1646.   E.G. Poem prefixed to Martin Llewellyn's *Men Miracles*.
[STC L2625. Cf. Thomas Corser, *Collectanea Anglo-Poetica*, Chetham Soc. Pubs., 1860-83.]

Sig. A 5 (Corser 4 [pt. 2] .366; Spurgeon 1.224-5):
So *Chaucers* learned soule in *Spencer* sung,
(*Edmund* the quaintest of the Fairy throng.)
And when that doubled Spirit quitted place
It fill'd up *Ben*: and there it gained grace. (FIC)
[Corser supposes E. G. to be Llewellyn's Oxford friend, Edward Gray.]

1646.   *A Latter Discovery of Ireland: Or, A Shamrokokive Gallemaufery. . . . Newly set forth by Peirce Plainman, an obscure Gentleman.*

Sig. A 2 [The author is commenting on his book]:
. . . . remember this dish is called a Gallemaufrey, which being neatly cookd is gustable and savoury; yet knowing what paines Doctor *Hanmer*, *Spencer*, and *Campion* have taken therein, I intend not to write the Annals, or History of Ireland.

Epilogue, sig. N 4ᵛ:
Now if the Authors meaning be so clouded here that a vulgar
Ed: Spencer   eye cannot discern it, then repair to the Dialogue betwixt
Eudoxus & *Irenæus*, there shall you finde it (in part) in plainer terms; one passage betwixt them I will give you for a farewell; *viz.* Right so *Irenæus*. (HER)

1646.   Francis Quarles (d. 1644). *The Shepheardes Oracles: Delivered in certain Eglogues.*
[STC Q114A. *Works*, ed. A. B. Grosart, 1880.]

Eglogue 1, pp. 11-2 (sig. C 2 - C 2ᵛ; Grosart 3.206):
      Towards bright *Titans* evening Court there lyes
      From hence ten miles not fully measur'd thrice,
      A glorious Citie, called by the name
      Of *Troynovant,* a place of noted fame
      Throughout the Christian world, of great renowne
      For charitable deeds, a place well knowne
      For good and gratious Government; in briefe,
      A place for common Refuge, and reliefe
      To banisht Shepheards, and their scatter'd Sheep;
      There our great *Pans* Vice-[reg]ent now does keep
      His royall Court. (DEM)

1646.   Samuel Sheppard. *The times Displayed in Six Sestyads.*
[STC S3170. Cf. S. Egerton Brydges, *British Bibliographer,* 1810, where
The Sixth Sestyad is quoted entire.]

The Sixth Sestyad, st. 7, p. 21 (Sig. C 3; Brydges 1.528):
      Although the *Bard,* whose lines unequalled,
      Who only did deserve a Poets name
      To my Eternal grief, be long since dead,
      His lines for ever shal preserve his Fame.   *Samuel*
      So *his who did so neer his foot paths tread   *Daniel.*
      Whose lines as neer as *Virgils Homers* came,
      Do equal *Spencers,* who the soul of verse
      In his admired Poems doth rehearse. (FIC)

1646-7.   George Daniel (d. 1657). *Poems written vpon Seuerall Occasions. Apud Biswicke: Anno Domini CD. iɔcxlvi,* B. M. Additional MS
19255.

[*Poems,* ed. A. B. Grosart, 1878.]
Vindication of Poesie, fol. 12ᵛ (Grosart, 1. 28):
      The Shepherds Boy; best knowen by that name
      Colin; vpon his homely oaten Reed.
      With Roman Titirus may share in ffame;
      But when a higher path hee seem's to tread,
      Hee is my wonder; for who yet has seene
      Soe Cleare a Poeme, as his Faierie Queene? (FIC)

Time and Honour, fol. 14 (Grosart 1.33-4; Bradley, p. 283):
      The proud Italian
      And iustly proud in Poesie, will allow
      The English (though not Equall) next him now;
      The noble Sidney crown'd with liveing Bayes;
      And Spencer cheif, (if a peculiar praise
      May pass, and from the rest not derogate)
      The learned Jonson, whose Dramaticke State
      Shall stand admir'd Example, to reduce
      Things proper, to the light, or buskind Muse. (JFB)

An Essay; Endevouring to ennoble our English Poesie by evidence of latter Qvills; and reiecting the former, fol. 31 (Grosart 1.82)

> And take the Radix, of our Poesie
> To honour more, in this last Centurie;
> The noble Sidney; Spencer liveing Still
> In an abundant fancie; Ionsons Qvill
> Ever admir'd; these iustly wee may call
> Father; high placed, in Apolloes Hall. (FIC)

Idyllia, fol. 270 (Grosart 4.211):

> And everie Tongve, can varnish or^e that Face
> W^ch is but now, the same, she ever was,
> The Ladie of the Wood, was never seene;
> Another Eccho, or the Fayerie Queene.

The Author, fol. III^v (Grosart 2.130-1):

> Next see in-imitable Colin, moves
> Our Admiration; Hee: poore Swaine; in bare
> And thin-set Shades, did sing; whil'st (ah) noe care
> Was had of all his Numbers; numbers which,
> Had they bene sung of old, who knowes, how rich
> A Fame, had Crown'd him? had he lived, when
> Phillips Great Son (that prodigie of men)
> Spread, like Aurora, in the Easterne light;
> Hee had not wish'd a Homer for to write
> His Storie, but ev'n Peleus Son, had sate
> A step below, in Fame, as well as Fate;
> But Hee, poor man, in an vngratefull Age
> Neglected lived; still borne downe, by the Rage
> Of Ignorance: for tis an Easier Thing
> To make Trees Leape, and Stones selfe-burthens Bring
> (As once Amphion to the walls of Thæbes',)
> Then Stop the giddie Clamouring of Pleb's;
> He poorlie dyed; (but vertue cannot dye)
> And scarce had got a Bed, in Death to lye
> Had not a noble Heroe, made a Roome,
> Heed beene an Epitaph, without a Tombe;
> For that Hee could not want; whilst verse or witt
> Could move a wing; they'd bene obliged to it;
> Or say, the bankrupt Age could none Afford;
> Hee left a Stocke, sufficient; on Record.

[Fol. III is dated 1647.] (DEM)

1647. Thomas Bradford. Poem prefixed to Robert Baron's 'EPOTO-ΠΑΙΓΝΙΟΝ, *Or the Cyprian Academy.* [STC B889.]

Sig. a 2 (Bradley, p. 292):

> Her'e is a *Chimist* which from a rude masse
> Extracts Elixar that death may well surpasse

Spencers ninth Canto in the fairy Queene,
Or Ben's Vulpony, oh had he but seene
Thy pregnant fancy, how could he forebeare
To rend his Cat'line and by Jove to sweare
Thy'ns the better. (JFB)

1647. Henry More. *Philosophical Poems Comprising Psychozoia and Minor Poems.*
[STC M2670. Ed. G. Bullough, Manchester, 1931.]

Cupid's Conflict, p. 300 (Bullough, p. 110):
    Lo! on the other side in thickest bushes
    A mighty noise! with that a naked swain
    With blew and purple wings streight rudely rushes
    He leaps down light upon the flowry green,
    Like sight before mine eyes had never seen.

    At's snowy back the boy a quiver wore
    Right fairly wrought and gilded all with gold:
    A silver bow in his left hand he bore,
    And in his right a ready shaft did hold.
[Cf. *S. C. Mar.* 78-84. For allusions to Spenser in the first edition of More's poems, see 1642.] (DEM)

About 1648. Nathaniel Sterry. *A direction for a good and profitable proceeding in study, by Mr. N. Sterry of E. C.* Bodleian, Tanner MSS, vol. 88, no. 5.
[Quoted in *TLS*, Aug. 31, 1933, by V. de S. Pinto.]

Fol. 5:
    After all this, if you can, before you are Batchelor read Spencer, & Daniels poëms for the furnishing of yor English tongue. for what good will all learning doe you, if you cannot make vse of it in the mother tongue? wch excellency few looke after, wch is an extraordinary folly. (DEM)

1648. Joseph Beaumont. *Psyche, or Loves Mysterie. In XX Canto's Displaying the Intercourse Betwixt Christ, and the Soule.*
[STC B1625. *Psyche*, with additions, ed. Charles Beaumont, 1702; *Works*, ed. A. B. Grosart, Chertsey Worthies' Library, 1880.]

Canto 2, Lust Conquered. [Aphrodisius, the deceiver of Psyche: cf. Archimago, *F. Q.* 1.1.29 ff. *et freq.*]

Canto 4, The Rebellion. [Psyche assailed by the senses: cf. *F. Q.* 2.11. 8-13; p. 45, sts. 52-7 (1702 ed., p. 44, sts. 60-4), Pageant of the seasons: cf. *F. Q.* 7.7.28-31.] (FMP)

Ibid., p. 48 (1702 ed. p. 47, st. 105):
    (Not farre from whom, though in a lower clime,
    Yet with a goodly Train doth *Colin* sweep:

Though manacled in thick and peevish Rhyme,
A decent pace his painful Verse doth keep
Well limm'd and featur'd is his mystick *Queen*,
Yet, being mask'd, her beauties less are seen.)
[*Whom* of first line refers to Homer, Pindar, and presumably Tasso.
In 1702 ed., the concluding couplet reads:
    Right fairly dress'd were his welfeatur'd Queen,
    Did not her Mask too much her beauties screen.] (FIC)

Canto 5, The Pacification. [Psyche, arrayed by Pride, rides forth in
coach of vanities, drawn by eight Passions, p. 72, sts. 188, 195 (1702
ed., sts. 214, 222): cf. *F. Q.* 1.4.16 ff.] (FMP)

Canto 6, The Humiliation. [Cave of Sleep, swarm of Dreams, pp. 87-8,
sts. 170 ff. (1702 ed. sts. 193 ff.): cf. *F. Q.* 1.1.39 ff.; 2.7.21 ff.]
(FIC)

Canto 15, The Poison, p. 288, st. 192 (1702 ed., Canto 18, p. 274, st.
61):
            He knew that they who once a foot had set
            In *Errors labyrinth*, would easily be
            Allured further to proceed in it
            By their own tickling Curiosity;
                And having turn'd from Truth's meridian light,
                Might soon inamored be of blackest Night. (DEM)

Canto 16, The Antidote. [Psyche taught and disciplined in Palace of
Ecclesia, p. 302, sts. 60 ff. (1702 ed. Canto 19, p. 286, sts. 77 ff.) cf.
F. Q. 1.10.]

Canto 18, The Persecution. [Palace of Persecution, p. 351, sts. 53-8
(1702 ed., Canto 22, pp. 329-30, sts. 60-6): cf. *F. Q.* 1.8.29 ff.]

Ibid. [Persecution's equipage and train, pp. 353-4, sts. 83-101 (1702
ed., pp. 331-2, sts. 92-113): cf. *F. Q.* 1.4.16 ff.]

Ibid. [Lion fawns upon Psyche, pp. 357-8, sts. 136-44 (1702 ed. pp.
334-5, sts. 151-60): cf. *F. Q.* 1.3.5 ff.]

Canto 19, The Dereliction, p. 373, st. 57 (1702 ed., Canto 23, p. 348,
st. 70):
            Thus cheerly Musick is but Torment to
            A pained Ear.
[Cf. *F. Q.* 1.8.44.4. 1702 ed. has *sounds* for *is.*] (FMP)

Ibid. [Psyche encounters Despair, pp. 376 ff., sts. 89 ff. (1702 ed., pp.
350 ff., sts. 106 ff.): cf. *F. Q.* 1.9.35 ff.] (FIC)

[In the volume of 1702 (*The Editor to the Reader*, sig. b 4), Charles,
the son of Joseph Beaumont, describes a principal difference between
the two editions: " The 16th Canto called *The Supply*, is wholly new . . .
Some Cantoes also of the First Edition are divided into Two Parts in

this Second Edition, under different Titles, which now increases the number of Cantoes to 24."]

1648.   John Dias. *Look to it London, Threatoned to be fired by Wilde-fire-zeal, Schismatical-faction, and Militant-Mammon.* [STC D1380.]

P. 2:
Yet, notwithstanding all this, my charity was of so large a size, that I thought it was but one Doctor *Dulmans* opinion, the *Ignis Fatuus,* or *Brutum Fulmen* of one Bragadochian soldier.

P. 8:
. . . all these felt and found what it was to fight against God, to kick against the prick, and to reckon without their Host, as this fond *Brag-gadocheo* sells the Fox skin before he be catcht. (JGM)

P. 16:
Lastly, this windy-gabs venting, *That if they conquer us, we shall be their slaves . . .* the humor of this fellow personating that bragging *Thraso* in *Terence,* and *Peripolinices* in *Plautus,* and of *Bragodocheo* in *Spencers Fairy* Queen. (GED)

1648.   *The Faerie Leveller: or, King Charles his Leveller descried and deciphered in Queene Elizabeths dayes. By her Poet Laureat Edmond Spenser, in his Unparaleld Poeme, entituled The Faerie Queene. A lively representation of our times.* [STC F81.]

A necessary Preface opening the Allegory, pp. 3-4 (sig. A 2 - A 2ᵛ):
. . . .[Levellers] were discryed long agoe in Queene *Elizabeths* days, and then graphically described by the Prince of English Poets *Edmund Spenser,* whose verses then propheticall are now become historicall in our dayes, I have now revised and newly published them for the un-deceiving of simple people. . . . The Booke out which this fragment is taken (called the *Faery Queene*) is altogether Allegoricall, and needs a little explanation: The drift and intention of the Author in it, is to set forth a compleat Gentleman, accomplisht with all vertues adorning a truly noble Person. The first Booke contains the Legend of Justice, the most universall Vertue. In the second canto *Arthegall* the Champion of Justice, with the Assistance of *Talus* his Groome betokening execution of Law, having overcome all illegall arbitrary oppressive power; under the person of *Pollente,* a barbarous *Saracen,* strengthened by his Daughter *Munera* importing bribes and taxes: He proceeds to suppresse the Gyant Ring-leader to the faction of Levellers, or applying all to these times; I suppose I may briefly give you this key of the work.
Arthegall Prince of justice. King Charles.
Talus his Executioner with his yron flayle. The Kings forces, or Gregory.
Pollente an oppressing Saracen. The prevalent over awing Faction in the two Houses.

Munera his assistant. The intolerable Tax-raisers the Countrey Committees Sequestrators and Excize-men: These must first be apprehended and brought to justice, ere the Army be quelled.
    The Gyant Leveller. Col. Oliver Cromwell, L. G. of the Sts. Army: the letters of whose name fall into this Anagram.
    Oliver Cromewell. Com' our vil' Leveller.

[The author of the tract quotes *F. Q.* 5.2.29-54, the account of Artegal and Talus.] (FIC)

1648.   Sir Richard Fanshawe. *Il Pastor Fido . . . with An Addition of divers other Poems* (2nd ed.). [STC G2175.]
    The Progress of Learning, sig. Kk 4ᵛ:
        Tell me O Muse, and tell me *Spencers* ghost. . . .
    [In Spenserian stanzas.] (FIC)

The Fourth Booke of Virgills Aeneis On the Loves of Dido and Aeneas, pp. 271-96.
    ["The translation is in Spenserian stanzas, a few of which suggest Spenser's handling of the form."] (EAS)

1648.   *Mercurius Elencticus,* No. 35, July 19-26.

P. 276:
    Courteous Reader you are desired to peruse A Book now extant, written by a learned hand, Intituled NOW or NEVER. The *Fairy Leveller,* or *King Charles* his *Leveller* described and decyphered in *Queen Eliz.* dayes by Edmund Spenser, Her *Poet Laureat,* in his unparallelld *poem* entitled the *Fairy* Queen. A lively representation of our times: is newly Printed, with *Annotations* worth your perusall. (HER)
    [See: 1648. *The Fairy Leveller.*]

1648.   Mathias Prideaux (d. before 1646?). *An Easy and Compendious Introduction for Reading all sorts of Histories.* [STC P3439.]

Sig. Xxᵛ:
    9. The *wandering Knights, Spencers Fairy Queene, Sir Philip Sidnies Arcadia,* with other pieces of like straine, may passe with singular Commendations for morall *Romances,* being nothing else but Poeticall *Ethicks,* that with apt contrivanse, and winning Language, informe Morality. (EG)

1648. [John Taylor.] *A Brown Dozen of Drunkards.* [STC T435.]

P. 16 (Spurgeon 4, App. A, p. 71):
    Though he doe not as exactly as *Virgil* imitate *Homer,* nor as our *Chaucer* and *Spenser Virgil.* (DEM)

1649.   John Milton. *Eikonoklastes.*
[STC M2112. *Works,* Frank A. Patterson, gen. ed., Columbia Univ. Press, 1931-40.]

P. 34 (*Columbia Milton* 5.110):
If there were a man of iron, such as *Talus*, by our Poet *Spencer*, is fain'd to be, the page of Justice, who with his iron flaile could doe all this, and expeditiously, without those deceitfull formes and circumstances of law, worse then cermonies in Religion; I say God send it don, whether by one *Talus*, or by a thousand. (FIC)
[Cf. *F. Q. 5.*]

1649. *Vaticinium Votivum: or Palaemon's Prophetick Prayer . . . with several Elegies.*
[STC W3206. Rptd Sp. Soc. Pub., 1885, quoted.]
P. 98:
> Up sad MELPOMENE, up and condole
> The Ruins of *three Realms;* attire thy Soul
> In sorrow's Robes: O let thy *Fountains* rise
> And over-flow the *Flood-gates* of thine eies.

[See *S. C. Nov.* 53. *Vaticinium Votivum* has been attributed to George Wither.] (DEM)

About 1650. Henry More. *Enthusiasmus Triumphatus, or, a Discourse,* 1656.
[STC M2655.]

P. 207 (sig. O 8):
I will show you now, not in the prose of More, but in the very Trot and Loll of *Spencer*, as this Naturall with his tongue lolling out of his driveling mouth, uncivilly calls it. [Quotes *F. Q.* 1.1.23]

P. 297 (sig. V 5):
You are first to consider what a showre of dirt my Antagonist had powred upon me in his foul Answer, endeavouring to tread me down into a dunghill if he could; and therefore it is more pardonable if I rise up with more courage and shake off all suspicion of being so pittifull a creature as he would make me; and truly I had a conceit that shewing the inward frame of my mind so freely to him, it might have proved as successfull as the flying open of Prince *Arthurs* shield in his combate with the Gyant Orgoglio; but it seems he had no eyes to behold that kind of lustre.
[Cf. *F. Q.* 1.8.19.] (DEM)

[1650 is assumed as the approximate date of composition and perhaps of an edition of the *Enthusiasmus Triumphatus*, since Thomas Vaughan evidently refers to the first passage quoted here, in his *Man Mouse taken in a Trap*, published in that year.]

1650. Jo. Bradford. Commendatory poem prefixed to Nicholas Murford's *Fragmenta poetica, or Miscelanies of Poetical Musings, Moral and Divine.*

[STC B3100. Quoted in G. E. Bentley, *Shakespeare & Jonson,* Univ. Chicago Press, 1945.]

Bentley 2.77 quoted:
Poetrie's now grown Staple-Merchandize
Free from Old Custome or the New Excise.
Silvester, Spenser, Johnsonn, Draiton, Donn,
May see Verse measured by the Last and Tunn,
While Dutch, French, Spanish, English liquours use
T' adorn thy house, their learning grace thy Muse. (GEB)

1650. Abraham Cowley. *The Guardian.*
[STC C6673. *Essays and Plays,* ed. A. R. Waller, Cambridge, 1906.]

Act 4, sc. 2, sig. D 2ᵛ (Waller, p. 205) [The poetaster Dogrel, after writing a line that is too long]:
The last is a little too long: but I imitate *Spencer.* (EG)

1650. Abraham Cowley. *To Sir William D'Avenant, upon his two first Books of Gondibert, finished before his Voyage to America,* prefixed to Davenant's *Discourse upon Gondibert,* Paris.
[STC D322. Rptd with eds. of *Gondibert,* 1651 (STC D324-6); *Poems of Abraham Cowley,* ed. A. R. Waller, Cambridge, 1905.]

Sig. A 3 (Waller, p. 42):
Methinks Heroick Poesie, till now
Like some fantastick Fairy land did show;
Gods, Devils, Nymphs, Witches, & Giants race,
And all but man, in mans best work had place.
Thou like some worthy Knight, with sacred Arms
Dost drive the *Monsters* thence, and end the Charms. (FIC)

1650. William Davenant. *A Discourse upon Gondibert. . . . With an Answer to it by Mr. Hobbs,* Paris.
[STC D322. Rptd as *Preface* to *Gondibert,* 1651 (STC D324-6).]

Pp. 11-3 (Chalmers 6.350-1):
Spencer may stand here as the last of this short File of Heroick Poets; Men, whose intellectuals were of so great a making, (though some have thought them lyable to those few censures we have mention'd) as perhaps they will in worthy memory out-last even Makers of Laws, and Founders of Empire, and all but such as must therefore live equally with them, because they have recorded their Names; and consequently with their own hands led them to the Temple of Fame. And since we have dar'd to remember those exceptions which the Curious have against them; it will not be expected I should forget what is objected against *Spencer;* whose obsolete language we are constrain'd to mention, though it be grown the most vulgar accusation that is lay'd to his charge.
Language (which is the onely Creature of Man's creation) hath, like a Plant, seasons of flourishing, and decay; like Plants, is remov'd from one

Soil to another, and by being so transplanted, doth often gather vigour and increase. But as it is false Husbandry to graft old Branches upon young Stocks: so we may wonder that our Language (not long before his time created out of a confusion of others, and then beginning to flourish like a new Plant) should (as helps to its increase) receive from his hand new Grafts of old wither'd Words. But this vulgar exception shall onely have the vulgar excuse; which is, That the unlucky choise of his *Stanza*, hath by repetition of Rime brought him to the necessity of many exploded words.

If we proceed from his Language to his Argument, we must observe with others, that his noble and most artfull hands deserv'd to be employ'd upon matter of a more naturall, and therefore of a more usefull kind. His Allegoricall Story (by many held defective in the Connexion) resembling (me thinks) a continuance of extraordinary Dreams; such as excellent Poets, and Painters, by being over-studious may have in the beginning of Feavers: And those morall visions are just of so much use to Humane application, as painted History, when with the cousenage of lights it is represented in Scenes, by which we are much lesse inform'd then by actions on the Stage. (FIC)

1650. Robert Heath. *Clarastella . . . Epigrams.* [STC H1338.]
[On p. 26 (sig. F 6ᵛ) the title "On *Braggadochio* Cit." occurs. Character is not modeled on Spenser's.] (FBW)

On Priscus, p. 48 (sig. G 5ᵛ):
> Priscus doth poetize now he's in love . . .
> Has th' *Amadis* and *Spencer* all by heart,
> Whence he extracts his sonnets, and his rime,
> And speaks them, dreaming, in and out of time. (JM)

1650? Andrew Marvell. *Miscellaneous Poems,* 1681.
[STC M872. *Poems & Letters,* ed. H. M. Margoliouth, Oxford, 1927.]

Tom May's Death, p. 37 (Margoliouth 1.92; Spurgeon 4.71-2):
> If that can be thy home where *Spencer* lyes
> And reverend *Chaucer,* but their dust does rise
> Against thee, and expels thee from their side,
> As th'Eagles Plumes from other birds divide. (CFES)

1650. Thomas Vaughan. *The Man Mouse taken in a Trap.* [STC V153.]
Epistle Dedicatory to Mr. Matthew Harbert, sig. A 2ᵛ:
You have here a simple *Bedlam* corrected, and whipt for his *mad Tricks.* A certain *Master of Arts* of *Cambridge,* & a *Poet* in the *Loll & Trot* of *Spencer.* It is suppos'd he is in *Love* with his *Fairie-Queen,* & this hath made him a very *Elf* in *Philosophie.* (DFA)

P. 25:
Doth *God* then compose *Anoticè,* so much of *each,* or do his *Scales* admit of *Imparities?* Answer me Positively, either in *Verse* of *Spencer,* or in *Prose* of *Moore.* (DEM)

P. 35:
   You are neither a *Modern* singer, nor yet an *Ancient one*; You live in *our dayes*, but you imitate *Spencer*, so that *your song* is both *old and new*, and Truth perhaps may be had *for it*. (DFA)

P. 101:
   This it is *Mastix* to *deal* with those *things* which you do not understand, to measure *Theo-Magic* by your *skill* in the *strain* of *Spencer*. (DEM)

[Apparently Vaughan is attacking Henry More; cf. the first quotation with that under: About 1650. Henry More. *Enthusiasmus Triumphatus*.]

Before 1651. John Milton. Marginalia.
[*Works*, Frank A. Patterson, gen. ed., Columbia Univ. Press, 1931-40.]

[Notes on copy of *Britannia's Pastorals*, 1613-6, are to the effect that in Book I, Song 2, line 180 on page 50, "Colin Clout" signifies "Spencer" (*Columbia Milton* 18.337); that in Book 2, Song 1, line 976 on page 26, "Spencer" is meant (*ibid.* 339); and that on page 27, line 995, his death is lamented (*ibid.* 339).] (FAP)

Before 1651. John Milton. Commonplace Book, B. M. Add. MS 36354.

Fol. 188 (*Columbia Milton* 18.189):
The wicked policies of divers deputies & governours in Ireland see Spenser dialogue of Ireland.

Fol. 242 (*Columbia Milton* 18.210):
Provisions for soldiers after yᵉ Warrs to be consider'd. Spenser dialogue of Ireland from p. 84 &c. (FIC)

1651. H. B. On Mr. *Cartwright's Poems* prefixed to William Cartwright's *Comedies, Tragi-Comedies, with other Poems*.
[STC C709. Cf. Joseph Hunter, *Chorus Vatum*, B. M. Additional MS 24489.]

Sig. *** 2 (Hunter, fol. 31):
           Here's Wit Stenography'd. No Compass steers
      A Course unknown to Him: He coasts the Spheres;
      For what Platonick *Spencer* did unfold,
      Or smooth-tongu'd *Carew* to the World hath told,
      What came in reach of *Fletcher's* searching mind,
      Or *Beaumont's* towring Brain could ever find,
      What other heads, who must unchristen'd go,
      Like Zanies to the Wits in Folio;
      All their rare Arts our Author does display:
      All Stars mix here, and make a *Milky-way*.
[H. B. is identified as Henry Bold.] (FIC)

1651. R. C. Prefatory remarks, in William Bosworth's *The Chast and Lost Lovers*. [STC B3799.]

The Epistle Dedicatory [to John Finch], Sig. A 2:
If Poetry be truly conceived to carry some *Divinity* with it, and *Poets*, on what Subjects soever their Fancies have discoursed, have bin intituled *Divine*, as the *Divine Mr. Spencer*, the *Divine Ronsard*, the *Divine Ariosto;* how much more properly may they be esteemed to be *Divine*, who have made chast Love their Argument.

To the Reader, sigs. A 3ᵛ - A 4:
The high, the fluent, and the pathetick discourse of his lovers, and the transformation of them after their death . . . you shall finde hath allusion to *Ovids Metamorphosis*. . . . The strength of his fancy, and the shadowing of it in words he taketh from Mr *Marlow* in his *Hero and Leander*. . . . The weaving of one story into another and the significant flourish that doth attend it is the peculiar Grace of Sir *Philip Sidney*, whom our Author doth so h[a]ppily imitate. . . . His making the end of one Verse to be the frequent beginning of the other (besides the Art of the Trope) was the labour and delight of Mr. *Edmund Spe[n]cer*, whom Sir *Walt. Raleigh* and S. *Kenelm Digby* were used to call the *English Virgill*. (FIC)

1651. William Cartwright. *The Lady-Errant. A Tragi-Comedy.*
[STC C710. *Plays and Poems*, ed. G. Blakemore Evans, Univ. Wisconsin Press, 1951.]

Act 2, sc. 1 (Evans, p. 105, quoted):
    Mach.   How I hate
    That Name of Madam, it befits a Chamber:
    Give me the words o'th'Field, such as you'd give
    To fairer Ladyes pricking o'r the Plains
    On foaming Steeds. (GBE)
[Cf. *F. Q.* 1.1.1.]

1651. Samuel Sheppard. *Epigrams Theological, Philosophical, and Romantick.* [STC S316.]

The Fourth Book, Epig. 10, *To* Clio, *having but begun my* Faerie King, pp. 78-9 (sigs G 3ᵛ - G 4):
    O Muse, what dost thou whisper in my eare?
    What thou suggests to me I dare not heare,
    Find thee an abler Agent, alas I
    Am all unfit for Warlike Poesie,
    To sing the Acts of *Heros*, and compile
    The Deeds of Kings, in a full heightned stile,
    Is such a task I dare not undergoe,
    How to begin, or end, I do not know:
    And more, if *Spencer* could not scape the spite
    Of tongues malevolent, whose gentle spright
    Prompted him, so meek as never man
    Before him could, nor (I think) ever can,

I then shall (sure) be bitt to death, but yet
If thou commandest that I forward set,
I will not be rebellious, but desire,
Thoult warme my bosome with my hottest fire. (EG)

Ibid., Epig. 12, *To the Illustrious Cardinall* Mazerine, *his Victory lately obtained over the* Spanish *Army under the Archduke* Leopold, p. 80 (sig. G 4ᵛ):

Now hast thou silenc'd Slander, par'd the clawes
O'th *Blatant* Beast.

Ibid., Epig. 17, *A Dialogue maintained by five, viz. the Poet, Clio, Povertie, Ignorance, Mammon*, p. 83 (sig. G. 6):

CLIO.

Hither direct thy steps, descend this Cave
Castalia call'd here, thou a place shalt have
To heare our Harmonie, here *Homer* sate,
When he his high immortal *Illiads* wrote,
Here *Orpheus* penn'd his *Hymns*, here *Maro* sung
Aeneas Travells with a golden tongue:
Here *Pindar*, and *Anacreon* did devise
Their *Odes*, which since none e're could equalize:
Here *Flaccus*, *Naso*, *Spencer*, hath been seen,
I help'd the last to frame his Faerie Queene. (JGM)

Ibid., Epig. 28, *On Mr.* Spencers *inimitable Poem, the* Faerie Queen, pp. 95-7 (sigs. H 4 - H 5):

Collin my Master, O Muse sound his praise
Extoll his never to be equal'd Layes,
Whom thou dost Imitate with all thy might,
As he did once in *Chawcers* veine delight
And thy new *Faerie* King, shall with Queen
When thou art dead, still flourish ever green.
Cease wealthy *Italy* to brag and boast,
That thou for Poesie art famed most
Of any Nation, *Ariostos* veine,
Though rare, came short of our great *Spencers* streine:
His great *Orlando* hath receiv'd great losse
By *Spencers Faerie* Knight of the Red Crosse:
Warrelike *Rogeros* honour clouded is
By his *Arthegall*, and much fame doth misse,
His sweet Angellica describ'd with Art,
Is wan withered, to his *Brittomart*,
His admirable Poems darkned quite,
As if he onely had known how to write,
Nor may that wonder of your Nation claime
Supremacie, before our *Spencers* Fame:
Admired *Tasso*, (pardon) I must do

That right the Muses all perswade me to,
Although to *Godfrey* by thy worthy Layes,
Thou dost a *Mausolean* Trophey raise,
Yet *Spencer* to *Eliza* hath done more,
And by his fullnesse lesseneth thy store:
He like the grand *Meonian* sits on high,
Making all Verse stoope to his Poesie;
Like to some mighty River *Nile* or *Po*,
All that obstruct him, hee'l soon overthrow:
And shallow Brooks, if any list to strive,
From forth his Ocean soon they may derive.
Hee next unto *Apollo* sits above
With *Homer*, and sweet *Maro*, who approve
Of his society, and joy to see
Him that did equall their fam'd Poesie.
Niggardly Nation be ashamed of this,
A Tombe for thy great Poet wanting is,
While fooles, not worth the naming, seated high
On Sepulchers of Marble God-like lie:
The learned in obscurity are thrust,
But yet their Names shall long out-live their dust:
Although Great *Spencer* they did thee interre,
Not Rearing to thy name a Sepulcher,
Yet thou hast one shall last to the last day,
Thy *Faerie* Queen, which never shall decay:
This is a Poets Priviledge, although
His person among sordid dolts do goe
Unto the Grave, his Name shall ever live,
And spite of Time, or Malice shall survive. (EG)

The Second Pastoral, pp. 235-6 (sig. R 5 - R 5ᵛ):
      They sorrow that thy Pipe is still,
      Which came so near to *Astrophill*,
      Yea, wont aswell to please the route,
      As the rare Layes of *Collin Clout*:
      Their Oaten Reeds they also break,
      And make great sorrow for thy sake. (DEM)

The Third Pastoral, pp. 246 [misprinted 462]-247 (sigs. S 2ᵛ - S 3):
      But I to thee will now display
      What I have heard my Father say.
      Next unto *Tytirus* there came
      One that deservd a greater name,
      Then was bestowed; but when She swaid,
      Whom to this day some call a Maid,
      Then *Collin Clout* his pipe did sound,
      Making both Heaven and Earth resound;
      The Shepheards all both farre and near

About him flock'd his layes to hear,
And for his songs he was so fam'd,
He was the Prince of Shepheards nam'd.

Ibid., p. 252 (sig. S 5ᵛ):
O gentle Shepheard still pipe on,
Stil take deep draughts of *Helicon,*
And thou'lt be rankt I make no doubt
With *Tytirus* and *Collin Clout.* (HER)

1652. Peter Heylyn. *Cosmographie in foure Bookes* (9th ed. of *Microcosmus*). [STC H1689.]

Book I. p. 268 (sig. Z 2ᵛ):
And finally for Poetrie, 1 *Gower,* 2 *Lidgate,* a Monk of *Burie,* 3 the famous *Geofrie Chawcer,* Brother in Law to *Iohn of Gaunt,* the great Duke of *Lancaster;* of which last Sir *Philip Sidney* used to say, that *he marvelled how in those mistie times he could see so cleerly, and others in so cleer times go so blindly after him.* 4 Sir *Philip Sidney* himself, of whom and his *Arcadia,* more when we come to *Greece.* 5 The renowned *Spencer,* of whom and his *Faerie Queen* in another place. 6 *Sam. Daniel,* the *Lucan,* 7 with *Michael Draiton,* the *Ovid* of the *English* Nation. 8 *Beaumont,* and 9 *Fletcher,* not inferiour to *Terence* and *Plautus;* with 10 My friend *Ben. Iohnson,* equall to any of the antients for the exactness of his Pen, and the decorum which he kept in *Dramatick* Poems, never before observed on the *English* Theatre.

Ibid., p. 308 (sig. Ee 2ᵛ) [After having named the principal Irish rivers]:
Of which, and others of like note, take this following Catalogue, out of the Canto of the mariage of the *Thames* and *Medway* in the *Faierie Queen.* [Quotes *F. Q.* 4.11.41, and concludes: "With many more, &c. So the renowned *Spencer* in his *Canto* of the mariage of *Thames* and Medway."]
[After a discussion of *Terra Incognita* in Book 4, Heylyn remarks (p. 195, sig. Bbbbb 3): "But being there is little certain of these last discoveries . . . therefore I will try my fortune, and without troubling the Vice-Royes of *Peru,* and *Mexico,* or taking out Commission for a new Discovery, will make search into this Terra Australis for some other regions." He discovers *Mundus Alter et Idem, Utopia, New Atlantis, Færie Land, The Painters Wives Iland, The Lands of Chivalrie, The New World in the Moon.* His description of *Færie Land* follows.]

P. 196 (sig. Bbbbb 3ᵛ):
4. *FAERIE LAND,* is another part of this *Terra Incognita;* the inhabitation of the *Faeries,* a pretty kind of *little fiends,* or *Pigmey devils,* but more inclined to sport then mischief; of which old Women, who remember the times of *Popery,* tell us many fine stories. A cleanyer and more innocent cheat was never put upon poor ignorant people, by

the *Monks* and *Friers*. Their habitation here or no where; though sent
occasionally by *Oberon* and their other Kings, to our parts of the World.
For not being reckoned amongst the *good Angels*, nor having malice
enough to make them *Devils* (but such a kind of midling *Sprites*, as
the *Latines* call *Lemures Larvae*) we must find out some place for them,
neither *Heaven* or *Hell*, and most likely this. Their Country never more
enobled, then by being made the Scene of that excellent Poem, called
the *Faerie Queen*. Intended to the honour of Queen *Elizabeth*, and the
greatest persons in her Court: but shadowed in such lively colours,
framed so exactly by the Rules of *Poesie*, and representing such *Idæas*
of all moral goodness; that as there never was a *Poem* more *Artificial*; so
can no *Ethical* discourse, more fashion and inflame the mind to a love
of vertue. *Invisurum facilius aliquem quàm imitaturam*, shall be *Spencers
Motto*; and so I leave him to his rest. (FRJ)

1652. *A Perfect Diurnall*, no. 130, Monday, June 7, 1652.
[Quoted *PMLA*, 37 (1922). 705.]

P. 1928:
He that desires to advance the Plantation of *Ireland*, can hardly find
better hints, then are in Mr. *Ed. Spencer* his view of the state of *Ireland*,
published almost three score years agoe, 1596. (EG)

1653. William Basse. *The Pastorals And Other Works*.
[Designed for publication at Oxford, 1653, but first published in 1870.
Poetical Works, ed. R. W. Bond, 1893.]

Dedication (Bond, pp. 170-1):
    The famous Shepheard Collin, whom we looke
    Never to match, (though follow him we may
    That follow sheep, and carry scrip and hooke)
    By iust aduantage of his time and way
    Has plac'd the moneths in his eternall booke,
    All in their owne due order and aray;
    (A Kalendar to last, we cannot say
    For one yeare, but as long as yeares shal bee);
    Yet of the weeke has left me euery day
    Vertues to sing, though in more low degree.
    And could they reach, my Lord, a higher key,
    Yours as the Shepheard is the songes should be.
    Great merit may claime grace in Noble breast;
    Favour is greatest where desart is least. (FIC)

Eclogue 1 (Bond, p. 180):
    His sheepe, that bore the brand of his neglect
    On their bare ribbes, resembled his desire;
    As if perceiuing where he did affect,
    From their owne vale attempt to clamber higher;
    But, like their gentle keepers loue, soon check't,
    To his and their owne miseries retire;

While her proud lambs mark'd with her like disdaine
Shew careles lookes to the despised playne. (DEM)
[Cf. *S. C.* Jan. 43-8.]

Eclogue 9 (Bond p. 248):
   When I survey my heap of youthfull song
   And Ditties quaint, to volumes neare arose,
   I whilome did, to please the amorous throng
   Of Nymphs and Swayns, to my green reed compose,
   And finde so small a number them among
   Of pious straine or vertues pure dispose,
   Then muse not (Hobbinoll) that my Muse growes
   Melancholly, but thinke her iustly sorry
   Four seeking earthly more then heau'nly glory.
[Cf. *H.H.L.* 8-14.]

Ibid. (Bond, p. 251):
   But aboue all, o blessed Majesty,
   Who by thy power and wisdome all hast wrought,
   And all dost rule, aboue and under skye,
   From greatest substance unto smallest thought,
   That we thy name aright may magnify,
   And sing thy works and wonders as we ought,—
   Grant with such streames our feeble hearts be fraught
   As thou doest giue, from forth thine euer-liuing
   Fountaine of grace, that more abounds by giuing. (FMP)
[Cf. *H.H.B.* 8-21.]

Ibid. (Bond, p. 253):
   Nor stand tall woods alone for goodly port,
   But each his proper businesse hath and state.
   The Oake a builder is of lasting sort,
   And him the Elme and Beech doe imitate.
   The Ash a souldier, Ewe is his consort:
   The Pine a Sayler, and the Fyrrhe his mate;
   The Cypresse mourner at the funerall gate;
   And Lawrell, that wee talked of but now,
   A crowne of Victors and of Muses brow.

   The Poplar can the climbeing workeman's wish
   As well advance as fan the sunny glade;
   The melancholly willow learne to fish
   Rather then bee for fooles the garland made;
   The Maple turne himselfe to Shep-heards dish,
   And Holly prentice be to Vintners trade,
   The hoary Palme the poore mans cottage shade:
   And all this crue to solace, Walnut-tree,
   And Box, and Plane, a set of Musique bee. (DEM)
[Cf. *F. Q.* 1.8-9.]

Ibid. (Bond, p. 259):

But he that fram'd this uniuersall globe
Aboue all Creatures here would Man his eye
Should upward lift, and contemplate on hye
Those glympses of the glorious life of blisse,
The more to striue for that life after this. (FMP)
[Cf. *H.H.B.* 295-301.]

1653. Theodore Bathurst. *Calendarium Pastorale, sive Æglogæ Duodecim, totidem Anni Mensibus accommodatæ. Anglicè olim Scriptæ ab Edmundo Spensero Anglorum Poetarum Principe: Nunc autem Eleganti Latino carmine donatæ A Theodoro Bathurst, Aulae Pembrokianæ apud Cantabrigienses aliquando Socio.*

[STC S4966. Alternate title of 1653 ed. of *S. C.* with English text and Bathurst's Latin tr. on opposite pages.] (FIC)

1653. John Davies, of Kidwelly (d. 1693). Prefatory remarks to his translation of Charles Sorel, *The Extravagant Shepherd. Or, The History of the Shepherd Lysis.* [STC S4703.]

Sig. A^v (1654 ed., STC S4704, quoted):

Nay, and thus many men not weighing discreetly the differences of *times, persons* and *places,* which they have had to represent, have fallen into error very misbecoming. The *Indecorum* of *Homers* gods, the fault in *Virgils* chronology, *Tasso* making Christians speak like *Heathens, Spencers* confusion, and different choice of names, are things never to be forgiven. (HH, JLL)

1653. [Sir John Denham, and others.] *Certain Verses Written By several of the Authors Friends; to be re-printed with the Second Edition of Gondibert.* [STC D992.]

To Dapane. On his Incomparable In[c]omprehensible Poem Gondibert, p. 12:

Virgil, thou hast no Wit, and *Naso* is
More short of *Will,* then is *Will's* Nose of his;
Can silence *Tasso,* and the *Fairy Queen,*
Thou all by *Will* unread and most unseen. (DEM)

1653. William Dillingham. *Viro eximio . . . Francisco Lane . . . ,* prefacing Theodore Bathurst's *Calendarium Pastorale.* [STC S4966.]

Sig. A 3^v:

Erat olim tibi *Spenserus* tuus in deliciis; quocirca nullus metuo nè ingratus hodie tibi fit, indutus idem Romanâ togâ; quæ ità quidem illum decet, tamq; aptè illi convenit, ut aut non aliâ cute natus, aut in eam non tam translatus, quam restitutus esse videatur. Erat quidem Poema Anglicè cum barbâ . . . imo & canitie suâ natum; ac si Poeta non tam in

Parnasso somniâsset, quàm cum *Endymione* in *Latmo* stertuisset, atqu; adèo post tertium indè seculum ad scribendum demum evigilâsset. (WW)

Sig. A 4:
. . . *Theophilus Bathurst* (Poeta non minùs elegans, quàm gravis idem postea Theologus) qui in eodem Collegio has æglogas latinè vertit, quo *Spenserus* ante aliquot annos poematia sua concepisse dicitur; & quidem ità vertit, ut & obscuris lucem, & facilitatem asperis, atq; omnibus ferè nitorem ac elegantiam fœneraverit; ac si unus ejusdem loci Genius idem carmen diuersis temporibus illi Anglicè, huic Latinè dictâsset. (FMP)

1653.   Sir Richard Fanshawe.   Letter to John Evelyn, Dec. 27, 1653, in B. M. Add. MS 28, 104.
[Transcribed William E. Simeone, "A Letter from Sir Richard Fanshawe to John Evelyn," *N & Q*, 196 (1951).315-6.]

Fol. 6 (Simeone, p. 316, quoted):
. . . . One thing I must needs acquaint you with: and it is, that this [translation by Evelyn of the first book of Lucretius] came to my hands just when I had made an end of reading a posthumous Translation, by mr or doctor Bathurst, lately printed at London (I presume you have seen it) of SPENCER'S SHEPHEARDS CALENDAR into Latine; as if opportunely to prevent my idolizing that Language: to the advantage whereof above ours, I doe not now impute that admirable worke, which (unlesse my Augury deceive mee) will, where it's true origine shall be vnknowne, passe for a Native of ould Rome, and that as farr, as the utmost bounds extend of ye commonwealth of Learning. ffor if the great wonder there bee, how a Poem, which the Author made it his buisinesse to cloathe in rugged English covld be capable of so smooth latine; certainly it is not lesse a one heere, how so rugged a latine poem . . . can be rendred in so smooth English. And if mr. Bathurst by that exported commoditie doe more honour to England Abroad; you, by this imported, will more inrich it at home: making our Income proportioable to our Expence. (WES)

1653.   *On Mr Edm. Spencer, Famous Poet*, in *Poems, by Francis Beaumont, Gent.* [STC B1602-3. Rptd in Alexander Chalmers, *English Poets*, 1810.]

Sig. M 2 (STC B1603 quoted; Chalmers 6.204):
At *Delphos* shrine, one did a doubt propound,
   Which by th'Oracle must be released,
Whether of Poets were the best renow'nd:
   Those that survive, or they that are deceased?
The Gods made answer by divine suggestion,
While *Spencer* is alive, it is no question. (DEM)
[Probably not by Beaumont: it is preceded by two poems lamenting Beaumont's death, by Basse's epitaph on Shakespeare, and by two epitaphs on Ben Jonson; it is followed by an epitaph on Michael Drayton.]

1653. Samuel Sheppard? *Merlinus Anonymous. An Almanack, And no Almanack. A Kalendar, and no Kalendar. An Ephemeris (between jest, and earnest) for the year, 1653.*

Sig. B 8 [Calendar for December under second column, *Fest dayes*): Semiramis. Pasiphæ. Canidia, Pilades, and Orestes. Hero and Leander. Duessa.

[Elsewhere in the second column four other months are listed, among many others, Sejanus, Bevis of Southampton, Circe, and Romeo and Juliet. Cf. sig. A 4 (describing the parts of the *Kalendar*): "In the second collumn the festivall Dayes (Martyrs quite forgotten by *Fox.*)"] (HER)

1653. James Shirley. *Cupid and Death, A Masque.*
[STC S3464. *The Dramatic Works and Poems,* ed. Alexander Dyce, 1833.]

Sig. B 3 (Dyce 6.351):
    Ch. Despair! my time's not come yet, what have I
    To do with thee? what com'st thou hither for?
    Des. To find out *Death;* life is a burden to me;
    I have pursu'd all Paths to find him out,
    And here i'th th'Forrest had a glimpse on him,
    But could not reach him with my feet, or voice;
    I would fain dy, but *Death* flies from me, sir. (FIC)
[Cf. *F. Q.* 1.9.21 ff.]

1654. Thomas Blount. *The Academie of Eloquence: Containing a Compleat English Rhetorique, Exemplified.* [STC B 3321. 1656 ed., STC B3322, quoted.]

P. 4 (sig. B 2ᵛ):
    Let Spencer tell you such a tale of a *Fairy Queen,* or *Ovid* of *Danae,* and 'tis a *Poetical Fiction.* (FIC)

[Blount is quoting, without acknowledgment, Hoskins' *Directions for Speech and Style;* see: 1599. John Hoskins.]

1654. Edmund Gayton. *Pleasant Notes upon Don Quixot.* [STC G415.]
P. 21 (Munro 2.36; Bradley, p. 304):
Let English men write of their owne wits, fancies, subjects, disputes, sermons, Histories; Romances are as good, vigorous, lasting, and as well worthy the reading, as any in the world. Our *Fairy Queen,* the *Arcadia,* Drayton, Beaumont and Fletcher, Shakespeare, Johnson, Rondolph; and lastly, Gondibert, are of eternall fame.

P. 150 (Munro 2.37; Spurgeon 1.229; Bradley, p. 304):
Our Nation also hath had its Poets, and they their wives: To passe the bards; Sr *Jeffery Chaucer* liv'd very honestly at Woodstock, with his Lady, (the house yet remaining) and wrote against the vice most wittily, which Wedlocke restraines. My Father *Ben* begate sonnes and daughters;

so did *Spencer, Drayton, Shakespeare* and more might be reckoned, who doe not only word it, and end in aiery *Sylvia's,* Galatæa's, Aglaura's;
——*sed de virtute locuti,*
Clunem agitant——
    It is possible to speak of holy life,
    And anon after Solace ones own wife. (JM)

About 1655. Samuel Sheppard. *The Faerie King Fashioning Love and Honovr. In an Heroicall Heliconian Dresse,* Bodleian MS Rawlinson poet. 28.
[Cf. introductory stanzas with *F. Q.* 1. proem 1.] (FMP)

2.5.20.1-5:
    there fell MEDEA & the SPARTANE QUEENE
    who ruin'd famous TROY, sterne AGAVE
    with PASYTHÆ, who clapsed a Bull uncleane
    (if wee may creddit NASO'S Poesie)
    ACRASIA and ARMIDA.
[For Acrasia, see *F. Q.* 2.1.51-5, *et freq.*] (DEM)

3.1.1:
    CLIO thou first of the Caelestiall Nine
    APOLLO'S DARLING, Sacred QUEENE of STORIES
    unto whose famous everlasting SHRINE
    (to their admired never-dying glories)
    great HOMER, VIRGILL, TASSO the Divine
    SPENCER (who Rules the two faire Promontories)
    offerd their Charming Volumes, & from thee
    were crowned with fulgent IM-MORTALLITIE. (HER)

3.5.7.1-4:
    th'Ruinians, had incampt themselves by this
    upon a spacious plaine, neare which there stood
    (SYLVANUS, & PRIAPUS Bower of Blisse)
    a most delightfull, flowry, shadie wood.
[Cf. *F. Q.* 2.5.27 ff.]

3.5.14:
    Deigne o' thou cheif'st of Muses, amply, now;
    to ayde in this great worke I undertake
    fill up my brest brim full, & show mee how
    to crowne thy Temples by the verse I make
    as once thou did'st to COLIN CLOUT allow
    let mee part of his sacred fire pertake
    so shall I raise a Trophey unto thee
    and purchase to my selfe Æternitie.

4.1.1.1-4
    Thou light[t]'st a candle to the glorious Sun
    dear Muse, & addst a drop unto the Sea

(wishing a glory that can nere bee won
as if great SPENSER could bee reach'd by thee) (DEM)

4.4.64,66:
    her hayre was halfe torn off, her garments too
    were curtail'd, her lanke meagre brests hung downe
    flapping upon her knee, of sanguine hiew
    was all her body, from her foot to crowne,
    for oft in madnesse, on her selfe she flew
    sometimes sheed hang her selfe, sometimes shee'd drowne
    her cursed corse, yet could not find a death
    for SATANS Essence, still supplide her breath.

    upon her wounded withered Arme shee bare
    a loade of rustie Swords, Knives, Daggers, Ropes,
    boxes of Poyson, & sharpe Hookes to tare,
    those whom shee frighted quite beyond their hopes,
    appointed thus, on ARIODANT shee doth stare
    a while (who strongly with her terror copes)
    Some times she stood, but could not long forbeare
    her luggage downe, thus thundered DESPAIRE. (FMP)
[Cf. *F. Q.* 1.9.21 ff.]

5.1.2.5-8:
    warme thee by Statius Immateriall fire
    or rather let great Spensers melody
    ravish thy Sense: o may his number be
    reverberated Artfully by thee.

5.2.30.5-8:
    compar'd with this dire Grot; those gloomie lands
    beneath the Scythian BOSPHORUS; where grow
    all balefull simples, paralelld with this
    might well be thought ACRASIAS BOWER OF BLISSE.
[Cf. *F. Q.* 2.5.27 ff.]

5.3.20.3-8:
        what Muse, wt Power, or wt thrice sacred herse
        by Homer, or by Spenser dignified.
        living Immortall in their mighty verse
        can lend mee such a holy light for guide
        as may declare Byanors Rapture now
        viewing Olivias hayre & pollisht brow. (DEM)

5.4.5.5-6:
                t'was indeede the Fort
    which Adam built (escapt from Errors Den) (FMP)
[Cf. *F. Q.* 1.1.13.6.]

5.6.44-5:
    SPENCER the next, whom I doe thinke't no shame
    to Immitate; if now his worke affords

so vast a Glory, o how faire a Fame
had hee not doated on Exploded words
had waited on him; let his honourd name
find veneration 'bove the Earths great Lords,
great PRINCE OF POETS, thou canst never die
lodg'd in thy rare Immortal History.

Immortal Mirrour of all Poesie
SPIRRIT OF ORPHEUS; bring your pretious Balms,
GOD OF INUENTION, to thy memory
we'l offer Incense, singing Hymns and Psalms,
joy to our Laurell, JOVES deare MERCURY
ingyrt his grave with Myrtle and with palms,
whose rare Desert first kindled my Desire
& gave me confidence, thus to Aspire. (HER)

[6.3.39.1-5 mentions, along with Semiramis, Camilla, Artemesia, " our
English PALLAS, glorious VAODICIA, / renowned BRITOMART."]
(DEM)

6.6.3:
    rise then thou sacred shade of COLIN CLOUT
    ENGLANDS APOLLO, whose renowned story
    shall live till Heavens Eye bee quite thrust out
    and courted as the Muses cheifest glory,
    if that they Genius Ayde, I shall not doubt
    to Tryumph over all things Transitory
    nor shall fell ATROPOS devouring Knife
    mince the tough Thread, of my farre better life. (HER)

Postscript, fol. 80ᵛ:
    Were not this worke of more worth then either my selfe will boast,
or permit others to divulge, I should thinke it Incompatible with that
modestie I have ever profest, to say the monstruositie of these times
merrit not a peice the least pollished & so much of kin to his miraculous
Minerva (Incomperable Spencer) whose Genius admits no Rivall. (DEM)

1655.   John Cotgrave. *Wits Interpreter, the English Parnassus.*
[STC C6370.]

[Engraved frontispiece, containing vignette portraits of Spenser, Shakespeare, Jonson, Randolph, More, Bacon, Sidney, Strafford, Richelieu, and
DuBartas.] (JGM)

1655.   Sir Richard Fanshawe. *The Lusiad, or Portugals Historicall Poem:
Written In the Portingall Language by Lvis de Camoens; and now newly
put into English by Richard Fanshaw Esq.* [STC C397.]

The Translator's Postscript, sig. b 2ᵛ:
    For (to name no more) the *Greek* HOMER, the *Latin* VIRGIL, *our*
SPENCER, and even the *Italian TASSO* (who had a *true,* a *great,* and

no obsolete story, to work upon) are in effect wholly *fabulous.* (DFA, EAS)

1655.   Thomas Fuller. *The Church-History of Britain.*
[STC F2416. Ed. James Nichols, 1842.]
Book 4, p. 152 (Nichols 1.469; Spurgeon 1.230):
He [Chaucer] lies buried in the South-Isle of *St. Peters, Westminster,* and since hath got the company of *Spencer* and *Drayton* (a pair-royal of Poets), enough (almost) to make passengers feet to move metrically, who go over the place, where so much *Poetical dust* is interred. (FIC)

1655.   Robert Johnston. *Historia Rerum Britannicarum . . . ab Anno 1572, ad Annum 1628,* Amsterdam.

Lib. VIII, 1598, p. 249 (sig. Ii):
   Annus & hic abstulit, apud *Anglos,* Maximum hujus ætatis Orna-mentum, *Edmundum Spenserum,* Londini in tenui re natum; qui omnes superioris Seculi *Poëtas Anglicos* longè superavit; & ad declinandam Paupertatem, in *Hiberniam,* cum *Graio Prorege* secessit; ut per Otium ac Requiem, *Apollini & Musis* operam daret: ubi à Prædonibus *Laribus* ejectus, & Bonis spoliatus, Inops in *Angliam* redijt; & Mestitiâ rebus humanis exemptus, in *Vestmonasterij Cænobio* sepultus est, apud Chaucerum, impensis *Essexia Comitis;* quia ut Creditur, in *Cecilium Quæstorem* acriter invehitur, in *Fabulâ Hubartae Vetulae.*   *Mother*
(FIC)   *Huberts*
                                                                                  tale.

1656.   *Choyce Drollery.*
[STC C3916. Ed. J. W. Ebsworth, Boston, England, 1876.]
On the Time-Poets, sig. B 4 (Ebsworth, p. 7; Spurgeon 1.1656; Bradley, p. 311):
          Old *Chaucer* welcomes them unto the Green,
          And *Spencer* brings them to the fairy Queene;
          The finger they present, and she in grace
          Transform'd it to a May-pole, 'bout which trace
          Her skipping servants, that do nightly sing,
          And dance about the same a Fayrie Ring. (CFES)

1656.   Abraham Cowley. *Poems: Viz. I. Miscellanies. II. The Mistress, or, Love Verses. III. Pindarique Odes. And IV. Davideis, or a Sacred Poem of the Troubles of David.*
[STC C6683. *Poems,* ed. A. R. Waller, Cambridge, 1905.]
Davideis, Book I, p. 7 (sig. Aaaa 4; Waller, p. 246):
          Envy at last crawls forth from that dire throng,
          Of all the direful'st; her black locks hung long,
          Attir'd with curling *Serpents;* her pale skin
          Was almost dropt from the sharp bones within,

And at her breast stuck *Vipers* which did prey
Upon her panting heart, both night and day
Sucking black *bloud* from thence, which to repaire
Both night and day they left fresh *poysons* there.
Her garments were deep stain'd in humane gore,
And torn by her own hands, in which she bore
A knotted whip, and bowl, that to the brim
Did with green gall, and juice of wormwood swim.
With which when she was drunk, she furious grew
And lasht herself; thus from th'accursed crew,
Envy, the worst of *Fiends*, herself presents,
Envy, *good* onely when she'herself *torments*. (FIC)

[Cf. *F. Q.* 1.4.30-2.]

1656. Peter Heylyn. *A Survey of the Estate of France*, and *France Painted to the Life. By a Learned and Impartial Hand.* See: 1626. Peter Heylyn.

1656. Samuel Holland. *Don Zara del Fogo. A Mock-Romance.* [STC H2437.]

Book 2, pp. 101-2 (sig. H 3 - H 3ᵛ; Munro 2.54; Bradley, p. 308):
The fire of Emulation burnt fiercely in every angle of this Paradise; the Brittish Bards (forsooth) were also ingaged in quarrel for Superiority; and who think you, threw the Apple of Discord amongst them, but *Ben Johnson*, who had openly vaunted himself the first and best of English Poets; this Brave was resented by all with the highest indignation, for *Chawcer* (by most there) was esteemed the Father of English Poesie, whose onely unhappiness it was, that he was made for the time he lived in, but the time not for him: *Chapman* was wondrously exasperated at *Bens* boldness, and scarce refrained to tell (his own *Tale of a Tub*) that his *Isabel* and *Mortimer* was now compleated by a Knighted Poet, whose soul remained in Flesh; hereupon *Spencer* (who was very busie in finishing his *Fairy Queen*) thrust himself amid the throng, and was received with a showt by *Chapman, Harrington, Owen, Constable, Daniel,* and *Drayton,* so that some thought the matter already decided; but behold *Shakespear* and *Fletcher* (bringing with them a strong party) appeared, as if they meant to water their Bayes with blood, rather then part with their proper Right, which indeed *Apollo* and the Muses (had with much justice) conferr'd upon them, so that now there is like to be trouble in Triplex; *Skelton, Gower* and the Monk of *Bury* were at Daggers-drawing for *Chawcer*: *Spencer* waited upon by a numerous Troop of the best Book-men in the World: *Shakespear* and *Fletcher* surrounded with their Life-Guard, viz. *Goffe, Massinger, Decker, Webster, Sucklin, Cartwright, Carew,* &c. (JM)

1656. Edward Leigh. *A Treatise of Religion and Learning, and of Religious and Learned Men.* [STC L1013.]

The Epistle to the Reader, sig. A 6 (Spurgeon 1.232; Bradley, p. 309):
I shall endeavour to marshall up some of our English Schollers. . . .
For Poets of old, *Chaucer, Spenser, Ockland.*

P. 91 (Spurgeon 1.232):
England hath been famous for Learned men, and for her Seminaries
of Learning, as well as other things. . . . For Poetry, *Gower, Chaucer,
Spencer, Sir Philip Sidnie, Daniel* and *Draiton, Beaumont and Fletcher,
Ben: Jonson.* . . .
Galfridus Chaucerus, Jeffery Chaucer, he was born in Oxfordshire.
He first of all so illustrated the English Poetry, that he may be esteemed
our English *Homer.* He is our best English Poet and *Spencer* the next.
(CFES)

1656. John Phillips (ed.). *Sportive Wits: The Muses Merriment. A
New Spring of Lusty Drollery.* [STC P2112.]

To his Friend: a censure of the poets, pp. 68-9:
> Graue *Spencer* shortly after there came in,
> Then whom I am persuaded there was none,
> Since the blind *Bard* his Iliads up did make,
> Fitter a task like that to undertake
> To set down boldly, brauely to indent
> In all high knowledge finely excellent. (FH)

1656. *Wit and Drollery.* [STC W3131.]

*Verses written over the Chair of Ben. Johnson, now remaining at Robert
Wilson's, at the signe of Johnson's head in the Strand,* p. 79 (Spurgeon
1.234):
> And though our Nation could afford no room,
> Near *Chaucer, Spenser, Draiton,* for thy tomb;
> What thou ordain'st, though for thy pleasures more
> Then Pyramids or Marbles guilded o're. (CFES)

1657. Oliver Cromwell. Letter to the Lord Deputy of Ireland and
Council, 27 March. Letters of Lord Protector and Council A / 28.
[Printed in Robert Dunlop, *Ireland under the Commonwealth,* Manchester, 1913; Pauline Henley, *Spenser in Ireland,* Cork Univ. Press,
1928; W. C. Abbott, *Writings and Speeches of Oliver Cromwell,* Harvard Univ. Press, 1937-47.]

Fol. 118 (Henley, pp. 206-7; Abbott, 4.437-8; Dunlop 2.659, item
936, quoted):
A petition hath been exhibited unto us by William Spencer, setting
forth that being but seven years old at the beginning of the Rebellion
in Ireland, he repaired with his mother, his father being then dead, to
the City of Cork, and during the Rebellion continued in the English
quarters, that he never bore arms or acted against the Commonwealth of

England, that his grandfather Edmund Spencer and his father were both Protestants . . . that his grandfather was that Spencer, who by his writings, touching the reduction of the Irish to civility, brought on him the odium of that nation, and for those works and his other good services Queen Elizabeth conferred on him that estate, which the said Wm Spencer now claims. . . . We judge it just and reasonable, and do therefore desire and authorize you that he be forthwith restored to his estate, . . . in doing whereof our satisfaction will be the greater by the continuance of that estate to the issue of his grandfather, for whose eminent deserts and services to the Commonwealth that estate was first given him. (FIC)

1657. Edward Fuscus (pseud.?) *Ovids Ghost: or, Venus overthrown by the Nasonian Polititian. With A remedy for Love-Sick Gallants. In a Poem. On the dispraise of all sorts of Wives.* [Folger F2566a.]

Epitaph on that pattern of Vertue, Thomas Beal, *Esq; Lievtenant of* Whittlewood Forrest Norton, *in imitation of* Doct. Alabaster *his Latine on one* Ed. Spencer, p. 92 (sig. G 3^v):

> Who lieth here? if any ask, 'tis one
> Whose very nam's enough to make him known.
> Reader, if that you'd see, look up, for there
> It's writ, but when th' hast read, tis *Beal* lies here:
> If after that you any further goe,
> And ask who's he? y'are worthy ne'r to know.
> *Heu Cervi! vester cecedit servator, & heu vos*
> *Imbelles Damae! quid nisi præda sitis?* (JGM)

1657. Joshua Poole. *The English Parnassus: or, A Helpe to English Poesie.* [STC P2814.]

[On p. 41 (sig. D 5; Bradley, p. 315) " Spencers fairy Queen " is included in *The Books principally made use of in the compiling of this Work.* On p. 562 (sig. Rr 2^v) under *Names of beauteous women* are listed, among others: Amoret, Florimel, Claribel, Belphebe, Pæana, Æmylia, Serena, Blandina.] (JFB, WW)

About 1658. Henry Oxinden. Commonplace Book, Folger MS 4018.
P. 16:

> Spencer erat magnus fama, et virtute poeta,
> Divinus major Nomine Spencer ad=est.

[These two verses comprise the only entry on the page.] (JGM)

1658. Sir Aston Cokayne. *Small Poems of Divers sorts.*
[STC C4898. *A Chain of Golden Poems,* STC C4894, is another issue: paginations noted below refer to either volume. Cf. S. Egerton Brydges, *Restituta* 2 (1815).]

A Remedy for Love, p. 8 (sig. B 4ᵛ; Brydges 2.138-9):

There thou upon the Sepulchre maist look
Of *Chaucer,* our true *Ennius,* whose old book
Hath taught our Nation so to Poetize,
That English rythmes now any equalize;
That we no more need envy at the straine
Of *Tiber, Tagus,* or our neighbor *Seine.*
There *Spencers* Tomb thou likewise maist behold,
Which he deserved, were it made of gold:
If honour'd *Colin,* thou hadst liv'd so long,
As to have finished thy Faery Song,
Not onely mine, but all tongues would confess,
Thou hadst exceeded old *Mæonides.*

Ibid., p. 11 (sig. B 6; Brydges 2.139-40):

For *Colins* sake (who hath so well exprest
The vertues of our Faery Elves, and drest
Our Poesie in such a gallant guise)
On happy *Pembroke-Hall* employ thine eyes.

Ibid., p. 16 (sig. B 8ᵛ; Brydges 2.139):

Though the *Arcadia* be a book approv'd,
Arcadia must not be by thee belov'd.
The Lady *Wrothes Vrania* is repleat
With elegancies, but too full of heat.
Spencers and *Daniels* Sonets do not view,
Though they are good, they are not so for you.
From feigned Histories refrain thy sight,
Scarce one is there but is an amorous Knight.
Musæus English'd by two Poets shun;
It may undo you though it be well done.
Harrington's Ariosto do not touch,
For wanton lines scarce any book hath such.
And my old friend *Drayton's* Epistles you
(Being too soft and languishing) eschew.

[Eclogues on pp. 24-34 (sigs. C 4ᵛ - Dᵛ) are faintly reminiscent of Spencer's style and diction.] (FIC, DEM)

Love Elegies, 12, pp. 51-2 (sig. E 2 - E 2ᵛ):

And unto the eternal praise
Of your rich Beauty I will raise
A fame so high, that times to come
Of your deare name shall ne're be dumbe;
So you with *Rosalinde* shall be
Eterniz'd unto Memorie,
With *Stella* live; names known as well
As *Colin Clout,* and *Astrophel.*

Funeral Elegies, 1. On the Death of my very good Friend Mr. *Michael Drayton,* p. 66 (sig. Fᵛ; Brydges 2.37):

> *Phoebus,* art thou a God, and canst not give
> A Priviledge unto thine own to live?
> Thou canst: But if that Poets nere should dye,
> In Heaven who should praise thy Deity?
> Else still (my *Drayton*) thou hadst liv'd and writ;
> Thy life had been immortal as thy wit.
> But *Spencer* is grown hoarse, he that of late
> Song *Gloriana* in her *Elfin* state;
> And so is Sydney, whom we yet admire
> Lighting our little Torches at his fire.
> These have so long before *Apollo's* Throne
> Carrol'd Encomiums, that they now are growne
> Weary and faint; and therefore thou didst dye,
> Their sweet unfinish'd Ditty to supply.
> So was the Iliad-writer rapt away;
> Before his lov'd *Achilles* fatall day,
> And when his voice began to fail, the great
> Unequal'd *Maro* did assume his seat:
> Therefore we must not mourn, unless it be
> 'Cause none is left worthy to follow thee. (DEM)

Encomiastick verses on several Books, To my friend, Mr. *Philip Massinger,* on . . . the *Emperour of the East,* p. 99 (sig. H 2; Brydges 2.39; Bradley, p. 168):

> Thou more then Poet! our *Mercury,* that art
> *Apollo's* Messenger, and dost impart
> Her best expressions to our ears, live long
> To purifie the slighted *English* Tongue.
> That both the Nymphes of *Tagus* and of *Po*
> May not henceforth despise our language so:
> Nor could they do it if they ere had seen
> The machless features of the Faery Queen. (JFB)

Ibid., To Mr. *Humphrey* C. on his Poem entitled *Loves Hawking Bag,* p. 105 (sig. H 5; Spurgeon 1.236):

> *Chaucer,* we now commit thee to repose,
> And care not for thy Romance of the *Rose.*
> In thy grave at *Saint Edmonds Bury,* thy
> *Hector* henceforth (*Lydgate*) may with thee ly;
> Old *Gower* (in like manner) we despise,
> Condemning him to silence for his Cryes.
> And *Spencer,* all thy Knights may (from this time)
> Go seek Adventures in another Clime.
> These Poets were but Footposts that did come
> Halting unto's, whom thou hast all outrun.
> For *Sol* hath lent thee *Pegasus* the Nag,

To gallop to us with Loves-Hawking Bag;
And welcome (mighty Poet) that alone
Art fit to sit with Phœbus in his throne. (DEM)

Epigrams The first Book, 37. Of *Edmond Spencer,* p. 155 (sig. L 6;
Brydges 2.140):
　Our *Spencer* was a Prodigie of wit,
　Who hath the Faery Queen so stately writ:
　Yield *Grecian* Poets to his Nobler Style;
　And ancient *Rome* submit unto our I'le.
　You modern wits of all the four-fold earth
　(Whom Princes have made Laureates for your worth)
　Give our great *Spencer* place, who hath out-song
　Phœbus himself with all his Learned Throng. (FIC)

1658. John Eliot. *Poems Consisting of Epistles & Epigrams.*
[STC E520.]

To the Lord Chamberlain, sig. G 7ᵛ :
　Inimitable *Spencer* ne'r had been
　　So famous for his matchless *fairie Queene,*
　Had he not found a *Sidny* to preferr
　His plain way in his shepherds *Callender.* (HH)

1658. Edward Phillips. *The New World of English Words: Or, a General
Dictionary.* [STC P2068.]

Sig. a 3 (Bradley, p. 316):
There will be occasion to persue the Works of our ancient Poets, as
Geffry Chaucer, the greatest in his time, for the honour of our Nation;
as also some of our more Modern Poets, as *Spencer, Sidny, Draiton, Daniel,*
with our reformers of the Scene, *Johnson, Shakesphear, Beaumont,* and
Fletcher, and among the renowned Antiquaries, *Cambden, Lambard,
Spelman, Selden,* and divers others. (JFB)

1658. S. W. *To his ingenuous Friend, the Author, on his imcomparable
Poems,* prefixed to *Naps upon Parnassus, A sleepy Muse nipt and pincht,
though not awakened.* [STC F1140.]

Sigs, B 4ᵛ - B 5 (Munro 2.78; Spurgeon 4.73; Bradley, pp. 316-7):
　If I may guess at Poets in our Land,
　Thou *beat'st* them all *above,* and *under hand.* . . .
　To thee compar'd four English Poets all stop
　And vail their Bonnets, even *Shakespear's* * *Falstop*　* It should
　Chaucer the first of all was'nt worth a farthing,　have been
　Lidgate, and *Huntingdon,* with Gaffer *Harding.*　Falstaff, *if*
　Non-sense the *Faëry Queen,* and *Michael Drayton,*　the rhyme
　Like *Babel's* Balm. (JM)　had per-
　　　　　　　　　　　　　　　　　　　　　　　mitted it.
[Wing attributes *Naps upon Parnassus* to Thomas Flatman.]

1658. William Sanderson. *Graphice. The use of the Pen and Pensil. or, The Most Excellent Art of Painting: In Two Parts.* [STC S648.]

Part I, *Of the disposition of the Parts,* pp. 50-1 (sigs. O^v - O 2):

Pourtray in your excellent *Pieces,* not only the dainty Lineaments of *Beauty,* but shadow round about, rude thickets, rocks; and so it yields more grace to the Picture, and sets it out: this *discord* (as in *musicke*) makes a comely *concordance;* a disorderly order of counterfeit rudeness, pleaseth: so much grace, doe mean and ordinary things, receive from a good and orderly *connexion.*

[Cf. E. K.'s epistle to Harvey, prefixed to *S. C.,* in defence of archaic language.] (FH)

1659. Richard Lovelace. *Lucasta. Posthume poems.* [STC L3241. Ed. C. H. Wilkinson, Oxford, 1925.]

The Triumphs of Philamore and Amoret, p. 53 (Wilkinson 2.158):

Whilst *Amôret* on the reconciled Winds
Mounted, and drawn by six Cælestial Minds;
She armed was with Innocence, and fire
That did not burn, for it was *Chast Desire;*
Whilst a new Light doth gild the standers by;
Behold! it was a Day shot from her Eye;
Chasing perfumes oth' East did throng and sweat,
But by her breath, they melting back were beat.
A Crown of Yet-nere-lighted stars she wore,
In her soft hand a bleeding Heart she bore,
And round her lay Millions of broken more.

[Cf. the description of Amoret, *F. Q.* 3.12.19-22.] (DEM)

1659. Henry Stubbe (?). *A Light Shining out of Darknes: or Occasional Queries submitted to the Judgment of such as would enquire into the true State of things in our Times.* [STC S6056.]

The Conclusion, pp. 175-6 [in the discussion of " changes and alterations as to the *Ministry* "]:

I shall recommend to the City of *London* some verses of their *Poet Laureate,* the famous *Spencer,* who dyed too many years ago that he should write out of favour to any *in our times,* and I think he was not deemed a *Sectarian.* In the Eclogue of *May* under the false Shepheard *Palinode,* he lively personates our *Presbyteriall Ministers,* whose whole life is a recantation of their pastorall vow, and whose profession to forsake the world, as they use the matter boggs them deeper into the world. Those he inveighes against (as I may say) not without some presage of these reforming times. [*S. C. May* 103-31 quoted, with marginal note: " cited by *I. M.*" ; see above: 1641. John Milton] (FIC) [On the title page of the B. M. copy is written in a contemporary hand: " By Sr Henry^e Vaine. K."]

1660-1. Samuel Hartlib. Letters to Dr. Worthington, in *Diary and Correspondence of Dr. Worthington.*
[Ed. James Crossley, Chetham Soc., 1847, 1855.]

Jan. 1, 1660 (Crossley 1.259 quoted):
I shall long to have your promises about the renowned Spenser, and shall very willingly make search after any pieces of his, as well in Ireland as in England.

Jan. 16, 1660 (Crossley 1.271 quoted):
I just now rec^d your last of Jan. 11, 1660. I thank you for the catalogue you sent of renowned Spenser. I shall enquire most diligently after all those pieces you have named as well in Ireland as in England. And if I speed in any place, you shall soon hear of it.

March 13, 1660 (Crossley 1.279 quoted):
I shall write into the Low C[ountries]. for the rest of Ainsworth's unpublished MSS., as I have done already about Spenser into Ireland.

Dec. 7, 1661 (Crossley 2.86 quoted):
I never received any answer out of Ireland concerning Spenser's works, but I purpose, God willing, to try once more, as I said before. (FIC)

1660. Henry More. *An Explanation of The grand Mystery of Godliness.* [STC M2658.]

Book 5, chap. 8, par. 2, pp. 152-3:
But that he [Christ] may have the Field clear to himself, it will not be amiss to digress a little further, and to take notice of some few others that put in for an *Equality* with him, or a *Superiority* above him: and the chief of them are these Three, *Mahomet, David George* and the *begodded Man of Amsterdam;* whom I dare not venture to bring into the list without a Preface for pardon and excuse for that which looks so like a piece of dishonour and disrespect to our blessed Saviour. But *Duessa* till unstripped will compare with *Una;* you know the story in *Spencer*: and the bold Ignorance of some does ordinarily make others take a great deal of pains to explain and evince that which to any indifferent man is usually true at first sight.
[Cf. *F. Q.* 1.2.20 ff., *et freq.*]

Ibid., chap. 14, par. 5, pp. 169-70:

* In his Fairy Queen, Book 1. Cant 6. Methinks * *Spencer*'s description of *Una*'s Entertainment by Satyrs in the Desart, does lively set out the condition of Christianity since the time that the Church of a Garden became a *Wilderness.* They danc'd and frisk'd and play'd about her, abounding with externall homages and observances; but she could not inculcate any thing of that *Divine law of life* that she was to impart to them. The Representation is so lively, and the Verses so musical, that it will

not be tedious to recite some of the chief of them; as Stanza
11. where he makes the Satyrs to lay aside their rudeness
and roughness as much as they could to revive the dismayed
Virgin after her great Distress. [Quotes st. 11, ll. 5-9; st.
12, ll. 5-9; st. 13 complete; st. 14, ll. 1-4.] But in all this
alacritie and activity in their Ceremonies and complemental
observances, *Una* could beat nothing of the *inward law of
life* into them, but all was spent in an outward Idolatrous
flattery, as the Poet complains Stanza 19 [st. quoted].
(DEM)

1660. Thomas Tanner. Verses contributed to *Epicedia Academiae
Oxonienses in obitum Serenissimae Mariae Principis Arausionesis,* Oxford.
[STC 0877.]

Sig. H 2ᵛ:
The rest of our poets may reherse
(I am but a Reformade in verse)
But sure, had she erst lived, she had been
Our SIDNEY's Stella, or our *Spencers Queen.* (LB)

1660. Henry White. ΘΥΣΙΑ 'ΑΙΝΈΣΕΩΣ, *Or, A Thank-offering To the
Lord, For the happy Recal of Our dread Soveraign Charles.*

P. 15:
By *builders* or architects here we are not forced to understand them to
whom the government was legally committed, not the *Archigubernists,*
but meer *Archimagoes,* which by crafty and cruel devices took upon them
the government, which snatched the reigns into their hands, and forced to
themselves the Title of the *Trustees of the Nation,* who under pretence
of keeping, utterly ruined the liberties of the People, who in stead of
holding forth a *Scepter of safety,* held over their heads a Sword of terror.
[According to the title-page this sermon was preached at Rougham,
Suffolk, May 24, 1660.] (GWS)

1660. William Winstanley. *England's Worthies. Select Lives of the Most
Eminent Persons from Constantine the Great to the death of Oliver
Cromwel late Protector.* [STC W3058.]

[In Frontispiece, the vignette portrait numbered 38 and bearing the
initials Eᵈ.S. apparently is intended as Spenser's likeness.] (WW)

[*The Names of Authors cited in this book,* sig. a⁸, includes *Spenser.*]

[In *The Life of Geoffrey Chaucer,* pp. 96-7, Winstanley reproduces almost
verbatim and without acknowledgement Speght's account of Spenser's
regard for Chaucer. See: 1598. Thomas Speght.] (DEM)

P. 98 [at the conclusion of remarks on Chaucer]:
I intended to have presented the world with the lives of three more
of the most eminent of our modern Poets, viz. Mr. *Edmond Spenser,*

Michael Drayton Esquire, and Mr. *Benjamin Johnson,* (not that I could thereby imagine to add unto their fames, they having built themselves everlasting Monuments in their never dying Works) but out of a desire to imitate forreign writers, who have ever done their Worthies that right, but as yet I cannot meet with any of their friends and honorers that are able to render me so full and happy an account, of them, as that I might have registred them in this volume to Posterity.
[Winstanley carries out his intention in the second ed.: see 1684, below.]

The Life of Sir Philip Sidney, p. 182:
The renowned Poet Spenser in his Ruines of Time, thus writes of him: [quotes ll. 323-9.] (WW)

P. 183:
[Sidney was] not altogether addicted to Arts, but given as much to the Exercise of Arms, being a follower of *Mars* as well as a Friend to the Muses; and although he himself used to say, *That Ease was the Nurse of Poesie,* yet his Life made it manifest, that the Muses inhabited the Fields of *Mars,* as well as the flowery Lawns of *Arcadia;* that Sonnets were sung in the Tents of War, as well as in the Courts of Peace; the Muses Layes being warbled forth by a Warlike *Sidney* in as high a tune, as ever they were sung by a peaceable *Spenser.* (DEM)
[See 1684 for additional references to Spenser in Winstanley's 2nd ed.]

1660-1.   John Worthington. Letters to Samuel Hartlib Jan. 11, 1660, and Dec. 2, 1661.
[*Diary and Correspondence of Dr. Worthington,* ed. James Crossley, Chetham Soc., 1847-86.]

Letter of Jan. 11, 1660 (Crossley 1.261-3 quoted):
Sir,
    Yours I receiv'd last week; which exprest a great desire of the catalogue of those pieces of the renowned Spenser, which are only mentioned, but were never printed. This I now give you, as it was collected out of several scatter'd intimations of them in his printed works.
    1. A Translation of Ecclesiastes.
    2. A Translation of Canticum Cantorum.
    3. The Dying Pelican.
    4. The Hours of the Lord.
    5. The Sacrifice of a Sinner.
    6. The 7 Psalms.
    7. His Dreams.   ) These two were promised by E. K. to be
    8. His English Poet.) set forth with his Comment. Which E.
    9. His Legends.   K. was he that did comment upon
    10. Court of Cupid.   Spenser's Kalendar.
    11. His Purgatory.
    12. The Hell of Lovers.
    13. A Sennights Slumber.
    14. His Pageants.

These are the smaller poems of his, besides many others in the hands of noble persons, and his friends. He had for his friends Sir Philip Sidney, (whom, as also the Countess of Pembroke, he highly honoured,) Sir Walter Raleigh, Mr. Gabriel Harvey, besides E. K. who wrote the Comment upon the Shepherd's Calendar; and others whose initial letters of their names only are set down, as R. S., H. B., W. L., G. W., senior, which need some Oedipus to discover them. But the greatest want is of the other six books of that incomparable poem, the Faery Queen; of which only 2 canto's and 2 stanza's of another canto are printed in the folio.

And this is an account of all that I have seen of his printed, except a short Discourse of Ireland in prose.

The printer in one place intimates, that divers of his poems were disperst abroad in sundry hands; and some were purloyn'd from him since his going into Ireland. These (if not quite lost) may perhaps lie hid in some libraries or closets. He lived heretofore in the north of England, and in the south, viz., Kent, as is intimated by the Kentish Downs, so often mentioned by him.

Next to his Faery Queen, I should most desire to see the English Poet, and the Divine Poems: for that in his latter years he most relish'd the more divine strain of poesie, appears by several passages in his printed poems.

Letter of Dec. 2, 1661. (Crossley 2.76 quoted):

In some former letters you desired me to give you a catalogue of the renowned Spenser's works unpublished. I made the best enquiry to find the intimations of them, which lay scattered at great distances in the epistles, prefaces, or notes of his works. I think about fourteen I recounted to you. And you told me you had written into Ireland, where his last being was. I suppose by your silence that you could never get any satisfactory answer. There are but few indeed that mind anything but what is in the road to profit. You could not but have been desirous to know the issue of that paper message, and to see your dove return with an olive leaf, or a laurel leaf, which hath a peculiar respect to poets.

1661.   S. P. *Mundorum Explicatio Or, The Explanation of an Hierogliphical Figure.* [STC P2974.]

P. 235:

Here lacks a *Tasso*, or a *Bartas*, or
A *Spencer's* Muse, a *Quarles*, or *Silvester*:
Or some such *Laureate*. (HH)

[Authorship by Samuel Pordage is probable.]

1662.   Elnathan Chauncy. Commonplace Book, late 17th Century.

[Cf. George Lyman Kittredge, "A Harvard Salutatory Oration of 1662," *Pub. Colonial Soc. Mass.*, 28 (1935).]

P. 22 (Kittredge, p. 5):

> [And allso turne your pleasant eulogys,
> [Into] ye most heart breaking elegys.

[Cf. *T. M.* 371-2. Kittredge observes that "Chauncy's Spenserian quotations, which run to more than a score of pages, cover almost all of Spenser's poems except the Faerie Queene. . . . Apparently he had at hand a mutilated copy" of 1611 or 1617 ed.] (EAS, FMP)

1662. Thomas Fuller. *The History of the Worthies of England.*
[STC F2440. Ed. P. Austin Nuttall, 1840.]

London, pp. 219-20 (Nuttall 2.379-80; Spurgeon 1.239):

EDMOND SPENCER born in this *City, was brought   *Camb. Eliz. in* up in *Pembroke-hall* in Cambridge, where he became   Anno 1598. an excellent Scholar, but especially most happy in English Poetry, as his works do declare. In which the many *Chaucerisms* used (for I will not say affected by him) are thought by the ignorant to be *blemishes,* known by the learned to be *beauties* to his book; which notwithstanding had been more salable, if more conformed to our modern language.

There passeth a story commonly told and believed, that *Spencer* presenting his Poems to Queen *Elizabeth*: She highly affected therewith, commanded the Lord *Cecil* Her Treasurer, to give him an hundred pound; and when the Treasurer (a good Steward of the Queens money) alledged that sum was too much, then *give him* (quoth the Queen) *what is reason;* to which the Lord consented, but was so busied, belike, about matters of higher concernment, that *Spencer* received no reward; Whereupon he presented this petition in a small piece of paper to the Queen in her Progress,

> *I was promis'd on a time,*
> *To have reason for my rhyme;*
> *From that time unto this season,*
> *I receiv'd nor rhyme nor reason.*

Hereupon the Queen gave strict order (not without some check to her Treasurer) for the present payment of the hundred pounds, the first intended unto him.

He afterwards went over into Ireland, Secretary to the Lord *Gray,* Lord Deputy thereof; and though that his office under his *Camd.* Lord was lucrative, yet he got no estate, but saith my *Author, *Eliz. in* *Peculiari Poetis fato semper cum paupertate conflictatus est.* . . . *Anno* 1598

Returning into *England,* he was robb'd by the Rebels of that little he had, and dying for grief in great want, *Anno* 1598. was honorably buried nigh *Chaucer* in Westminster, where this Distick concludeth his Epitaph on his Monument,

Anglica te vivo vixit plausitque poesis,
Nunc moritura timet te moriente mori.

Whilst thou dids't live, liv'd English poetry,
Which fears, now thou art dead, that she shall die.
Nor must we forget, that the expence of his funeral and monument, was defrayed at the sole charge of *Robert*, first of that name, Earl of *Essex*. (FIC)

Ibid., p. 234 (Nuttall 2.411):
    I will not pry too nearly and narrowly into the fancy of our *Bella* in his *Poet, speaking of the ruins of old Rome, [quotes *R. R.*
Bella in his   39-42.] (FH)
ruins of
Rome trans-
lated by
Spencer.

Warwick-Shire, p. 126 (Nuttall 3. 285; Spurgeon, App. A, 3. 108) [In review of Drayton's career]:
He was born within a few miles of *William Shakespeare*, his Countryman and fellow-Poet and buried within fewer paces of *Jeffry Chaucer*, and *Edmund Spencer*. (DEM)

1662.   Henry More. *Philosophical Writings of Dr. Henry More.*
    [STC M2672.]

The Defence of the Moral Cabbala, Chap. 3:
    It is much that *Philo* should take no notice of that which is so particularly set down in the Text, *the subtilty of the Serpent*, which methinks is notorious in *Pleasure*, it looking so smoothly and innocently on't, and insinuating it self very easily into the minds of men upon that consideration, and so deceiving them; whenas other Passions cannot so slily surprise us, they bidding more open warre to the quiet and happiness of mans life, as that judicious Poet *Spenser* has well observed in his Legend of Sir *Guyon* or *Temperance*.
[Cf. *F. Q.* 2.]

An Appendix to the Defence of the Philosophic Cabbala, Chap. 11, p. 148:
    Whereas therefore it is said that these *Flaming Cherubims* keep the way to the Tree of Life, being placed before the Garden of *Eden*, it is but in such a sense as when Hesiod says,
    That God has made Labour the porter of the Gate of Vertue; and in such as *Virgil* places *Grief*, and *Care*, and *Sickness*, and *Old Age* at the entrance of *Orcus*. . . . Of which certainly there is no other sense in either place, then that by being *laborious* a man shall attain unto Vertue, and no otherwaies; and that by being overcharged with *Care*, *Grief*, *Sickness*, or *Old Age*, a man shall be sent packing into the state of the dead. So *Spencer*, to omit several other instances in him, in making those two grave personages, *Humilita* and *Ignaro*, the one the

Porter of the House of Holiness, the other of the Castle of *Duessa,* can understand nothing else thereby but this, That he that would enter into the House of Holiness must be like *Humilita,* an humble man; and he that can conscientiously passe into the communialty of the imposturous *Duessa,* must be a very *Ignaro.*
[Cf. *F. Q.* 1.10.5, 1.8.30-4.] (DEM)

1664.   William Bold. *To my dear Brother Mr. H. B. on his Poems,* prefixed to Henry Bold's *Poems Lyrique, Macaronique, Heroique, &c.* [STC B3473.]

Sigs. A 4ᵛ - A 5:
  For he that writes to imitate thy Vein
  May write, and keep the paper for his Pain.
  As He that thought to write like Princely *Spencer,*
  Prov'd in his Faculty, a very Fencer:
  No more to be compar'd then *Trigg* to *Frazier*
  Or Turvy-Tinker to an Acon-Brazier. (EG)

1664.   William Cavendish, Duke of Newcastle. *To the Lady, on her Booke of Poems,* prefixed to *Poems and Phancies,* by the Marchioness of Newcastle, 2nd ed. [STC N870.]

Sig. A (Bradley, p. 331):
  I saw your *Poems,* and then Wish'd them mine,
  Reading the *Richer Dressings* of each Line;
  Your *New-born, Sublime Fancies,* and such store,
  May make our *Poets* blush, and Write no more:
  Nay *Spencers Ghost* will haunt you in the Night,
  And *Johnson* rise, full fraught with *Venom's Spight.*
  Fletcher, and *Beaumont,* troubl'd in their *Graves,*
  Looke out some deeper, and forgotten *Caves:*
  And Gentle *Shakespeare,* weeping, since he must
  At best, be Buryed, now, in *Chaucers Dust.*
  Thus dark Oblivion covers their each *Name,*
  Since you have Robb'd them of their *Glorious Fame.* (JFB)
[Not in 1st ed. of 1653.]

1664.   Richard Flecknoe. *A Short Discourse of the English Stage,* in *Love's Kingdom.* [STC F1229.]

Sig. G 6 - G 6ᵛ (Spingarn 2.94):
  Beaumont and *Fletcher* were excellent in their kinds, but they often err'd against *Decorum,* seldom representing a valiant man without somewhat of the *Braggadoccio,* nor an honourable woman without somewhat of *Dol Common* in her. (JGM)

1664.   Thomas Killigrew. *The Parsons Wedding,* in *Comedies and Tragedies.*
[STC K450. Ed. Montague Summers, *Restoration Comedies,* 1921.]

Act 1, sc. 3, p. 81 (sig. L; Summers, pp. 20-1):
Joll. Who, Mr. Jeoffrey? *Hobinol* the second; By this life 'tis a very
Veal, and he licks his Nose like one of them; By his discourse you'ld
guess he had eaten nothing but Hay. (RHP)
[Cf. *S. C. Jan.* 55 ff.]

1664.   Henry More. *The Apology of Dr. Henry More,* in *A Modest In-
quiry into the Mystery of Iniquity.* [STC M2666.]

His Answer Touching Episcopacy, Chap. 5, par. 5, pp. 514-5:
    My observation of Passages in the late great change of affairs in this
Nation has given me too great occasion to surmise so, and made me look
upon *Spencer* as a *Prophet* as well as *Poet,* in his second *Eclogue,* he
has so lively set down the effects of the extirpation of *Episcopacy* upon
the *Presbyters* themselves, when once that great shelter of Church-
Government was removed. For when the Lord of the Field had cut
down the aged and sacred *Oak,* having been complained to by the
busie *Briar* that had a minde to domineer alone, pretending forsooth
that the spreadng *Oak* hindered his tender growth, keeping off the
light of the Sun, and spoiling his beautiful Flowers with dropping of
his hoary moss upon them; the *Briar* wanting this shelter against greater
storms was utterly born down by the next Winterly weather, and
troden into the dirt by Beasts. His condition is so lively described in
the Poet, that I have thought it worth transcribing. After he has set out
the dismal fall of the Oak, [*S. C. Feb.* 219-37, quoted.]
    The *Apodosis* is easie, though it were demanded in rhyme.
But no semblance of mirth can well suit with so sad a consideration.
Nothing were more desirable than that all men would lay aside any sense
they have of their popular faculties, and make use of their talents to the
common Interest of the Reformed Christianity, and not seek a victory
over those who are their most impregnable shelter against their greatest
enemies. This intimation is enough for them that are willing to see, and
all that I can say will be nothing to as many as are wilfully blind. (DEM)

1664.   Katherine Philips (d. 1664). *Poems by the Incomparable, Mrs.
K. P.* [STC P2032.]

No. 12. *To the Noble* Palaemon, *on his incomparable Discourse of
Friendship,* p. 30 (sig. C 7ᵛ):
            Sure the Litigious as amaz'd would stand,
            As Fairy Knights touch'd with *Cambina's* Wand.
[Cf. *F. Q.* 4.3.37 ff.]

No. 18. *Content, To my dearest* Lucasia, p. 45 (sig. D 7; Saintsbury
1.520):
            Content, the false World's best disguise,
            The search and faction of the Wise,
            Is so abstruse and hid in night,
            That, like that Fairy Red-cross Knight,

Who treach'rous Falshood for clear Truth had got,
Men think they have it when they have it not. (FIC)
[Cf. *F. Q.* 1.2.13 ff.]

1665. Joseph Beaumont. *Some Observations upon The Apologie of Dr.
Henry More for his Mystery of Godliness.* [STC B1628.]

P. 64:
   In his 5. Sect. I presume he found himself at very good leisure: for
he gives us good store of verses out of *Spencer,* wherein he saith, he
describes the effect of the extirpation of Episcopacy, upon the Presbyters
themselves. (DEM)

1665.   Lord Edward Herbert of Cherbury (d. 1648). *Occasional Verses.*
[STC H1508. *Poems,* ed. C. G. Moore Smith, Oxford, 1923.]

[*Loves End,*] pp. 6-7 (Smith, pp. 6-7):
   . . . there only rests but to unpaint
   Her form in my mind, that so dispossest
   It be a Temple, but without a Saint.
[Cf. *Am.* 22.]

To a Lady who did sing excellently, p. 45 (Smith, p. 45):
2.
   When they again, exalted by thy voice,
   Tun'd by thy soul, dismiss'd into the air,
      To us repair,
   A living, moving, and harmonious noise,
   Able to give the love they do create
      A second state,
   And charm not only all his griefs away,
      And his defects restore,
   But make him perfect, who, the Poets say,
   Made all was ever yet made heretofore.
[Cf. *Col.* 841-2. The date 1618 follows the poem.]

To the C. of D., p. 55 (Smith, p. 55):
3.
   Thus, as in your rare temper, we may find
   An excellence so perfect in each kind,

   That a fair body hath a fairer mind;
      So all the beams you diversely do dart,
      As well on th' understanding as the heart,
      Of love and honour equal cause impart.
[Cf. *Am.* 15.11, 13-4; 21; 79. The poem is to be dated before 1631.]

The IDEA, p. 75 (Smith, p. 75):
   Some of her figures therefore, foil'd and blurr'd,
   Shew as if Heaven had no way concurr'd
   In shapes so disproportion'd and absurd.

Which being again vex'd with some hate and spite,
That doth in them vengeance and rage excite,
Seem to be tortur'd and deformed quite.
[Cf. *H. B.* 141-6. The poem is dated 1639.] (DEM)

1665. R. Monsey. *Scarronides: or, Virgile Travestie, A Mock-Poem.*
[STC M2455.]

P. 57 (sig. E 5):
    Æneas then his light head bound. . . .
    He dreamed that Fountains did him go by
    Of Fairy Queens, and Women Sprights. (JGM)

1667. John Evelyn. *Diary.*
[Ed. William Bray, 1889.]

Letter to the Lord Chancellor, March 18, 1666/7, Bray 2.40.
[Evelyn advises " what pictures might be added to the Assembly of the
Learned and Heroic persons of England " which his Lordship has col-
lected. Of those " Wanting " among the " Learned " he lists " Edmund
Spencer " along with William Lilly, Dr. Sanderson, Roger Bacon, and
others.] (EG)

Item under date of August 3, 1667, Bray 2.30:
    Went to Mr. Cowley's funeral, whose corpse lay at Wallingford
House, and was thence conveyed to Westminster Abbey. . . . He was
interred next Geoffry Chaucer, and near Spenser. (DEM)

1667. John Milton. *Paradise Lost.*
[STC M2136-42, with title-pages bearing dates 1667-9. *Works,* Frank
A. Patterson, gen. ed., Columbia Univ. Press, 1931-40.]

Book 2, ll. 927-8 (*Columbia Milton* 2.71):
                At last his Sail-broad Vannes
        He spreads for flight.
[Cf. *F. Q.* 5.4.42-4.]

Ibid., ll. 1024-7 (*Columbia Milton* 2.74):
                Sin and Death amain
        Following his track, such was the will of Heav'n,
        Pav'd after him a broad and beat'n way
        Over the dark Abyss.
[Cf. *F. Q.* 2.7.21.1-4.]

Book 3, ll. 681-5 (*Columbia Milton* 2.101-2):
                So spake the false dissembler unperceivd;
        For neither Man nor Angel can discern
        Hypocrisie, the only evil that walks
        Invisible, except to God alone,
        By his permissive will, through Heav'n and Earth.
[Cf. Una's mistaking Archimage for the Redcrosse Knight, *F. Q.* 1.3.26.]

Book 4, l. 37 (*Columbia Milton* 2.107):
    O Sun, to tell thee how I hate thy beams.
[Cf. *F. Q.* 2.1.36.7; 2.1.45.9; 6.12.35.5; *Daph.* 47, 407.]

Book 7, ll. 621-2 (*Columbia Milton* 2.233):
    and every Starr perhaps a World
    Of destind habitation. (DEM)
[Cf. *F. Q.* 2. proem 3.]

[Parallels between *Paradise Lost* and Spenser's verse previously noted
in *An Index to the Columbia Milton,* Frank L. Patterson and French
R. Fogle (Columbia Univ. Press, 1940) 2.1849-50, are listed below.
Numbers in parentheses refer to pages in vol. 2 of the *Columbia Milton;*
unless otherwise noted, *F. Q.* is the Spenser reference.

Book 1:   63 (10):   1.1.14.5-6; 193-4 (15):   1.11.14.1-2; 225-6
          (16):   1.11.18.1-4; 287 (18):   5.5.3.6-8; 667-8 (32):
          1.4.40.3-4; 712 (34): 3.1.40.4.

Book 2:   1-4 (38):   1.4.8.1-6; 3 (38): 3.4.23.4; 40-3 (39): 7.6.21.
          6-9; 492 ff. (55):   Am. 40; 650-6 (61):   1.1.14-5, 6.6.10;
          666-8 (61):   7.7.46.4-5; 675-6 (62):   1.7.8.4-6; 729 (64):
          3.1.5.9; 823 (67):   1.5.33.7; 941-2 (77):   1.11.8.2.

Book 3:   11 (77):   1.1.39.2; 380 (91):   H. H. B. 93-4, 118-9.

Book 4:   108 (110):   1.5.43.3-4; 140-1 (111):   6.10.6.4-8; 264
          (116):   3.1.40.3-4; 304-6 (117):   4.1.13.2-5; 337 (118):
          3.8.14.2; 605 (128):   *Epith.* 288.

Book 5:   1-2 (144):   4.5.45.3-4; 44 (145):   3.11.35.8-9; 130-3
          (148):   3.7.9.1-4.

Book 9:   2 (260):   1.10.56.2-3; 390 (274):   1.6.16.9; 1086 (299):
          1.1.7.4-5.

Book 10:   850 (335):   6.4.40.3-4; 858-9 (335):   *Daph.* 355.]

1668.   Walter Charleton. *The Ephesian and Cimmerian Matrons, Two
Notable Examples of the Power of Love and Wit.* [STC C3670.]

To the Author of the Ephesian Matron, sig. B^v:
    But, *you'll* say (I presume) as poor *Malbecco* said in excuse of his
jealousie; that you grounded your command of Secresie, not upon distrust of the *Matrons* virtue, but upon fear of having your judgment and
honour brought into question.
[The faithless wife is described as "his dear *Fidessa*" on p. 6, and the
jealous husband as "the inraged *Malbecco*" on p. 18.] (JGM)

1668.   Abraham Cowley (d. 1667). *Several Discourses by way of Essays,
in Verse and Prose,* in *The Works of Mr Abraham Cowley.*
[STC C6649. *Essays and Plays,* ed. A. R. Waller, Cambridge, 1906;
Essays and Other Prose Writings, ed. A. B. Gough, Oxford, 1915.]

260 Spenser Allusions

11. *Of Myself,* p. 144 (sig. S 4ᵛ; Waller, pp. 457-8; Gough, p. 218):
I believe I can tell the particular little chance that filled my head first with such Chimes of Verse, as have never since left ringing there: For I remember when I began to read, and to take some pleasure in it, there was wont to lie in my Mothers Parlour (I know not by what accident, for she her self never in her life read any Book but of Devotion) but there was wont to lie *Spencers* Works; this I happened to fall upon, and was infinitely delighted with the Stories of the Knights, and Giants, and Monsters, and brave Houses, which I found every where there: (Though my understanding had little to do with all this) and by degrees with the tinckling of the Rhyme and Dance of the Numbers, so that I think I had read him all over before I was twelve years old, and was thus made a Poet as irremediably as a Child is made an Eunuch. With these affections of mind, and my heart set upon Letters, I went to the University. (FIC)

1668.   Sir John Denham. *Poems and Translations, with The Sophy.*
[STC D1005. *Poetical Works,* ed. Theodore Howard Banks, Jr., Yale Univ. Press, 1928.]

On Mr. Abraham Cowley His Death and Burial amongst the Ancient Poets, pp. 89-90 (Munro 2. 159; Bradley, p. 347; Banks, pp. 149-50):

Old *Chaucer,* like the morning Star,
To us discovers day from far,
His light those Mists and Clouds dissolv'd,
Which our dark Nation long involv'd;
But he descending to the shades,
Darkness again the Age invades.
Next (like *Aurora*) *Spencer* rose,
Whose purple blush the day foreshows. . . .

Time, which made them their Fame outlive,
To *Cowly* scarce did ripeness give.
Old Mother Wit, and Nature gave
Shakespeare and *Fletcher* all they have;
In *Spencer,* and in *Johnson,* Art,
Of slower Nature got the start. (JM)

1668.   Richard Flecknoe. *Sir William D'avenant's Voyage to the Other World: With His Adventures in the Poets Elizium.* [STC F1235.]

P. 8 (sig. A 4ᵛ; Bradley, p. 339):
Nor was he less amaz'd than they, to find never a Poet there, Antient nor Modern, whom in some sort or other he had not disoblig'd by his discommendations, as Homer, Virgil, Tasso, Spencer, and especially Ben. Johnson. . . . Nay, even Shakespear, whom he thought to have found his greatest Friend, was as much offended with him as any of the rest, for so spoiling and mangling of his Plays. (JFB)

1668.   Thomas Sprat. *An Account of the Life of Mr. Abraham Cowley,* printed with *The Works of Mr. Abraham Cowley,* ed. Thomas Sprat. [STC C6649.]

Sig. A 2 (Spingarn 2.121):
The occasion of his first inclination to Poetry, was his casual lighting on *Spencer's Fairy Queen,* when he was but just able to read. That indeed is a Poem fitter for the examination of men,than the consideration of a Child. But in him it met with a Fancy, whose strength was not to be judged by the number of his years.

Sig. e 2 - e 2ᵛ (Spingarn 2.145):
His Body was attended to *Westminster Abby,* by a great number of Persons of the most eminent quality, and follow'd with the praises of all good, and Learned Men. It lies near the Ashes of *Chaucer* and *Spencer,* the two most Famous *English* Poets, of former times. (FIC)

About 1669.   Verses set to music, in B. M. MS Harleian 6947.

Fol. 401 (Spurgeon 1.247; Bradley, p. 352):
To heauen once ther caime a Poett a friend of mine swore hee did
                                        know itt. . . .
Ould Chauser mett him in great state Spenser and Johnson at the
                                        gate
Beamon and Flettchers witt mayd one butt Shakspeers witt did goe
                                        aloane. (CFES)

1669.   Edward Howard. *The British Princes: An Heroick Poem.* [STC H2965.]

Preface to the Reader, sigs. A 5ᵛ - A 6:
And now to pay a due esteem to such Poets of our own Country, who are justly dignified by the Heroick muse . . . yet have these our Native Poets deservedly merited esteem, perhaps above those any other Nation has produced in the times they lived; and of these the most considerable, I think must be granted our famous Spencer, and the late Sir *William Davenant,* (not considering *Daniel, Drayton,* and the like, rather Historians than Epicke Poets) the first of whom is by many granted a parallel to most of the Antients, whose genius was in all degrees proportion'd for the work he accomplished, or for whatsoever structures his Muse had thought fit to raise, whose thoughts were like so many nerves and sinews ready with due motion and strength to actuate the body he produced; nor was the success of his Poem less worthy of Admiration, which notwithstanding it be frequent in words of obsolete signification, had the good fortune to have a reception suitable to its desert, which tells us the age he writ in, had a value for sense above words, though perhaps he may have received deservedly some censure in that particular, since our Language (when he writ) was held much improved, that it has been the wonder as well as the pity of some, that so famous a Poet should so much obscure the glory of his thoughts, wrapt

up in words and expressions, which time and use had well nigh exploded: And though words serve our uses but like Counters or numbers to summe our intellectual Products, yet they must be currant as the money of the Age, or they will hardly pass: Nor is it less ridiculous to see a man confidently walk in the antiquated and mothy Garments of his Predecessors, out of an obstinate contempt of the present Mode, than to imitate the expressions of obsolete Authors, which renders even Wit barbarous, and looks like some affront to the present Age, which expects from Writers due esteem of the tongue they speak. But this objection which I have presumed to mention against Renowned *Spencer,* (though it be a Common one, and the most is laid to his charge,) shows us that his building was rather mighty than curious, and like the Pyramids of Egypt, may expect to be a long Companion of times. (JM, FIC)

1670. John Milton. *The History of Britain.*
[STC M2119. *Works,* Frank A. Patterson, gen. ed., Columbia Univ. Press, 1931-40.]

Chap. 1, sig. Cᵛ (*Columbia Milton* 10.17):
Brutus therefore surnamed *Greenshield* succeeding, to repair his Fathers losses as the same *Lessabeus* reports, fought a second Battail in *Henault* with *Brunchild* at the mouth of *Scaldis,* and Encamp'd on the River *Hania.* Of which *our Spencer* also thus Sings. [Quotes F. Q. 2.10.24.1-7] (FIC)

1670. William Penn. *The Great Case of Liberty of Conscience Once more Briefly Debated & Defended.*
[STC P1299. Cf. Austin C. Dobbins, " More Seventeenth-Century Chaucer Allusions," *MLN* 68 (1953).33-4.]

Pp. 39-40 (Dobbins, p. 33, quoted):
10. *Tenthly,* And here let me bring in honest *Chaucer,* whose Matter (and not his Poetry) heartily affects me: 'twas in a time when *Priests* were as rich, and lofty as they are now, and Causes of Evil alike. [Quotes *S. C. May* 109-37; line 109 has the note: " The Primative State of things observed by a Poet, more than 300. year old, by which the Clergy may *read* their own Apostacy and Character."] (ACD)

1670. Edward Phillips. *Tractulus de Carmine Dramatico Poetarum Veterum,* in John Buchler's *Sacrarum Profanarumque Phrasium poeticarum Thesaurus,* 1669. [STC B5303.]

Pp. 396-7 (sigs. R 6ᵛ - R 7):
Edmundus Spenserus vir immortali memoria dignus, qui carmine Heroico descripsit Encyclopædiam Christianarum & moralium virtutum, saltem maxima ex parte, siquidem miserâ morte præveniente (nam vertur inediâ periise) Opus imperfectum reliquit, hócque magis est mirum cum Reginæ, quam in poemate summis laudibus in cœlum evexerat, minimè

ignotus esset. Stichi seu Stanzæ hujus poematis constant versuum Congerie post Italicum sonettum pulcherrimâ, nempe novenariâ, & postremo versu cæteris dissyllabam longiore, Majestatis gratia; in hos Sticho quomodo versus inter se respondeant hoc exemplum docebit. [Quotes *F. Q.* 2.12.71, omitting line 5.] Sunt etiam præterea ex operibus ejus quæ extant, ut Calendarium pastorale atq; alia quaedam, at multa desiderantur. (DEM)

1670. Richard Graham, 1st Viscount Preston. *Angliae Speculum Morale; The Moral State of England, with The several Aspects it beareth to Virtue and Vice.*

[STC P3310. Quoted in *Works of Spenser*, ed. H. J. Todd, 1805.]

The Poet, pp. 66-8 (Todd 2.cxli):

The Bards and Chroniclers in the Isles of *Britain* and *Ireland* have been in former times even ador'd for the Ballads in which they extoll'd the Deeds of their forefathers; and since the ages have been refined, doubtless, *England* hath produced those, who in this way have equall'd most of the Antients: and exceeded all the Moderns. *Chaucer* rose like the morning Starr of Wit, out of those black mists of ignorance; since him, *Spencer* may deservedly challenge the Crown; for though he may seem blameable in not observing *decorum* in some places enough, and in too much, in the whole, countenancing Knight-errantry; yet the easie similitudes, the natural Pourtraicts, the so refined and sublimated fancies, with which he hath so bestudded every Canto of his subject will easily reach him the Guerdon; and though some may object to him that his Language is harsh and antiquated; yet his design was noble; to shew us that our language was expressive enough of our own sentiments; and to upbraid those who have indenizon'd such numbers of forreign words. (FIC)

1670. John Worthington. Letter to Henry More, Nov. 4.

[*Diary and Correspondence of Dr. Worthington*, ed. James Crossley, Chetham Soc., 1847-86.]

Crossley 2.344-5 quoted:

That of Spenser of the Briar and Oake, is done into Latin by one Mr. Bathurst (an ancient Minister deceas'd) who hath translated all Spenser's Shepherd's Calendar into verse, much like Virgil's Eclogues. Dr. Dillingham of Emanuel published Mr. Bathurst and Spenser in 8vo. (FIC)

After 1670. Alexander Cunningham. *On the much lamented death of that dearest Darling of the muses Mr Pat: Schaw Doctor of Medicine*, Folger MS 1302.2.

> You sacred offspring of the thundring Iove
> who doe Inhabit the Heliconian Grove;

And ffork'd parnassus; from whose mouthes divine
  drops Eloquence most pure and most refine   I find Mr
Infuse into me some Heroick streams   Alex: Cun-
  which doe proceed from your more purer beams, ningham who
Into me Suada's warrow do Instill   was then but
  that from my lugent and deepe mourning Quill a student
I may proclaime the praises great of one   at ye Colleg
In Galems Crew inferior unto none   was ye
But who can his Encomiums declare   author of
Call Spensers Ghost Ben Johnstons, Couleys rare?   this.
Poetick Hero's of the former dayes.
Yea Dryden Orrerie*—of this present age,
and others who doe crown the famous stage.
These Divin mortals be the only men
who can his vertues celebrate w^t pen. . . . (JGM)

                    Animitus

[*The " Orrerie " alluded to is clearly Roger Boyle, first Earl of Orrery
(1621-1679), who was a dramatist and poet, friend of Dryden, etc.
Alexander Cunningham was probably the A. C. (1655-1730) who edited
Horace, Virgil, etc., as he was educated in part at Edinburgh and later
was professor of civil law there, whereas Alexander Cunningham, the
historian (1654-1737), often confused with the above, was educated at
Selkirk school and in Holland. As the poem was seemingly written before
the death of Boyle and while Cunningham was still a student, a date in
the 1670's seems logical. F. M. P.]

1671.   Samuel Clarke. *A Geographical Description Of all the Countries
In the Known World,* published with the 4th ed. of *A Mirrour or Looking-
Glass.* [STC C4552.]

P. 199:
    4. *Showre,* &c. of which *Spencer* makes these Verses. [Quotes *F. Q.*
4.11.41 and stanza 44.1-5] (HH)

1671.   Sir Thomas Culpepper. *Essayes or Moral Discourses On several
Subjects.* [STC C7556.]

P. 118 (Spurgeon 1.247):
Some have thought to honour Antiquity by using such [words] as were
obsolete, as hath been done by our famous *Spencer,* and others, though
the times past are no more respected by an unnecessary continuing of
their words then if wee wore constantly the same trimming to our Cloaths
as they did, for it is not Speech, but things which render antiquity
venerable, besides the danger of expressing no Language, if as *Spencer*
made use of *Chaucers,* we should likewise introduce his. (FIC)

1671.   John Milton. *Paradise Regain'd. A Poem. In IV Books To which
is added Samson Agonistes.*

[STC M2152. *Works*, Frank A. Patterson, gen. ed., Columbia Univ. Press, 1931-40.]

[Parallels to Spenser in *Paradise Regained* and *Samson Agonistes* noted in *An Index to the Columbia Milton*, Frank L. Patterson and French R. Fogle (Columbia Univ. Press, 1940) 2.1849-50, are noted here. Numbers in parentheses indicate volume and page in the *Columbia Milton*; unless otherwise noted, *F. Q.* is the Spenser reference.]

Paradise Regained: 1.1 ff. (2.405): 1.proem 1; 1.294 (2. 415): H. H. L. 170.

Samson Agonistes: 118 (1.341): 2.5.32.1; 136 (1.341): 1.7.11.1-2; 184-6 (1.343): 1.10.24.3-8, 2.8.26.6-7; 535-6 (1.356): 2.6.14.6-7; 623-6 (1.359): 3.2.39.4-6, 6.6.5.1-4.]

Before 1672. Peter Sterry. *A Discourse of the Freedom of the Will*, 1675. [STC S5477.]

Pt. 1, p. 43 (sig. G 2):
I have indeed willingly taken every fair occasion, as I have past along through this Land of Love and Bliss, amidst the Gardens of true *Adonis*, the eternal Son, to stay thy self and me some moments, upon the contemplation of the charming Prospect, as also to gather and present thee with some of the *Paradisical* Flowers and Fruits which grow so plentifully there.
[Cf. *F. Q.* 3.6.29 ff.]

Pt. 2, p. 179 (sig. Aa 2):
A Poetical History, or work framed by an excellent Spirit, for a pattern of Wisdom, and Worth, and Happiness, hath this, as a chief rule, for the contrivance of it, upon which all its Graces and Beauties depend. That persons and things be carried to the *utmost extremity*, into a state where they seem altogether uncapable of any return to Beauty or Bliss: That then by just degrees of harmonious proportions, they be raised again to a state of highest Joy and Glory. You have examples of this in the Divine pieces of those Divine Spirits, (as they are esteemed and stiled) *Homer, Virgil, Tasso*, our English *Spencer*, with some few others like to these; The *Works* of these persons are called *Poems*. So is the Work of God in Creation, and contrivance from the beginning to the end, ποίημα τῷ θεῷ, God's Poem. (DEM)

1672. John Dryden. *The Conquest of Granada by the Spaniards*. [STC D2256. *Works*, ed. Walter Scott (1808), rev. and corr. George Saintsbury, Edinburgh, 1882-93.]

Of Heroique Playes. An Essay, sig. a 4 (Scott-Saintsbury 4.23):
For my part, I am of opinion, that neither *Homer, Virgil, Statius, Ariosto, Tasso*, nor our *English Spencer*, could have form'd their Poems half so beautiful, without those Gods and Spirits, and those Enthusiastick

parts of Poetry, which compose the most noble parts of all their writings. and I will ask any man who loves Heroick Poetry, (for I will not dispute their tastes who do not) if the Ghost of *Polydorus* in *Virgil,* the Enchanted wood in *Tasso,* and the Bower of bliss, in Spencer (which he borrows from that admirable *Italian*) could have been omitted without taking from their works some of the greatest beauties in them. (FMP)

1672. William Ramesay. *The Gentlemans Companion: Or, A Character of True Nobility, and Gentility.* [STC R206.]

Pp. 127, 129 (Munro 2.184; Spurgeon 1.246; Bradley, p. 351):
A few good Books is better than a Library, and a main part of Learning. I shall here contract this Study into these few Books following; in which he may indeed reade all that is requisite, and of Substance. . . . *Homer, Horace, Virgil, Ovid, Buchanan* the *Scot,* not inferiour to any Poet. And among our selves, old Sr. *Jeffrey Chaucer, Ben. Johnson, Shakespear, Spencer, Beaumont* and *Fletcher, Dryden.* (JM)
[Furnivall observes that, before Munro, W. C. Hazlitt had noted this allusion to the English poets.]

1672. Henry Wotton. *Essay on the Education of Children,* 1753.
[Rptd *The Works of Sir Thomas Browne,* ed. Geoffrey Keynes, 1928-31.]

P. 58 (Keynes 6.423):
Certificate for William Wotton
I do hereby declare and certify, that I heard William Wotton, Son to Mr. Henry Wotton, of Wrentham, of the age of six Years, read a Stanza in Spencer very distinctly, and pronounce it properly.
As also some Verses in the first Ecologue of Virgil, which I purposely chose out, and also construed the same truly.
Also some Verses in Homer, and the Carmina Aurea of Pythagoras, which he read well and construed.
As he did also the first Verse of the 4th Chapter of Genesis, in Hebrew, which I purposely chose out.
July 20, 1672   Tho. Browne (EAS)

1674. John Ray. *A Collection of English Words not Generally Used.* [STC R388.]

North Countrey words. Y., pp. 55-6:
Yewd or *Yod*: Went. . . . *Chaucero* Yed, Yeden, Yode eodem sensu. Spencer also in his Fairie Queen lib. 1. c. 10 [quotes stanza 53.3-5].
(EG)

1674. Thomas Rymer. *The Preface of the Translator,* in René Rapin's *Reflections on Aristotle's Treatise of Poesie.* [STC R270.]

Sigs. A 6ᵛ - A 7 (Spingarn 2.167-8):
Spencer, I think, may be reckon'd the first of our *Heroick Poets*; he had a large spirit, a sharp judgment, and a *Genius* for *Heroick Poesie,* perhaps

above any that ever writ since *Virgil*. But our misfortune is, he wanted a true *Idea*, and lost himself, by following an unfaithful guide. Though besides *Homer* and *Virgil* he had read *Tasso*, yet he rather suffer'd himself to be misled by *Ariosto*; with whom blindly rambling on *marvellous* Adventures, he makes no Conscience of *Probability*. All is fanciful and chimerical, without any uniformity, without any foundation in truth; his Poem is perfect *Fairy-land*.

They who can love *Ariosto*, will be ravish'd with *Spencer*; whilst men of juster thoughts lament that such great Wits have miscarried in their Travels for want of direction to set them in the right way. But the truth is, in *Spencer's* time, *Italy* it self was not well satisfied with *Tasso*; and few amongst them would then allow that he had excell'd their *divine Ariosto*. And it was the vice of those Times to affect superstitiously the *Allegory*; and nothing would then be currant without a mystical meaning. We must blame the Italians for debauching great *Spencer's* judgment; and they cast him on the unlucky choice of the *Stanza*, which in no wise is proper for our Language. (FIC)

1674.   Samuel Speed. *Fragmenta Carceris: or, The Kings-Bench Scuffle; with the Humours of the Common-Side.* [STC S4900.]

The Legend of . . . His Grace Humphrey, Duke of St. Pauls *Cathedral Walk*, sig. F 4 (Munro 2.206; Bradley, p. 377):

> . . . Fire began not in *his Graces* house,
> But thither came, and Burnt both Rat and Mouse.
> On which the DUKE, to shun a scorching doom,
> Perambulated to *Ben Johnson's* Tomb,
> Where *Shakespear, Spencer, Cambden,* and the rest,
> Once rising Suns, are now set in the West;
> But still their lustres do so brightly shine,
> That they invite our Worthies there to Dine. (JM)

Ibid., sig. F 4ᵛ:

> Our DUKE by this time spies a *Fairy Queen*,
> And as a man surpriz'd with Fits o'th'Spleen,
> Such strange infusions did his passions move,
> That he must live to dote, or dye in love. (WW)

1675.   Charles Cotton. *Burlesque upon Burlesque: Or, The Scoffer Scoft. Being some of Lucians Dialogues Newly put into English Fustian.* [STC C6380a.]

Pp. 148-9:

> Too mean mans skill without dispute is,
> To judge of your immortal Beauties!
> To judge of such Cælestial Lasses,
> A Swains capacity surpasses!
> Or that if any humane wit
> Were capable of doing it,

Some Courtier it should be no doubt,
Much rather than a Collin Clout. (JGM)

1675?   Andrew Marvell. *Britannia and Raleigh By A. M.* in *A Collection of Poems on Affairs of State,* 1689.
[STC C5176. *The Poems & Letters of Andrew Marvell,* ed. H. M. Margoliouth, Oxford, 1927.]

P. 8 (sig. A 4ᵛ; Margoliouth 1.185):
Brit[annia to *Raleigh].* . . . The other day fam'd *Spencer* I did bring
    In lofty Notes *Tudor's* blest Race to sing;
    How Spain's proud Powers her Virgin Arms controul'd,
    And Golden Days in peaceful Order roul'd;
    How like ripe Fruit she dropt from off her Throne,
    Full of grey Hairs, good Deeds, and great Renown.

[Margoliouth (1.308, n. to line 42) suggests that the line may allude to the publication of the third folio ed. of Spenser in 1678, the year of Marvell's death. The identification of *A. M.* in the title with Andrew Marvell the younger may be incorrect.] (EG)

1675.   Edward Phillips. *Theatrum Poetarum, or a Compleat Collection of the Poets.* [STC P2075. Ed. S. Egerton Brydges, 1800.]

The Preface, sigs. **3ᵛ - **4 (Spingarn 2.265; Brydges, p. xxv):
There is certainly a decency in one sort of Verse more then another which custom cannot really alter, only by familiarity make it seem better; how much more stately and Majestic in Epic Poems, especially of Heroic Argument, *Spencer's* Stanza (which I take to be but an Improvement upon *Tasso's Ottava Rima,* or the *Ottava Rima* it self, used by many of our once esteemed Poets) is above the way either of Couplet or Alternation of four Verses only, I am perswaded, were it revived, would soon be acknowledg'd. (FIC)

Ibid., sigs**9 - **9ᵛ (Spingarn 2.271; Munro 2.221; Brydges, p. xxxvi):
Nay, though all the Laws of *Heroic Poem,* all the Laws of *Tragedy* were exactly observed, yet still this *tour enterjeant,* this Poetic *Energie,* if I may so call it, would be required to give life to all the rest, which shines through the roughest most unpolish't and antiquated Language, and may happly be wanting, in the most polite and reformed: let us observe *Spencer,* with all his Rustie, obsolete words, with all his rough-hewn clowterly Verses; yet take him throughout, and we shall find in him a graceful and Poetic Majesty. (JM)

The Modern Poets, pp. 34-6 (sigs. Bb 5ᵛ - Bb 6ᵛ; Brydges, pp. 148-9):
    Edmund Spencer, the first of our *English* Poets that brought Heroic Poesie to any perfection, his *Faery queen* being for great Invention and Poetic heighth judg'd little inferiour, if not equal to the chief of the ancient Greeks and Latins or Modern *Italians,* but the first Poem that brought

him into Esteem was his *Shepherds Calendar,* which so endear'd him to that Noble Patron of all Vertue and Learning *Sir Philip Sidny,* that he made him known to Queen Elizabeth, and by that means got him preferr'd to be Secretary to his Brother *Sir Henry Sidny,* who was sent Deputy into *Ireland,* where he is said to have written his *Faerie Queen,* but upon the return of *Sir Henry,* his Employment ceasing, he also return'd into *England,* and having lost his great Friend *Sir Philip,* fell into poverty, yet made his last Refuge to the Queens Bounty, and had 500 *l.* order'd him for his Support, which nevertheless was abridg'd to 100 by *Cecil,* who hearing of it, and owing him a grudge for some reflections in Mother *Hubbards* Tale, cry'd out to the Queen, What all this for a Song? This he is said to have taken so much to Heart, that he contracted a deep Melancholy, which soon after brought his life to a Period: So apt is an Ingenious Spirit to resent a slighting, even from the greatest Persons; and thus much I must needs say of the Merit of so great a Poet from so great a Monarch, that as it is incident to the best of Poets sometimes to flatter some Royal or Noble Patron, never did any do it more to the height, or with greater Art and Elegance, if the highest of praises attributed to so Heroic a Princess can justly be term'd Flattery. (FIC)

Ibid., pp. 111-2 (sig. Ee 8 - Ee 8ᵛ):
Iohn Lane . . . [may deserve] a name not much inferiour, if not equal to *Drayton,* and others of the next rank to *Spencer.*

Ibid., p. 136 (sig. Ff 8ᵛ):
Michael Drayton. Contemporary of *Spencer* and Sr *Philip Sidny,* and for Fame and renoun in Poetry, not much inferiour in his time to either.

Ibid., pp. 139-40 (sig. Ff 10 - Ff 10ᵛ):
Nicholas Breton, a writer of Pastoral, Sonnets, Canzons and Madrigals, in which kind he keeps company with several other Contemporary Æmulators of *Spencer* and Sr *Philip Sidny.*

Ibid., p. 174 (sig. Hh 3ᵛ):
Th. Campion, a Writer of no extraordinary fame; but who hath the honour to be nam'd by *Cambden* with *Spencer, Sidny, Drayton,* and other the Chief of our English Poets.

Ibid., p. 178 (sig. Hh 5ᵛ):
Thomas Kid . . . quoted among some of the more fam'd Poets, as *Spencer, Drayton, Daniel, Lodge. &c.* with whom he was either Contemporary, or not much later.

Ibid., p. 195 (sig. Ii 2):
William Warner . . . may be rekoned with several other Writers of the same time, *i. e.* Queen *Elizabeth's* Reign; who though inferiour to *Sidny, Spencer, Drayton* and *Daniel,* yet have been thought by some not unworthy to be remember'd and quoted. (WW)

1678.   John Dryden. *All For Love: or, the World well lost.*
[STC D2229. *Works,* ed. Walter Scott (1808), rev. and corr. George
Saintsbury, Edinburgh, 1882-93.]

Act 1, sig. Bᵛ (Scott-Saintsbury 5.344):
Serap. Last night, between the hours of Twelve and One,
     In a lone Isle o'th'Temple while I walk'd,
     A Whirl-wind rose, that, with a violent blast,
     Shook all the *Dome*: The Doors around me clapt,
     The Iron Wicket, that defends the Vault,
     Where the long Race of *Ptolomies* is lay'd,
     Burst open, and disclos'd the mighty dead.
     From out each Monument, in order plac'd,
     An Armed Ghost start up. (AWC)
[Cf. *F. Q.* 3.12.3.]

1678.   Thomas Rymer. *The Tragedies of the Last Age Consider'd and
Examin'd by the Practice of the Ancients, and by the Common sense
of all Ages.* [STC R2430.]

P. 10 (sig. B 5ᵛ; Spingarn 2.186):
Nor will it, I hope, give offence that I handle these *Tragedies* with the
same liberty that I formerly had taken in examining the *Epick Poems*
of *Spencer, Cowley,* and such names as will ever be *sacred* to me. (DEM)

1678.   George Starkey. *Ripley Reviv'd.* [STC S5286.]

An Exposition upon Sir G. Ripley's Fifth Gate, p. 371:
     Of uncouth subjects now shall be my Song,
     My mind intends high wonders to reveal,
     Which have lain hidden heretofore full long,
     Each artist striving them how to conceal,
     Lest wretched Caitiffs should these Treasures steal:
     Nor Villains should their Villanies maintain
     By this rare Art; which danger they to heal,
     In horrid Metaphor veil'd an Art most plain,
     Lest each fool knowing it, should it when known disdain.
[Cf. *F. Q.* 1. proem 1-2. Starkey employs the pseudonym Eirenaeus
Philalethes; see Edward Payson Morton, *MP,* 4 (1907). 647.] (FMP)

About 1679.   Sir Thomas Herbert. *Carolina Threnodia,* MS published
with title, *Memoirs of the Two last Years of the Reign of that unparallel'd Prince of ever Blessed Memory King Charles I,* 1702.

P. 21 (*Memoirs,* p. 43, quoted):
The sacred Scripture was the Book he most delighted in, read often
in Bishop *Andrews* Sermons, *Hooker's* Ecclesiastical Polity, Dr. *Ham-
mond's* Works, *Villalpandus* upon *Ezekiel,* &c. *Sands's* Paraphrase upon
King *David's* Psalms, *Herbert's* divine Poems; and also *Godfrey of Bul-*

loigne writ in *Italian* by *Torquato Tasso,* and done into *English* Heroick Verse by Mr. *Fairfax,* a Poem his Majesty much commended, as he did also *Ariosto,* by Sir *John Harrington* a facetious Poet, much esteem'd of by Prince *Henry* his Master; *Spencer's* Fairy Queen and the like, for alleviating his Spirits after serious Studies. (HH)
[Thomas Wagstaffe quotes the passage in his *Vindication of King Charles I,* 1711, p. 83.]

1679. *A Summary of the Life of Mr. Edmond Spenser* in 1679 ed. of the *Works.* [STC S4965.]

Sigs. A - A 2:

Mr. *Spenser* was born in *London,* (as his *Epitaph* says) in the Year of our Lord 1510, by his Parent liberally Educated, and sent to the University of Cambridge, where he continued a Student in *Pembrook-Hall*; till upon the vacancy of a Fellowship, he stood in competition with Mr. *Andrews,* (afterwards *Lord Bishop of Winchester*) in which he miscarried; and thus defeated of his hopes, unable any longer to subsist in the *College,* he repair'd to some Friends of his in the North, where he staid, fell in Love, and at last (prevail'd upon by the perswasions, and importunities of other Friends) came to *London.* His fame in the Art of *Poetry* soon made way to his acquaintance with those that were that way enclin'd, by whose means he quickly inform'd himself who, in likelyhood, might give him Encouragement, and Patronage. Mr. *Sidney* (afterward Sir *Philip*) then in full glory at *Court,* was the Person, to whom he design'd the first Discovery of himself; and to that purpose took an occasion to go one morning to *Leicester-House,* furnish't only with a modest confidence, and the Ninth *Canto* of the First Book of his *Faëry Queen:* He waited not long, e're he found the lucky season for an address of the Paper to his hand; who having read the Twenty-eighth *Stanza of Despair,* (with some signs in his Countenance of being much affected, and surpris'd with what he had read) turns suddenly to his Servant, and commands him to give the Party that presented the Verses to him Fifty Pounds; the Steward stood speechless, and unready, till his Master having past over another *Stanza,* bad him give him an Hundred Pound; the Servant something stagger'd at the humour his Master was in, mutter'd to this purpose, That by the semblance of the Man that brought the Paper, Five Pounds would be a proper Reward; but Mr. *Sidney* having the following *Stanza,* commands him to give Two Hundred Pounds, and that very speedily, least advancing his Reward, proportionably to the heigth of his Pleasure in reading, he should hold himself oblig'd to give him more than he had: Withal he sent an invitation to the Poet, to see him at those hours, in which he would be most at leasure. After this Mr. *Spenser,* by degrees, so far gain'd upon him, that he became not only his Patron, but his Friend too; entred him at *Court,* and obtain'd of the *Queen* the Grant of a Pention to him as *Poet Laureat*: But in this, his Fate was unkind; for it prov'd only a *Poetical Grant,* the payment, after a very short time, being stopt by a

great Councellour, who studied more the Queen's Profit than her Diversion, and told Her, 'twas beyond Example to give so great a Pention to a *Ballad-maker*: Of This, the grieved Poet thus complains in his *Tears of the Muses*: [Quotes R. T. 449-55]
How much deeper his resentment wrought in *Mother Hubbard's Tale,* may appear to those that list to read it with reflection.

He was in great esteem, and good favour with many of the Nobility whom he Celebrates in his Honorary Verses, and encourag'd by their kindness, he continued in Town, a Poet, a Lover, and a man of Business: A Poet indeed, without a Rival, but not so successful a Lover, for tho' *Hobbinol* as a Gentleman, rather lov'd in Concert with him, than to his grievance, yet *Menalcas* put him to't, whose treachery, together with the Apostacy of his Mistress, gave him occasion bitterly to complain, and having eas'd himself that way, he apply'd himself to Business. Sir *Henry Sidney* had bin three times Deputy of *Ireland,* and after the third being recall'd, *Arthur Lord Grey of Wilton,* was chosen to that Employment, to whom Mr. *Spenser* was recommended for *Secretary.* Shortly after, for his Services to the Crown he had bestow'd upon him by *Queen Elizabeth* 3000 Acres of Land in the County of *Cork:* there he finisht the latter part of his *Faëry Queen,* which was soon after unfortunately lost by the disorder, and abuse of his Servant, whom he had sent before him into *England,* being then (in the Rebellion of the *Earl of Desmond*) *á rebellibus* (as *Camden's* words are) *e Laribus ejectus, & bonis spoliatus*: His House was in *Kincolman,* the River *Mulla,* so often celebrated by him, running through his Grounds. In this ill posture of his Affairs he returned into *England,* where he his losses redoubled by the loss of his generous Friend Sir *Philip Sidney*; And thus, yielding to the impressions of a Fortune obstinately adverse to him, he died, without the help of any other Disease save a broken Heart; and was Buried in the Collegiate Church at *Westminster,* near the renowmed *Chaucer* (as himself desired) at the Charge of the most Noble *Robert Earl of Essex,* in the year 1596.

His great-Grandchild *Hugolin Spencer* was, after the *King's Return,* restor'd by the *Court of Claims,* to so much of the Lands as could be found to have bin his Ancestors. The remainder of his Works were embezill'd when he was in *Ireland*; for (besides his *Poems* in this Volume, The *View of the State of* Ireland, and some few Letters between himself and his intimate Friend Mr. *Harvey* which have bin Printed) many other excellent Pieces of his, highly valued by his learned Friends, are either wholly lost, or unkindly conceal'd from the Publique by private hands: mongst others these his *Nine Comedies,* so much esteemed by Mr. *Harvey.* The *Canticles* paraphras'd. The *Ecclesiastes,* and *Hours of our Lord.* His *Seven Psalms.* The *dying Pelican.* The *Sacrifice of a Sinner. Stemmata Dudleiana,* and *Purgatory. A Sennight's Slumber. Epithalamium Thamesis. The Hell of Lovers.*

He was a man of extraordinary Accomplishments, excellently skill'd in all parts of Learning: of a profound Wit, copious Invention, and solid Judgment: of a temper strangely tender, and amorous; as appears every where in his Writings, but particularly in his Laments on the Death of Sir *Philip Sidney*, and in his incomparable *Daphnaida*. He excelled all other Ancient and Modern Poets, in Greatness of Sense, Decency of Expression, Height of Imagination, Quickness of Conceit, Grandeur and Majesty of Thought, and all the Glories of Verse. Where he is passionate, he forces commiseration and tears from his Readers; where pleasant and airy a secret satisfaction and smile; and where Bold, and Heroique, he inflames their breasts with Gallantry and Valour. His Descriptions are so easie and natural, that his Pen seems to have a power of conveying *Idea's* to our mind, more just, and to the Life, than the exquisite Pencils of *Titian*, or *Raphael*, to our eyes. He was, in a word, compleatly happy in every thing that might render him Glorious, and Inimitable to future Ages. (FMP)

1679. Samuel Woodford. *A Paraphrase Upon the Canticles, And Some Select Hymns Of The New and Old Testament, With other occasional Compositions in English Verse.*
[STC W2632A. Cf. A. C. Judson, " Samuel Woodford and Edmund Spenser," *N & Q*, 189 (1945). 191-2.]

The Preface, sig. b 2:
Among the several other Papers that we have lost of the Excellent and Divine *Spenser*, one of the happiest Poets that this Nation ever bred, (and out of it the World, it may be (all things considered) had not his Fellow, excepting only such as were immediately Inspired) I bewail nothing me-thinks so much, as his Version of the *Canticles*. For doubtless, in my poor Judgment, never was Man better made for such a Work, and the Song it self so directly suited, with his Genius, and manner of Poetry (that I mean, wherein he best shews and even excels himself, His *Shepherds Kalender*, and other occasional Poems, for I cannot yet say the same directly for his *Faery Queen* design'd for an Heroic Poem) that it could not but from him receive the last Perfection, whereof it was capable out of its Original.

Ibid., sig. c 2ᵛ:
If therefore Our selves, or the *French* will use Blank Verse, either in an Heroick Poem, where they should be I think Couplets, as in Mr. *Cowley's Davideis* (for the Quadrains of Sir *William Davenant*, and the Stanza of Nine in *Spensers Faery Queen*, which are but an Improvement of the Ottava Rima, to instance in no more, seem not to me so proper) or in an Ode or Sonnet, (which remains yet to be attempted). . . let us give it the Character, as to its Form, which it anciently had.

Ibid., sig. c 4 - c 4ᵛ [commenting upon his own " epode," *The Legend of Love*, appended to the Canticles]:
The *Legend* further of Love I have stiled it, for honours sake to the great *Spenser*, whose Stanza of Nine I have used, and who has Intituled the six Books which we have compleat of his *Faery Queen*, by the several Legends of *Holiness, Temperance, Chastity, Friendship, Justice* and *Courtesy*, and

to any who knows what the word Legend there, or in its true and first notion signifies, it will neither seem strange, ridiculous, or improper.

Ibid., sig. c 8ᵛ:
I might amongst the rest [of my published poems] have added the Muses Complaint, but beside that I thank God I have no great need, being content with my Fortune, I never yet found any good come of it, and Mr. *Cowley's*, and Mr. *Spenser's* before him, will indifferently serve for any of the Trade, and he values himself too highly who dares expect better fortune than they met. (FMP)

ΕΠΩιΔΗ. *The Legend of Love*, pp. 54-118 (sigs. E 3ᵛ - I 3ᵛ). [A. C. Judson (*N & Q*, 189 (1945). 191-2) observes that this poem, written in 189 Spenserian stanzas which are disposed in three cantos, has no close verbal parallels to Spenser; but that the Platonic ascent to God, Canto 1. 24-36 (pp. 62-6, sigs. E 7ᵛ - Fᵛ) is to be compared with *H. H. B.*, and the procession of Idleness, Desire, Folly, Mirth, and the rest, Canto 2.43-62 (pp. 90-6, sigs. G 5ᵛ - G 8ᵛ), with the processions in *F. Q.*]

To the Honourable Sir JOHN DENHAM, upon his New Version of the Psalms, pp. 147-8 (second pagination; sig. Kk 2 - Kk 2ᵛ):

VII.
'Twas you, great Sir, who like the Redcross Knight,
To save the Damsel Poesy, arose;
Like him did with th'Enchanted Dragon fight,
And made her Reign a Queen, amidst her Foes.

[Poem dated 1668; see p. 149, sig. Kk 3.]

The Voyage. Ode, p. 174 (second pagination; sig. Ll 7ᵛ) [Woodford's muse is addressing him]:

X.
" Try me this once, and once more tempt the Main!
  " Thou shalt not unattended go,
" For when thou next putst forth to Sea again,
" I'll be thy Pilot, and the Passage show.
  " Nay, wonder not, for 'tis no more
" Than what I several times have done before,
" When *Tasso* I through unknown Straits did guide,
"And made my *Bartas* o're the Surges ride,
"And *Collins* sacred *Mulla* deifid."

[A note at the end of the poem, p. 175, sig. Ll 8: " *Made first* 1666, *and some time after review'd.*"] (ACJ)

After 1679. John Dryden. Marginal note in Dryden's copy of Spenser's *Works*, ed. 1679; in the Library of Trinity College, Cambridge. [*Works*, ed. Walter Scott (1808), rev. and corr. George Saintsbury, Edinburgh, 1882-93.]

P. 335 (Scott-Saintsbury 11.170):
In *Faerie Queene*, VII.vii.12 the words in line 6 are underlined in
Dryden's hand:

Where Phoebus self, that god of Poets hight

After stanza 12 the following note is inserted:

Ground-work for a Song
on St Cecelias Day. (DEM)

About 1680. Thomas Plume (d. 1704). Fragment in Dr. Plume's
" pocket-book."
[Printed in *Essex Rev.*, 14 (1905)]

P. 14:
Spencer's Fidessa is Queen Elizabeth and Duessa is Queen Mary of
Scotland for which all papists speak ill of him. (EG)

1680-81. John Aubrey. *Brief Lives*, Parts 1 and 3, Bodleian Lib. MSS
Aubrey 6 and 8.
[Ed. Andrew Clark, Oxford, 1898; ed. Oliver Lawson Dick, 1949.]

[*Sir Walter Raleigh*,] MS Aubr. 6, fol. 77^v(Clark 2.191 quoted):
He was somtimes a poet, not often. Before Spencer's Faery Q. is
a good copie of verses, which begins thus:—
Methinkes I see the grave wher Laura lay.

[*Mary Herbert, Countess of Pembroke*,] MS Aubr. 6, fol. 81 - 81^v
(Clark 1.311 [omits last sentence of quotation]; Dick, pp. 138-9,
quoted):
In her time, Wilton house was like a College, there were so many
learned and ingeniose persons. She was the greatest Patronesse of witt
and learning of any Lady in her time. . . . And I cannot imagine that
Mr. Edmund Spencer could be a stranger here.

[*Sir Philip Sidney*,] MS Aubr. 6, fol. 82 - 82^v (Dick, p. 279; Clark
2.248-9 quoted):
He was of a very munificent spirit, and liberall to all lovers of
learning, and to those that pretended to any acquaintance with Parnassus;
in so much that he was cloyd and surfeited with the poetasters of those
dayes. Among others Mr. Edmund Spencer made his addresse to him,
and brought his *Faery Queen*. Sir Philip was busy at his study and his
servant delivered Mr. Spencer's booke to his master, who layd it by,
thinking it might be such kind of stuffe as he was frequently troubled
with. Mr. Spencer stayd so long that his patience was wearied, and went
his way discontented, and never intended to come again. When Sir Philip
perused it, he was exceedingly delighted with it, that he was extremely
sorry he was gonne, and where to send for him he knew not. After much
enquiry he learned his lodgeing, and sent for him, mightily caressed
⟨him⟩, and ordered his servant to give him . . . pounds in gold. His
servant sayd that that was too much; ' No,' said Sir Philip, ' he is . . .,'

and ordered an addition. From this time there was a great friendship between them, to his dying day.

[*Edmund Spenser,*] MS Aubr. 8, fol. 41 (Dick, p. 282; Clark 2.232-3 quoted):

Mr. Edmund Spencer was of Pembrooke-hall in Cambridge; he misst the fellowship there which bishop Andrews gott. He was an acquaintance and frequenter of Sir Erasmus Dreyden. His mistris, Rosalind, was a kinswoman of Sir Erasmus' lady's. The chamber there at Sir Erasmus's is still called Mr. Spencer's chamber. Lately, at the College takeing-downe the wainscot of his chamber, they found an abundance of cards, with stanzas of the 'Faerie Queen' written on them.— from John Dreyden, esq., Poet Laureate.

Mr. Beeston sayes he was a little man, wore short haire, little band and little cuffs.

Ibid., MS Aubr. 6, fol. 83 (Dick, pp. 282-3; Clark 2.233 quoted):

Mr. Samuel Woodford (the poet, who paraphras'd the Psalmes) lives in Hampshire neer Alton, and he told me that Mr. Spencer lived sometime in these parts, in this delicate sweet ayre; where he enjoyed his muse, and writt good part of his verses. I have said before that Sir Philip Sydney and Sir Walter Ralegh were his acquaintance. He had lived some time in Ireland, and wrote a description of it, which is printed with Morison's History, or Description, of Ireland.

Sir John Denham told me, that archbishop Usher, Lord Primate of Armagh, was acquainted with him, by this token: when Sir William Davenant's *Gondibert* came forth Sir John askt the Lord Primate if he had seen it. Said the Primate, 'Out upon him, with his vaunting preface, he speaks against my old friend, Edmund Spenser.'

In the south crosse-aisle of Westminster abbey, next the dore, is this inscription:

'Heare lies (expecting the second comeing of our Saviour Christ Jesus) the body of Edmund Spencer, the Prince of Poets of his tyme; whose divine spirit needs no other witnesse then the workes which he left behind him. He was borne in London, in the yeare 1510, and dyed in the yeare 1596.'

[*Michael Drayton,*] MS Aubr. 8, fol. 8ᵛ (Clark 1.239-40 quoted):
Vide his inscription given by the countess of Dorset
In Westminster Abbey, neer Spencer. [Drayton's epitaph follows.]
(FIC, WW)

1680. Nathaniel Lee. *Theodosius: Or, The Force of Love, A Tragedy.* [STC L877.]

Prologue, sig. A4ᵛ:
On Poets onely no kind Star e're smil'd;
Curst Fate has damn'd 'em every Mothers Child:
Therefore he warns his Brothers of the Stage
To write no more to an ingrateful age.

Think what penurious Masters you have serv'd;
Tasso ran mad, and noble *Spencer* starv'd.
Turn then, who e're thou art that canst write well,
Thy Ink to Gaul, and in Lampoons excell. (EG)

1681. J. Bankes. Verse prefixed to Charles Saunders' *Tamerlane the Great.* [STC S741.]

Sig. A^v:
> Not *Spencer* dead, nor *Spencer* now alive
> Cou'd ever find a way by Wit to thrive.
> It is a Dream of Wealth, a Fairy Land,
> A fickle Treasure grasp'd like Golden Sand,
> Which, as 'tis held, does vanish through the Hand. (RB)

1681. John Dryden. *The Spanish Fryar, or, the Double Discovery.* [STC D2368. *Works*, ed. Walter Scott (1808), rev. and corr. George Saintsbury, Edinburgh, 1882-93.]

To the Right Honourable John Lord Haughton, sig. A 3 (Scott-Saintsbury 6.407):
Thus an injudicious Poet who aims at Loftiness runs easily into the swelling puffie style, because it looks like Greatness. I remember, when I was a Boy, I thought inimitable *Spencer* a mean Poet, in comparison of *Sylvester's Dubartas.* (FMP)

1681. Thomas D'Urfey. *Sir Barnaby Whigg: or, No Wit like a Womans.* [STC D2778.]

To the Right Honourable George Earl of Berkeley, sigs. A 2^v - A 3:
My Lord, 'tis not only a nice, but a very difficult thing to write a good Comedy; and therefore a tolerable one should be the more excusable; for there is not only Wit, but Plot, Invention, and a quick and ingenious fancy requir'd: Fancy! the brightest Jewel of Poetry, of which the Famous *English Spencer* was the great and only Master, as we may see in all his Descriptions, but more particularly in his Legend of Temperance, when he speaks of *Mammon* or Covetousness. [Quotes F. Q. 2.7, sts. 3 and 5.]
But this is a sort of Poetry of a different nature from *Dramaticks*; and therefore the fancy must of necessity vary, bcause in one it is digested into Characters, that are to speak before a carping Audience: and in the other, perhaps, only to be read or spoken of before one or two persons. (ECW)

1681. John Oldham. *Some New Pieces Never before Publisht. By the Author of the Satyrs upon the Jesuites.* [STC O248.]

Horace His Art of Poetry, Imitated in English, p. 6 (sig. A 4^v):
> If *Spencer's* Muse be justly so ador'd
> For that rich copiousness, wherewith he stor'd

Our Native Tongue; for Gods sake why should I
Straight be thought arrogant, if modestly
I claim and use the self-same liberty? (DEM)

1682. Henry Keepe. *Monumenta Westmonasteriensa.*
[STC K126; 1683 ed., STC K127, quoted below.]

P. 46:

§. 36. On the South side of this Cross, hard by the
little East door, is a decayed Tomb of grey Marble, very
much defaced, and nothing of the antient Inscription remaining, which was in Latine, but of late there is another
Edmund Spen- in English to inform you that *Edmund Spencer,* a most
cer. vid. Ep. excellent *Poet,* lies there intombed, who indeed had a sweet
28. and luxuriant fancy, and expressed his thoughts with admirable success, as his FAIRY-QUEEN, and other Works of
his sufficiently declare; and pity it was such true Poetry
should not have been imployed in as true a subject; he died
in the year 1596.

P. 208.
[Spenser's English epitaph recorded.] (FIC)

1682. *Poeta de Tristibus: Or, the Poets' Complaint.* [STC P2727.]
[*The Author's Epistle,* sig. A 3, quotes lines from Lee's Prologue to
Theodosius; see: 1680. Nathaniel Lee.] (JGM)

1682. John Sheffield, Earl of Mulgrave. *An Essay upon Poetry.* [STC
B5339.]

P. 21 (sig. C 4; Spingarn 2.296):
Who can all Sciences exactly know?
Whose fancy flyes beyond weak reason's sight,
And yet has Judgment to direct it right?
Whose nice distinction, *Virgil-like,* is such,
Never to say too little nor too much?
Let such a man begin without delay,
But he must do much more than I can say,
Must above *Cowley,* nay and *Milton* too prevail,
Succeed where great *Torquato,* and our greater *Spencer* fail. (FIC)

1682. *The Tory Poets: A Satyr.*
[STC T1948. Rptd *Complete Works of Thomas Shadwell,* ed. M. Summers, 1927.]

P. 9 (sig. C; Summers 5.285):
Such Vices now amongst the Poets Reign,
The very Fops do of their Faults complain:
Dead *POETS* Ashes in their Tombs do grieve,
And to rebuke their crimes do seem to live.

Spencers old bones about do toss and turn
With Indignation kicks his rusty Urn. (RHP)
[Sometimes attributed to Thomas Shadwell.]

1683.   John Chalkhill. *Thealma and Clearchus*. See 1600.

1683.   Thomas Flatman. *To my worthy Friend Mr. Isaac Walton; On the Publication of this Poem*, prefacing John Chalkhill's *Thealma and Clearchus*. [STC C1794.]

Sig. A 4ᵛ (Saintsbury 2.378):
> As long as *Spencer*'s noble flames shall burn,
> And deep Devotions throng about his Urn;
> As long as *Chalkhill*'s venerable Name,
> With humble emulation shall enflame
> Ages to come, and swell the Rolls of Fame:
> Your memory shall ever be secure. (FIC)

[Flatman's poem is dated June 5, 1683.]

1683.   James Montagu. Verses in *Hymenæus Cantabrigiensis*, Cambridge. [STC C338.]

Sig. Q 3ᵛ:
> Come, youth, to thy enlightened eyes I'll show
> What mighty mighty Blessings hence shall flow.
> Here in this Mirror, this fam'd Magick glass,
> Thou shalt behold all Revolutions pass.
> Here *Britomart* did *Arthegal* espy,
> And the brave race of her long Progeny. (LB)

[Cf. *F. Q.* 3.2.]

1683.   Sir William Soame and John Dryden. *The Art of Poetry, written in French by The Sieur de Boileau*, tr. with amplifications. [STC B3464. Rptd in *The Art of Poetry*, ed. A. S. Cook, 1892.]

Canto 1, pp. 7-8 (sig. A 6 - A 6ᵛ; Cook, p. 165):
> Our ancient Verse, (as homely as the Times,)
> Was rude, unmeasur'd, only Tagg'd with Rhymes:
> Number and Cadence, that have Since been Shown,
> To those unpolish'd Writers were unknown.
> *Fairfax was He, who, in that Darker Age,
> By his just Rules restrain'd Poetic Rage;
> *Spencer* did next in Pastorals excel,
> And taught the Noble Art of Writing well:
> To stricter Rules the Stanza did restrain,
> And found for Poetry a richer Veine.
> Then *D'Avenant* came.

*Fairfax in his Translation of *Godfrey of Bullen*. (FIC)

1683. Edmund Waller (?). *To Mr. Creech on his Translation of Lucretius*, in *Titus Lucretius Carus His Six Books of Epicurean Philosophy*, Thomas Creech's tr. of the *De Rerum Natura*, third ed. [STC L3449. Verses rptd *Poems of Edmund Waller*, ed. G. Thorn Drury, 1893.]

Sig. D 3 (Drury, p. 218; Bradley, p. 404):

These scribbling Insects have what they deserve,
Not Plenty, nor the Glory for to Starve.
That *Spencer* knew, That *Tasso* felt before,
And Death found surly *Ben*. exceeding poor.

[The poem is signed " E.W." and dated " London, Feb. 6." As Thorn Drury points out, the authenticity of the poem was questioned by E. Fenton in his edition of Waller, 1729 (p. lxxviii of the notes).] (JFB, DB)

1684. Knightly Chetwood. *To the Earl of Roscommon, on his Excellent Poem*, prefixed to *An Essay on Translated Verse*. [STC R1930.]

Sig. A 4ᵛ (Munro 2.304; Bradley, p. 406):

As when by *labouring* Stars new Kingdoms rise
The mighty *Mass* in *rude* confusion lies,
A Court *unform'd, disorder* at the Bar,
And even in *Peace* the *rugged Meen* of War,
Till some wise States-man into *Method* draws
The parts, and Animates the frame with *Laws*;
Such was the case when *Chaucer's early* toyl
Founded the *Muses* Empire in *our* Soyl.
Spencer improv'd it with his painful hand
But *lost* a *Noble* Muse in *Fairy-land*.
Shakespear say'd all that Nature cou'd impart,
And *Johnson* added *Industry* and *Art*. (JM)

1684. Nathaniel Lee. *Constantine the Great; A Tragedy*. [STC L848.]

Prologue, sig. A 3ᵛ:

Therefore, all you who have Male Issue born,
Under the Starving Sign of *Capricorn*;
Prevent the Malice of their Stars in time,
And warn them early from the Sin of Rhime:
Tell 'em how *Spencer* starv'd, how *Cowley* mourn'd,
How *Butler's* Faith and Service was return'd. (EG)

[Prologue is assigned to Otway in 1812 edition of *Works*, 2.455.]

1684. George Sandys. *Anglorum Speculum, or the Worthies of England in Church and State*. [STC S672.]

Pp. 497-8 (Spurgeon 1.257):

Edm. Spencer, bred in *Camb*. A great Poet who imitated *Chaucer*, 'Tis said that he presented Q. *Eliz.* with a Poem, with which she was so well pleased, that she commanded the Lord Treasurer *Cecil* to give him 100 *l.* and when he alledged that Sum was too much, *then give him,* (Quoth the Q.) *what is Reason,* but being delayed he presented these Lines to the Queen:

> I *was promised on a time*
> *To have Reason for my Rhyme;*
> *From that time unto this Season,*
> I *receiv'd nor Rhyme nor Reason.*

Hereupon the Q. gave strict Order for the present payment of the 100 *l.* He was afterwards Secretary to the Lord *Gray,* Deputy of *Ireland.* He was an excellent Linguist, Antiquary, Philosopher, Mathematician, yet so poor (as being a Poet) that he was thought *Fami non Famae scribere.* Returning into *England,* he was robb'd by the Rebels of that little he had, and dying for Grief in great Want 1598, was honourably buried nigh *Chaucer* in *Westminster.* The expence of his Funeral and Monument was defrayed at the sole charge of *Rob.* first of that Name, E. of *Essex.* (DEM)

[Sandys' account appears to be a careless abridgment of William Winstanley's compilation also published in 1684. See below.]

1684.   William Winstanley. *England's Worthies. Select Lives of the most Eminent Persons of the English Nation, From Constantine the Great Down to these Times.* [2nd ed.] [STC W3059.]

The Life of Mr. Edmond Spenser, pp. 224-7:

Next to this incomparable Knight Sir *Philip Sidney,* we shall add the Life of his fellow-Poet and contemporary, Mr. *Edmond Spenser,* who was born in the City of *London,* and brought up in *Pembroke-hall* in *Cambridge,* where he became a most excellent Scholar, but especially very happy in English Poetry, as his Learned elaborate Works do declare. In which the many *Chaucerisms* used (for I will not say, affected by him) are thought by the ignorant to be blemishes, known by the learned to be beauties to his book: which notwithstanding (saith a learned writer) had been more Saleable, if more conformed to our modern Language.

His first flight in Poetry was that Book of his called *The Shepherds Kalendar,* applying an old name to a new work, being of Eglogues fitted to each moneth in the year: of which work hear what that worthy Knight, Sir *Philip Sidney* writes, in his *Defence of Poesy: The Shepherds Kalendar* (saith he) *hath much Poetry in his Eclogues, indeed worthy the reading if I be not deceived. That same framing his Stile to an old rustick Language I dare not allow, since neither* Theocritus *in Greek,* Virgil *in Latine, nor* Sanazara *in Italian did affect it.* Afterwards he translated the *Gnat,* a little fragment of *Virgils* excellency. But his main Book, and which indeed I think Envy its self cannot carp at, was his *Fairy Queen,* a Work of such an ingenious composure, as will last as long whilest times shall be no more.

Now as you have heard what esteem Sir *Philip Sidney* had of his Book, so you shall hear what esteem Mr. *Spenser* had of Sir *Philip Sidney*, writing thus in his *Ruines of Time*. [Quotes lines 323-9.]

There passeth a story commonly told and believed, that Mr. *Spenser* presenting his Poems to Queen *Elizabeth*, she highly affected therewith, commanded the Lord Cecil, her Treasurer to give him an hundred pound; and when the Treasurer (a good Steward of the Queens money) alledged that Sum was too much for such a matter; then give him (quoth the Queen) *what is reason*; to which the Lord consented, but was so busied, belike, about matters of higher concernment, that Mr. *Spenser* received no reward: whereupon he presented this Petition in a small piece of Paper to the Queen in her Progress.

> *I was promis'd on a time,*
> *To have reason for my Ryme;*
> *From that time unto this season,*
> *I receiv'd nor Rhyme nor Reason.*

[For an early appearance of this quatrain, see: 1602-3. John Manningham.]

Hereupon the Queen gave strict order (not without some check to her Treasurer) for the present payment of the hundred pounds she first intended unto him.

Now what esteem also this our Poet had amongst learned men may be seen in these verses.

> *At* Delphos *shrine one did a doubt propound* . . . .

[Quotes epitaph ascribed to Francis Beaumont; see 1653. *On Mr. Edm. Spencer, Famous Poet* above.]

He afterwards went over into *Ireland*, Secretary to the Lord Gray, Lord Deputy thereof; and though that his Office under his Lord was Lucrative, yet got he no estate; *Peculiari Poetis fato semper cum paupertate conflictatus est*, saith the reverend *Cambden*; so that it fared little better with him, than with *William Xilander* the *German*, (a most excellent Linguist, Antiquary, Philosopher, and Mathematician) who was so poor, that (as *Thuanus* writes) he was thought *Fami non famae scribere*.

Thriving so bad in that Boggy Country, to add to his misery, he was Rob'd by the Rebels of that little he had left; whereupon in great grief he returns into *England*, and falling into want, which to a noble Spirit is most killing, being heart broken, he died *Anno* 1598. and was honourably buried at the sole charge of *Robert*, first of that name Earl of Essex, where this Distick on his Monument.

> *Anglica te vivo, vixit plausitque Poetis;*
> *Nunc moritura, timet te moriente mori.*

> *Whilest thou didst live, liv'd English Poetry,*
> *Which fears, now thou art dead, that she shall die.*

A modern Author writes, that the Lord *Cecil* owed Mr. *Spenser* a grudge for some Reflections of his in Mother *Hubbard's Tale*, and therefore when the Queen had ordered him that Money, the Lord

Treasurer said, What all this for a Song? And this he is said to have taken so much to Heart, that he contracted a deep melancholy, which soon after brought his life to a period: So apt is an ingenious Spirit to resent a slighting even from the greatest persons. And thus much I must needs say of the merit of so great a Poet from so great a Monarch, that it is incident to the best of Poets sometimes to flatter some Royal or Noble Patron, never did any do it more to the height, or with greater art and elegance, if the highest of praises attributed to so Heroick a Princess can justly be termed flattery. (FIC)
[RH has called attention to The Life of Spenser in transcript of part of the 1633 ed. of John Stow's *Survey of London* with additions, Huntington MS HM727, fol. 221-221ᵛ. Apparently a draft of part of Winstanley's 1684 *Life,* it repeats the Epitaph ascribed to Beaumont, the English translation of the Latin distich, the reference to Spenser's esteem of Sidney reflected in *R. T.,* the anecdote of the riming petition to the Queen, and the paragraph mentioning Cecil and *M. H. T.*]

The Life of Mr. Michael Drayton, p. 340:
He was in his time for Fame and Renown in Poetry, not much inferior to Mr. *Spencer,* or Sir *Philip Sidney* himself.

Ibid., p. 341:
He changed his Lawrel for a Crown of glory, *Anno* 1631. and was buried in *Westminster-Abby,* near the South-door, by those two eminent Poets, *Jeffrey Chaucer* and *Edmond Spencer.* (DEM)

[*The Life of Mr Wil. Shakespeare,* p. 347, quotes Basse's elegy on Shakespeare. See: 1622. William Basse, above.] (FMP)

[For the first ed. of *England's Worthies,* see: 1660, above.]

1685. John Dryden. *Sylvæ: or the Second Part of Poetical Miscellanies.* [STC D2379. *Works,* ed. Walter Scott (1808), rev. and corr. George Saintsbury, Edinburgh, 1882-93.]

The Preface, sig. a 6 (Scott-Saintsbury 12.298) [discussing the pastoral excellencies of Theocritus]:
Even his Dorick Dialect has an incomparable sweetness in its Clownishness, like a fair Shepherdess in her Country Russet, talking in a *Yorkshire* Tone. This was impossible for Virgil to imitate; because the severity of the *Roman* Language denied him that advantage. *Spencer* has endeavour'd it in his Shepherds Calendar; but neither will it succeed in *English,* for which reason I forbore to attempt it. (FMP)

1685. John Evelyn. *The Immortality of Poesie* in *Poems by Several Hands . . . Collected by N. Tate.* [STC T210.]

P. 91 (Bradley, p. 408):
Old *Chaucer* shall, for his facetious Style
Be read, and prais'd by warlike *Britains,* while
The Sea enriches, and defends their Isle.

While the whole Earth resounds *Elisa's* Fame,
Who aw'd the *French*, and did the Spaniard tame,
The *English* will remember *Spencer's* Name.
[Continues the roll call of English poets by naming Jonson, Shakespeare,
Cowley, Milton, Dryden, Wycherley, Lee and Otway, Sidley, and
Etheridge.] (JFB)

1685. *Miscellany Poems and Translations by Oxford Hands.*
[STC M2232.]

[Ovid's] *Elegy the Fifteenth, Book the First Imitated,* p. 156 (Spurgeon
1.258):

Spencer's Heroick Lines no death shall fear,
His Fairy Queen, and Shepherd's Kalendar,
Shall be admired, whilst to our *Room**   *London
The Vassal Isle to pay their Tribute come. (DEM)

1685. *Mixt Essays Upon Tragedies, Comedies, Italian Comedies English
Comedies and Opera's. Written Originally in French By the Sieur de
Saint Euvremont.* [STC S307.]

Preface to the Translation, sig. A 4 (Bentley 2.188) [on criticism]:
The *Dutch* and *Germans* (as though frozen up) have produced little in
this kind; yet we must confess that *Grotius, Heinsius, Scaliger,* and *Vossius*
were Learned *Criticks.* Some of the *English* have indeed rais'd their
Pens, and soar'd as high as any of the *Italians,* or *French*; yet *Criticism*
came but very lately in fashion amongst us; without doubt *Ben. Johnson*
had a large stock of Critical Learning; *Spencer* had studied *Homer,* and
Virgil, and *Tasso,* yet he was misled, and debauched by *Ariosto,* as
Mr. *Rymer* judiciously observes. (GEB)

1685. *A Pastoral, Written at Dublin, in May 1683* in *Poems by Several
Hands . . . Collected by N. Tate.* [STC T210.]

Pp. 45-6:

Thyrsis. O Coridon! Who shall presume to sing?
Who to these Groves shall foreign Numbers bring?
Where once great *Spencer* did triumphant reign,
The best, the sweetest, of the inspir'd Train;
Scarce from the God of Wit such Verse did flow,
When he vouchsaf'd to follow Sheep below:
Here sigh'd the love-sick Swain, here fed his Sheep
Near *Mullas* Stream, whose Waves he taught to weep:
While hungry'st Herds forgot the flowry Meads,
And the unshorn Hills inclin'd their list'ning Shades;
Oft as I've heard the Muses hither came,
The Muses slighted the inspiring Stream,
Charm'd with the merit of their *Colins* fame:
While hoarser Goatherds in some wretched strain
Invok'd the absent Deities in vain.

Ah! liv'd he now, what Subjects might he chuse,
The deathless Theams of his immortal Muse,
O God-like *Ossory* his Song would tell,
How much belov'd he liv'd, how much bewail'd he fell.
In War unconquer'd, but betray'd in Peace
By fraud of Death, and snares of a Disease.

P. 47:

Say happy Bard! immortal *Spencer* say!
What numbers would'st thou choose, what Praise display,
When of *Armagh* thy mighty Song should be,
Of *Armagh*'s Justice and his Piety? (FMP)

1685. Nathaniel Thompson. *A Collection of 86 Loyal Poems.* [STC T1005.]

P. 64:

The Bad- And yet I have Sense Children and Fools to scar,
ger in the By teaching *Ben* and *Franck* to Write great Lies;
Fox-Trap, How mighty monsters quarrel in the Skies,
or a Satyr Visions at *Hatfield,* either White or Green,
upon Far more Prodigious than the *Fairy Queen.* (HER)
Satyrs

1685. Samuel Wesley. *Maggots: or, Poems on Several Subjects, Never before Handled.* [STC W1374.]

On the Bear-fac'd *Lady,* p. 30:

He who to meet a *Devil* does prepare,
Like *Spencer*'s Knight, may find an Angel there.[f]

Note [f] [referring to the passage above], p. 32 :
See *Spencer*'s *Fairy Queen;* In one of the first Cantos—instead of
an old Witch, the Knight found a brisk young Lady. (JM, FIC)

1685. John Wilmot, Earl of Rochester (d. 1680). [John Fletcher's]
Valentinian: A Tragedy. As 'tis Alter'd by the late Earl of Rochester.
[STC F1354. *Collected Works,* ed. John Hayward, 1926.]

P.27 (sig. E 2; Hayward, pp. 188-9):

Lucin[a]. Dear solitary Groves where Peace does dwell,
Sweet Harbours of pure Love and Innocence!
How willingly could I for ever stay
Beneath the shade of your embracing Greens,
Listning to Harmony of warbling Birds,
Tun'd with the gentle Murmurs of the Streams,
Upon whose Banks in various Livery
The fragrant offspring of the early Year
Their Heads like graceful Swans bent proudly down,
See their own Beauties in the Crystal Flood? (JM)

[Cf. *F. Q.* 2.12.71.]

1687. Philip Ayres. *Lyric Poems, made in Imitation of the Italians.*
[STC A4312.]

Preface, sig. A 5ᵛ (Saintsbury, 2.269):

If any quarrel at the Oeconomy, or Structure of these Poems, many
of them being Sonnets, Canzons, Madrigals, &c. objecting that none
of our great men either Mr. WALLER, Mr. COWLEY, or Mr. DRYDEN,
whom it was most proper to have followed, have ever stoop'd to any
thing of this sort; I shall very readily acknowledge, that being sensible of
my own Weakness and Inability of ever attaining to the performance of
one thing equal to the worst piece of theirs, it easily disswaded me from
that attempt, and put me on this; which is not without President; For
many eminent Persons have published several things of this nature, and
in this method, both Translations and Poems of their own; As the famous
Mr. SPENCER, Sir PHILIP SIDNEY, Sir RICHARD FANSHAW, Mr. MILTON,
and some few others. (EG)

1687. John Dryden. *The Hind and the Panther. A Poem, In Three
Parts.*
[STC D2281. *Works,* ed. Walter Scott (1808), rev. and corr. George
Saintsbury, Edinburgh, 1882-93.]

The Second Part, pp. 71-2 (Scott-Saintsbury 10.191):
This peaceful Seat my poverty secures,
War seldom enters but where wealth allures;
Nor yet despise it, for this poor aboad
Hast oft receiv'd, and yet receives a god;
A god victorious of the stygian race
Here laid his sacred limbs, and sanctified the place.
This mean retreat did mighty *Pan* contain.
Be emulous of him, and pomp disdain,
And dare not to debase your soul to gain. (DEM)
[Cf. *S.C. May* 54.]

The Third Part, pp. 73-4 (Scott-Saintsbury 10.195):
Much malice mingl'd with a little wit
Perhaps may censure this mysterious writ:
Because the Muse has peopl'd *Caledon*
With *Panthers, Bears* and *Wolves,* and Beasts unknown,
As if we were not stock'd with monsters of our own.
Let *Æsop* answer, who has set to view,
Such kinds as *Greece* and *Phrygia* never knew;
And mother *Hubbard* in her homely dress
Has sharply blam'd a *British Lioness,*
That *Queen,* whose feast the factious rabble keep,
Expos'd obscenely naked and a-sleep. (FIC)

Ibid., p. 77 (Scott-Saintsbury 10.199):
This heard, the *Matron* was not slow to find
What sort of malady had seiz'd her mind;

Disdain, with gnawing envy, fell despight,
And canker'd malice stood in open sight.
Ambition, int'rest, pride without controul,
And jealousie, the jaundice of the soul.
Revenge, the bloudy minister of ill,
With all the lean tormentors of the will. (DEM)

1687. *The Revolter. A Tragi-Comedy Acted between the Hind and Panther, and Religio Laici, &c.* [STC R1206.]

Pp. 1-2 (sig. A 2 - A 2ᵛ) [commenting on Dryden]:
Truly, one would think the *Author* might have bethought himself of Allusions much more proper for his purpose than such Beastiall *Prosopopeia's* as these; now altogether Antiquated, notwithstanding his idle Apology for what he has done, and his miserable President of Mother *Hubbard*, as much out of fashion, as *Hellen* of *Troys* Wardrobe, or his Eye-sore of Q *Elisabeth's* Fardingale. (RHP)

1687. *Spencer Redivivus Containing the First Book of the Fairy Queen, His Essential Design preserv'd, but his obsolete Language and manner of Verse totally laid aside. Delivered in Heroick Numbers.* [STC S5969.]

Folger copy quoted:
" The Preface," sigs. A 3 - A 4v:
There are few of our Nation that have heard the Name of *Spencer*, but have granted him the repute of a famous Poet.

But I must take leave to affirm, that the esteem which is generally allow'd to his Poetical Abilities, has rather been from an implicite or receiv'd Concession, than a knowing Discernment paid to the Value of this Author: Whose Design, in his Books of the *Fairy Queen*, howsoever admirable, is so far from being familiarly perceptible in the Language he deliver'd it in, that his Stile seems no less unintelligible at this Day, than the obsoletest of our *English* or *Saxon* Dialect.

On which ground I believe it ought to have been long ago wish'd, as well as readily embrac'd, by all politely judicious, that something of this Eminent Poet had been genuinely and succinctly convey'd by the Purity of our Tongue.

An Endeavour undertaken by me, supposing it could not be less acceptable to others than my self. By which I have not only discharg'd his antiquated Verse and tedious Stanza, but have likewise deliver'd his Sense of Heroick Numbers: much more sutable to an Epick Poem, the deserv'd Denomination of his, than can possibly be accomplish'd by any sort of Measures in Stanza's, both in respect of their Freedom & Pleasure above any other Form that can be us'd in a Poem of this Nature.

For at the Writing in Stanza's must render Verse sententious and constrain'd, the most weighty part of their meaning still being to be expected at the Period of the Stanza; so, in that consideration, their Composure must needs be less difficult than where the force of each single line is to be weigh'd apart. As who can judge, had *Virgil* writ or been render'd by any alternate Meeter, that either his design or expressions had appear'd so unconfin'dly elevate, as he is to be acknowledg'd in his own, or in such measures as should not resemble the unlimited nature and freedom proper to the greatness of his Subject.

As for the essential Story of *Spencer*, contain'd in this one Book of his *Fairy Queen*: I have entirely preserv'd his Matter and Design, except where both are abreviated, and, as I conceive, improv'd by my thoughts.

Nor do I doubt but every impartial Reader will find, that in the way I have undertaken to delineate and express him by, he is render'd what he ought to have been instead of what is to be found in himself.

Not that I believe, his Language being wav'd, any *Poetical Genius*, since the incomparable *Virgil*, has exceeded the wonderful Variety, Beauty, and Strength of Conception that is to be found in our famous *Spencer*.

If we consider him as an extraordinary Inventer or Tale teller, the main Engine and Fabrick of Poesie, we shall find him more fruitfully new and delicate than any that have preceded him to the Age in which *Virgil* liv'd.

The most esteem'd of whose Successors, in the Heroick way, *Statius* and *Tasso*, have borrow'd so much from their great Poetical Predecessor, that it may be said of them, as *Scaliger* does of *Statius*, that they had very probably been greater in themselves, had they not endeavour'd to be like *Virgil*, whose Excellency was above all subsequent Imitation.

Wheras the Compositions of our wonderful *Spencer* are not only purely created throughout his Works by his unally'd Invention, but vary'd in every *Canto* with such a singular Method, that he is granted, at this day, abating his Expressions and manner of Verse, to compleat a distinct Original of Heroick Poesie.

The late ingenious Sir *William Davenant* taking occasion in his Preface before his *Gondibert* to commend this author, compares his Poem of the *Fairy Queen* to an admir'd Course of Poetical Dreams and Extasies, or an Allegory of Things and Persons deliver'd from extraordinary Result of Imagination. And I conceive him so far in the right in his judicious esteem of this Poet, that, in his kind, perhaps he may remain perpetually unparallel'd.

Having thus far explain'd the Value and Form of this Author's Work, I will take leave to present my Reader with a Taste of what I judge the Essential Parts of Heroick Poesie.

Sigs. A7 - A7ᵛ:

True it is, that according to holy Religion, we must not presume to transform our Hero's into demi-gods, which I confess was some advantage to the Ancients in magnifying their Heroicks above the ordinary Exaltation and Endowments of men: However I believe that the sublime Piety and Fortitude incident to a Christian Hero duely convey'd by the

Poet in reference to Exploits of highest Admiration and Glory, may well compare with what could be feign'd of the best of theirs.

And this I suppose is sufficient for their Conviction, who affirm that an *Epike Poem* is not to be produc'd within the bound of Christianity. Not but I grant that it is a Work of highest difficulty, and no less to be admir'd, if perfect, than some wondrous Architecture hardly to be equall'd in point of Design, Magnitude, and Beauty.

But not impossible to be effected since there needs not be urged a surer Refutation of all Opposers, than the marvellous esteem of this Author, notwithstanding the Obsoleteness of his *English* and Verse, who liv'd within a hundred years of our time. But how to excuse the choice of the Language he writ in, that he could not but know, was of too antiquate a Date, if not generally exploded by all Writers in the time he liv'd; or why he should not conceive himself oblig'd to impart the Tongue of that season as currant as he found it, I cannot apprehend.

Unless he was resolv'd as is reported of him, to imitate his ancient Predecessor *Chaucer,* or affected it out of design to restore our *Saxon English.* However it was, the Reader may peruse him here, as far as I have gone, in more fashionable *English* and Verse; and I hope without Diminution to his Fame in any regard.

" To the Author of *Spencer Redivivus,*" sig. A8:
>Well to improve dead Author, and refine
>His proper worth, resembleth power divine.
>Or as Faith does of Resurrection tell,
>When Souls by future Glory shall excel.
>Thus does your Pen in this your Work provide,
>That *Spencer*'s Fame shall still renew'd abide,
>So clear by you his deep Invention's told,
>That in your words him perfect I behold.
>His Stanza's, Language, old as *Saxon* Rhyme,
>From you receive fit Epithites and Chime.
>What could your pregnant *Genius* higher raise,
>Than with smooth Verse to polish ancient Bayes?
>Of *English,* he had the most the Epike Vein,
>And first does by your Lines advantage gain.
>I'le not trust Painters, who no Pencil say
>Can warmly liken Life the copy'd way.
>Since I affirm, that *Spencer* figur'd here
>Does in his lively Pattern best appear.
>And who reads that with a discerning mind,
>Must wish that more of him such Change may find:
>Or be your happy Emulator seen
>In copying, where you leave, the *Fairy Queen.*

Beginning of Canto I, p. 1 (sig. B):
>The Argument
>*The Patron of True Piety*
>*Foul Error doth Defeat,*

> But Snares of vile Hipocrisy
> His Virtue Next do Cheat.
> A Worthy Knight was Riding on the Plain,
> In Armour Clad, which richly did Contain
> The Gallant Marks of Many Battels fought,
> Tho' he before no Martial Habit sought;
> How Warlike ere his Person seem'd to Sit
> On a Bold Steed, that scarce obey'd the Bit:
> Upon his Breast a Bloody Cross display'd,
> The Precious drops for him his Saviour paid;
> And on his Mighty Shield the same did bear,
> To shew his Faith was made his Valours Care. (FIC)

[The paraphrase comprises some 4600 verses. On probable grounds Professor Leicester Bradner (*Review of English Studies*, 14. 323-6) identifies the author of *Spencer Redivivus* with Edward Howard; see 1669 above, and 1689 below.]

About 1688. *A Journal from Parnassus.*
[First printed from MS now in the Bodleian Library, by Hugh Macdonald, 1937.]
Macdonald, p. 38 (Bentley 2.9):
   The Examination of Heroics was assign'd to Spencer: of Epics & Pindarics to Mr Waller: of Satyrs to Mr Oldam: For Stage-Poetry the supervising of Tragedies was committed to Shakespear; Of Comedies to Ben. Johnson: of Tragi-Comedies to Beaumont & Fletcher: of Prologues, Songs & all the Garniture & Appurtenances of this sort of Poetry (especially Prefaces,) to Bays. (GEB)

1688. "Philaster." *To Madam Jane Barker on Her Incomparable Poems*, prefixed to *Poetical Recreations: Consisting of Original Poems, Songs, Odes, &c. In Two Parts. Part I. Occasionally Written by Mrs. Jane Barker. Part II. By several Gentlemen of the Universities, and Others.* [STC B770.]
Sig. A 5ᵛ:
   Bald and Bombastick equally you shun,
   In ev'n paces all your Numbers run.
   Spencer's aspiring fancy fill your Soul
   Whilst lawfull Raptures through your Poems rowl,
   Which always by your guidance do submit,
   To th'curb of Judgment, and the bounds of Wit.
[Signed, sig. A 6, " *St.* John's *Colledge.* PHILASTER."] (JM)

1688. J. Whitehall. Poem addressed to Mr. Thomas Wright, in *Poetical Recreations: Consisting of Original Poems, Songs, Odes, &c. . . . In Two Parts. Part I. Occasionally Written by Mrs. Jane Barker. Part II. By several Gentlemen of the Universities, and Others*, [STC B770.]

Pt. 2, p. 39:
    To tell thy Fame, I want great *Spencer's* Skill. (JM)

1689. Charles Cotton. *Poems on several Occasions.*
[STC C6389. Poems, ed. John Beresford, 1923.]

Eclogue. Corydon, Clotton, pp. 108-9 (Beresford, p. 77):
    Corydon. Rise, *Clotten,* rise, take up thy Pipe & play,
    The Sheepherds want thee, 'tis Pan's Holy-day;
    And thou, of all the Swains, wert wont to be
    The first to grace that great Solemnity.
    Clotten. True, *Corydon,* but then I happy was,
    And in *Pan's* favour had a Minion's place:
    Clotten had then fair Flocks, the finest Fleece
    These Plains and Mountains yielded then was his.
    In these auspitious times the fruitfull Dams
    Brought me the earliest and the kindli'st Lambs;
    Nor nightly watch about them need I keep,
    For *Pan* himself was Sheepherd to my Sheep;
    But now, alas! neglected and forgot
    Are all my off'rings, and he knows me not.
    The bloudy Wolf, that lurks away the day,
    When night's black palm beckons him out to prey
    Under the cover of those guilty shades,
    No Folds but mine the rav'nous Foe invades;
    And there he has such bloudy havock made,
    That, all my Flock being devour'd or stray'd,
    I now have lost the Fruits of all my pain,
    And am no more a Sheepherd but a Swain.

The Morning Quatrains, st. 15, p. 231 (Beresford, p. 50):
    Fair *Amarillis* drives her Flocks,
    All night safe folded from the Fox,
    To flow'ry Downs, where *Collin* stays,
    To court her with his Roundelays.

Noon Quatrains, st. 7, p. 235 (Beresford, p. 53):
    The lagging Ox is now unbound,
    From larding the new turn'd up ground,
    Whilst *Hobbinal* alike o'er-laid,
    Takes his course dinner to the shade.

To my Friend, Mr. John Anderson. From the Countrey, st. 7, p. 379
(Beresford, p. 112):
    We have too errant *Knights* so stout,
    As honest *Hobinol* and *Clout.* (DEM)

1689. John Evelyn. *Diary.*
[Ed. William Bray, 1889.]

Letter to Samuel Pepys, 12 August, Bray 3.301 (Munro 2.337):

. . . For there were the Pictures of Fisher, Fox, Sir Thomas More, Thomas Lord Cromwell, Dr. Nowel, &c. And what was most agreeable to his Lordship's general humour, old Chaucer, Shakespeare, Beaumont and Fletcher, who were both in one piece, Spencer, Mr. Waller, Cowley, Hudibras, which last he plac'd in the room where he used to eat and dine in public, most of which, if not all, are at the present at Cornbury in Oxfordshire. (JM)

1689.   Edward Howard. *Caroloiades, or, The Rebellion of Forty One.* [STC H2966-7.]

The Preface, sig. A 4 - A 4ᵛ:

In the mean time, to come closer to my purpose by alledging such Authorities as have the most undoubted Modern reception: I need but mention the Great *Tasso,* and our famous *Spencer,* by whose Poems, tho' the Productions of Latter Times, and agreeable to Evangelical persuasion, it is very clear that neither as to Fiction or Allegory, they wanted any necessary Ingredients or supplements, if compar'd with such Poets who had been precedent to Christian Belief. I shall not present my Reader with any Inspections into the Poem of *Spencer,* it being upon the matter wholly Allegory, and therefore not so proper to the Application I intend.

P. 137 (Munro 2.328; Spurgeon 1.261; Bradley, p. 416):

Of which he *Chaucer, Spencer,* much beheld,
And where their Learned Poems most excell'd.
Tho' words now obsolete express their Flame,
Like Gemms that out of Fashion value Claim. (JM)

1690.   Francis Atterbury (?). Preface to *The Second Part of Mr. Waller's Poemes.*
[STC W521. *Poems of Edmund Waller,* ed. G. Thorn Drury, 1893.]

Sig. A 4ᵛ (Drury, p. xxiii):

In the mean time, 'tis a surprizing Reflection, that between what *Spencer* wrote last, and *Waller* first, there should not be much above twenty years distance: and yet the one's Language, like the Money of that time, is as currant now as ever; whilst the other's words are like old Coyns, one must go to an Antiquary to understand their true meaning and value. Such advances may a great Genius make, when it undertakes any thing in earnest! (FIC)

1690.   John Dryden. *Don Sebastian, King of Portugal: A Tragedy.*
[STC D2262. *Works,* ed. Walter Scott (1808), rev. and corr. George Saintsbury, Edinburgh, 1882-93.]

Act 2, sc. 1, p. 36 (Scott-Saintsbury 7.364):

Seb. . . . *Brutus* and *Cato* might discharge their Souls,
And give 'em Furlo's for another World:

But we, like Centry's, are oblig'd to stand
In starless Nights, and wait the pointed hour. (RHP)
[Cf. F. Q. 1.9.41.]

1690.   Sir William Temple. *Upon Poetry,* the fourth essay in his *Miscellanea. The Second Part.* [STC T652.]

Pp. 46-7 (sigs. Ccc 7ᵛ - Ccc 8; Spingarn 3.99). Temple is speaking of the revival of poetry after the " Gothic " night]:
Petrarch, Ronsard, Spencer, met with much Applause upon the Subjects of Love, Praise, Grief, Reproach. *Ariosto* and *Tasso* entered boldly upon the Scene of *Heroick* Poems, but having not Wings for so high Flights, began to Learn of the old Ones, fell upon their Imitations, and chiefly of *Virgil,* as far as the Force of their Genius or Disadvantage of New Languages and Customs would allow. The Religion of the Gentiles had been woven into the Contexture of all the antient Poetry, with a very agreable mixture, which made the Moderns affect to give that of Christianity, a place also in their Poems. But the true Religion, was not found to become Fiction so well, as a false had done, and all their Attempts of this kind seemed rather to debase Religion than to heighten Poetry. *Spencer* endeavoured to Supply this, with Morality, and to make Instruction, instead of Story, the Subject of an *Epick* Poem. His Execution was Excellent, and his Flights of Fancy very Noble and High, but his Design was Poor, and his Moral lay so bare, that it lost the Effect; 'tis true, the Pill was Gilded, but so thin, that the Colour and the Taste were too easily discovered. (FMP)

1691.   *The Athenian Mercury,* vol. 2, no. 14, Saturday, July 11.

" Questions " [no pagin. or sig.] (Munro 2.378; Bradley, p. 423; Spurgeon 1.263):
Quest. 3. Which is the best Poem *that ever was made and who in your Opinion, deserves the* Title *of the best* Poet *that ever was?*
Answ. . . . *Plautus* wrote *wittily, Terence* neatly—and *Seneca* has very fine thoughts. But since we can't go through all the world, let's look home a little. *Grandsire Chaucer,* in spite of the Age, was a Man of as much wit, sence and honesty as any that have writ after him. Father *Ben* was excellent at *Humour, Shakespeare* deserves the Name of sweetest, which *Milton* gave him.—Spencer was a noble poet, his *Fairy-Queen* an excellent piece of Morality, Policy, History. *Davenant* had a great genius.—Too much can't be said of *Mr. Coley. Milton's Paradice lost,* and some other Poems of his will never be equal'd. *Waller* is the most *correct* Poet we have. (JM)

1691.   James Harrington.   Preface to Anthony Wood's *Athenae Oxonienses.* [STC W3382. Ed. Philip Bliss, 1813.]

Sig. Aᵛ (Bliss 1.clix-clx):
An old word is retain'd by an Antiquary with as much Religion as a

Relick; and few are by him receiv'd as English, but such as have been naturaliz'd by *Spencer.* (LB)

1691. Gerard Langbaine. *An Account of the English Dramatick Poets,* Oxford. [STC K373.]

Abraham Cowley, p. 79 (sig E):
His first Inclinations to Poetry, proceeded from his falling by chance on *Spencer's Fairy Queen,* " With which he was so infinitely delighted, and which by degrees so fill'd his head with that tinkling of the Rhime, and dance of the Numbers, that he had read him all over before he was Twelve years old, and was thus made a Poet as immediately as a Child is made an Eunuch."
[Quotation from Cowley's *Essay of Himself;* see 1668, above.]

[*Ibid.,* p. 83 (sig. F 2), quotes Denham's verses on Shakespeare, Fletcher, Spenser, and Jonson; see 1668, above.]

Ibid., p. 86, (sig. F 3ᵛ):
He was buried at *Westminster* Abby, near Two of our most Eminent English Bards, *Chaucer,* and *Spencer.*

[*Samuel Daniel,* p. 105 (sig. G), quotes Charles Fitzgeffrey's epigram on Daniel containing reference to Spenser; see 1601, above.]

Sir *John Denham,* p. 127 (sig. H 8):
He was Buried the twenty-third Instant [March 1668] at *Westminster,* amongst those Noble Poets, *Chaucer, Spencer,* and *Cowley.*

Sir *Richard Fanshaw,* pp. 196-7 (sigs. N 2ᵛ - N 3):
Besides these Pieces, Mr Philips (*Modern Poets,* p. 156) and Mr. Winstanley (*Acc. of the Poets,* p. 196) attribute to him the *Latin* Version of Mr. *Edmund Spencer's* Shepherds Calender, which I take to be a mistake of Mr. *Philips'* whose Errors Mr. *Winstanley* generally copies; not having heard of any other Translation than that done by Mr. *Theodore Bathurst,* sometime Fellow of *Pembroke-Hall* in *Cambridge,* and printed at the end of Mr. *Spencer's* Works in fol. *Lond.* 1679.
(DEM)

1691. Matthew Morgan. *A Poem to the Queen upon the King's Victory in Ireland and his Voyage to Holland,* Oxford.
[STC M2735.]

Sig. D 2:
Judicious *Spencer* shakes his Reverend Head,
Depress'd when living, slighted now he's dead. (DFA)

1691. William Mountfort. *King Edward the Third, with the Fall of Mortimer Earl of March. An Historicall Play.*
[STC B635. Ed. John Cadwalader, Univ. Pa. Diss., 1949.]

Dedication to Henry, Lord Viscount Sidney of Sheffrey, sig. A 2 (Cadwalader, p. 32):

I must not omit the Renowned Sr. *Philip Sidney* (whose Father was thrice Lord Deputy of *Ireland*) which was not only an Admirable Writer (besides his vast Accomplishments in other things) But so Indulgent a Patron to the Sons of the Muses, that the famous *Spencer* Dedicated his Works to him as the only Person Capable of Espousing 'em. (EG)

[The play is sometimes attributed to John Bancroft on weak evidence; for a summary of the problem of authorship see Cadwalader, pp. 8-10.]

1691. N. N. *The Blatant Beast Muzzled or Reflections on a Late Libel Entitled The Secret History.* [STC N28.]

[Title prompted by Spenser's Blatant Beast.] (JGM)

1691. Anthony Wood. *Athenæ Oxonienses.*
[STC W3382-3. Ed. P. Bliss, 1813-20.]
Vol. 1, col. 379 (Bliss 2.269; Bentley 2.216):
Our author *Daniel* had also a good faculty in setting out a Mask or a Play, and was wanting in nothing that might render him acceptable to the great and ingenious men of his time, as to Sir *Joh. Harrington* the Poet, *Camden the learned*, Sir *Rob. Cotton*, Sir *H. Spelman*, *Edm. Spencer*, *Ben. Johnson*, *John Stradling*, little *Owen* the Epigrammatist, &c. (GEB)

1692. Charles Gildon. *The Post-boy rob'd of his Mail: or, The Paquet Broke Open.* [STC G735 A.]
Pp. 166-7:
If I may judge my own, I think it far excels this of *Spencers;* which I have seen quoted for an Excellence,
> The joyous Birds shrouded in cheerful shade,
> Their Notes unto the Voice attemper'd sweet.
[Cf. *F. Q.* 2.13.71.1-2.]

P. 267:
Spencer (pursu'd Summer) *is of your mind* Chappel, *when he says,*
> Nought under Heav'n so strongly doth allure,
> The Sense of Man, and all his Mind possess.
[Cf. *F. Q.* 5.8.1.1-2.] (HER)

1693. *The Athenian Mercury,* vol. 12, no. 1, Oct. 24.
" Questions " [no pagin. or sig.] (Bradley, pp. 442-3; Spurgeon 1.265):
Quest. 4. What Books of Poetry wou'd you Advise one that's Young, and extreamly delights in it, to read, both Divine and other?
Answ. For Divine, *David's* Psalms, *Sandys's* and *Woodford's* Versions, *Lloyd's* Canticles, *Cowley's* Davideis, Sir *J. Davis's* Nosce Teipsum, *Herbert's* and *Crashaw's* Poems, *Milton's* Paradices, and (if you have Patience) *Wesley's* Life of Christ. For others, Old Merry *Chaucer,* *Gawen Douglas's* Æneads (if you can get it) the best Version that ever

was, or We believe ever will be, of that incomparable Poem; *Spencer's*
Fairy Queen, &c., *Tasso's* Godfrey of Bulloign, *Shakespear, Beaumont*
and *Fletcher, Ben. Johnson, Randal, Cleaveland,* Dr. *Donne, Gondibert,*
WALLER, all DRYDEN, *Tate, Oldham, Flatman, The Plain Dealer*—and
when you have done of these, we'll promise to provide you more. (JFB)

1693.   John Dryden. *The Satires of Decimus Junius Juvenalis. Translated*
into English Verse.
[STC J1288. *Works*, ed. Walter Scott (1808), rev. and corr. George
Saintsbury, Edinburgh, 1882-93.]

Dedication To the Right Honourable Charles Earl of Dorset and Middle-
sex, p. vii (Scott-Saintsbury 13.16):
    And those who are guilty of so boyish an Ambition in so grave a
Subject, are so far from being consider'd as Heroique Poets, that they
ought to be turn'd down from *Homer* to the *Anthologia*, from *Virgil* to
Martial and *Owen's* Epigrams, and from *Spencer* to *Fleckno;* that is,
from the top to the bottom of all Poetry. (DEM)

Ibid., pp. viii-ix (Scott-Saintsbury 13.17-9):
    The *English* have only to boast of *Spencer* and *Milton* who neither
of them wanted either Genius, or Learning, to have been perfect Poets;
and yet both of them are liable to many Censures. For there is no Uniformity in the Design of *Spencer*: He aims at the Accomplishment of
no one Action: He raises up a Hero for every one of his Adventures;
and endows each of them with some particular Moral Virtue, which
renders them all equal, without Subordination or Preference. Every
one is most Valiant in his own Legend; only we must do him that
Justice to observe, that Magnanimity, which is the Character of Prince
Arthur, shines throughout the whole Poem; and Succours the rest, when
they are in Distress. The Original of every Knight, was then living
in the Court of Queen *Elizabeth*: And he attributed to each of them
that Virtue, which he thought was most conspicuous in them: An
Ingenious piece of Flattery, tho' it turned not much to his Account. Had
he liv'd to finish his Poem, in the six remaining Legends, it had certainly
been more of a piece; but cou'd not have been perfect, because the
Model was not true. But Prince *Arthur*, or his chief Patron, Sir *Philip*
Sidney, whom he intended to make happy, by the Marriage of his
Gloriana, dying before him, depriv'd the Poet, both of Means and Spirit,
to accomplish his Design: For the rest, his Obsolete Language, and the
ill choice of his Stanza, are faults but of the Second Magnitude: For
notwithstanding the first he is still Intelligible, at least, after a little practice; and for the last, he is the more to be admir'd; that labouring under
such a difficulty, his Verses are so Numerous, so Various, and so Harmonious, that only *Virgil*, whom he profestly imitated, has surpass'd him,
among the *Romans*; and only Mr *Waller* among the *English*. . . .
    [Milton's] Antiquated words were his Choice, not his Necessity; for
therein he imitated *Spencer*, as Spencer did *Chawcer*. (FIC)

Ibid., p. xiii (Scott-Saintsbury 13.31) [In the discussion of a projected epic]:

Wherein, after *Virgil* and *Spencer,* I wou'd have taken occasion to represent my living Friends and Patrons of the Noblest Families, and also shadow'd the Events of future Ages, in the Succession of our Imperial Line.

Ibid., p. xxviii (Scott-Saintsbury 13.67) [Writing of satirical verse]:

In the English I remember none, which are mix'd with Prose, as *Varro's* were: But of the same kind is Mother *Hubbard's* Tale in *Spencer.*

P. 1 (Scott-Saintsbury 13.117)[On looking for " beautiful turns of words and thoughts "]:

I consulted . . . *Milton.* . . . I found in him a true sublimity, lofty thoughts, which were cloath'd with admirable *Grecisms,* and ancient words, which he had been digging from the Mines of *Chaucer,* and of *Spencer,* and which, with all their rusticity, had somewhat of Venerable in them. But I found not there neither for which I look'd. At last, I had recourse to his Master, *Spencer,* the Author of that immortal Poem call'd the *Fairy Queen;* and there I met with that which I had been looking for so long in vain. *Spencer* had studi'd *Virgil* to as much advantage as *Milton* had done *Homer.* And amongst the rest of his Excellencies had Copy'd that. (DEM)

1693. John Hacket. *Scrinia Reserata: A Memorial Offer'd to the Great Deservings of John Williams D. D.* [STC H171.]

Pt. 1, sect. 59, p. 49 (sig. H):

The Castle of *Munera* (as I borrow it from Mr. *Spenser's* Divine Wit) must be quite defaced.
[Cf. *F. Q.* 5.2.]

Ibid., sect. 95, p. 81 (sig. M):

An Evill befall that Archimago, that Fiend of Mischief, that set Variance between the Head and the Body. . . . And for his part, he [John Williams] was willing . . . to be unto him [the King] as the Black Palmer was to the Fairy Knight in Mr. *Spencer's* Moral Poem, to guide his Adventure from all distemperate Eruptions.

Ibid., sect. 212, p. 206 (sig. Dd 3ᵛ):

Virtue is beholding to Good Times to act its part in, as well as Good Times are beholding to Virtue. Our most Laureat Poet *Spenser,* Lib. I. Cant. 3. tells of a sturdy Thief *Kirkrapine,*

> Who all he got he did bestow,
> To the daughter of Corceca *blind and slow;*
> And fed her fat with Feasts of Off'rings,
> And Plenty which in all the Land did grow.

To meet with him, and give him his hire, *Una* had a fierce Servant for her Guard that attended her, a Lyon who tore the Church-robber to pieces. And what is meant by *Una's* Lyon? That's not hard to guess at. But rather what's become of *Una's* Lyon? The Poet says afterwards that *Sans-Loy*, a Paynim-Knight had slain him. Belike none is left now to defie *Kirkrapine*. (EG)

Pt. 2, sect. 153, p. 160 (sig. U 4ᵛ) [In the discussion of Williams' attitude towards Strafford]:
Says our Arch-Poet *Spencer*, lib. 3. Can. 1. st. 10.
> *Great hazard were it, and Adventure fond,*
> *To lose long-gotten Honour with one evil Hand.* (HH)

1693. *The Humours and Conversations of the Town, Expos'd in two dialogues, The first of the Men. the second, of the Women.*
[STC H3720.]

Pp. 81-4 (sigs. E 5 - E 6ᵛ):
But the incomparable *Spencer* describes the Court very well; as it has generally in all Ages merited the good Word of the Poets, especially when they speak their Minds: In their Flatteries of Great Men, we may observe a Violence offer'd to themselves, and some words cast in, lest the World shou'd think they meant really what they writ; but when they speak against the Court, you may easily see they are in earnest: But now to *Spencer*, I'll repeat 'em; for the delight I took in 'em, made me learn them without book. [Quotes *Col.*, ll. 680-730]
I'll make no Apology for the Length of the Quotation, because I am sure, Mr. *Sociable*, you are no little admirer of *Spencer*.
Soc. Prithee, in what part of the Poet is this? For I don't remember it.
Jov. '*Tis in his Colin Clouts, come home again.* (RH)

1693. Thomas Wright. *The Female Vertuoso's. A Comedy.*
[STC W3711.]

Act 3, p. 26 (Bentley 2.330):
Sir Maur[ice]. But I tell you Lady, that I will have a Reformation in my House, that this Plague of Wit has infected all my Servants, even my little Boy, forsooth, can not turn the Spit now without a *Pharamond*, or a *Cassandra* in his hand; if I call for Drink, the Butler brings me a *Spencer*, or a *Ben Johnson*. (GEB)

1694. Joseph Addison. *An Account of the Greatest English Poets. To Mr. H.S. Apr. 3, 1694*, in *The Annual Miscellany: for the Year 1694. Being the Fourth Part of Miscellany Poems.* [Ed. John Dryden.]
[STC D2237. *The Miscellaneous Works of Joseph Addison*, ed. A. C. Guthkelch, 1914.]

Pp. 318-9 (Guthkelch 1.31-2):
> Old *Spencer* next, warm'd with Poetick Rage,
> In Antick Tales amus'd a Barb'rous Age;
> An Age that yet uncultivate and Rude,
> Where-e're the Poet's Fancy led, pursu'd

Through pathless Fields, and unfrequented Floods,
To Dens of Dragons, and Enchanted Woods.
But now the Mystick Tale, that pleas'd of Yore,
Can Charm an understanding Age no more;
The long-spun Allegories fulsom grow,
While the dull Moral lyes too plain below.
We view well-pleas'd at distance all the sights
Of *arms* and *Palfries*, Cattel's, Fields and Fights,
And Damsels in Distress, and Courteous Knights.
But when we look too near, the Shades decay,
And all the pleasing Lan-skip fades away. (JWS)

1694.   Thomas Pope Blount. *De Re Poetica: or, Remarks upon Poetry*
[Vol. 1], *with Characters and Censures of the most Considerable Poets*
[Vol. 2], *Extracted out of the Best and Choicest Cricks.*
[STC B3347. Since Blount does not quote or paraphrase exactly, and
so reveals his own attitudes, Spenser allusions from the *De Re Poetica*
are given in full, for purposes of comparison.]

1.114 (sig Q^v):
Spencer had studied *Homer,* and *Virgil,* and *Tasso,* yet he was mis-led,
and debauch'd by *Ariosto,* as Mr. *Rimer* judiciously observes.
[Cf. 1674. Thomas Rymer, above.]

Abraham Cowley, 2.52 (sig. H 2^v):
    The Character that Sir John Denham gave of Abraham Cowley, you
may take in these his following Verses:
            Old Mother Wit, and Nature gave
            Shakespear *and* Fletcher *all they have*;
            In Spencer, *and in* Johnson, Art
            Of slower Nature got the Start. . . .
                        DENHAM's Poems, *pag.* 90, 91 of the 3d Edition.
[Cf. 1668. Sir John Denham, above.]

Ibid.:
    Rimer tells us, That a more happy *Genius* for *Heroick Poesie* appears
in *Cowley,* than either in *Spencer,* or *D'avenant.*

John Milton, 2.135-7 (sigs. S 4 - T):
    Dryden tells us, That in *Epique* Poetry, the *English* have only to boast
of *Spencer* and *Milton;* neither of whom wanted either *Genius* or *Learning,* to have been perfect Poets; and yet both of them are liable to many
Censures. . . . His [Milton's] Antiquated Words were his Choice, not
his Necessity; for therein he imitated *Spencer,* as *Spencer* did *Chaucer.*
And tho', perhaps, the love of their Masters, may have transported *both*
too far, in the frequent use of them; yet in my Opinion, says *Dryden,*
Obsolete words may then be laudably reviv'd, when either they are more
Sounding, or more *Significant* than those in practice: And when their
Obscurity is taken away, by joyning other Words to them which clear the

Sense; according to the Rule of *Horace,* for the admission of *New Words. . . .* DRYD. *Dedic:* before the *Translat.* of *Juvenal,* pag. 8, 9.

I consulted (says *Dryden*) a greater Genius than *Cowley,* (without offence to the *Manes* of that Noble Author) I mean *Milton,* for the *Beautiful Turns* of *Words* and *Thoughts.* But as he endeavours every where to express *Homer,* whose Age had not arriv'd to that *fineness,* I found in him (says *Dryden*) a true Sublimity, lofty Thoughts, which were cloath'd with admirable *Grecisms,* and *Ancient Words,* which he had been digging from the Mines of *Chaucer,* and of *Spencer,* and which, with all their *Rusticity,* had somewhat of *Venerable* in them: But, says *Dryden,* I found not *there* what I look'd for, *viz.* any *Elegant Turns,* either on the *Word,* or on the *Thought.* DRYD. *Ibid.* pag. 50. [Cf. 1693. John Dryden, above.]

2.213-6 (sigs. Ee 3 - Ee 4ᵛ):
					Edmund Spencer,
A Famous *English* Poet, born in the City of *London,* and brought up in *Pembroke-Hall* in *Cambridge;* He flourish'd in the Reign of Queen *Elizabeth.* His great Friend was Sir *Philip Sidney,* by whose means he was preferr'd to be *Secretary* to his Brother Sir *Henry Sidney,* who was sent *Deputy* into *Ireland,* where he is said to have written his *Fairy-Queen;* but upon the return of Sir *Henry,* his Employment ceasing, he also return'd into *England,* and having lost his great Friend Sir *Philip,* fell into Poverty; whereupon he addrest himself to Queen *Elizabeth,* presenting her with a Poem, with which she was so well pleas'd that she had order'd him 500 *l.* for his support, which nevertheless was abridg'd to One Hundred Pounds by the Lord Treasurer *Cecil,* who hearing of it, and owing him a grudge for some Reflections in *Mother Hubbard's Tale,* cry'd out to the Queen, *What all this for a Song?* This he is said to have taken so much to Heart, that he contracted a deep Melancholy, which soon after brought his life to a Period, *Anno Dom.* 1598.

Edward Phillips, in his *Theatrum Poetarum,* says, That *Spencer* was the first of our *English* Poets that brought *Heroick Poesie* to any perfection; his *Fairy-Queen* being for great Invention and Poetick Heighth, judg'd little Inferiour, if not Equal to the Chief of the Ancient *Greeks* and *Latins,* or Modern *Italians*; But the first Poem that brought him into Esteem, was his *Shepherds Kalendar.* This *Piece* was highly admir'd by Sir *Philip Sidney.*

Cambden, in his *History* of Queen *Elizabeth,* says, That *Edmund Spencer* was a *Londoner* by Birth, and a Scholar also of the University of Cambridge, born under so favourable an Aspect of the *Muses,* that [h]e surpass'd all the *English* Poets of former Times, not excepting *Chaucer* himself, his Fellow-Citizen. But by a *Fate* which still follows *Poets,* he always wrestled with Poverty.

Dr. *Fuller,* in his *Worthies of England,* affirms, That *Edmund Spencer* was an Excellent Linguist, Antiquary, Philosopher, and Mathematician; yet so poor (as being a *Poet*) that he was thought *Famem* non *Famæ scribere.*

Sir *William Temple*, in his *Essay* of *Poetry, pag.* 46, 47. remarks, That the *Religion* of the *Gentiles*, had been woven into the *Contexture* of all the *Ancient Poetry*, with a very agreeable Mixture; which made the *Moderns* affect, to give that of *Christianity* a place also in their Poems. But the *true Religion*, was not found to become *Fiction* so well, as a *False* had done, and all their Attempts of this Kind, seem'd rather to debase *Religion*, that to heighten *Poetry*. *Spencer*, says *Temple*, endeavour'd to supply *this* with *Morality*, and to make *Instruction*, instead of *Story*, the Subject of an *Epick* Poem. His Execution was Excellent, and his Flights of Fancy very Noble and High, but his Design was poor, and his *Moral* lay so bare, that it lost the Effect; 'tis true, says *Temple*, the Pill was Gilded, but so thin, that the Colour and the Taste were too easily discover'd.

Rimer, in the *Preface* to his Translation of *Rapin's* Reflexions on *Aristotle* of *Poesie*, tells us, That in his Judgment, *Spencer* may be reckon'd the first of our *Heroick* Poets; He had a large Spirit, a sharp Judgment, and a Genius for *Heroick Poesie*, perhaps above any that ever writ since *Virgil*. But our Misfortune is, says *Rimer*, he wanted a true *Idea*; and lost himself, by following an unfaithful Guide. Though besides *Homer* and *Virgil* he had read *Tasso*, yet he rather suffer'd himself to be misled by *Ariosto*; with whom blindly rambling on *marvellous Adventures*, he makes no Conscience of *Probability*. All is Fanciful and Chimerical, without any Uniformity, or without any foundation in Truth; in a Word, his Poem (says *Rimer*) is perfect *Fairy-Land*.

Dryden, in his *Dedication* to the *Earl* of *Dorset* before the Translation of *Juvenal, pag.* viii. says, That the *English* have only to boast of *Spencer* and *Milton*, in *Heroick Poetry*; who neither of them wanted either *Genius*, or *Learning*, to have been perfect *Poets*; and yet both of them are liable to many Censures. For there is no *Uniformity* in the Design of *Spencer*: He aims at the Accomplishment of no one Action: He raises up a *Hero* for every one of his Adventures; and endows each of them with some particular *Moral Vertue*, which renders them all equal, without Subordination or Preference. Every one is most valiant in his own *Legend*; only (says *Dryden*) we must do him that justice, to observe, that *Magnanimity*, which is the Character of Prince *Arthur*, shines throughout the *whole Poem*; and Succours the rest, when they are in distress. The Original of every Knight, was then living in the Court of Queen *Elizabeth*: And he attributed to each of them that Virtue, which he thought was most conspicuous in them: An Ingenious piece of flattery, tho' it turn'd not much to his Account. Had he liv'd to finish his Poem, in the six remaining *Legends*, it had certainly been more of a piece; but cou'd not have been perfect, because the Model was not *true*. But Prince *Arthur*, or his chief Patron, Sir *Philip Sidney*, whom he intended to make happy, by the Marriage of his *Gloriana*, dying before him, depriv'd the Poet, both of Means and Spirit, to accomplish his Design: For the rest, his *Obsolete Language*, and the *ill Choice* of his *Stanza*, are faults but of the Second Magnitude: For notwithstanding the *first* he is still Intelligible, at least, after a little practice; And for the *last*, he is the more to be admir'd; that labouring under such a difficulty, his Verses are so Numerous, so Various, and so Harmonious, that only *Virgil*, whom he has profestly imitated, has surpass'd him, among the *Romans*; And only Mr. *Waller* among the *English*, says *Dryden*.

The Expence of his Funeral and Monument was defray'd at the sole charge of *Robert*, first of that Name, Earl of *Essex*. He lies buried in *Westminster-Abbey*, near *Chaucer*, with this *Epitaph*:

> Edmundus Spencer, *Londinensis, Anglicorum Poetarum nostri seculi fuit Princeps, quod ejus* Poemata, *faventibus Musis, & victuro genio conscripta comprobant. Obiit immaturâ morte, Anno salutis,* 1598. *& prope* Galfredum Chaucerum *conditur, qui fælicissimè* Poesin *Anglicis literis primus illustravit. In quem hæc* Scripta *sunt* Epitaphia.
>
> Hîc prope Chaucerum *situs est* Spenserius, *illi*
> Proximus Ingenio, proximus ut Tumulo.
> Hîc prope Chaucerum Spensere *poeta poetam*
> Conderis, & versu! quam tumulo proprior.
> Anglica te vivo vixit, plausitque Poesis;
> Nunc moritura timet, te moriente, mori. (FMP)

Theocritus, 2.232 (sig. Gg 4ᵛ):
Even his [Theocritus'] *Dorick* Dialect has an incomparable Sweetness in its *Clownishness,* like a *fair Shepherdess* in her *Countrey Russet,* talking in a *Yorkshire* Tone. This (says *Dryden*) was impossible for *Virgil* to imitate; because the severity of the *Roman* Language denied him that advantage. *Spencer* has endeavour'd it in his *Shepherds Calendar;* but neither will it succeed in English, for which reason, *Dryden* says, he forbore to attempt it. (WW)
[Cf. 1685. John Dryden, above.]

Edmund Waller, 2.244-6 (sigs. Ii 2ᵛ - Ii. 3ᵛ):
In the mean time, 'tis a surprizing Reflexion, that between what *Spencer* wrote last, and *Waller* first, there should not be much above Twenty Years distance; and yet the *One's* Language, like the Money of that Time, is as currant now as ever; whilest the *Other's* Words are like Old Coyns, one must go to an *Antiquary* to understand their true Meaning and Value. . . . See the *Anonymous Writer* of the *Preface,* before the *Second Part* of Mr. *Waller's Poems.* (LL)
[Cf. 1690. Francis Atterbury, above.]

1694. Charles Gildon, ed. *Chorus Poetarum: or Poems on Several Occasions by The Duke of Buckingham . . . , Sir John Denham, Sir Geo. Etheridge, Andrew Marvel, Esq; The famous Spencer, Madam Behn, And several other Eminent Poets of this Age.* MDCLXIXIV [for MDCXCIV]. [STC B5309.]

A Satyr against Poetry. In a Letter to the Lord D.—, pp. 124-5 (Munro 2.202):

Were *Shakespear*'s self alive again he'd ne'er
Degenerate to a Poet from a Player.
For now no *Sidneys* will three Hundred give,
That needy Spencer and his Fame may live;
None of our poor Nobility can send
To his *Kings-Bench,* or to *Bedlam* Friend.

By SPENCER, pp. 172-3:

Phillis is both blithe and young;
Of *Phillis* is my Silver Song:
I love thilk Lass, and in my Heart
She breeds full many a baleful Smart.
Kids, cracknels, with my earliest Fruit,
I give to make her hear my Suit;
When *Colin* does approach o'erjoy'd,
My Hopes, alass! are all accoy'd.
Were I not born to love the Maid,
Yet she calls Miracles to her Aid.
When storm Stou'rs had dress'd the year,
In shivering Winters wrathful Chear:
Phillis, that lovely cruel wight,
Found me in a dreerie Plight;
And Snow-balls gently flung at me,
To wake me from my Lethargie.
Fire I ween there was y pent
In all those frozen Balls she sent
For Ah! woe's me, I felt them burn,
And all my Soul to Flames I turn.
Ah! *Phillis,* if you'd quench my Fire,
Burn your self with as fierce Desire. (JM)

[As Malone noted long ago, the poem is certainly not by Spenser; it is
quoted in full here because of its imitative effects.]

1695. T. B. *A Dedication of These and the foregoing Verses,* prefixed to
the 1695 ed. of Drayton's *England's Heroical Epistles.* [STC D2145.]

Sig. A 3ᵛ (Bradley, p. 445):

Time has devour'd the Younger Sons of Wit,
Who liv'd when *Chaucer, Spencer, Johnson* writ:
Those lofty Trees are of their Leaves bereft,
And to a reverent Nakedness are left. (JFB)

1695. Sir Richard Blackmore. *Prince Arthur. An Heroick Poem. In
Ten Books.* [STC B3080.]

The Preface, sig. b 2 (Spingarn 3.238):

But *Ariosto* and *Spencer,* however *great Wits,* not observing this judicious
Conduct of *Virgil,* nor attending to any sober Rules, are hurried on with

a *boundless, impetuous* Fancy over Hill and Dale, till they are both lost in a Wood of Allegories. Allegories so *wild, unnatural,* and *extravagant,* as greatly displease the Reader. This way of writing mightily offends in this Age; and 'tis a wonder how it came to please in any. (FIC)

1695. William Congreve. *The Mourning Muse of Alexis.*
[STC C4549. *Works,* ed. Montague Summers, 1923.]

P. 2 (sig. A 2v; Summers 4.39-40):
Of *ALBION*'s Loss, and of *PASTORA*'s Death,
Begin thy mournful Song, and raise thy tuneful Breath. . . .

O could I sing in Verse of equal Strain,
With the *Sicilian* Bard, or *Mantuan* Swain;
Or melting Words, and moving Numbers chuse,
Sweet as the British *Colins* mourning Muse;
Could I, like him, in tuneful Grief excel,
And mourn like *Stella* for her *Astrofel*;
Then might I raise my Voice, (secure of Skill,)
And with melodious Woe, the Valleys fill;
The list'ning *Echo* on my Song should wait,
And hollow Rocks *PASTORA*'s Name repeat;
Each whistling Wind, and murmuring Stream should tell
How Lov'd she liv'd, and how Lamented fell. (DEM)

1695. John Dryden. *De Arte Graphica. The Art of Painting, by C. A. Du Fresnoy. with Remarks. Translated into English.*
[STC D2458. *Works,* ed. Walter Scott, rev. and corr. George Saintsbury, Edinburgh, 1882-93.]

Observations on the Art of Painting, pp. 108-9 (Scott-Saintsbury 17. 418-9):
And other Books of the like Nature, the reading of which are profitable to warm the Imagination [of the painter]: such as in *English,* are *Spencer's Fairy Queen; The Paradise lost* of *Milton; Tasso* translated by *Fairfax;* and the History of *Polybius,* by Sir *Henry Shere.* (FIC)

1695. Thomas D'Urfey. *Gloriana. A Funeral Pindarique Poem. Sacred to the Blessed Memory of that Ever-admired and most excellent Princess, Our late Gracious Sovereign Lady Queen Mary.*
[Use of *Gloriana,* in praise of a royal princess.] (JGM)

1695. John Gadbury. *In Ephemeris. Or, A Diary, Astronomical, Astrological, Meteorological, For the Year of Grace, 1695.* [STC G1774.]
Sig. B 7:
It was this most Bountiful Native [Sir Philip Sidney] that encouraged the delicate Muse of Mr. Spencer, as he did also most of the Shining Wits of that Age. (BH)

1695. Patrick Hume. *Notes on Milton's Paradise Lost,* bound with the Sixth Edition of *Paradise Lost.*

[STC M2151; also STC H3663, *Annotations on Milton's Paradise Lost, 1695.*]

P. 92, note on *P. L.* 2.965:
Our Poet has followed *Spencer* in placing this terrible Bugbeare in the immense Abyss. [Quotes *F. Q.* 4.2.47.6-9; 1.5.22.5-6.]

P. 134, note on *P. L.* 4.151 ff. [after comparing the topography of Paradise to Alcinous' garden and Calypso's " shady Grotta " in Homer]:
But to make a Comparison more obvious to most Understandings, read the Description of the *Bower of Bliss,* by a Poet of our own Nation, and famous in his time; but 'tis *impar congressus!* and Rhyme fetter'd his Fancy. [Quotes *F. Q.* 2.12.42.4-9, with ref. given as 2.11.42.]

P. 157, note on *P. L.* 4.703:
Now if we compare the foregoing Description of this blissful Bower, with one of a Poet our Country-man, and deservedly famous in his time, we shall find the difference of their Genius to be as great as that of their Language. [Quotes *F. Q.* 2.5.29, omitting ll. 5-6] as far short of ours, as his Garden of *Adonis,* Bo.3.C.6.Stan.30. is of inimitable *Eden,* V.210.

P. 232, note on *P. L.* 8.152:
Of the Probability of a *Plurality of Worlds,* hear what another of our Country-men, and a Poet excellent in his time, said: [Quotes *F. Q.* 2. Proem 3,6-9, with ref. given as 2.1.3.]

P. 314, note on *P. L.* 11.180:
IMBOSS—A Word used by our *Spencer.* [Quotes *F. Q.* 1.9.29.1-2.]
(DEM)

1695. W. J. *The Preface of the Translator,* in *Monsieur Bossu's Treatise of the Epick Poem.* [STC L804.]

Sig. a 2 [in a synopsis of Rymer's criticism of English poets]: *Spencer,* whom he reckons the first of our *Heroick* Poets, yet falls under his Censure, and is tax'd for his want of a true Idea, for his rambling after marvellous adventures, for making no Conscience of Probability, for making his Poem a perfect *Fairy-Land,* and for his unlucky Choice of the Stanza, which in no wise is proper for our language.

Sig. a 3ᵛ:
This therefore must be own'd by all, that he has made a happy Choice of his *Subject* and *Hero,* whereby he signalizes his own Country; which is more than any of our *English* Poets have done before him, besides the *Romantick Spencer.*

Sig. a 7 [on Homer]:
'Tis likely he was admir'd and esteem'd by all, but receiv'd no other reward that we know of, for his Deserts, but what our poor *Spencer* did,

namely a Courtiers Smile; insignificant Promises, and a few fawning
Compliments. (DEM)

1695.   Henry Killigrew. *A Book of New Epigrams. By the same Hand
that Translated Martial.* [STC K443.]

> Pt. II, Ep. 101. *To the soft modern Muse,* p. 73 (sig. E 5):
> Thou wert all Painting, Garniture, and Fan;
> Lame and mishapen oft; and didst disclose,
> Thy Beauty not in Features lay, but Clothes;
> And while to be fair *Una* thou didst brag,
> Uncas'd, thou art *Duessa,* and a Hag.
> * In *Spencer's* Fairy Queen [Cf. 1.8.46 ff.]   (JGM)

1697.   John Dryden. *The Works of Virgil: Containing His Pastorals,
Georgics, and Æneis. Translated into English Verse.*
[STC V616. *Works,* ed. Walter Scott, rev. and corr. George Saintsbury,
Edinburgh, 1882-93.]

Dedication of the Pastorals, *To the Right Honourable Hugh Lord Clifford,*
p. 3 (sig. A 2; Scott-Saintsbury 13. 324-5) [After commenting on Virgil
and Theocritus as pastoral poets]:
> Our own Nation has produc'd a third Poet in this kind not inferiour
to the two former. For the Sphepherd's Kalendar of *Spencer,* is not to be
match'd in any Modern Language. Not even by *Tasso's Amynta,* which
infinitely transcends *Guarini's Pastor-Fido,* as having more of Nature in
it, and being almost wholly clear from the wretched affectation of Learning. I will say nothing of the *Piscatory Eclogues* [of Sannazaro], because
no modern *Latin* can bear Criticism. 'Tis no wonder that rolling down
through so many barbarous Ages, from the Spring of *Virgil,* it bears
along with it the filth and ordures of the *Goths* and *Vandals.* Neither
will I mention Monsieur *Fontenelle,* the living Glory of the *French.*
'Tis enough for him to have excell'd his Master *Lucian,* without attempt-
ing to compare our miserable Age with that of *Virgil,* or *Theocritus.* . . .
But *Spencer* being Master of our Northern Dialect; and skill'd in
Chaucer's English, has so exactly imitated the *Doric* of *Theocritus,* that
his Love is a perfect Image of that Passion which God infus'd into both
Sexes, before it was corrupted with the knowledge of Arts, and the
Ceremonies of what we call good Maners. (FMP)

Dedication of the *Aeneid, To . . . John, Lord Marquess of Normanby,
Earl of Mulgrave,* p. 208 (sig. Dd^v; Scott-Saintsbury 14.144):
> *Spencer* has a better plea for his Fairy-Queen, had his action been
finish'd, or had been one. (FIC)

Ibid., p. 213 (sig. Dd 4; Scott-Saintsbury 14.157) [On the worship of
Trojan ancestry]:
> *Spencer* favours this Opinion, what he can. His Prince *Arthur,* or
whoever he intends by him, is a *Trojan.* Thus the Heroe of *Homer*
was a *Grecian,* of *Virgil* [a] *Roman,* of *Tasso* an *Italian.*

Ibid., p. 217 (sig. Ee 2; Scott-Saintsbury 14.166):
  Ariosto, the two *Tasso's, Bernardo* and *Torquato,* even our own *Spencer;* in a word, all Modern Poets have Copied *Homer* as well as *Virgil.*

Ibid., p. 237 (sig. Gg 4; Scott-Saintsbury 14.208):
  I must acknowledge that *Virgil* in Latin, and *Spencer* in English, have been my Masters. *Spencer* has also given me the boldness to make use sometimes of his *Alexandrin* Line, which we call, though improperly, the *Pindarick;* because Mr. *Cowley* has often employ'd it in his Odes.
(DEM)

Ibid., p. 238 (sig. Gg 4ᵛ; Scott-Saintsbury 14.210):
  Spencer wanted only to have read the Rules of *Bossu;* for no Man was ever Born with a greater Genius, or had more Knowledge to support it. (FIC)

Ibid., p. 240 (sig. Hhᵛ; Scott-Saintsbury 14.214-5):
  Spencer and *Milton* are the nearest in English to *Virgil* and *Horace* in the Latin.

Ibid., p. 243 (sig. Hh 3; Scott-Saintsbury 14.221) [On Pindaric and triplet rhyme]:
  Spencer is my Example for both these priviledges of *English* Verses.

Ibid., pp. 243-4 (sig. Hh 3 - Hh 3ᵛ; Scott-Saintsbury 14.222):
  There is another thing in which I have presum'd to deviate from him [Cowley] and *Spencer.* They both make Hemysticks (or half Verses) breaking off in the middle of a Line. I confess there are not many such in the *Fairy Queen:* And even those few might be occasion'd by his unhappy choice of so long a Stanza.

Ibid., p. 246 (sig. Hh 4ᵛ; Scott-Saintsbury 14.227):
  Lay by *Virgil,* I beseech your Lordship, and all my better sort of Judges, when you take up my Version, and it will appear a passable Beauty, when the Original Muse is absent: But like *Spencer's* false *Florimel* made of Snow, it melts and vanishes when the true one comes in sight.
(DEM)

1697. Nahum Tate. *Upon the Present Corrupted State of Poetry,* prefixed to *The Original, Nature, and Immortality of the Soul,* by Sir John Davies (d. 1626), ed. of 1697.
[STC D405.]

Sig. b 4 - b 4ᵛ:
  Our Poets, when Deserters they became
  To Virtue's Cause, declin'd as much in Fame.
  That Curse was on the lewd Apostates sent,
  Who, as they grew Debauch'd, grew Impotent.
  Wit's short-liv'd Off-springs in our later Times
  Confess too plain their vicious Parents Crimes
  No *Spencer's* Strength, or *Davies,* who sustain'd.
  Wit's Empire when Divine *Eliza* reign'd. (RHP)

1698.   John Hughes. *Of Style*, in *Poems on Several Occasions. With some Select Essays in Prose*, 1735.

[Ed. Willard H. Durham, *Critical Essays of the Eighteenth Century*, Yale Univ. Press, 1915.]

1.249-50 (Durham, p. 81):

There is another Particular which I shall mention here, because I think it differs but little from *Propriety*, and that is *Purity*, which I take more particularly to respect the Language, as it is now spoke or written. The Rule of this is *modern Use*, according to that of *Horace*,

> *Multa renascentur quae jam cecidere, cadentque*
> *Quae nunc sunt in honore vocabula, si volet usus,*
> *Quem penes arbitrium est, & jus & norma loquendi.*

By this Rule, all obsolete Words are to be avoided. But to a Man of long Practice and Reputation in the Language, the Privilege may be allow'd sometimes of reviving old, or bringing in new Words, where the common ones are deficient. For this reason, we dare not censure so great a Man as *Milton* for his antiquated Words, which he took from *Spenser*. (EG)

1698.   Luke Milbourne. *Notes on Dryden's Virgil. In a Letter to a Friend.*
[STC M2035. The quotation of the passage to which the following note applies is given above; see: 1697. John Dryden. *The Works of Virgil. . .* , p. 237 (sig. Gg 4).]

P. 25:
The Alexandrine *Line, which we call, tho' improperly the* Pindaric*; tho' sillily*, he means sure; for none who understood any thing of *Pindaric Poetry*, could call that the *Pindaric Line* in contradistinction to Lines of other Measures: And since Mr. *Spencer* uses it to close his *Stanza*, without any Thought of *Pindarizing* in it, why should Mr. *Cowley's* using it give it that Name now. (RHP)

1699.   Richard Bentley. *A Dissertation upon the Epistles of Phalaris*, 2nd ed.
[STC B1929. Quoted J. L. Moore, *Tudor-Stuart Views on the Growth, Status and Destiny of the English Language*, Halle, 1910.]

P. 406 (sig. Dd 3ᵛ; Moore, p. 172):
Nay even *Oppian* himself, who took the allow'd privilege of using antiquated Words (as among Us *Spencer* and *Milton* did, though a little more sparingly) could not be understood in his own Town, except by the Learned. (DEM)

1699.   Charles Davenant. *An Essay upon the Probable Methods of Making a People Gainers in the Ballance of Trade.* [STC D309.]

Pp. 107-8:

From king *John, Henry* the 3d, and their Successors, the ancient *Irish* and the first Adventurers (of whom many as *Mr. Spencer* has observ'd, have taken the Names, Manners and Humours of the Natives) derive several Franchises and Immunities, and among the rest to hold a Parliament. The Story of those Times is it self dark, but the Reason of their Councils is yet darker. From *Mathew Paris,* and *Giraldus Cambrensis* it appears, That these Concessions were made to the Body of the Old *Irish,* tho' but few, in Practice, submitted to them; for to use Mr. *Spencer's* own Words, *To whom did King Henry the 2d impose those Laws? Not to the* Irish, *for the most of them fled from his Power into Desarts and Mountains, leaving the wide Country to the Conquerour, who in their stead eftsoons plac'd* English *Men, who possess'd all their Lands, and did quite shut out the* Irish, *or the most part of them. And to those new Inhabitants and Colonies he gave his Laws, to wit, the same Laws under which they were born and bred, the which it was no difficulty to place among them, being formerly well inur'd thereunto; unto whom afterwards there repair'd divers of the Poor distress'd People of the* Irish, *for Succour and Relief of whom, such as they thought fit for Labour, and industriously dispos'd, as the most part of their baser sort are, they receiv'd unto them as their Vassals, but scarcely vouchsaf'd to impart unto them the benefit of those Laws, under which they themselves liv'd, but every One made his Will and Commandment a Law unto his own Vassal: Thus was not the Law of* England *ever properly apply'd unto the* Irish *Nation, as by a purpos'd Plot of Government, but as they could insinuate and steal themselves under the same, by their humble Carriage and Submission.*

*Edmund Spencer's View of the State of Ireland, p. 222.

[The volume is attributed only to " The Author of *The Essay* on Ways and *Means.*"] (JRM)

1699. John Toland. *Amyntor: or, a Defence of Milton's Life.* [STC T1760.]

Pp. 138-9:

Now, to shew further how cautiously People should rely on Sir WILLIAM DUGDALE, and Historians like him, we shall produce another remarkable Instance. In the Book before quoted, he expresly writes, That Mr. HERBERT did often see the *Icon Basilike* while he waited on the King in the *Isle of Wight;* wheras all that Sir THOMAS (for he was Knighted after the Restoration) has said in the Manuscript which Sir WILLIAM perus'd, and wherof Mr. WAGSTAFF has printed an Abstract is, that he " had there the Charge of the King's Books; and that those he most read, after the Sacred Scriptures, were Bishop ANDREWS's Sermons, HOOKER's Ecclesiastical Polity, VILLALPANDUS on EZEKIEL, SANDY's Paraphrase on the *Psalms,* HERBERT's Poems, the Translation

of GODFREY of Bulloign by Mr. FAIRFAX, of ORLANDO FURIOSO by Sir JOHN HARRINGTON, and SPENCER's Fairy Queen (to which he might have added PEMBROKE's *Arcadia*)."
[Cf. 1679. Sir Thomas Herbert, above.] (HH)

Before 1700. John Dryden. *On the Death of Amyntas: A Pastoral Elegy,* in *Poetical Miscellanies: the fifth part,* 1704.
[*Works,* ed. Walter Scott, rev. and corr. George Saintsbury, Edinburgh, 1882-93.]

Pp. 16-21 (Scott-Saintsbury 11.140-3).
[Strong relation to Spenser's pastoral elegiac vein, especially the bright closing of hope for the departed. Cf. the Lament for Dido, *S.C. Nov.*]
(DEM)

About 1700. Samuel Cobb. *Poetae Britannici. A Poem.*
[STC C4773.]

P. 10 (Spurgeon 1.271):
> Sunk in a Sea of Ignorance we lay,
> Till *Chaucer* rose, and pointed out the Day.
> A Joking Bard, whose Antiquated Muse,
> In mouldy Words could solid Sense produce.
> Our *English Ennius* He, who claim'd his part
> In wealthy Nature, tho' unskilld in Art.
> The sparkling Diamond on his Dung-hill shines,
> And Golden Fragments glitter in his Lines.
> Which *Spencer* gather'd for his Learning known,
> And by successful Gleanings made his own.
> So careful Bees, on a fair Summers Day,
> Hum o'er the Flowers, and suck the Sweets away.
> Of *Gloriana,* and her Knights he sung,
> Of Beasts, which from his pregnant Fancy sprung.
> O had thy Poet, *Britany,* rely'd
> On Native Strength, and Foreign Aid deny'd,
> Had not wild Fairies blasted his design,
> *Mœnides* and *Virgil* had been Thine!
> Their finish'd Poems he exactly view'd,
> But *Chaucer's* Steps Religiously pursued.
> He cull'd and pick'd, and thought it greater praise
> T'adore his Master, than improve his Phrase.
> 'Twas counted Sin to deviate from his Page;
> So sacred was th' Authority of Age! (CFES, FIC)

1700. *A Description of Mr. D[ryde]n's Funeral,* appended to *Luctus Britannici: or The Tears of the British Muses; for the Death of John Dryden.* [STC L3451.]

Spurgeon 1.288:
> A Crowd of Fools attend him to the Grave,
> A Crowd so nauseous, so profusely lewd,

With all the Vices of the Times endu'd,
That *Cowley's* Marble wept to see the Throng,
Old *Chaucer* laugh'd at their unpolish'd Song,
And *Spencer* thought he once again had seen
The Imps attending of his *Fairy Queen.* (DFA)

1700. John Dryden. *Fables Ancient and Modern; Translated into Verse, from Homer, Ovid, Boccace, & Chaucer: with Original Poems.* [STC D2278. *Works,* ed. Walter Scott, rev. and corr. George Saintbury, Edinburgh, 1882-93.]

Preface, sig. A (Scott-Saintsbury 11.209-10):
For *Spencer* and *Fairfax* both flourish'd in the Reign of Queen *Elizabeth*: Great Masters in our Language; and who saw much farther into the Beauties of our Numbers, than those who immediately followed them. *Milton* was the Poetical Son of *Spencer.* . . . *Spencer* more than once insinuates, that the Soul of *Chaucer* was transfus'd into his Body; and that he was begotten by him Two hundred years after his Decease. *Milton* has acknowledg'd to me, that *Spencer* was his Original.

Ibid., sig. B 2ᵛ (Scott-Saintsbury 11.226):
We must be Children before we grow Men. There was an *Ennius,* and in the process of Time a *Lucilius,* and a *Lucretius,* before *Virgil* and *Horace*; even after *Chaucer* there was a *Spencer,* a *Harrington,* a *Fairfax.*

Palamon and Arcite, Book 3, p. 54 (Scott-Saintsbury 11.302):
Creator *Venus,* Genial Pow'r of Love,
The Bliss of Men below, and Gods above,
Beneath the sliding Sun thou runn'st thy Race,
Dost fairest shine, and best become thy Place.
For thee the Winds their Eastern Blasts forbear,
Thy Month reveals the Spring, and opens all the Year.
The, Goddess, thee the Storms of Winter fly,
Earth smiles with Flow'rs renewing, laughs the Sky,
And Birds to Lays of Love their tuneful Notes apply.
[Cf. *F.Q.* 4.10.44, and see Saintsbury's footnote.] (DEM)

1700. *Gallus,* appended to *Luctus Britannici: or The Tears of the British Muses; for the Death of John Dryden.* [STC L3451.]
P. 6:
Expectat Cowleus amans, viridiq; decorus
Spencerus lauru, & major Miltonus utroque.
Ex. Aul. C. (DEM)

1700. Henry Hall. Verses in *Luctus Britannici: or The Tears of the British Muses; for the Death of John Dryden, Esq.* [STC L3451.]

P. 19:
　　Let us look back, and Noble Numbers trace
　　Directly up from Ours, to *Chaucer's* days;
　　Chaucer, the first of Bards in Tune that Sung,
　　And to a better bent reduc'd the stubborn Tongue.

　　Spencer upon his Master much Refin'd,
　　He Colour'd sweetly, tho he ill Design'd;
　　Too mean the Model for so vast a Mind.
　　Thus while he try'd to make his stanza's Chime,
　　Good *Christian* Thoughts Turn *Renegade* to Rhime. (DEM)

Before 1701? Charles Gildon. *The Vision. A Fable. Inscribed to Dr. Garth,* in *Examen Miscellaneum,* 1702.

Pp. 62-3:
　　　　　But from the true and genuine Race of Heav'n,
　　Spring Heroes; and beneficent to Man
　　Patriots and Poets, ...
　　Euripides, and *Virgil, Dryden, Garth,*
　　Athenian *Sophocles,* the British Bard,
　　Whose song above the *Aonian* Mountain soars:
　　Homer, and *Horace, Tasso,* and *Racine.*
　　Shakespear, and *Otway, Spencer, Denham, Donn,*
　　And various more, not nam'd, to Fame ally'd
　　Of Ancient Bards, and Poets yet unknown.

[The poem, a Miltonic imitation, in which this passage occurs is evidently by the compiler of the miscellany, who is supposed to be Charles Gildon.] (HH)

Before 1701? Nahum Tate. *The Kentish Worthies. A Poem,* 1701.

P. 1:
　　Shall *Britain* and Applauding Nations round
　　The Fame of *Kentish* Loyalty resound,
　　And *Britain's* Poets, who should loudest raise
　　Their Voice, and give the first Alarm to Praise,
　　Shall they be Mute? They who in Glory's Cause
　　Should fire th'Admiring World into Applause!
　　No—*Spencer* first from *Faiery-Land* shall rise,
　　And *Milton* from his Bow'rs of Paradise,
　　Waller return from blissful Fields of Light,
　　E'er such Desert shall want Poetick Right
　　And sink, Unsung, to deep Oblivion's Night. (JGM)

Undated. Quotation from *The Shepheardes Calender* in B. M. MS Sloane 1489.

[The roundelay in *Aug.* is quoted, fols. 17ᵛ - 18, no author's name being given.] (WBA)

ERRATA

P. 113.   In the last line of the entry, " 1607. Richard Niccols," for the reference to *F. Q.*, " 2.127.1," read 2.12.71.

P. 172.   Delete the last entry, " Before 1626. Sir John Davies." Its replacement is the entry, " 1653. John Davies, of Kidwelly (d. 1693)" on p. 235.

P. 284, fifth line from the top of page, *read* Sedley *for* Sidley.

P. 295.   In the entry, " 1692. Charles Gildon," for the reference to *F. Q.*, " 2.13.71.1-2," read 2.12.71.1-2.

INDEXES

1. AUTHORS AND TITLES

2. ALLUSIONS TO CHARACTERS
   AND PASSAGES

3. ALLUSIONS TO PERSONS
   OTHER THAN SPENSER

The editors wish to thank the Duke–University of North Carolina Cooperative Program in the Humanities for a grant to aid the preparation and printing of these Indexes.

1. AUTHORS AND TITLES

2. ALLUSIONS TO CHARACTERS AND PASSAGES IN SPENSER

Acrasia, 77 J. M., 117 Tomkis, 119 Wybarne, 121-2 Fletcher, 238-9 Sheppard (2 refs).

Aemylia, 244 Poole.

Alma, 170 Aylett, 191 Fletcher, 199 Austin.

Amaryllis, 197 Heywood, 291 Cotton.

Amoret, 42 Edwards, 199 Heywood, 200 Milton, 218 Waller, 244 Poole, 248 Lovelace.

Amoretti, general, 23 Daniel, 29 Barnes, 56 Salusbury, 154 Drummond.
  No. 15, 104-5 Baxter, 257 Herbert of Cherbury.
  18, 49 Linche.
  22, 257 Herbert of Cherbury.
  40, 259 Milton.
  54, 49 Griffin.
  56, 49 Linche.
  75, 124 Byrd.
  76.3, 113-4 Niccols.
  77, 104-5 Baxter.
  79, 257 Herbert of Cherbury.
  80, 30-1 Drayton.

Ape and the Fox, The, see: *Mother Hubberds Tale*, general.

Archimago, 120 Wybarne, 179 Quarles, 181 *Pathomachia*, 207 Shirley, 221 Beaumont, 250 White, 297 Hacket.

Artegall, 152 *A maske at Coleoverton*, 223-4 *The Faerie Leveller*, 230 Sheppard, 279 Montagu.

Arthur, 29 Barnes, 36 *Masque of Proteus*, 152 *A maske at Coleoverton*, 217 Waller, 225 More, 296 Dryden, 301 Blount (2 refs), 306 Dryden.

Astrophel, ll. 1-8, 75 *Englands Helicon*.

Belge, 131 Heywood.

Belphoebe, 22-3 Raleigh, 37 I. O., 78 Lane, 95 Niccols, 95 T.W., 124 Stanford, 169 Browne, 244 Poole.

Blandamour, 185 Burton.

Blandina, 244 Poole.

Blatant Beast, The, 109 *Returne from Parnassus* (II), 154 Jonson, 158 Fletcher, 202 Hayward, 205 Jonson, 218 Cleveland, 230 Sheppard.

Braggadochio, 27 Nashe, 32-3 Harvey, 34 and 37 Nashe, 40 H. C., 58 Chapman, 61 Rankins, 68 Weever, 72 *Returne from Parnassus* (I), 77 J. M., 78 Lane, 81-2 Vaughan, 90 Marston, 92 Niccols, 104 Baxter, 129 Taylor, 130 Dekker, 144 Overbury, 145 Browne, 156 Robinson, 183 Lenton, 193 Gower, 206 Mennes, 223 Dias (3 refs), 227 Heath, 255 Flecknoe.

Britomart, 12 Lyte, 36 Drayton, 102 Baxter, 196 Tooke, 197 *King and Queenes Entertainement*, 200 Milton, 230 and 240 Sheppard, 279 Montagu.

Busirane, 200 Milton.

Calidore, 152 *A maske at Coleoverton*.

Cambina, 256 Philips.

Charissa, 157 Quarles, 205 Holme.

Claribell, 111 Barnes, 244 Poole.

Colin, 6 Peele, 11 Fraunce, 27 Nashe, 29 Barnes, 30-1 Drayton, 33 Lodge, 35 R. B., 35 Barnfield, 36 Drayton, 39 Barnfield, 40 E. C., 41-2 Drayton, 43 Edwards, 48 Davies, 52-3 Smith, 55 Hall, 59 Marston, 68 Roche, 69 Weever, 69 Chalkhill, 76 *Englands Helicon*, 87-8 Basse, 88-9 Davison, 92 Chettle, 94 Lane, 95 Niccols, 97 Markham, 98 Hall, 98 *In Calvum Poetam*, 103 Chettle, 108 Drayton, 118 Clapham, 130 Browne, 131 Heyward, 137 Niccols, 145-6 Browne, 176 Drayton, 190-2 Fletcher (7 refs), 193 Papillon, 221 Beaumont, 228 Milton, 231-2 Sheppard (3 refs), 233 Basse, 238 and 240 Sheppard, 254 Cokayne (4 refs), 268 Cotton, 274 Woodford, 284-5 *A Pastoral, Written at Dublin*, 291 Cotton (2 refs), 303 Gildon, 304 Congreve.

3-6, 11 Fraunce.
11-4, 91 Rowlands.
17-8,
41-4,
65-6, and
71-6, 11 Fraunce.
71-84, 89 Davison.
74, 31 Drayton.
77-83, 192 Fletcher.
87-90, 11 Fraunce.
92, 171 Aylett.
102ff., 11 Fraunce, 159 Aylett, 176 Wotton.
143-6, and
169-86, 11 Fraunce.
219-37, 256 More.
March.
ll. 1-6, 9 Webbe.
10-11, 11 Fraunce.
61 ff., 172 Alleyn.
61-101, 11 Fraunce.
78-84, 221 More.
115-7, 11 Fraunce.
April, general, 86-7 Morley (Norcombe).
ll. 1-8, 135 Davies.
13-6, 190 Fletcher, 196 Rutter.
23-4, 190 Fletcher.
33, 139 Wither.
33-6, 14 Peele (*Farewell*).
36, 5 Blenerhasset, 20 Vallens.
37-45, 9 Webbe, 11 Fraunce, 103 Baxter.
37-153, 9 Webbe, 10 Daye, 30 Drayton, 71 *Hymnus Pastoralis,* 75 *Englands Helicon.*
55-63, 5 Blenerhasset, 11 Fraunce.
62, 203 Milton.
64-72, 11 Fraunce.
74, 65 Davies.
91-2, 11 Fraunce.
115ff., 13 Lodge.
136-44, 11 Fraunce, 155 Robinson, 189 Fletcher, 195 Quarles.
May, general, 76 *Englands Helicon.*
ll. 9-14, 11 Fraunce.
35-6, 89 Davison.
38-54, 190 Fletcher.
39-44,

43-4, and
45-50, 11 Fraunce.
54, 92 Chettle, 103 Baxter, 210 More, 286 Dryden.
71-2, and
95-100, 11 Fraunce.
103-31, 208 Milton, 248 Stubbe.
109-37, 262 Penn.
117-9, and
121, 11 Fraunce.
127, 203 Milton.
139-40, 91 Rowlands.
142, 203 Milton.
164-7, 91 Rowlands, 11 Fraunce.
168,
182-8,
195-7,
205-6,
215-26,
227-8,
235-48, and
268-9, 11 Fraunce.
Glosse "Great pan', 216 Milton.
June,
ll. 1-8,
9-16, and
17-8, 11 Fraunce.
33ff., 139 Wither.
65-80, 30 Drayton.
67, 203 Milton.
81 and glosse, 134 Browne.
81-2, 171 Aylett.
89, 96 T. W.
93-112, 11 Fraunce.
108-12, 192 Fletcher.
109, 6 Desainleins.
115-6, 11 Fraunce.
July, general, 76 *Englands Helicon.*
ll. 9-12,
18-24, and
39-52, 11 Fraunce.
49, 210 More.
53-6, and
57-60, 11 France.
81, 190 Fletcher.
97-100,
101-4,
113-6,
129-32,
145-8,
153-6,

(*Shepheardes Calender*)
169-77, and
173, 11 Fraunce.
183-203, 190 Fletcher.
191, 108 *Plough-mans Tale*.
Aug., general, 51-2 Rollinsou, 117-8
    Davison.
ll. 5-6, 11 Fraunce.
16-7, 192 Fletcher.
25-42, 11 Fraunce, 55 Hall.
26-7, and
26-36, 11 Fraunce.
47-8, 190 Fletcher.
53ff., 172 Alleyn.
53-6, 9 Webbe.
53-124, 75-6 *Englands Helicon*,
    Quotation from B. M. MS
    Sloane 1489.
61-72,
69-72, and
137-8, 11 Fraunce.
151-7, 9 Webbe.
151-62, 10 Fraunce.
151-89, 53 Smith.
Sept., general, 76 *Englands Helicon*.
ll. 1-2, 11 Fraunce (2 refs).
36-9, 91 Rowlands.
44-6,
58-61, and
80-5, 11 Fraunce.
82-3, 91 Rowlands.
90-3,
106-7,
120-1, and
128-9, 11 Fraunce.
130-5, 91 Rowlands.
134-5, and
150-3, 11 Fraunce.
141, 91 Rowlands.
236-41, 11 Fraunce.
Oct., general, 13 Lodge.
Argument, 251 Worthington.
ll. 7-18, 194 Heywood.
13-4, 118 Davison.
17, 6 Vallans.
19, 203 Milton.
55-78, 135-6 Davies, 194 Hey-
    wood.
61-2, 6 Vallans.
79-96, 30 Drayton.
83-4, 59 Meres.

91-6, 11 Fraunce.
105, 216 Milton.
116-8, 190 Fletcher.
Nov., general, 310 Dryden.
ll. 14-6, and
20-1, 118 Davison.
53, 6 Melbancke, 6 Lodge, 78
    Kemp, 225 *Vaticinium Vo-*
    tivum.
53-6, 9 Webbe.
53-62, 30 Drayton, 56 Kirbye.
58, 11 Fraunce.
58-9, 96 T. W.
58-62, 107 Chapman.
115-6, and
128, 11 Fraunce.
153-4, 209 Kynaston.
169, and
183-92, 11 Fraunce.
Dec., general, 31 Drayton.
ll. 1-2, 12 Byrd.
4, 171 Aylett.
19-20, and
19-36, 11 Fraunce.
19-50, 190 Fletcher.
53-4,
67-70, and
77-80, 11 Fraunce.
70 and glosse, 123 Guillim.
77, 217 Milton.
83-4, 181 Fletcher.
91-4, 11 Fraunce.
Sonnet *To Lo. Burghley*, ll. 3-6, 101
    Fletcher.
Speranza, 205 Holme.
Squire of Dames, The, 184 and 186
    Burton.

Talus, 66-7 Hall, 203 Whiting, 218
    Waller, 223 *The Faerie Leveller*,
    225 Milton.
Teares of the Muses, The, general, 44
    Southwell, 45 B. M. MS Harleian
    6910, 58-9 Guilpin, 61 Rogers, 69
    Weever, 80 Shakespeare, 194 Hey-
    wood, 201 Adamson.
l. 53, 203 Milton.
ll. 115-72, 22 Nashe.
262, and
301-2, 216 Milton.
371-2, 252-3 Chauncy.

DATE DUE
